SINCE 1948

SUNY SERIES IN CONTEMPORARY JEWISH LITERATURE AND CULTURE

EZRA CAPPELL, EDITOR

Dan Shiffman, *College Bound:
The Pursuit of Education in Jewish American Literature, 1896–1944*

Eric J. Sundquist, editor, *Writing in Witness:
A Holocaust Reader*

Noam Pines, *The Infrahuman: Animality in Modern Jewish Literature*

Oded Nir, *Signatures of Struggle:
The Figuration of Collectivity in Israeli Fiction*

Zohar Weiman-Kelman, *Queer Expectations:
A Genealogy of Jewish Women's Poetry*

Richard J. Fein, translator, *The Full Pomegranate:
Poems of Avrom Sutzkever*

Victoria Aarons and Holli Levitsky, editors,
*New Directions in Jewish American and
Holocaust Literatures: Reading and Teaching*

Jennifer Cazenave, *An Archive of the Catastrophe:
The Unused Footage of Claude Lanzmann's Shoah*

Ruthie Abeliovich, *Possessed Voices:
Aural Remains from Modernist Hebrew Theater*

Victoria Nesfield and Philip Smith, editors,
The Struggle for Understanding: Elie Wiesel's Literary Works

Ezra Cappell and Jessica Lang, editors,
Off the Derech: Leaving Orthodox Judaism

Nancy E. Berg and Naomi B. Sokoloff, editors,
Since 1948: Israeli Literature in the Making

SINCE 1948
Israeli Literature in the Making

Edited by
Nancy E. Berg and Naomi B. Sokoloff

Cover: The Shrine of the Book under construction 1964–65.
Photo by Alfred Bernheim © The Israel Museum, Jerusalem.

Translation of "Beterem" by Yehuda Amichai from *Mishkan HaNefesh: Machzor for the Days of Awe, Yom Kippur* copyright © 2015, by Central Conference of American Rabbis, under copyright protection by the Central Conference of American Rabbis and reprinted for use by permission of the CCAR. All rights reserved.

Published by State University of New York Press, Albany

© 2020 State University of New York

All rights reserved

No part of this book may be used or reproduced in any manner whatsoever without written permission. No part of this book may be stored in a retrieval system or transmitted in any form or by any means including electronic, electrostatic, magnetic tape, mechanical, photocopying, recording, or otherwise without the prior permission in writing of the publisher.

For information, contact State University of New York Press, Albany, NY
www.sunypress.edu

Library of Congress Cataloging-in-Publication Data

Names: Berg, Nancy E., editor. | Sokoloff, Naomi B., editor.
Title: Since 1948 : Israeli literature in the making / [edited by] Nancy E. Berg, Naomi B. Sokoloff.
Description: Albany : State University of New York, 2020. | Series: SUNY series in contemporary Jewish literature and culture | Includes bibliographical references and index.
Identifiers: LCCN 2020002269 (print) | LCCN 2020002270 (ebook) | ISBN 9781438480497 (hardcover) | ISBN 9781438480480 (pbk.) | ISBN 9781438480503 (ebook)
Subjects: LCSH: Israeli literature—History and criticism.
Classification: LCC PJ5021 .S56 2020 (print) | LCC PJ5021 (ebook) | DDC 892.4006—dc23
LC record available at https://lccn.loc.gov/2020002269
LC ebook record available at https://lccn.loc.gov/2020002270

10 9 8 7 6 5 4 3 2 1

Contents

List of Illustrations — vii

Acknowledgments — ix

Introduction
Under Construction: A Kind of Festschrift for Israeli Literature — 1
   Nancy E. Berg and Naomi B. Sokoloff

PART ONE:
THROUGH TIME: SILENCES, VOICES, ECHOES

Not One, but Five Moments of Silence: On the Poetics and
Politics of Asking for Silence — 27
   Eran Tzelgov

Sounding the Mizrachi Voice: *Ḥafla* Thematics from the
Ma'abarah to the Post-Arabic Novel — 43
   Michal Raizen

Anthological Poetics: Reading Amichai and Halfi in Liberal
Prayerbooks — 59
   Wendy I. Zierler

PART TWO:
ACROSS LANGUAGE AND TERRITORY: LITERATURE AND IDENTITY

When Yiddish Was Young in Israel — 83
   Shachar Pinsker

A Canaanite Story: Language, National Identity, and the 1948 War — 103
   Yael Dekel

Hebrew Unbound: Alternative Homelands in the New World   123
   Melissa Weininger

Part Three:
Between the Lines: Rethinking Genres

From Here to Elsewhere and Back in Israeli-Hebrew Children's Literature   143
   Shai Ginsburg

"The pigs were my best friends": Animals and the Holocaust in Alona Frankel's Memoirs   163
   Naomi B. Sokoloff

Stalagim: At the Limits of Israeli Literature   183
   Eric Zakim

Part Four: Concerning Canons

Disruptive Nativity: The Poetry of Rina Shani and the Sixties in Israel   207
   Riki Traum

Asaf Schurr and the Critique of Postmodernism in Contemporary Hebrew Literature   229
   Yaron Peleg

"And the Winner Is . . .": The Economy of Literary Awards   247
   Nancy E. Berg

Appendix
A Canaanite Story: "The Lord Be Praised"   267
   Eitan Notev

On Our Bookshelf   277

Contributors   279

Index   283

Illustrations

Figure 1.1	Carmit Rosen, "chorus"	35
Figure 3.1	Psalm 95 and Yehuda Amichai, "*Shir shel shabbat*"	65
Figure 3.2	Psalm 92 and Avraham Halfi, "*Tefilah*"	68
Figure 3.3	S'lichot and Yehuda Amichai, "*Beterem*"	72
Figure 4.1	Photograph of Yung Yisroel Members (courtesy of Tzvi Eisenman)	91
Figure 4.2	Cover of the journal *Yung Yisroel*, December 1954	92
Figure 4.3	Cover of Mendel Mann, *In a farvorloztn dorf*	96
Figure 4.4	Cover of Tzvi Eisenman, *Di ban: dertseylungen*	97
Figure 9.1	Cover of Ivan Spasky, *Stalag Stalingrad*	189
Figure 9.2	Cover of Roy Adams, *Stalag banot hasatan (Devil Girls Stalag)*	192

Acknowledgments

This book grew out of a conference at Washington University in St. Louis, "Enshrining the Book: Israeli Literature at 70," that we directed in April 2018. We are grateful to all the academic units in the School of Arts and Sciences at Washington University that provided financial support: the Center for the Humanities, the Department of Jewish, Islamic, and Near Eastern Languages & Cultures (now known as Jewish, Islamic, and Middle Eastern Studies), the Department of History, and the Programs in Comparative Literature, Religious Studies, and International and Area Studies. The Israel Institute awarded a generous—and deeply appreciated—grant.

The administrative support provided on the ground by Stephen Scordias, as well as media assistance by John Moore and accounting by Leslie C. Smith, made the conference possible; the emotional support from those individuals made the planning enjoyable. We have loved working with all of the conference participants-turned-contributors: those who were timely, receptive, and simple to edit, as well as those who struggled with deadlines, writing, and revisions. They have shaped this volume. We hope that the reader learns as much from the end product as we have learned from the process.

We also want to thank Tim Huskey for his guidance. Much appreciation goes to our editorial team at SUNY Press, and to our anonymous readers for their comments on the manuscript. Special acknowledgment is due both to the Weiner Fund at Washington University and to Hebrew Union College-Jewish Institute for Religion for providing funds for reprinting poetry in this volume.

We were both on sabbatical leave for part of the time we were preparing the manuscript for publication. For the freedom to complete this work, Nancy is grateful to both Washington University in St. Louis and the Katz Center for Advanced Jewish Studies at the University of Pennsylvania; Naomi thanks the University of Washington and, in particular, Professor Selim Kuru and Patrick Gibbs in the Department of Near Eastern Languages and Civilization for their support.

As always, love and gratitude to Stan and Doug.

Acknowledgment is made for permission to include the following material:

Yehuda Amichai, "Beterem" ["Before"]; from *Mishkan HaNefesh: Machzor for the Days of Awe, Yom Kippur* (2015), Copyright by Central Conference of American Rabbis.

Yehuda Amichai, "Shir leil Shabbat," in Wendy Zierler's English translation, by permission of Hana Amichai.

Haim Gouri, "Ani vehasheket," by permission of Hakibbutz Hameuchad-Sifriat Poalim Publishing House.

Avraham Halfi, "Tefilah," copyright by Avraham Halfi—ACUM—Israel.

Tehila Hakimi, "T'nu li yom echad," copyright by Tangier Publishing, Israel.

Eitan Notev [Shraga Gafni], "Praised Be the Lord," translation by Yael Dekel of "Hashevach le'elohim." By permission of Avner Gafni.

Carmit Rosen, "Chorus," by permission of Hakibbutz Hameuchad-Sifriat Poalim Publishing House.

Rina Shani, "Alibi," "Ani ratsiti et ha'ir zarah," "Perach zar," "Shalom le'adoni hamelekh," and "Zeh Shavuot," from *Mivchar shirim*, ed. Riki Traum (2019), copyright by Hakibbutz Hameuchad-Sifriat Poalim.

Yona Wallach, "Tishlach li sheket," by permission of Eikhut Publishing,

Natan Zach, "Rega' echad," *Shirim Shonim*, copyright by Natan Zach—ACUM—Israel.

Introduction

Under Construction
A Kind of Festschrift for Israeli Literature

NANCY E. BERG AND NAOMI B. SOKOLOFF

> Festschriften persist and multiply. Why? Because they are not just retrospective, but prospective. That is to say the Festschrift is a Beruf, a call to further work, effort, and energy, a call to the improvement of learning, of a discipline, a science, an artistic vision, or an intellectual position. Even in this age of mass Festschriften, they remain a special literary genre.
>
> —Irving Louis Horowitz, *Communicating Ideas: The Politics of Scholarly Publishing*

Building and Being Built

Until recently, Israeli literature has been viewed as Hebrew literature and as a well-defined corpus of works established by a limited number of writers. Even into the late twentieth century, a generally accepted historiography stipulated a mostly agreed-upon set of must-reads. In the last few decades, though, an explosion of writing has altered the scene. New creative voices have proliferated since the 1990s, as have new approaches to reading their work and the work of their predecessors. Diversity has replaced consensus, and agreement about the past is itself up for question and revision. Multiple languages vie for recognition. New genres, such as the graphic novel and science fiction, demand consideration. In addition, greater attention to voices from the margins has led both to discovery and recovery of literary works, as well as a rethinking of literary history. Now, on the occasion of Israel at seventy, we have produced this volume to think about and reevaluate the startling trajectories of Israeli literature. At the seventy-year mark, a time that scholars often honor their teachers with a festschrift, we have the opportunity to reexamine Israeli writing, to gain new perspectives through a retrospective, and so offer a kind of festschrift to a now venerable yet still dynamic and ever-changing literature.

Our work here explores the opening up of Israeli literature to definitions that do not insist on linguistic, religio-ethnic, political, or even territorial correlations. Rather than limiting Israeli literature to work written in Hebrew by Jews living in the State of Israel, we take into account texts written in Hebrew and in other languages as well, texts by Israelis abroad as well as in Israel, texts by both Jews and non-Jews. And, even as the category "Israeli literature" stretches linguistically and geographically, we are mindful of the complexities that emerge from ideological and aesthetic implications of creativity in Hebrew—a new-old language with a remarkable history, remarkable richness, remarkable limitations (of size and number of native speakers), and no less remarkable political entanglements. It is important to keep all of this in mind when assessing the ways that artistic conventions have exhibited rupture and continuity. While the essays here tend to highlight peripheries, that which is innovative or has been overlooked, they do not neglect the center. Rather, the commentary offered uses observations about outliers to enrich, complement, and reinterpret canonical texts. Furthermore, as we take up implicit questions of canon, master narrative, and predominant motifs that are crucial for examining a national literature, we also reconsider the implications of defining a body of writing *as* a national literature.

The idea of a unified single narrative of Israeli literature has never been more than a myth. There have always been Israeli authors working in languages other than Hebrew, as well as authors undervalued by the literary establishment (some of whom later became major figures). Alternative artistic cross-currents and undercurrents have circulated in diverse Israeli communities. As with most myths, though, there is an element of truth at the core of the idea that Israeli culture once enjoyed considerable cohesion. For many years, broad agreement prevailed regarding the boundaries of the literature, whom and what to read, and even—to large degree—how to read it. So too, there was a reigning history: a sense of changing generations. It was generally accepted, for instance, that the New Wave and Young Poets of the 1960s shook up the convictions held in the 1950s by the State Generation, that poet Natan Zach challenged the conventions of Natan Alterman. In short, the dominant perception was of the center holding even as new, rebellious, and subversive trends worked their way from marginal to central positions. Well into the 1990s, it seemed that everyone shared the same media experiences—for example, that everyone watched the Mabat news program at 9 p.m. daily on the sole Israeli television station. Before that time, in an era of much more unified and homogeneous cultural production, ideas and values circulated through even more centralized media: a few publishing houses (all affiliated with ideological movements); a limited number of radio stations; educational curricula and public ceremonies shaped by establishment institutions.[1] So, too, it appeared that everyone interested in literature shared the same reading list and, for the most part, similar ways of reading and of thinking about what everyone was reading. At least, they were all part of a shared conversation. General agreement reigned regarding which books and cultural values had been enshrined in communal debate. Today things are different. It is not just that a fractured literature now prevails along with many readerships; in addition, the corpus of texts by Israelis—transnational in production and written in multiple languages—defies categorization. To take an example: Is Dina Rubina, who writes in Russian and is famous among Russian language readers throughout the world, part of the Israeli canon or the Russian canon? Both or neither? What about Shahar Bram, who publishes in English in Israel, or Shani Boianju, who writes in English and publishes in America?[2] Consider, too, the emerging Hebrew literary scene in Berlin.[3] These cases indicate how difficult it is to delineate the boundaries of Israeli literature.[4]

Furthermore, the very idea of canon has shifted. Canon as a topic of study has held high visibility for well over a half-century, but it has undergone a sea change during that time. In 1948—the same year, coincidentally, that Israel achieved statehood—F. R. Leavis's *The Great Tradition* appeared in Britain. Its stringent pronouncements of what belonged in the category of great English writing, and what didn't, were highly influential. However, as time went by, such narrow gatekeeping was widely mocked.[5] Subsequently, canon turned from a noun into a verb, from product to process. Scholarship shifted from defining what is in the canon to asking how it got there. Questioning the canon then continued to gain momentum as a topic of academic inquiry. It peaked sometime in the 1980s, as various scholarly approaches—feminist studies, identity politics, gender studies, ethnic studies, etc.—called attention to and scrutinized hierarchies of power.[6] Debate on such topics has been ongoing in Europe and North America ever since. Israeli literature should be understood within this context of global inquiry, but Israel presents a particularly acute case: because it is a cauldron of multilingualism and different cultures, because its demographics have evolved at breathtaking speed, because the sheer number of publications is stunning.

The fragmentation of Israeli literature and the copious amount of writing available is such that the notion of attempting an encyclopedic historiography is now considered passé. Yet, even as the idea of canon itself becomes less determinative, canon study persists in other guises. The quantity of literature coming out of Israel may feel overwhelming and consensus elusive, but formative forces at work still raise compelling questions: What is produced and consumed? Who gets published, reviewed, translated, adapted, taught, honored? What are the factors that shape bestseller lists, prizes, curricula, and scholarship? These are significant processes worthy of deliberation. Moreover, once upon a time, discussions of canon—whether constructive or deconstructive—necessarily acknowledged how the Zionist project was integral to understanding the evolution of Hebrew literature. It wasn't possible to talk about one without the other, whether that literature was allied with cultural endeavors expressed in the slogan "to build and be built" or, on the contrary, was critical of Zionism and Zionist discourse. Today it is clear that Israeli literature is still very much under construction. Indeed, it is experiencing boom times, expanding in many directions, gaining acclaim nationally and internationally, and it is not so closely linked to Zionism, either for or against. The idea of canon in these circumstances is very much a construct—that is, merely a concept and not a full, complex reality. Nonetheless, for all the limitations of canon-making, debate about canon still plays a crucial role as it provides conceptual frameworks to try to make sense of how things have developed, to decide what matters, and to consider why certain authors and works merit attention.

Any account, however brief, of the first seventy years of Israeli literature must surely deal with some fundamental tensions that persist over the decades. These include the construction of "Hebrewness (Ivriut) as an 'authentic' local culture" and "an act of national invention,"[7] along with the ways that Israeli writing has pushed back against that idealized project, measuring gaps between dreams and realization; tensions between universalism and the particularities of Israeli experience; tensions between dominance of Ashkenazi, secular, male writers and other voices that long remained peripheral. What we offer here, much more modestly, as a lead-in to our collection of essays is a brief look at three moments of canon formation that are significant in both reflecting and influencing the development of Israeli literature. These three snapshots in time help trace the arc of a process that has transformed Israeli literature from a literature with an emerging common core to a literature that has prospered and expanded and splintered and become much more elastic. Along the way, we get a glimpse of multiple factors that have contributed to canon making—not only scholarship and education, but also the changing nature of the media; the role of publishing houses and their marketing strategies in shaping culture; the compilation of anthologies and awarding of prizes; artistic trends and influences from abroad; and the swiftly transforming demographics in Israeli society. The first moment, 1977, finds scholars and readers building a shared bookshelf (albeit not without dissent; alternative trends were already evident and had long been emerging). The second moment, 1993, features a highly acclaimed and influential TV series. While the show still argued for a cohesive narrative about Israeli literature, it was also adopting a new (and competing) medium to achieve popular outreach, even as it acknowledged more diverse content. This moment, too, was marked by competing claims—there was much that the show elided or overlooked, alternative literary developments that were gaining increasing attention in other forums. During the third moment, 2009–10, rival lists of recommended reading duel, making evident that one bookshelf no longer suffices. These events ushered in an era in which not just new authors but also multiple new genres and perspectives clamored for attention. These moments show the making and unmaking of the Israeli canon(s) to be rapid, intense, and palpably self-reflexive.

1977—Building a Canon

By this date, it seems, Israeli literature was well established, on the threshold of fulfilling thirty years. Significantly, 1977 marked the appearance of the first volume of Gershon Shaked's magnum opus, *Hasipporet ha 'ivrit, 1880–1980* (*Modern Hebrew Literature, 1880–1980*) which, over the coming years, was followed by multiple further installments.[8] The idea was to provide a grand overview, grounded in the fundamental Zionist value of return to the land and a concomitant revival of the Jewish people. According to Yaron Peleg, Shaked's concept of the "Zionist metanarrative" created "an overarching framework of references that encompassed all aspects of life in the new Jewish society in Erets Israel, including the creation of literature."[9] Shaked's first volume concentrated decidedly on precursors to Israeli literature (Hebrew writers of the diaspora and in the Yishuv, only a few of whom even lived till 1948), yet it proved foundational, for it envisioned what would become the most influential of interpretive frameworks for many years into the future.

Also in 1977, the journal *Modern Hebrew Literature* was launched by the Institute for the Translation of Hebrew Literature and two significant English-language anthologies made their debut;[10] these publications represent efforts to set the canon (though in a less deliberate way than that of the literary historian), and they suggest a calculated effort to reach an Anglo-American audience.[11] Most of these endeavors unsurprisingly posit the land—and often the nation—at the center of Israeli writing. Even writers who place characters in other settings seem to reinforce the centrality of Israel, and even texts that question the Zionist narrative respond to it as a central preoccupation. These collections helped introduce readers outside of Israel to S. Y. Agnon, Amos Oz, A. B. Yehoshua, Yoram Kaniuk, David Shachar, Haim Gouri, Yitzhak Orpaz, Uri Orlev, Pinchas Sadeh, Yehuda Amichai, Aharon Appelfeld, Yizhak Ben-Ner, and Dan Tsalka. (Readers of today might notice the minimal diversity; almost all these authors are male and Ashkenazi)

Alongside the model of the Zionist metanarrative and consensus building, in 1977 Itamar Even-Zohar presented an alternative model of literary study: a dynamic, layered model of sociocultural systems that affect the world of literature.[12] While Shaked took into account many genres of prose, Even-Zohar's ideas about the "literary polysystem" opened space to consider multiple additional kinds of literary production and genres, from highbrow to lowbrow, thus opening possibilities for shaking up assumptions and complicating the picture. Mainstream fiction at the time was itself shaking up assumptions and exploring new paths. Note, too, that 1977 was a year of political upheaval, when Likud defeated the long-dominant Labor party in national elections and Mizrachi voters gained new clout, and societal cataclysms were beginning to manifest in Israeli novels as well. The year 1977 saw the publication of A. B. Yehoshua's *Hame'ahev* (*The Lover*), Sami Michael's *Hasut* (*Refuge*), Yaakov Shabtai's *Zikhron dvarim* (*Past Continuous*), and Amalia Kahana-Carmon's *Sadot magnetiyim* (*Magnetic Fields*). *The Lover* reflects on the trauma of the 1973 war. The novel is still very much grounded in the Zionist metanarrative, yet interrogates it by featuring multiple characters' perspectives, including that of the young Arab, Naim. In *Refuge*, Michael goes farther in giving voice to the hitherto unrepresented, introducing Arab and Jewish characters, each with his—and her—own perspective. His roman à clef of a communist cell in Haifa presents an alternative to the Zionist metanarrative. That foundational framework of reference is still present, but the author highlights relations between Jews and Arabs in ways that are distinct from mainstream views. In turn, Shabtai's tale of disillusionment presents itself through scenes of disintegration of family and societal values in Tel Aviv. Though this author is preoccupied with the dreams and experiences of Israel's founding generations, his novel suggests that what was once the center is no longer holding. Kahana-Carmon, for her part, moves outside the metanarrative parameters altogether. She formulates a "personal and original discourse of love" that features women characters and emphasizes the significance of individuals and relationships.[13]

These deviations from and variations on the Zionist metanarrative are harbingers of more radical changes to come. Shaked's comprehensive overview of Hebrew literature—which would eventually come to foreground such Israeli writers as S. Yizhar, Moshe Shamir, Aharon Megged, Natan Shaham, Benjamin Tammuz, Amos Kenan, Nisim Aloni, Yotam Reuveni, Ruth Almog, David Schutz, along with all those named above—was by design limited to a hundred-year span: 1880–1980. As that end date was approaching, the literary scene was rapidly changing and soon to veer off into post-Zionist and postmodernist directions.

MOMENT TWO: THE CANON IN THE MIRROR

In 1993, Shaked's series *Leshon hamar'ot* (*The Language of Mirrors*) premiered on Israeli television on the new Channel Two. Informed by his multivolume history and its conclusions, this enormously ambitious project proved to be a major cultural event. The programs aimed to present an overview of modern Hebrew literature in seventeen 35–45 minute episodes comprising three dozen novels and a handful of shorter fictional pieces. Dramatizations of excerpts were interspersed with remarks by Shaked, occasional stills, bits from documentaries, and scenes from previous cinematic adaptations.

The criteria for inclusion seem to balance aesthetics, and the significance of the writer and specific work, with the thematics of the individual episodes and the series as a whole. There were also, as ever, extraliterary factors to take into account—technical considerations such as the ease of dramatizing, excerpting, and adapting works, as well as copyright and budgeting. The series focused on the relationship between literature and Israeli society, and especially the conflict between the individual and the collective in Israel. Each episode was organized by a topic, and—except for the one on women writers—contributed to the overall thematic flow of the entire program. Commentary on Y. H. Brenner frames the series, and S. Yizhar's *Yemei Tziklag* (*Days of Ziklag*) sits at the center of the inquiry: What does it mean to be Israeli? What are the social implications of the status of Zionism? The series sought to demonstrate how literature reflects these questions, and what kinds of answers it offers.

Shaked's series has been read as a fascinating experiment to counter television's threat to literature. It approached the relatively new medium as a potential partner instead of as competition,[14] and, at the time it aired, *Leshon hamar'ot* was received with excitement and enthusiasm. Despite its dismal placement on Saturday mornings, the reception was positive and the reviews were strong. They labeled the series quite an achievement, an exceptional experience, and they remarked on its good sense and good taste. The only criticism at the time was that the program offered "too much richness."[15] *Leshon hamar'ot* was to Hebrew literature as *Pillar of Fire* to Israeli history (or Alex Haley's *Roots* to the African American story).

And yet, missing from the program is much of what was emerging in Israeli literature during the 1980s—perhaps because the process of bringing the series to the air purportedly took ten years. From today's vantage point, it is clear that the *Leshon hamar'ot* presented a rather conservative canon. The 1980s was a decade in which exile, not homeland, gained overt dominance as a theme, while the stories of Jews from Arab and Islamic lands gained greater audiences. Fissures in the national hegemony were becoming visible to the naked eye, whether due to the trauma of '73 or the political upheaval in its wake, the coming of age of different immigrant communities, military scandals that threatened idealism, or all of the above and more.[16] By the mid-1990s, when the series was broadcast, change was well underway; this new decade was dominated by women writers, and hyphenated identities and ethnic writing flourished—not to mention LGBT themes, religious subject matter, and personal writing. In the television series, though, these developments went largely unremarked.

Mizrachi writers, like women writers, were confined to their own episode. Shaked did attend to the second generation to the Holocaust (concentrating primarily on David Grossman's *See Under: Love*), but he did not delve into works by many of the prominent writers on this topic (Nava Semel, Savyon Liebrecht, Amir Gutfreund) nor did he underscore the year 1986 as a watershed moment. Later scholarship has emphasized the innovations and turning points associated with that year, in response to Anton Shammas's novel *Arabeskot* (*Arabesques*) and Yehoshua Kenaz's *Hitganvut yechidim* (*Infiltration*), along with Grossman's *See Under: Love* and groundbreaking short story collections such as Ruth Almog's *Nashim* (*Women*) and Savyon Liebrecht's *Tapuchim min hamidbar* (*Apples from the Desert*).

Shaked at one time or another penned reviews and analysis of all those writers and many other contemporary authors as well.[17] The fact that not all made it into *Leshon hamar'ot* indicates that canon setting is a matter of perspective and of making space for and conferring value on a chosen few artists and texts. As the '90s continued and literary production grew, scholars paid attention to a wide variety of authors and poets, including—to name just some examples—Amnon Shamosh, Batya Gur, Shulamit Lapid, Ronni Someck, Yona Wallach, Yehoshua Sobol, but literary critics were also attentive to new genres, introducing serious analysis of the family saga, the mystery novel, and chick lit to the more panoramic view of the literary scene. So, while this second moment that we've highlighted in some way continues or echoes the first, it does so in a way that embraces new media and branches out in multicultural directions. It anticipates the third moment, in which another deliberate attempt to produce canon is undercut not only by fragmentation and diversity, but by heightened awareness of the inevitable limitations of canon making.

MOMENT THREE: DUELING CANONS

In 2009, in honor of the seventieth anniversary of the newspaper *Yediot aharonot*, its publishing house decided to reissue twenty novels. This was a deliberate attempt to designate a sealed canon by creating a list of significant Hebrew books. The initiative, called "Am hasefer—prozah yisraelit," was a sister project to the earlier publication series "Jewish bookcase" (*Aron hasefarim hayehudi 2007*).[18] A few months later, in parallel, publishing house Hasifriyah Hechadashah reached its twentieth anniversary, and editor Menachem Perry marked the occasion by publishing twenty-two volumes of choice selections.

Clear differences set this list apart from the one produced by *Yediot*. *Yediot*'s list spans the years 1948–2008, is limited to novels, and consciously sets out to establish "the essential bookshelf." The approach was conservative and, indeed, the effort covered much the same material and many of the same writers as Shaked's earlier work.[19] Perry's collection, on the other hand, was drawn from the backlist of publishing house Siman Kri'ah. Novels dominated, but poetry, translation, drama, and shorter fiction were also included. At the time, most of the works had been newly revised and edited. The complete set of books purports to comprise landmark works of Israeli literature, volumes that "changed the face of Hebrew [literature] in their time."[20] Some of the titles overlap with the canon presented in *Leshon hamar'ot*, as well as with the competing list from 2010, but Perry's choices skew more recent. They are slightly edgier and, in some ways, make for more challenging reads.

Each list, of course, is informed by the personal knowledge, taste, and agenda of its respective editor, and each list is shaped by its missions—both stated and unstated—as well as by market forces. *Yediot*, for example, wants to offer an overview of Israeli literature, choosing the most representative works. Hasifriyah Hechadashah is conscious of "attracting new readers and challenging new writers." That helps explain why *Yediot* begins with Shamir's *Hu halakh basadot* (*He Walked in the Fields*) and Pinchas Sadeh's *Hachayim kemashal* (*Life as a Parable*)—books whose time, by then, may have passed—and Hasifriyah Hechadashah's includes two titles each from Shabtai, Yehoshua, and Grossman. Together, however, the two lists suggest that Shaked's historiography still dominated thinking about Israeli literature. The regnant views focused mostly on male, Ashkenazi writers who had contributed to the so-called Zionist narrative, even when contesting it. This way of constructing the canon barely nodded toward the unraveling of the master narrative, which had already begun to take place a generation before, and, it did not foresee the very dynamic, innovative literary arena that has been materializing since the turn of the twenty-first century.

However, between the time of the 1993 television series, *Leshon hamar'ot*, and the more recent rival canons, many scholarly works appeared that directly undertook analysis of canon formation and questioned the processes by which canons become fixed. A special issue of the journal *Teoria uvikoret* (1991) provided a forum for scholars interested in the influence of identity politics on the canon.[21] In addition, clusters of scholars began to debate at length the limits of writing literary history and mapping canons, demonstrating the need to recognize careful negotiations between centers and peripheries.[22] Dan Miron's important book *From Continuity to Contiguity* (2005) pointed out the complexities of the relationship between "Jewish" and Israeli literatures, where the two overlap, and how both test the meaningfulness of the term *national literature*.[23] By the time the dueling lists were produced, they followed more than a decade of fevered research and discussion in the area of canon formation in Hebrew and Israeli literature. In addition, other studies offered partial correctives to the national narrative by redefining and expanding the canon to include, respectively, writing by women; writing by Israelis who hailed from the Mediterranean region; Israeli writing in Yiddish, Russian, and English; American Hebrew literature; and the concept of minor literature.

These efforts, together, greatly raised awareness of Diaspora writers (such as David Vogel) and new appreciation for others who wrote about Jewish experience outside of Israel (for instance, Aharon Appelfeld, who often wrote about the European past; Eleonora Lev; and Sami Berdugo, particularly in his evocation of Moroccan life in *Zeh hadvarim*). Critical attention to new genres and to previously marginal ones—diaries, genre fiction (e.g., detectives, romance, sci fi), flash fiction, and the graphic novel—contributed to widening conversations about literature and to a concurrent opening of the canon.[24] Recognition now went to any number of authors—including Eshkol Nevo, Nir Baram, Vaan Nguyen, Alex Epstein, Rutu Modan, Alon Hilu, Asfu Beru, and Assaf Gavron—who were virtually unknown a decade before, and who introduced or reintroduced genres and modes of writing to Israeli literature. It became a widely accepted assumption that young Israeli authors were likely to strive for highly personal and individual art, to "shun political relevancy, whether as writers or activists" and to decline to serve as "spokesmen for the collective."[25] They differ qualitatively from writers of the '60s who wrote about the individual to counter the narrative of the collective, or who wrote from the perspective of sons who cannot live up to their fathers' self-sacrifice. Those writing from a generation later chose not to engage with questions of the collective, of self-sacrifice, and of heroic fathers. Such questions were not even part of their vocabulary.

This third moment, then, like the earlier ones, displays a central tension between attempts to designate a canon and a lively, messy, expansive, and rapidly changing literary scene that overpowers and defies efforts at canon building. The result is not just cultural fragmentation—which was emerging already in 1977—nor the flourishing of multiculturalism, which has itself attained the status of metanarrative. More to the point: any number of writers in the 2000s no longer felt a need to engage with the Zionist metanarrative. The rise of a literature that no longer sets the nation at its center gives rise to a crisis of canon. That crisis is a symptom of challenge to the very idea of a national literature.

To Be Determined

Nevertheless, even while the borders of national literature are being breached, people are still trying to make sense of the literary scene and to assign priorities. While canon remains an elusive entity, as slippery as soap in a bathtub, reports of the death of the canon have been greatly exaggerated. The canon represents "that which is assumed to be 'good' literature, in fact the 'best' literature: that which is worth preserving and passing on from one generation to the next"[26] or "the limited field we criticize and theorize about."[27] Multiple canons are constantly in the process of forming and re-forming themselves. The scholarly canon is likely to differ from popular and commercial ones; the academic bookshelf differs from best-seller lists. Yet, while scholarship neither determines nor is determined by market forces, it informs and is influenced by them. In addition, overseas canons are necessarily distinct from the Israeli, homegrown canon, but they have been growing in recent years.[28] Consider the Israeli list of the Dalkey Archives, begun the same year as the Hebrew bookshelves of Hasifriyah Hechadashah and Proza Yisraelit discussed above: starting with Castel-Bloom's *Dolly City* and Eshkol Nevo's *Homesick,* Kaniuk's, Asaf Schurr's, and Gabriela Avigur-Rotem's works quickly followed. Toby Press has brought ever more Israeli writers to the attention of the world in English translation.[29]

Fishel Lachower's early history of modern Hebrew literature (1946–48) has been described as part of a "conscious Zionist effort to establish a Hebrew literary tradition where there was none before."[30] That project was, in concert with the spirit of the Zionist slogan "To build and be built," an act of determination to forge a new culture. Now, by contrast, the canon remains "to be determined"; it is fluid and multifaceted and as yet unknowable.

In the midst of this complicated scene, our volume *Since 1948* offers interim assessments of and commentary on how this remarkable literature has evolved and is evolving. This project includes reports from the field of literary studies and provides state of the art readings, but also aims for rereading, recovery, and reinterpretation. The essays take a look back over seventy years and reconsider some of the ways we have gotten to where we are today.

The contributors, who include a mix of established and new scholars and writers from both sides of the Atlantic, address a wide range of issues. They present diverse viewpoints, topics, genres, and approaches. Approximately half of us are Israeli, half American, although in keeping with the central assumptions of this book, it could be argued that national categories are neither as significant nor as fixed as they were once thought to be. In every case, the contributors have each had experience in the Israeli academy as well as in American academia. We hope that our variously transnational backgrounds help us bring discussion of Israeli literature in the making to an English-speaking audience.

As editors, we considered many possible ways of constructing the table of contents. The numerous options reflect the many facets of Israeli literature, and, indeed, the difficulties we encountered indicate the very reason for writing this book: so as to present an enlarged view of the diversity and heterogeneity of Israeli literature now and also so as to rediscover the past. New perspectives on the past call for reclaiming it, recasting or reconfiguring the historiography in order to allow for a wider lens and consideration of more voices. We entertained the possibility of including one section oriented to a chronological arc, focusing on developments from early to more recent texts; we thought about thematic divisions; we weighed the idea of pairing texts with similar critical approaches, or just placing essays in a random order. The upshot of this process is that we have arranged the pieces into four sections. All four in one way or another point to the question of voice: which voices have been sounded, which have been silenced in Israeli literature? In which ways do they connect, emerge from another, quarrel, contradict, or stand independently? The notion of canon—as that word is used in the musical sphere—comes to mind, and we cannot help but think of how the multiplicity of voices we are dealing with is *not* canonic. In music, a canon is a contrapuntal composition in which "each successively entering voice presents the initial theme usually transformed in a strictly consistent way."[31] In contrast, the voices in Israeli literature are neither rigidly structured, nor are they strictly in counterpoint; that is, they do not combine "two or more independent melodies into a single harmonic texture." Rather, they are polyphonic—sometimes complementing, sometimes harmonic, often contrasting, at times filled with tensions or discordant, certainly independent but also part of a complicated weave of interconnected expression. Together, the essays in this volume illustrate a primary observation that challenges the model of a national literature: in the case of Israeli writing land, literature, and people do not line up neatly.

For Part One, "Through Time: Silences, Voices, Echoes," we have singled out three essays that most boldly highlight how new voices have succeeded old ones and emerged in subsequent generations, as well as how they have reverberated with one another and built on intertextual references. Our second section, "Across Language and Territory: Literature and Identity," emphasizes the point that the words *Hebrew, Jewish, Israeli, Erets Yisraeli*, and *Zionist* are not coterminous. Sometimes they overlap, but not always, and often in startling configurations. This section takes into account Israeli authors who write in languages other than Hebrew, Hebrew-speaking Israeli citizens who are not Zionists, and Israelis writing outside of Israel. Part Three, "Between the Lines: Rethinking Genres," turns to genres that were long seen as outside of the canon but that have become more central in recent years: children's literature, memoir of childhood, and pulp fiction geared to teen readers. It is a sign of the maturity of Israeli literature that scholars now can see how such once-marginalized genres fit into the grand scheme of literary productivity in Israel. The essays aim to show how these genres rejuvenate, energize, and contribute original approaches to mainstream literature. Finally, in Part Four, we have placed the three essays that deal most directly or most self-consciously with questions of constructing canon. Grouped under the title "Concerning Canons," these pieces raise questions with regard to established canon even as they acknowledge consternation over the conundrums of canon building. Canons, like the boundaries of national literature, are constantly and continuously being prodded, provoked, and imploded.

The volume opens with "Not One, but Five Moments of Silence" by Eran Tzelgov. Looking at poems that overtly call for silence, beginning with Nathan Zach's famous line "One moment, silence" (1960) and ending with a poem from Tehila Hakimi's debut collection (2015) that calls for one day of silence, this essay highlights shifts and changes in the making of an authentic speaker in Israeli poetry. Tzelgov's historiography derives not from a top-down theory, but from a series of texts, each of which constitutes its own *ars poetica* and each of which responds to another that preceded it. This analysis thereby uncovers a chain of voices that assert themselves in evolving fashion. The essay also provides new readings of classic texts while introducing texts that are most likely altogether new to English-reading audiences.

In the next essay, Michal Raizen also identifies a chain of literary creativity—one that links together song and story, Hebrew and Arabic. Raizen explores the emergence of Mizrachi voices in Israeli literature by examining the trope of the *hafla*, a kind of traditional musical and story-telling performance widely popular throughout the Arab world. One of Raizen's key insights here is that this Arabic literary genre has been incorporated into recent Hebrew fiction in a way that enables cultural transmission across generations. Her analysis makes accessible several novels that make accessible the *hafla*, a cherished part of the culture of Middle Eastern Jews before they came to Israel, and so the novels make that heritage more legible to Hebrew readers. The written, printed word aspires to retrieve and express an art form of the past, to sound the sounds of the *hafla* through a non-sound medium, and thereby also to introduce innovative themes and style into Hebrew prose.

Wendy Zierler's essay on "Anthological Poetics" points out resonances generated by placing modern poems side by side with traditional prayers. Her essay is grounded in the nascent Israeli phenomenon of *Hitchadshut Yehudit*—a contemporary Israeli religious renaissance that makes extensive use of secular song and poetry within synagogue liturgy. Zierler argues that conscious editorial juxtapositions of varied materials in newly compiled prayer books produce new meaning, encourage new readings of texts, and continue the tradition of *piyyut* in an innovative way. With the recent rise of liberal Judaism, new worship communities, and the secular *beit midrash*, *siddurim* are disseminating Hebrew verse in significant, energizing ways, showing how ancient and modern texts speak to one another.

While the majority of the literature we consider in this collection is Hebrew literature, the second section of essays here readily acknowledges the multilingual landscape. Shachar Pinsker examines the place of Yiddish writing in our evolving understanding of what constitutes Israeli literature and its history. His essay argues for including Yiddish in our reading of Israeli culture, showing how bilingual Hebrew-Yiddish writers strengthen his case. At the heart of the chapter is an analysis of Yiddish poems, stories, and a novel written between 1948 and 1966, by Avrom Sutzkever, H. Binyomin, Mendel Mann, Tzvi Eisenman, and Yossl Birshteyn. These texts deal with questions about the relationship between Yiddish and Hebrew, the authors' encounter with the Israeli landscape, and the traumas suffered by those uprooted from their homes. Against the prevalent notion that Israeli literature is synonymous with Hebrew literature, Pinsker demonstrates a better understanding of Israeli literature by attending to the "Yiddish that lurks behind."

Yael Dekel's article on short fiction from the 1950s also directs attention to formative times in Israel, to territory, and to languages in contact. She focuses on largely overlooked stories published in *Alef*, the magazine of the Canaanite movement—an ideological and cultural movement from the pre-State era that aimed to create a Hebrew nation disconnected from the Jewish past. Her close look at a story from 1950, Eitan Notev's "Praise Be to God," offers fresh perspectives on the 1948 Arab-Israeli war and on fictional representation of encounters between Hebrew speakers and Arabic speakers. Engaging with theories of translation to elucidate relations between Canaanite and Zionist ideology, she argues that Notev's story poses critical questions concerning the very definition of Hebrew literature and Israeli literature. Dekel's translation of this story—the first English translation of it—appears in the appendix to this volume.

In "Hebrew Unbound: Alternative Homelands in the New World," Melissa Weininger further explores the boundaries of Israeli literature by addressing Hebrew works and English language works by Hebrew speakers, largely written and published outside of Israel. Both linguistically and geographically, this body of work challenges what we think of as "Israeli" or "Hebrew" literature, complicating the linear narrative of Israeli literary history from Statehood Generation onward. Focusing on Ruby Namdar's 2015 novel *Habayit asher nechrav* (*The Ruined House*) and Nava Semel's 2006 *Iysra'el* (*IsraIsle*), this essay explores fiction that, in the wake of globalization, imagines alternative histories and entertains visions of alternative homelands.

The following section treats literature for and about children and teenagers, delving into genres that fall outside the conventional boundaries of canon. Shai Ginsburg examines the (relatively late) emergence of fantasy and make-believe in Israeli children's literature through works by Yigal Mossinsohn, Avraham Shlonsky, Devorah Omer, Nurit Zarchi, and Yanetz Levi. Rather than categorizing these stories and poems of imaginary travel as escapism, this chapter reads between the lines to analyze political contexts and nuance that only adults would discern, not child audiences/readers. Children's literature is an especially rich area of inquiry, not only because of its significance in formulating a national narrative, and its paradoxical capacity for experimentation, but also because Israeli children's literature was consciously and deliberately developed in large part by established, canonical writers Here, Ginsburg looks at the ways in which fantasy is employed in children's literature as a response to politics of the here and now by use of "there" and "then." Even while timeless and universal, these works are grounded in Israeli place and time.

Naomi Sokoloff's essay focuses on memoir by Alona Frankel, a renowned Israeli children's author. In a trilogy aimed at adult readers, Frankel incorporated conventions of juvenile fiction in order to present the story of her own childhood experiences in Nazi-occupied Poland. Sokoloff posits that Frankel's autobiographical writing can help put into relief a whole strain of Hebrew literature, from the 1960s till today, that approaches the topic of the Holocaust through animal themes. By challenging and dismantling the notion of the "dumb" animal, narratives dealing with trauma signal that their verbal art ventures into a realm of extremes beyond ordinary human language. Drawing on the field of critical animal studies, Sokoloff draws a noncanonical genre firmly into the canon.

Eric Zakim looks at the *stalagim*, stories—published as pulp fiction—about World War II POW camps. Generally considered a vulgar curio, or at best as examples of popular culture geared to the pubescent male, these stories are treated here as serious literary works. This approach adds to (and complicates) our understanding of the role of the Holocaust in literary history as Israel transitioned to statehood. The masquerade that these texts were imported—the very fiction that these texts were translations—allows the works their initial entry into Israeli writing, and Zakim shows how the noncanonical nature of the *stalagim* allows the writers to give expression to taboos, to test the very limits of acceptable literature, and to contest the repression of individual desire. He argues that the distinctiveness of the *stalagim*—and part of what brought them so much opprobrium—relates to the ways subjects in these texts float freely, detached from national identities; so too, shifting narrative points of view destabilize subjectivity. Indeterminability, and not simple vulgarity, is what makes these texts so unsettling and controversial a phenomenon.

Having moved outside the canon to a marginalized subgenre, we then turn in our final section to essays that directly consider issues of canonicity and the challenges of historiography.

In "Disruptive Nativity: The Poetry of Rina Shani and the Sixties in Israel" Riki Traum recovers an almost forgotten poetic voice, analyzing Shani's aesthetics of resistance to the idea of belonging. In countering tensions between home and exile, Shani employed nomadism as a strategy in both her life and her art. This essay puts her poetry in dialogue with that of the more canonical Leah Goldberg, her teacher, mentor, and friend, noting that where Goldberg offers the solution of two homelands, Shani questions the option of even one.

Yaron Peleg brings us to the present and beyond in his piece on Israeli millennial literature. He returns our focus to the Zionist meta-narrative in the twenty-first century, an age that is at one and the same time post-nationalist and post-globalist. By looking at the work of Asaf Schurr, who published five novels in quick succession between the years 2007 and 2014, Peleg addresses the attempts of more contemporary Israeli works to overcome the limitations of postmodernism. Read together, Schurr's novels invoke the crisis of representation in the postmodern age while at the same time offering a tentative solution. His project eschews the idea of an "imagined national community" in favor of smaller but more cohesive social units.

In the concluding essay, "'And the winner is . . .': The Economy of Literary Awards," Nancy E. Berg observes that prizes for Israeli literature have proliferated. While recognizing the largely reactive nature of literary prizes, this chapter reads such competitions as expressions of national identity and values, as discussions of changing times and tastes, and as opportunities for dissent. Berg presents the Sapir Prize as a test case, examining its triumphs, its scandals, and its impact on the economics of the book markets and publicity in Israel. Recent controversies have revealed significant fissures between society and culture and speak to the concerns in a number of this volume's other essays; so too, the overtly political aspect(s) shed light on both the Israeli literary landscape at seventy, and on literary prizes in general.

We hope that the order of our table of contents—as the prepositions in the titles of the sections suggest—will indicate relationships among the essays as well as cross-connections among the multiple factors that converge in shaping Israeli literature. Emerging out of those entwinements are possibilities for constructing new understandings of Israeli literature. A very different order for these essays is possible. For instance, Zierler deals with cultural exchange between North America and Israel, noting that American Jewish thinkers have joined with Israelis to redesign prayer books. She asks not only what is going into the Israeli prayer canon, but also which aspects of Israeli writing will enter the American prayer canon. Her piece, then, might well be compared with Melissa Weininger's—which similarly deals with America as well as Israel—to spur reflection on contemporary interactions between the two major Jewish populations in the world today. Another example: Tzelgov, Pinsker, and Traum all comment on poetry and poets who have responded to their precursors. Joint consideration of those essays could contribute to an enhanced sense of intertextuality and implied conversations within Israeli literature. Ginsburg and Peleg, for their part, both raise questions about the political and the personal, pulling us to think about shifting trends in Israeli literature that place varying emphasis, over time, on the collective versus the individual.

Yael Dekel's piece, in particular, lends itself to various alternate pairings, because it highlights multifaceted qualities of Israeli writing and one of the basic issues our volume confronts: the rather complex ways in which land, language, and national identity do and do not overlap. In that regard, it makes sense to group her essay with Melissa Weininger's, which similarly focuses on geography and language and raises questions about who is counted as an Israeli writer. Distilling out those nuances and complexities is central to the task of redefining the scope of Israeli literature. However, Dekel also analyzes how Canaanite prose stretches the boundaries of Hebrew so as to allow Arabic voices to be heard, and in that regard her work is closer to Michal Raizen's acknowledgment of Arabic song within Israeli culture. Note, too, that Dekel and Sokoloff both call attention to voices that once were suppressed in Hebrew literature—Holocaust survivors and Arabs. In the literature they consider, the silencing of such voices has been connected to animal themes. Arab characters in early Israeli literature often were presented by Jewish authors as mute, as animals, and remained that way for some decades until the 1980s and after, with the prominence of writers Anton Shammas, Siham Daoud, Sayed Kashua, Ayman Sikseck, Salman Masalha, Ayat Abou Shmeiss, and others. Sokoloff shows how Alona Frankel approaches animal themes to work through and break out of the traumatic silences of her childhood during the Holocaust—a time when Jews were viewed as subhuman. Finally, the pairing of Dekel's and Zakim's essays is thought-provoking, for both grapple with representations of language itself. Dekel shows how Notev imports Arabic dialogue into his prose by translating it into varying registers of Hebrew. Zakim reports on a faux translation: he examines Hebrew fiction that pretends to have been written originally in English. These essays together put into relief ways that Israeli literature has reckoned with its own linguistic boundaries.

We hope our readers will combine and recombine these essays, mix and match them, consider how they speak to one another, and realize that Israeli literature is wonderfully flexible and elastic. It can contain many challenges—of language, geography, and genre. Israeli literature is multifaceted and that makes it harder to grasp the contours of a canon, but understanding these dimensions yields an enriched overall picture of this exciting and dynamic literature. Given these considerations, at the end of this volume we have provided a combined list of authors mentioned in the essays. The purpose is to give readers some indication of the literature we are covering here and what we have focused on, out of the myriad possibilities that presented themselves to us. This select sample of Israeli authors can provide some sense of the scope of the phenomena in question.

This volume aims to provide a meaningful range of perspectives on Israeli literature, indicating its ongoing vitality and the need to reread and reconsider aspects of what has come before. It should be clear that we are not necessarily endorsing the phenomena we describe, and we are not aiming to replace the so-called Zionist metanarrative with an alternative, unified narrative—nor do we advocate attempting that. We do, however, hope to open up conversation about Israeli literature to multiple narrative strands. The essays here are in conversation with one another and with larger conversations in comparative literature contexts. We invite the reader to join in those conversations. While these essays will interest and challenge scholars of Hebrew literature along with those readers who have broad and deep knowledge of Israeli culture, we hope it will also speak to others, too: readers who follow modern Jewish literature; anyone who has a stake in the changing values of Jewish culture and identity; everyone interested in Middle Eastern writing or in transnational literary developments. At a time when Humanities are questioning the model of the national literature department and the frameworks that associate language with nation, Israeli literature provides an intense and illuminating example of efforts to construct a national identity as well as the pressures and complexities that deconstruct those efforts. It can serve as a test case for considering the relevance of the category "national literature." Going beyond a national lens, this volume of essays aims to help reinvigorate the study of Israeli texts and culture and also create new audiences for them within the context of world literature. Israeli literature can no longer be defined by a homogenized national narrative; indeed, it never could. In fact, it offers an exemplar of a culture forged by both local and global forces and influences. Israeli literature is not a minor regional literature, but one that is transnational, multilingual, and worthy of global attention.

Notes

1. On the history of Israeli media and the circulation of culture in the early years of statehood, see for instance Motti Regev and Edwin Seroussi, *Popular Music and National Culture in Israel* (Berkeley and Los Angeles: University of California Press, 2004), 15–41.

2. For more on recent Israeli expat writing, see https://www.timesofisrael.com/7-internationally-acclaimed-israeli-expat-writers-to-watch/.

3. Germany has become a hub of Hebrew writing and the home of some notable Hebrew writers (such as poet Admiel Kosman and novelist Mati Shmuelof). Berlin boasts several Hebrew literary journals: *Shpitz, Aviv,* and *Mikan ve'eilakh.*

4. Rachel Harris refers to contemporary Israeli writing in the twenty-first century as "transcultural." See her introduction to "Israeli Literature in the 21st Century: The Transcultural Generation," in *Shofar: An Interdisciplinary Journal of Jewish Studies* 33, no. 4. On the question of what constitutes Israeli literature, see also, Shai Ginsburg: "Israeli Literature," *Oxford Bibliographies*, 2016. http://www.oxfordbibliographies.com/abstract/document/obo-9780199840731/obo-9780199840731-0130.xml?rskey=gut0qz&result=1&q=shai+ginsburg#firstMatch; accessed Oct. 15, 2018.

5. Leavis, *The Great Tradition* (London: Chatto and Windus, 1948).

6. Stanley Fish, *Is There a Text in This Class? The Authority of Interpretive Communities* (Cambridge: Harvard University Press, 1980); John Guillory, "The Ideology of Canon-Formation: T. S. Eliot and Cleanth Brooks," *Critical Inquiry* 10, no. 1 (1983): 173–98; Barbara Herrnstein Smith, *Contingencies of Value: Alternative Perspectives for Critical Theory* (Cambridge: Harvard University Press, 1988); Cornel West, "Minority Discourse and the Pitfalls of Canon Formation" *Yale Journal of Criticism* 1, no. 1 (1987): 193–201; Itamar Even-Zohar, "Polysystem Theory," *Poetics Today* 1, no. 1–2 (1979): 287–310.

7. Rachel Harris, introduction to "Israeli Literature in the 21st Century: The Transcultural Generation," *Shofar* 33, no. 4 (2015): 4.

8. Volume 2 appeared in 1983, volume 3 in 1988, volume 4 in 1993, and volume 5 in 1998. A highly condensed and abbreviated version in English appeared as *Modern Hebrew Fiction*, trans. Yael Lotan, ed. and adapted Emily Miller Budick, bibliography Jessica Cohen (New Milford, CT: Toby Press, 2000).

9. Yaron Peleg, "The Critic as a Dialectical Zionist," *Prooftexts: A Journal of Jewish Literary History* 23, no. 3 (2003): 384. For other excellent overviews of Shaked's five-volume history and its impact, see Yigal Schwartz's review in *Partial Answers: Journal of Literature and the History of Ideas* 5, no. 2 (June 2007) and Shachar Pinsker, "The Challenges of Writing a Literary History of Early Modernist Hebrew Fiction: Gershon Shaked and Beyond," *Hebrew Studies* 49 (2008): 291–98.

10. Elliott Anderson and Robert Friend, *Contemporary Israeli Literature* (Philadelphia: Jewish Publication Society, 1977) and Ezra Spicehandler and Curtis Arnson, eds, *New Writing in Israel* (New York: Schocken Books, 1976).

11. Yaakov Besser, who would go on to found the General Union of Hebrew Writers, launches '*Iton 77.*

12. Even-Zohar, "Polysystem Theory."

13. Hannah Naveh. "Context and Authorial Intent," in Alan Mintz, *Reading Hebrew in America* (Hanover, NH: Brandeis University Press; University Press of New England, 2003), 198. It's worth noting that Lesley Hazelton's path-breaking book *Israeli Women: The Reality behind the Myths* was published in 1977 (New York: Simon and Schuster).

14. Nancy E. Berg, "A Cavalcade of Hebrew Literature," *Prooftexts* 24, no. 2 (1993): 43–51.

15. Hannah Zemer, "Leshon hamar'ot," *Shishi*, Jan. 21, 1994.

16. http://www.jewishvirtuallibrary.org/jsource/isdf/text/ben-horin.html.

17. See, for instance, Shaked's *Gal achar gal basiporet ha'ivrit* (Jerusalem: Keter, 1985).

18. Oryan Aryeh Morris, "Hachatirah lakanon" Musaf Shabbat *Makor rishon*, June 9, 2011; https://musaf-shabbat.com/2011/06/09/אורין-אריה-מוריס-/החתירה-לקנון.

19. Of the twenty titles, only three authors debuted after 1993.

20. http://www.newlibrary.co.il/page_1249.

21. *Teoria uvikoret* is published by the Van Leer Institute in Jerusalem.

22. Chana Kronfeld, *On the Margins of Modernism: Decentering Literary Dynamics* (Berkeley: University of California Press, 1996); Yerach Gover, *Zionism: The Limits of Moral Discourse in Israeli Hebrew Fiction* (Minneapolis: University of Minnesota Press, 1994); Ammiel Alcalay, *Remaking Levantine Culture* (Minneapolis: University of Minnesota Press, 1993); Yael Feldman, *No Room of Their Own: Gender and Nation in Israeli Women's Fiction* (New York: Columbia University Press, 1999) (also in Hebrew: *Lo cheder mishelahen: Migdar ule'umiyut beytsiratan shel sofrot yisra'eliyot* [Tel Aviv: Hakibbutz Hameuchad], 2002).

23. *Harpayah letsorekh negi'ah: likrat chashiva chadashah 'al sifruyot haYehudim* (Tel Aviv: Am Oved, 2005). An English version appeared as *From Continuity to Contiguity: Toward a New Jewish Literary Thinking* (Stanford: Stanford University Press, 2010).

24. Cinema and literary adaptations to cinema open up new worlds of debate altogether.

25. Miriam Shaviv, "A Literary Blank Ballot," *The Jerusalem Post*, March 9, 2001.

26. A. Thompson, "The Literary Canon and the Classic Text," in *King Lear. The Critics Debate* (London: Palgrave, 1988), 60.

27. Alastair Fowler, "Genre and the Literary Canon," *New Literary History* 11 (1979): 97.

28. Authors published in translation by Toby Press include S. Yizhar, Haim Hazzaz, and much more recent writers Zeruya Shalev, Shulamit Lapid, and Yehudit Katzir. The question of how overseas canons compare to trends in Israeli reading preferences is beyond the scope of our volume; it is a topic that deserves research and scrutiny of its own. Two comprehensive sources of information on Hebrew and Israeli authors are *Leksikon heksherim lesofrim yisra'elim* [*The Heksherim Lexicon of Israeli Authors*], ed. Yigal Schwartz and Zisi Stavi (Beersheva: Ben Gurion University, 2014), and Yosef Galron-Goldschlager's *Leksikon hasifrut ha'ivrit hechadashah* (https://library.osu.edu/projects/hebrew-lexicon/). The Institute for the Translation of Hebrew Literature (http://www.ithl.org.il/) is an indispensable resource for information about which authors and titles are available in which languages.

29. Yael Halevi-Wise notes that Hebrew literature in translation has been mostly fiction, with less poetry, and little drama or children's books. "Hebrew Literature in the 'World Republic of Letters': Translation and Reception, 1918–2018" (with Madeleine Gottesman), *Israel Studies Review* 33, no. 2 (2018): 1–25.

30. Peleg, "The Critic as a Dialectical Zionist," 384.

31. https://www.merriam-webster.com/dictionary/canon augu 22 2018.

Part One
Through Time: Silences, Voices, Echoes

Not One, but Five Moments of Silence
On the Poetics and Politics of Asking for Silence

Eran Tzelgov

Introduction

This paper offers an alternative way of writing the historiography of modern Hebrew poetry. Unlike the works of previous scholars (*inter alia* Gershon Shaked and Dan Miron), this paper will demarcate the shifts and changes in Israeli poetry not through the lenses of literary groups, literary generations, magazines, best-seller books or literary debates. Though all of the above will be at the backdrop of this paper, at its foreground will be an attempt to outline the changes in Israeli poetry through a close reading of a recurring theme: the request and need for silence, its absence and its nature. Reading poems by Nathan Zach, Haim Gouri, Yona Wallach, Carmit Rosen, and Tehila Hakimi, I show how the trope of pleading for silence is used and reused differently, thus offering a glimpse into the changes in the poetics and politics in each period or what might be labeled as a "poetical generation."

In that sense, this paper offers a genealogical reading of (the need for) silence in different generations in Israeli poetry, as it relates to power relations in Israel poetry and society in general. Consequently, there will be gaps, stalls, breaks, and jumps in the depiction of the notion in different eras. My observations stress moments of change, rather than a linear development. Though each and every poet in the following discussion asks, begs, or calls for silence, the differences between them are striking, mainly:

1. In the manner the silence is being asked for.
2. In the speaker's position and tone.
3. In the addressees of the request for silence.

Yet each in some way responds to precursors. As T. S. Eliot maintained in his seminal essay from 1921 *Tradition and the Individual Talent*,

> No poet, no artist of any art, has his complete meaning alone. His significance, his appreciation is the appreciation of his relation to the dead poets and artists. You cannot value him alone; you must set him, for contrast and comparison, among the dead.[1]

Following his advice, I offer close readings of poems that stress their differences from preceding poetry but that also allow us to see—borrowing Eliot's term—an Israeli poetry "tradition." At the same time, this approach offers a peek at the shifts and breaks from the specific tradition these poems themselves help create.

My reading also draws on Hamutal Tzamir's *Book in the Name of The Land: Nationalism, Subjectivity and Gender in The Israeli Poetry of The Statehood Generation*.[2] In the opening chapter Tzamir offers new readings and a new understanding of the poetry of Statehood Generation.[3] In my reading of the aforementioned poets, while echoing Hamutal Tzamir's discussion, I will ask these questions: In each poem, whom does the speaker in each poem hush and why? What are the power relations between the speaker and the addressee? What is the nature of this noise? And finally—what does this call for silence teach us as readers?

Natan Zach's One Moment of Silence

One Moment

One moment of silence Please. If you please. I
would like to say something. He walked
and passed by me. I could have touched the hem
of his gown. I did not touch. Who could have
known what I did not know.

The sand clung to his clothes. In his beard
twigs were entangled. Apparently, he had slept
last night by the ricks. Who could have
known that the following night he would be
empty as a bird, hard as a stone.
I could not have known. I do not blame
him. Sometimes I feel him rise
in his sleep, moonstruck as the sea, passing by me, saying to
me my son.
My son. I did not know that you are, this much, with me.

From the first moment of its publication, Nathan Zach's Poem "One Moment" [*rega' echad*], marked a sea change in Hebrew poetry.[4] The poem became the epitome and the prime example for the poetics of the Statehood Generation of readers and critics alike ever since. See, for example, Nissim Calderon's summary:

> These words opening the poem "One Moment" . . . became the passcode for huge cultural domains in Hebrew. They carried within the core of Zach's influence on the literary taste of his generation, the inter-relations between poetry and critical thinking, influencing texts and popular music alike.[5]

In a similar manner, Ruth Kartun-Blum maintains:

> The poem "One Moment" turned into a central poem not only in Zach's poetical corpus but also in Israeli poetry in general. It can be stated that it is one of the greatest poems ever written in Hebrew poetry. In fact, it can be labeled as the identity-mark of a generation.[6]

For those familiar with the history of modern Hebrew poetry and Israeli poetry, Zach's innovations are clear: his use of the first person singular not as a trope but rather as reaction to the "royal we" of the previous generation; the simplicity in diction and syntax; favoring understated rhetoric and subtle irony over pathos, and favoring the mundane over glorifying the dead or the nation; shifting from the rigid rhythmic style of the Shlonsky-Alterman-Goldberg school into more flexible and surprising rhyming schemes and patterns, in an attempt to reflect the natural flow of conversational Hebrew; refraining from symbolistic obscurity and "flowery" and flashy metaphors.[7] These "rules" or poetic toolbox became, and still are to this very day, the major tone in Hebrew poetry, nearly sixty years after they were first introduced.

Even though no explicit *ars-poetic* statements are made throughout the poem, the poem was often understood as the "Statehood Generation's" rite-of-passage poem, dealing with the role of a new poet in a new era of new poetry. One way to support this metapoetic reading of the poem is through culling the many allusions to the Elijah-Elisha story in the poem (Kings II 1-2).[8] The biblical story portrays Elisha, Elijah's disciple and most devoted follower, taking his role as the leading spiritual leader after the ascension of his teacher and master to the sky. However, it is important to note that this story is a very masculine one: both (spiritual) leaders are men.

Another way to understand this poem as a call for a change in Israeli poetry, poetically and thematically, is through comparing the poem's opening line, "One moment of silence Please. If you please. I / Would like to say something," to Zach's own words in his new (for the period) literary journal from 1961, *Yochany*. In it Zach asserted, "The aim of this new literary magazine is to hush the choirs for the individual to be heard." Note the need for silence, and the binary opposition: the choirs versus the individual.

Moreover, the poem's seemingly simple opening can be read as an "interpellation," as coined by the French Marxist philosopher Louis Althusser. Althusser explains: "All ideology hails or interpellates concrete individuals as concrete subjects." Althusser's famous example is of an officer hailing, "Hey, you there!" Elaborating on this example, Althusser explicates: "Assuming that the theoretical scene I have imagined takes place in the street, the hailed individual will turn round. By this mere one-hundred-and-eighty-degree physical conversion, he becomes a subject."[9]

Zach's seemingly naive pleading, his *rega' echad sheket . . . ana ani*, interpellates and produces a subject but in more than one way. First, and most simply, the addressees: the poem interpellates an audience, namely, readers willing to listen to the speaker. And by the same token, as the readers-addressees are interpellated as such, a new speaker, the new speaker of Hebrew poetry to come, by gaining an audience and a stage, finally emerges. This double interpellation, of speaker and addressees, offers yet another layer to the understanding of how this poem became so important for poets and readers alike.

Various critics suggested that unlike earlier generations, the Statehood Generation poets are a-national poets: they are neither nationalists or antinationalists. They do not define themselves vis-à-vis the nation. Put differently, though labeled as the "Statehood Generation" (a label suggesting their connection to the nation-state) the poets themselves did not relate to political or national issues in their work. Nonetheless, as Tzamir showed in her book, while stressing the individual, this poetry is still connected to the nation-state.[10] Though the poets of the Statehood Generation did not mention the state of Israel in their poetry, they took the state of Israel for granted without posing questions, criticizing it, or referring to its origins and problematic existence (the Palestinian defeat or the *Nakba*). In this way, they did not explicitly partake in the national apparatus, yet at the same time they supported it. Put differently, their seemingly neutral and national-less themes made the Israeli nation-state always already "natural" (i.e., unquestionable), and in that sense the poems are nonetheless part of the hegemonic national Israeli discourse.

To sum it up, Zach's pleading for silence is in fact a non-naive call. It is a call of a masculine national speaker looking for his place in the national Israeli poetry. It is a pleading that constitutes himself as a poet and at the same time it constitutes the voice of many. The bi-directional interpellation makes this poem special and the individual "I" becomes the "I" of a generation.

Haim Gouri and the Silence

The Silence and I

I heard of the silence.
I haven't met it yet.
It belongs to a land
I do not know its name.
It belongs to a city
I did not pass through.
It resides in a house—
I did not lean upon its windows.
It seems, that the silence
Is when all ends.
And I am not yet.
Like hunger.

I would like now to stall and not move forward in time, but rather "sideways" and listen more to the voices and silences of the era. In order to do so, I "look" sideways at one of Israel's most celebrated poets—Haim Gouri. A distinguished poet who has influenced generations with his patriotic poems, Gouri (1928–2018) served in the *Palmach* and fought in the 1948 War. Although his poetry evolved over the years, Gouri was the poet most identified with the poetics of the *Palmach* Generation poetry due to his debut collection *Pirchei esh* (1949).

Important to our discussion here is a poem not from his first, but rather from his third book *Shoshanat ruchot*, published only a few months after Zach's *Shirim shonim* (1960). *Shoshanat ruchot* (*Compass Rose*) marks Gouri's harsh break from the Palmach Generation's poetics and aesthetics, after a failed attempt to do so in his second book *Shirei chotam* (1954).[11]

Gouri's *Shoshanat ruchot* meditates, as its title suggests, on the speaker's displacement and estrangement, as well as on his disillusionment from the war and its goals, and the need for an immediate change. The displaced speaker, estranged from a land-not-his, introverted and insecure in his own powers (marked by phrases such as "apparently"—*nidmeh li*), was identified by readers and critics as the "voice of the generation. Gouri's generation, our generation."[12] This voice was the voice of the disillusioned soldiers after the war, or in the words of literary historian Gershon Shaked: "The affinity between the world described in Gouri's poetry and the lives of his cohort is clear. He articulates well the voice of the 'Odysseus-generation' returning from the hazardous journey of war, being strangers at their own home."[13]

The first section of the book is named after the poem with which it ends: "The Silence and I." This may suggest how highly Gouri thought of this poem. While there is no explicit or implicit call for silence, the poem reinforces some of the notions found in Zach's poem. It is almost as if Gouri's speaker meditates on the silence Zach's speaker asked for—he knows it exists, but it is yet to come.

First and foremost, the title of Gouri's poem suggests that the speaker and the silence are not one; they are separate entities, and yet there is a relationship between them. As the situation develops, it is clear that the speaker longs for silence: he is willing to wait for it, though he is a stranger to it, as it is clearly not a part of his life nor of his geography at the present time.

In a sense the two poems, Zach's and Gouri's, capture the *Zeitgeist*. One cannot claim to know whether either of the poets read the other, however both of them share a similar thought and need for a change—a change had happened in their world, a change is needed in poetry and its "acoustics." Put differently, the war is over, things have changed and now both speakers feel detached from their surroundings. Therefore, there is a need for a change in this surrounding, in the sounds around them; perhaps silence or even just a moment of silence could help them familiarize with and within a world that had changed. Hereafter, there is a desire for silence, so a new sound or a different voice might finally be heard. A silence that will allow an expression of new ideas in a new way that is a new poetics for a new generation of poets writing new poetry.

By the end of the poem, the speaker likens himself to hunger. "Hunger" is a natural feeling that cannot be simply ignored and should be treated. Like other biological necessities, hunger signals that the time has come. But what for? Shaked's reading may provide an answer: "[Gouri] stands between an ethical biological surrender to time and a revolution against it. His rebellion signifies an aspiration for the everlasting 'not yet,' unwilling to compromise with the 'when all ends' . . . his poetry secretly desires a 'new beginning.'"[14] In that sense, Gouri's secret yearning for a new beginning completes and complements Zach's call for silence discussed earlier.

Yona Wallach's Explicit *Sheket*

Send Me Silence

> Send me well protected silence
> Send me silence from a cloud
> Send me mechanical silence
> So I can hear silence not from here
> Send me a boxed silence
> From a faraway country
> Silence, silence, exemplary silence
> From the day I was born until the day I die.
> Exemplary silence
> Until the day I die
> Send me organized silence
> Send me updated silence
> Send me magnificent silence
> Send me silence from the countryside
> Send me a boxed silence

> From a faraway country
> Send me decorated silence
> Send me improvised silence
> Send me lunar silence
> Send me intergalactic silence
> Send me a boxed silence
> From a faraway country

It is 1966, six years have passed, Yona Wallach has published her debut poetry collection *Dvarim*, and a massive sea change has taken place. According to Calderon, Wallach was the last "Israeli national poet. . . . [Since] Yona Wallach was the last Israeli poet that Israeli intelligentsia read and could possibly even quote."[15] Calderon suggests that, like Zach in his time, Wallach offered a new poetry "code." Her code is at once a continuum to Zach's code, and on the other hand is a drastic break from it. Accordingly, Calderon concludes, "[O]ne must read Wallach's work alongside Zach's, and at the same time against it."[16]

In Wallach's poem published posthumously, "Send me Silence,"[17] the speaker literally asks for silence over and over again. Wallach's editor and publisher of the poem, Dror Green—a psychotherapist by profession—offered a biographical-psychological reading of the poem. He remarks that, following the trauma of the death of her father, "[the poem] is a cry for help of the little girl Yona had been all her life."[18] I beg to differ.

To begin with, if one follows Calderon's advice of reading Wallach against the backdrop of Zach's poetry, Wallach's poem can be read as one depicting the passing of the baton. From one poet to another. From the poet who gained a "moment of silence" to another asking it from him.[19]

Interestingly, Wallach's silence is different and surprising. It seems silence in Wallach's poem is something physical: it can be bought, packed, and even sent. Her "silence" undermines the common meaning of silence: "the fact of abstaining or forbearing from speech or utterance."[20]

This repetitive utterance of "send me silence" brings to mind George Bataille's famous discussion: "[The word silence] is already, as I have said, the abolition of the sound which the word is; among all the words it is the most perverse, or the most poetic: *it is the token of its own death*" (emphasis added).[21]

In that sense, Wallach's poem exemplifies exactly what Calderon suggested about the poetic code. Her poem, read alongside Zach's, shows a similar request for (the signifier) "silence." While at the same time their requests aim at gaining two different things. Stated differently, in a similar manner to the avant-garde North American "Language Poets" of the late 1960s and 1970s, Wallach pleads for "silence" only to raise a question about the signifier "silence" and its meaning.

After reading Wallach's almost playful poem, one could argue that the speaker actually does not understand the full meaning of silence—or, on the other hand, that only Wallach's speaker knows the true meaning of silence while others, such as Zach and his cohort, do not. The latter reading implies Wallach's "silence" undermines Zach's use of the signifier "Silence" and consequently undermines his success in gaining one.

Thus, Wallach's poem can be read almost as mocking "the code" of the Statehood Generation and its moment of nascence: its pleading for silence. Wallach's speaker annuls the poetic voice of Zach (and his generation) by suggesting they never really understood the meaning of the word *silence*. By parodying the old code, she offers a reexamination of it, thus allowing new understanding of words, and a new language to rise.

Carmit Rosen: Old Kings and a New Queen?

chorus

"One moment silence. If you please. I would like to say something."

"One moment silence. If you please. I would like to say something."

"One moment silence. If you please. I would like to say something."

"One moment silence. If you please. I would like to say something."

"One moment silence. If you please. I would like to say something."

"One moment silence. If you please. I would like to say something."

"One moment silence. If you please. I would like to say something."

"One moment silence. If you please. I would like to say something."

"One moment silence. If you please. I would like to say something."

"One moment silence. If you please. I would like to say something."

"One moment silence. If you please. I would like to say something."

"One moment silence. If you please. I would like to say something."

"One moment silence. If you please. I would like to say something."

"One moment silence. If you please. I would like to say something."

"One moment silence. If you please. I would like to say something."

"One moment silence. If you please. I would like to say something."

"One moment silence. If you please. I would like to say something."

"One moment silence. If you please. I would like to say something."

"One moment silence. If you please. I would like to say something."

"One moment silence. If you please. I would like to say something."

"One moment silence. If you please. I would like to say something."

Figure 1.1. Carmit Rosen, "chorus."

Fast forward to 2013 and to Carmit Rosen's debut poetry collection *Kahal yachid* ("Sole Audience"): while lauding Rosen's book, critic Eli Hirsch points out the poet's interrelations with other poets. Hirsch writes:

> Rosen writes against the backdrop of a noisy, crowded lingual domain, infested with authoritative voices, often violent, mainly masculine . . . the world of poetry, as Rosen sees it, is a world of well-established kingdoms ruled by male kings. Rosen desires to write in their high literary language and thus to win their approval, and at the same time, being a young poet and also a woman, she desires to rebel and destroy them, building her kingdom over their ruin.[22]

Hirsch had an amazing insight, one almost too clear to note, too bright to see: the Israeli poetic domain is a masculine one. Consequently, women poets must struggle to find their place in it. Hirsch then concludes: "Rosen is totally committed to the *masculine-Ashkenazi* poetic tradition, and in order to be heard, she adopts its values and tries to rebel against it from the inside."[23] The "Ashkenazi" adjective adds another layer to the "walls" of the Israeli poetic tradition, yet Hirsch unfortunately refrained from discussing this at all and focused solely on the gender issue.

Surprisingly, though Hirsch mentions many male poets in his essay, he fails to mention Natan Zach. In a poem titled "chorus" [*sic*], Rosen repeatedly copy-pasted Zach's opening lines that were discussed earlier, enclosing the quote within quotation marks. This "readymade" poem may seem at first like a funny or unserious one. Nonetheless, I would like to suggest that this poem is a key to understanding the speaker's struggle to find her own voice. The quotation marks should be understood as "scare quotes" since "scare quotes indicate disagreement with the quoted material, or indicate sarcasm, irony or euphemism."[24] And indeed, as I will show by and by, Rosen parodies Zach's "achievement."

To begin with the poem's title, "chorus": first, it suggests a choir and implies the grand achievement of the Statehood Generation, favoring the "I" over the "we," was in fact a failure; it is a *faux* first person singular. Or as Haviva Pedaya wrote on Zach and his work:

> The Universal I . . . became the most replicated model in the poetry domain. Furthermore, the very thing that aimed at

expressing the individual, the singular I, became a replicating apparatus more than anything else.²⁵

It is not hard to see how this replicating apparatus, stripping the first person singular from its original meaning, is evident also through literally reprinting, "replicating," Zach's famous lines. This redundancy, this reprinting, works as a graphic visual representation of the idea behind it.

Additionally, the poem's title "chorus," and not choir, brings to mind the Greek tragedy and the role of the choir it. As such, the poem's title implies it may know more than what is explicitly "said." In a subtle manner, this again recalls Zach's original poem, where the speaker asserts "I could not have known." Hence, the knowledge, so crucial to the role of the prophet, or its reincarnation as the poet, is missing in Zach's poem, while it is present in a poem of a female poet mocking it.²⁶ Rosen finds her place in the realm of modern Hebrew poetry shouting over and over again: "The king [of Hebrew poetry] is naked!"

Consider, too, the echo created through the repetitions here. *The Oxford English Dictionary* defines "echo" as a "secondary or imitative sound produced by reflected waves."²⁷ Feminist critics maintain that echo has a subversive potential. Orly Lubin argues that, although the myth of Echo suggests women do not have their own voice nor the capability to speak for themselves, "as a matter of fact, by echoing, mythical Echo slyly creates her own text . . . ," a text that often has the opposite meaning.²⁸ Accordingly, the nature of the echo is dual: it both copies the source, and simultaneously, by dispossessing and changing that source, it creates a new phrase, text, and meaning. Rosen's poem does precisely that—by echoing Zach's request, it effectively empties the phrase of all meaning. No more "I" singular of the hegemonic tone—but rather an attempt to open a new space for a new voice.

Moreover, the repetitions in the poem can also be understood as either a stutter or even a hysterical attack. This is indeed a cry for help: if it is a stutter, it is an acting-out of the traumatic event that caused the stutter. The speaker was not allowed to speak, specifically by the hegemonic code that demanded she speak in a "Universal *I*" that was actually a masculine one. Thus, she is now stuck, begging silence, in a voice that is not her own. According to Hélène Cixous, hysteria is itself a way to rebel against the patriarchal order, since it is a "nuclear example of women's power to protest."²⁹ Taking all of the above into account, it is clear that

Rosen's poem undermines Zach's hegemonic tone in Hebrew poetry while appropriating his own words. Rosen's poem exposes Zach's seemingly universal and neutral "I" as instead a very masculine one.

Tehila Hakimi—The Time Has Come to Say Shut Up

I would like now to go back to the brilliant essay by Haviva Pedaya that I briefly mentioned above. In her essay, the critic and poet aims to shape a new revolution in modern Hebrew poetry. She traces the various events that have shaped the field of Israeli poetry since the rise of Zach, favoring the universal "I" and excluding other models of poetry. Pedaya suggests that the Universalistic "I" at the center of Zach's poetics, which became the hegemonic tone of Hebrew poetry from the 1960s on, was always already a Western/*Ashkenazi* one. Since, in the name of liberation from the collective tone and from the recruitment in the poetry of Alterman and the Palmach Generation (which preceded the Statehood Generation), all "poems engaged deeply and intensively with immigration and identity were rejected, labeling them as either 'religious,' 'peripheral' or 'ethnic.' "[30]

Pedaya, writing in 2006, stresses that the time for a change has come, a change in the "I." Pedaya's call for a new "I" was ahead of its time. It took nearly six more years for the breakthrough of what is called today Ars Poetika, a group of young Mizrachi (or Arab-Jews) poets writing the new "I" of Hebrew poetry. Judging by their popularity, the sales of their books, their fans, critics, and haters, Hebrew poetry will never be the same. You can either love or hate the new "kick 'em in the balls" style or their portrayal of a very specific "I" that presents young Mizrachi experience—but Ars Poetika is here to stay. It is noteworthy for our discussion that one of their leading figures is a woman: Adi Keissar.

However, I will not discuss Keissar's work, but instead offer a reading of a poem by her close friend and colleague, another female poet: Tehila Hakimi. Hakimi's poem "Give Me One Day" is from her debut poetry collection *Tomorrow We Will Work* (2016). My reading aims to show how this poem offers an alternative, a change, a break from the hegemonic discourse and tone. While Hakimi's speaker asks once again for a silence, just as Zach's speaker did, the tone could not be more different.

Give Me One Day

I want you to allow me to finish a sentence
Do not explain anything
I want you to shut up
For one whole day
Do not speak about anything
Take a vow of silence
Silence will fall in the hallways of government
The IDF's command will also be quiet

Leaves will rustle outside

I request one day of relative silence
On the borders and in the bus stations
No whistles on the way to the beach
No catcalls from car windows
Around the kitchen tables mothers will discuss politics
Daughters will laugh at their sisters' jokes
You will shut up.

This is yet again a poem whose speaker asks for silence, but note the striking difference—for the first time, the speaker speaks in the first person *feminine*. Neither Rosen's nor even Wallach's speaker revealed their gender. In those two poems there might have been a feminine speaker, however, in each, the Universal "I" hid its sex/gender.[31]

Another striking difference between Wallach's poem and Hakimi's is the tone. Unlike Wallach (almost) begging for silence from a male addressee, Hakimi's uses a very authoritative tone. She demands silence; not because the masculine addressee has it (and hence the privilege, that is, the power to grant or deny the speaker what the latter lacks), but because times have changed, or, finally, "time has come," as in Pedaya's aforementioned essay.[32] The speaker claims her right to speak, she does not need any explanation, she knows what she wants: she demands it. In the first stanza, the feminine speaker demands silence, silencing of the constant noise of generals and of the government, two realms often associated with male/masculine authority.

As the first stanza ends, one stanza separates it from the third and last one: "Leaves will rustle outside." When silence falls, nature will be nature;

it will make the sounds of nature. And this Nature—of the nature-culture divide often associated with the feminine—will not be hushed.[33] On the contrary: it makes noise, a noise that, it seems, is welcome.

At the opening of the last stanza, the readers get more details about this silence—silence at the borders and also, no less important, at the bus stations: no catcalls or whistles. Sounds that bother and (sexually) harass women and the (female) speaker. As the poem reaches its ends, it is clear why the speaker demands a day of silence. On that day, the revolution will be complete: in kitchens (the "feminine domain"), women will talk politics, daughters and sisters (that is, females, or members of what is often labeled as "the humorless gender") will laugh at jokes, and you, a seemingly "neutral" you[34]—yet specifically the second person plural masculine *atem*—will finally shut up.

Before taking this advice personally, I would like to suggest that Hakimi's poem rips the final layer off the universalistic "I" Zach introduced into Hebrew poetry. Tehila Hakimi's poem can and should be read as a protest, aimed principally at the universalistic "I," one that kept women, specifically but not solely Mizrachi women, hidden under its cloaking, "neutral" language.

My reading through various stations in modern Hebrew poetry reveals that the universalistic "I," the seemingly neutral "I," was from its nascent moments a masculine Ashkenazi one. Hakimi's poem is, for the time being, the final step in deconstructing this "I," opening the reader's eye to see new "I"s, a different way to write poetry and also a more critical way to understand and read the old "masters" of Hebrew poetry.

Notes

1. T. S. Eliot, "Tradition and the Individual Talent," in *The Sacred Wood* (New York: Alfred A. Knopf, 1921), 44.

2. Hamutal Tzamir, "Where Is the State in the Statehood Generation Poetry?" In *In the Name of The Land: Nationalism, Subjectivity, and Gender in The Israeli Poetry of The Statehood Generation.* (Jerusalem and Beer Sheva: Keter and Ben-Gurion University, 2006).

3. Ibid., 17–58.

4. Regarding its major role in what was later labeled as "the revolution of the 1950s in Israeli poetry" or the poem of the Statehood Generation, the poem was not included in Zach's first book *"Shirim rishonim"* (1955) but rather in his second *"Shirim shonim"* (1960). Furthermore, though printed in Zach's second book five years later, Zach did not open the book with it.

5. Nissim Calderon, "Nathan Zach," in *The Heksherim Lexicon of Israeli Authors* (Tel-Aviv and Beer Sheva: Dvir and Ben Gurion University, 2014), 410. For more on Zach's role in shaping new poetics and a new "I" see: Hamutal Tzamir, " 'The Landscape Loses Its Name': Nathan Zach's National-Israeli Subject," *Jerusalem Studies in Hebrew Literature* 19: 219–44.

6. Ruth Kartun-Blum, *Reflections on Psycho-theology in Natan Zach's Poetry* (Tel Aviv: Hakibbutz Hameuchad,2009), 20. It is noteworthy how the critic widens the scope of her appraisal as it unfolds. Kartun-Blum begins with "Zach's corpus," then shifts into "Israeli poetry" (i.e., Hebrew poetry from 1948 onward), and ends with "Hebrew poetry" in general.

7. For more on Zach's set of rules for poetry, read his own summary at: Nathan Zach, "*La'akliman hasignoni shel shnot hachamishim vehashishim beshiratenu*," *Haaretz*, July 29, 1966. At first Zach's essay may seem to be a descriptive summary but it is in fact a prescriptive manifesto of the Statehood Generation and a demonstration of Zach's authoritative power as the new arbiter of taste and style.

8. See for example Dan Miron's reading in "The Epistemological Quest and the (Im)Possibility of Prophecy in the Early Poetry Of Natan Zach," in *The Prophetic Mode in Modern Hebrew Poetry* (New Milford, CT: Toby Press, 2010), 526–96.

9. Louis Althusser. *Lenin and Philosophy, and other Essays*, trans. Ben Brewster (New York and London: Monthly Review Press, 1971), 174.

10. Ibid., 69.

11. Zach concludes his review of Gouri's second book with these harsh words: "[After reading the book] it is clear that the poet of "*Pirchei esh*" [i.e., Haim Gouri] has embarked on a journey, however the poet of the book did not yet reach not even the first station." *Mevo'ot* 15, Nov. 8, 1954.

12. Moshe Shamir, "*Barak shehitpayes*," *Ma'ariv*, Oct. 21, 1960.

13. Gershon Shaked, "*Hapgisha 'im haprozah*," *Lamerchav/Masa*, Nov. 25, 1960.

14. Ibid.

15. Nissim Calderon, "Yona Wallach's Room," in *The Second Day: On Poetry and Rock in Israel after Yona Wallach* (Jerusalem and Beersheba: Keter and Ben-Gurion University, 2009), 69–83.

16. Ibid.

17. Yona Wallach, "Tishlach li sheket," in *Or Pere* (Jerusalem: Eichut, 1990), 46.

18. Dror Green, "Yona Wallach: Tishlach li sheket"; http://www.psychom.com/Poetry_803_he.html.

19. Notably, Wallach's addressee, the one that can provide the ungendered speaker with "silence," is masculine.

20. *Oxford English Dictionary*, Online Edition; http://www.oed.com/view/Entry/179646.

21. George Bataille, *Inner Experience* (Albany: State University of New York Press, 1988), 16.

22. Eli Hirsch, "Kor'e shirah: Na'ama Gershy and Carmit Rosen," *Yediot Aharonot*, July 12, 2013; emphasis added.

23. Ibid.; emphasis added.

24. Elke Brendel, Jörg Meibauer, Markus Steinbach, and Walter de Gruyter, *Understanding Quotation* (Berlin and New York: Walter de Gruyter, 2016), 20.

25. Haviva Pedaya, "The Time Has Arrived to Say *I* Differently in Hebrew Poetry," *Haaretz*, May 1, 2006.

26. The notion of "knowledge" or lack thereof is reinforced by comparing this poem to Wallach's "Send Me Silence" discussed earlier.

27. *Oxford English Dictionary*, Online Edition; http://www.oed.com/view/Entry/59326.

28. Orly Lubin, *Ishah kor'et ishah* (Haifa: Haifa University and Zmora Bitan, 2003), 69.

29. Hélène Cixous and Catherine Clément, *The Newly Born Woman*, trans. Betsy Wing (Minneapolis: University of Minnesota Press, 1986), 154.

30. Ibid.

31. This is almost contrary to Wallach's claim in a different poem: "Hebrew is a sex maniac/wants to know who's talking/almost a mirror almost a picture." Yona Wallach, "Ivrit." *Tat hakarah niftachat kemo menifah* (Tel-Aviv: Hakibutz Hameuchad, 1992), 180–82.

32. Ibid.

33. For more on this, see, for example, Carol P. MacCormack and Marilyn Strathern, eds., *Nature, Culture, and Gender* (Cambridge: Cambridge University Press, 2001).

34. More on the seeming neutrality of masculinity, see Simone de Beauvoir, *The Second Sex* (New York: Vintage Books, 1989). In her introduction, the critic writes: "[M]an represents both the positive and the neutral, as is indicated by the common use of man to designate human beings in general; whereas woman represents only the negative . . . there is an absolute human type, the masculine" (xv).

Sounding the Mizrachi Voice

Ḥafla *Thematics from the* Ma'abarah *to the Post-Arabic Novel*

Michal Raizen

In 2018, the Arabic word *ḥafla* sounds entirely familiar to the average Israeli speaker of Hebrew. The mass immigration of Jews from the Arabic-speaking world in the 1950s marked a point of entry for the term to make its way into the Israeli lexicon: first in the relative insularity of the *ma'abarah* (transit camp) where new immigrants tuned into Arabic-language radio; then in the predominantly Mizrachi urban peripheries and development towns where the *ḥafla* came to be associated with neighborhood gatherings and weddings; then through the kiosks of the old Tel Aviv central bus station where *muzikah mizrachit* (Mizrachi music) rose to prominence in the 1970s through the circulation of cassette tapes; and finally, to the mainstream popular sphere where the term has landed, thoroughly Hebraized and unmoored from its Arabic antecedents. As a contemporary turn of phrase, *ḥafla* merely denotes a party with Middle Eastern flair. Popular Hebraized usage of the term largely ignores the Arabic poetic universe evoked by the great twentieth-century all-stars of Arabic song during the epic *ḥafla* performances through which they staked a claim to fame. The Egyptian artist Umm Kulthum, with whom the word *ḥafla* assumed an almost tautological association, was widely known as the artist who brought Arabic poetry to the masses. Her Thursday night *ḥafla* reached audiences across the Middle East through powerful radio broadcasts out of Cairo and catapulted certain literary tropes into the public consciousness: ruins as a repository for memory, youth spent and irrecoverable, the lost beloved, and the ever-present longing for a homeland. Her famous declaration, "My audience is in a Sufi state," points to an element of ecstatic transcendence and to one of the hallmarks of *ḥafla* poetics: the constant gesture toward an elsewhere in time, place, or interpersonal relationships. For new immigrants in the transit camps, the act of gathering around the radio for the Thursday night Umm Kulthum *ḥafla* provided an avenue for the collective expression of loss and longing for a cultural life left behind. Today's *ḥaflot* (the Hebraized plural of *ḥafla*) are, for the most part, thoroughly associated in the Israeli public consciousness with widespread airplay and popular concerts.

The linguistic trajectory of the term *ḥafla* from the *ma'abarah* to the mainstream Israeli public sphere has a parallel artistic arc in the realm of Israeli literature. My essay probes this literary arc through a reading of *ḥafla* thematics in novels: the Iraq Trilogy (*Tarngol kaparot*, 1983; *Mafriach hayonim*, 1992; and *Yasmin*, 2005) by Eli Amir and *Tchachla veḤezkel* (*Rachel and Ezekiel*, 2005) by Almog Behar.[1] By placing these works in a comparative framework and reading them along a continuum, I ask what avenues of expression emerge when Mizrachi authors make space in their writing for an Arabic literary idiom couched in musical affect. Unlike the linguistic domestication/Hebraization of the word, a process through which each subsequent generation has grown increasingly estranged from the Arabic cultural context of the *ḥafla* and its original performance practices, literary usage of the term has engendered an Arabic afterlife that contests and stretches the boundaries of the printed Hebrew word. A generation apart, Amir and Behar have different relationships to the Arabic language and to cultural memory, and these differences are marked in their writing. Nevertheless, their respective usages of the word *ḥafla* and its musico-poetic purview points to an Israeli literature that absorbs and transforms an Arabic literary idiom. The quintessential gesture toward an elsewhere serves as an indication that Israeli literature written by Jews in Hebrew has the capacity for transcending conceptual, linguistic, and geopolitical borders.[2] Moreover, the semiautobiographical nature of all four novels, when coupled with the proverbial elsewhere of *ḥafla* poetics, suggests that both authors, whether drawing upon direct or inherited traumatic memory, engage the Iraqi-Jewish past.

Though it is beyond the scope of my essay to provide a comprehensive survey of *ḥafla* thematics in Mizrachi literature, a few preliminary observations bear mentioning. In their respective novels, Amir and Behar foreground the language and sounds of the Arab Jewish past, not only through their usage of the aforementioned *ḥafla* tropes, but through an extended representation of the repertoires and personas of the Arabic musical all-stars who turned those tropes into a cultural currency legible throughout the Middle East. My reading of the Iraq Trilogy and *Tchachla veḤezkel* as case studies points to a dimension of Israeli literature that I have termed, "sounding the Mizrachi voice." Collectively, these works illuminate an increasingly salient and direct engagement with Arabic language and cultural memory and mark the *ḥafla* as a poignant representation of cultural and linguistic rupture and return in the Mizrachi context.[3]

Amir and Behar both set up the *ḥafla* as a dramatization of the generational schisms and processes of deterritorialization that have typified the Iraqi Israeli experience. In these works, the *ḥafla* signals critical nodes or turning points in the lives of the protagonists and their communities. Acknowledging some overlap, I argue that Amir's trilogy is melancholic and largely oriented toward the past, whereas Behar uses the affective index of the *ḥafla* to reshuffle the interior world of his protagonist and gesture toward a future in which this interiority might manifest itself in Israeli space and place.[4] Behar makes no mention of Umm Kulthum and pushes back against Egyptian cultural hegemony by focusing on the legacy of Jewish Iraqi musicians: Salima Pasha, the Kuwaiti Brothers, and Nazem Al-Ghazali. Amir's representations fluctuate but roughly break down along preimmigration and postimmigration settings. *Tarnegol kaparot* and *Yasmin* are set in Israel and predominantly feature Umm Kulthum and other Egyptian artists, whereas *Mafriach hayonim* is set in Iraq and features Salima Pasha in the *ḥafla* scene. In both cases, the quintessential nod to an elsewhere serves myriad narrative functions. In literature and critical scholarship, the term *ḥafla* serves as an index for Mizrachi experiences eclipsed by the Zionist metanarrative: the erasure of cultural memory, the process of estrangement from the Arabic language, loss of citizenship and homeland, socioeconomic and artistic marginalization. Refigured in Mizrachi literature as a bridge between the here and now of Israel and the Arab Jewish past, the emphatic elsewhere of *ḥafla* poetics serves to destabilize both Zionist and Pan-Arab epistemological frameworks and creates a narrative space for marginalized voices.[5]

Since the 1970s, the word *ḥafla* has gained increasing visibility in Israel. Literary and cinematic representations of the performance genre, postcolonial readings of community listening practices, and contemporary literary salons and soirées fashioning themselves in the vein of a *ḥafla* have all contributed to the legibility of the term in the Israeli public sphere. As previously mentioned, popular usage of the word simply denotes a party with Middle Eastern flair. Beyond the seeming simplicity of this current turn of phrase there exists an initiative among Mizrachi poets and activists to repurpose the term and reclaim its poetic depth as an intervention into the epistemological frameworks that relegate Mizrachi literature to a heritage corner. For the artistic conglomeration known as Ars Poetika, spearheaded by Adi Keissar, the word *ḥafla* has come to signify a loud, proud, and profane reclamation of Arab Jewish culture. The name *Ars Poetika* itself proclaims this attitude. A double-entendre, it refers to both Horace's renowned poetic treatise and to the Arabic term *ars* (pimp) which came to be used as a racial slur for Mizrachi men. When asked about the rowdy nature of Ars Poetika events, Keissar noted: "Mizrachi culture is loud and passionate. As such . . . its poetry should be a *hafla—a party.*"[6] In his poem "The State of Ashkenaz," Roy Hassan, a prominent member of the group, echoes Keissar's sentiments: "I am *Haflah*/I am Honor/I am lazy/I am everything that was never here before/when everything was white . . . / . . . I am an Ars" (ibid.). An activist in his own right and a contemporary of Keissar and Hassan, Behar demonstrates some overlap with regard to the political interests of Ars Poetika, but his writing draws heavily on liturgical and Midrashic language.[7] These approaches, respectively iconoclastic and idiosyncratic, represent two distinct but interrelated streams of new Mizrachi writing. Eli Amir belongs to a previous generation, and his writing reflects a perspective based on his experience in the transit camps, in a kibbutz youth absorption program, and in the role of advisor to the Israeli government on Arab affairs.

A comparative reading of Amir and Behar requires some context, and the first aspect to consider is the degree to which these writers incorporate Arabic into their prose. A point of departure for this assessment is Nancy Berg's *Exile from Exile: Israeli Writers from Iraq*, in which she discusses the language shift in Mizrachi writing.[8] Berg offers a periodization that breaks down largely along the lines of pre-exile literature composed in Iraq, *ma'abarah* (transit camp) literature, and post-*ma'abarah* literature. Within this periodization, we see some variation. Amir's *Tarnegol kaparot* (1983) offers a transition between *ma'abarah* and post-*ma'abarah* literature but can still be grouped with the latter due to its extensive treatment of the protagonist's rift with the cultural milieu of the *ma'abarah*. In *Poetic Trespass: Writing Between Hebrew and Arabic in Israel/Palestine*, Lital Levy expands this periodization with a discussion of the "third generation" of Mizrachi authors.⁹ I follow Levy's use of the term *generation* as a "means of understanding patterns in Mizrachi writing vis-à-vis authors' relationship to Hebrew (and corresponding distance from Arabic) rather than age or place of birth" (199). I apply the term post-Arabic to refer to the largely monolingual third generation of Mizrachi Hebrew writers, among them Almog Behar and the Ars Poetika poets.¹⁰ Unlike first and second-generation authors, with their varying degrees of Arabic language proficiency, few of the post-Arabic authors have access to Arabic outside of the colloquial phrases and expressions heard at home. In an experience akin to (re)acquiring one's mother tongue as a second-language learner, Behar and some of his contemporaries have become proficient in Arabic as adults. In a related cultural shift, a number of prominent Mizrachi musicians have returned to the Arabic of their grandparents and produced Arabic-language albums with massive popular appeal in Israel and throughout the Middle East.¹¹ Levy suggests that the use of Arabic among the *ma'abarah* and post-*ma'abarah* writers does not indicate a struggle with language itself or a challenge to the "linguistic integrity of Hebrew" (210). By contrast, use of Arabic among the post-Arabic authors presents a challenge to the contours of Israeli Hebrew by questioning the mapping of Hebrew onto Jewish national territory.

Eli Amir's Iraq Trilogy and the Melancholia of No Return

My analysis opens with a look at Eli Amir's *Mafriach hayonim* (1992). Shot through with the pain of impossible return, the *ḥafla* scene portends the dramatic mass exodus of the Iraqi Jewish community, simultaneously marking a poetic turn and presaging a new political reality. The Iraqi Jewish experience is encoded with the melancholia of "no-return" and the millennia-long history of Iraqi Jewry is subsumed by the Israeli melting pot narrative. *Tarnegol kaparot* (1983) picks up the chronological thread of *Mafriach hayonim* and captures the protagonist's departure from the immigrant transit camps and painful acculturation process on the Israeli kibbutz. The *ḥafla* scene in *Tarnegol kaparot* marks the protagonist's irreversible break with the Iraqi home and family, portrayed in the novel as a handicap to upward mobility in the Israeli polity. *Yasmin* (2005), the final installment of Amir's Iraq Trilogy, takes place during the 1967 Arab-Israeli War and its aftermath. Amir's protagonist, Nuri, is serving as a reserve officer in the Israeli army and is tasked with translating the radio broadcasts out of Egypt. Nuri's intelligence gathering is disrupted by the Umm Kulthum ḥafla. By introducing an element of pathos and performativity to an intelligence mission with seemingly fixed rules of engagement, Amir makes room for ambivalence and throws into question the finality of the rupture depicted in *Tarnegol kaparot*.

Mafriach hayonim presents an account of the Amari family's final months in Iraq leading up to the large-scale revocation of Iraqi Jewish citizenship.[12] Structured as a bildungsroman, the novel features parallel coming-of-age narratives. On an individual level, Amir's protagonist, Kabi, develops a political awareness at the crosscurrents of the multiple ideologies espoused by his family and peers. On a collective and allegorical level, the Babylonian Jewish community awakens to a new political reality in which being Jewish and being an Iraqi patriot are refigured as incompatible. Cast as a quasi-spiritual encounter, the ḥafla scene in *Mafriach hayonim* signals both an exit from the body politic and a traumatic re-scripting of the 2,500-year dictate of Psalm 137. The original lamentation over the Jewish exile to Babylon in 586 BCE is recast in the novel as a reverse exile to Zion. This reverse exodus is foregrounded with the image of the community boarding planes bound for Israel. The community leave-taking is marked in the novel by a "performance on the occasion of the departure to Israel" (311).[13] "The entire neighborhood will be there," remarks Abu Kabi as he tries to convince his son that the ḥafla featuring Salima Pasha is an event not to be missed.[14] Amir's use of the loaded term *yetsi'ah* in reference to the community's exodus *to* Israel situates the scene as a rupture of epic proportions and identifies the imperiled group as migrants.[15] Salima uses the space of the performance to guide the audience on a journey through memory and lost love—romantic love unrequited or cut tragically short, love of homeland, love of the family and tribe. Her repertoire grows progressively melancholic throughout the evening until she enacts an Arabic evocation of *tefilat haderekh* (the Jewish prayer for travel) to the tune of an Iraqi folk melody:

> Who can foresee the paths of migration?
> May it be willed that the journey be a success.
> Long is the road to Erets habechira,
> Tomorrow the planes alight for the promised land
> Who can foresee the paths of migration?
> May it be willed that the journey be a success. (314)

Amir likens the audience members to supplicants in a synagogue, swaying in a state of *hit'alut* or spiritual exaltation (ibid.). "In her singing," writes Amir, "[Salima] gave voice to their desires, and they showered her with all of their love for Baghdad, their city that they would leave behind never to return" (ibid.). The particular combination of a typical *ḥafla* experience and Arab Jewish liturgical practices situates the scene as a lamentation on a syncretic cultural firmament that would all but disappear in the crosscurrents of Zionism, Arab nationalism, and postcolonialism.[16] Amir's depiction of Salima Pasha in *Mafriach hayonim* follows the singer's real-life decision to stay behind in Iraq.

Published almost a decade after *Mafriach hayonim*, *Tarnegol kaparot* presents the Hebraized term *ḥaflot* as an extended metaphor for the rupture experienced by Iraqi youth brought to the kibbutz from a neighboring *ma'abarah*. Amir's protagonist, Nuri, experiences a crisis precipitated by the clash between the musical culture of the local youths and that of the Iraqis. Eager to forge ties with the kibbutz community, the Iraqi group plans a cultural showcase, an Arabic play with musical accompaniment following the Zionist tale of a Jew from Basra who immigrates to Palestine and dies fighting for Israeli independence. Not a single kibbutz member or local youth shows up for the performance, and in an effort to temper their disappointment, the Iraqis decide to hold a *ḥafla*. The word *ḥafla* gets lost in translation from the very beginning of the scene when Sonia, the sympathetic kibbutz sponsor, inquires about the meaning. Nuri answers glibly, "It's a party" (106). In the privacy of their clubhouse, the Iraqi youth fervently express their longing for the past, night after night: "And on the following nights, the flame of the *ḥaflot* would ignite, as if we were leaving the kibbutz for another world, the world from which we came" (108). At the center of these melancholic gatherings is a character named Matzul, a crooner who plays the *'ūd* (Middle Eastern lute) and constantly challenges the Zionist tenet of leaving behind the "Generation of the Wilderness" and its diasporic ways. Matzul's fierce and transgressive claim on the exilic past finds expression in the nightly *ḥaflot* and eventually antagonizes the kibbutz members who perceive the nightly event as "Arab noise."[17] A character named Ze'evik releases a torrent of xenophobic rage: "What is this? An Arab café? Quit your wailing or we'll move your clubhouse to the forest where you belong" (111). Though *Tarnegol kaparot* is peppered with Arabic terms, they are largely calibrated against the Zionist metanarrative and its frames of reference. Matzul's songs, for example, consistently open with a transliterated Arabic phrase followed immediately by a Hebrew translation:

'ala baladi al-maḥbūb wada'īnī,
Lemoladeti ha'ahuvah kachini
[Take me to my beloved homeland]
My yearning for you—a burning fire.
Oh, my sad and lonely soul. (113)

As a marker, *ḥafla* indeed gestures in *Tarnegol kaparot* to an elsewhere—the Iraqi homeland, the long-lost beloved, irrecoverable youth—but it is always framed in reference to the Israeli here and now.

Yasmin falls more decisively into the category of post-*ma'abarah* literature. Set in Israel/Palestine during the 1967 Arab-Israeli War, the novel addresses a number of considerations: Israel's occupation of the West Bank and Gaza Strip, the ongoing implications of reconstituted borders, the emergent opportunities for social mobility granted to Israeli speakers of Arabic, and the cultural schizophrenia that has accompanied such opportunities, particularly among members of the Israeli intelligence community. *Yasmin* features a scene in which Nuri, a reserve officer in the Israeli army, has been called to duty and awaits orders on the outskirts of Gaza City. To kill time and calm his nerves, he volunteers to translate the radio broadcasts out of Egypt. As the only Arabic speaker in his platoon, he is entrusted with the task of faithfully relating sensitive information. All of a sudden, the news broadcasts are cut off to make way for a musical performance by Umm Kulthum. The lieutenant in charge of communications turns to Nuri in a panic: "We lost the Egyptian broadcast! The radio waves are full of songs! What the hell are they singing about?" (44) Nuri lingers, soaking up the words and the melody: "Your eyes took me back to bygone days/they taught me to regret the past and its wounds/what I saw before I set eyes on you/was a lifetime wasted."[18] The lieutenant cuts in: "What's taking you so long?" Buying himself a little time, Nuri replies: "Just a minute, a little patience . . . let me understand what's going on here" (44). For a moment, Nuri forgets about his duty as an Israeli officer gathering intelligence. He finds himself transported by the music into an alternate reality characterized by "musical inebriation, a quiver of excitement, unfettered joy, intoxication by sound, bodily pleasures, spiritual transcendence, radiance of the soul" (ibid.). Nuri turns back to the lieutenant: "I think that they muted the broadcasts and are playing Umm Kulthum. Someone is saying to his friend over the network that the connection will resume after the *ḥafla*." Alarmed, the lieutenant asks: "Are you serious? How long will it take?" Nuri replies dismissively, "An hour, two, three, it depends" (44–45). In a sense, Nuri demonstrates an internalization of the notion of "Arab noise." He experiences ecstatic transcendence privately, even furtively. When asked about the experience by Israelis, Sonia and the lieutenant respectively, he gives lackluster and simplistic translations. In *Tarnegol kaparot*, one of the kibbutz veterans, Yishai, expresses genuine interest in Nuri's musical heritage but lacks the vocabulary to ask nuanced questions. "Who were the greatest composers in Iraq?" asks Yishai. Irritated by the question, Nuri replies curtly, "Jews" (120). "The only one I've heard of is Abdul . . . Abdul," continues Yishai. "Wahhab," answers Nuri impatiently, "That's something else entirely" (ibid.). The idea of a "something else entirely" illegible to the Israeli listener/reader creates a field of tension between private ecstatic moments and public displays of feigned indifference. Hollowed out of meaning, or rather, too private to translate, the term *ḥafla* serves in *Tarnegol kaparot* and *Yasmin* as a placeholder for a cultural life left behind in Iraq. Amir's Iraq Trilogy situates this cultural life as irreconcilable with the Israeli melting pot narrative. Nuri's "stolen moment" in *Yasmin* is notable for the role of music, specifically the *ḥafla*, in subverting hierarchies. In *Music and the Play of Power in the Middle East, North Africa, and Central Asia*, Laudan Nooshin notes that "music is quixotic in its ability to serve both dominant power positions and ideologies and at the same time give voice to those disempowered by them" (30).[19] As the only Arabic speaker in his platoon and the only officer with an understanding of the ecstatic temporality that typifies an Umm Kulthum *ḥafla*, Nuri maintains complete control of sensitive military information and the pace with which it is relayed. He is at once an Israeli patriot and a subversive lover, not only of Umm Kulthum, but of Egypt's president Nasser, whose voice elicits similar feelings of elation. In his official capacity, Nuri insists on the untranslatability of the *ḥafla* experience and even wields his cultural knowledge as a source of power over his monolingual Israeli peers. Through the character of Nuri, Amir selectively translates the melancholia of no return and invites the Israeli reader to consider the semiautobiographical arc of his departure from the *ma'abarah*, socialization on the Israeli kibbutz, and intelligence work for the Israeli army. The musical personae, Salima Pasha and Umm Kulthum respectively, morph from a symbol of fierce Iraqi Jewish self-assurance in *Mafriach hayonim* to an index of torn allegiances and stolen moments in *Yasmin*.

A Bilingualism of Hebrew and Silence: Almog Behar's *Tchachla veHezkel*

If Amir's depiction of Salima Pasha represents a rupture, a decisive break with the Iraqi-Jewish past, Almog Behar's 2010 novel *Tchachla vdeHezkel* casts Salima as a symbol of return. The idea that Salima Pasha never left Iraq functions in the former as a portrait of irremediable loss and in the latter as a suggestion that her musical legacy and its affective purview might be reanimated in contemporary Israel. *Tchachla veHezkel* follows the trials and tribulations of a working-class Mizrachi couple in Jerusalem in the early 2000s. Behar's protagonist Hezkel Al-Ghazali is an aspiring poet who seeks solace in the literary world. Through his frequent visits to the iconic Tmol Shilshom café and bookstore, he is exposed to the works of renowned Mizrachi poets Erez Biton and Haviva Pedaya. His foray into poetry is narrated with a flashback to his youth and a profound meditation on Mizrachi cassette culture and the value of listening *as* a community. The idiosyncratic musical habits of Hezkel's childhood home differ somewhat from the communal behaviors associated with the Umm Kulthum Thursday night *hafla*. His parents would wait for the late-night cassette ritual of their elderly neighbor and open their windows to the sounds of Nazem Al-Ghazali, Salima Pasha, and the Kuwaiti Brothers. When prompted by Hezkel to buy their own cassettes, they refuse and offer the following explanation: "This is just how we are. Our memories come from the windows, the sky, the streets, from the outside. How would we rejoice in the music if we played it for ourselves and listened alone in a closed house? It would be better to intone the songs for ourselves, in the silence of our hearts" (38). Deeply intimate, this flashback situates *Tchachla veHezkel* as a reflection on the act of creating poetry or song in exile. The marked shift away from Egypt shows that Arab Jewish culture in Israel is no less vast and varied than Arab culture at large. Iraqi musical heritage is the fulcrum here, and Behar plugs into a larger challenge to the grand narratives propagated by Egyptian media, a hegemonic cultural force with deep ties to Pan-Arab ideology.

As a point of comparison, both Amir and Behar refigure Psalm 137 as a reverse exile, but the ways in which they orient their protagonists vis-à-vis the *longue durée* of Arab Jewish cultural syncretism varies in tone and implication. In a passage reminiscent of the linchpin of Psalm 137 (How shall we sing the song of the Lord on foreign soil?), Hezkel's parents reject musical recommendations from their Egyptian and Moroccan neighbors, declaring their undying devotion to Salima Pasha: "Once, when Salima Pasha was the greatest singer in all of Iraq, from the North to the South, we had never heard of Zohra Al-Fassiya. Who needed other singers? Who would have given his heart over to Laila Murad? We got to know them *here*, but Salima was our *muṭriba*, an Iraqi *muṭriba*. . . . How could she leave song to come here to silence? She had to stay [behind], and we listened to her from afar, glued to our radios" (38–39; emphasis mine).[20] Rather than leaving the resounding *how* unanswered, Behar begins to string together a talk-back to the impossibility of writing and consuming poetry in exile. Narrated through a series of chapters titled *shirah* (poetry or song) and culminating in a chapter titled *muzikah* (music), Ḥezkel's development as a poet unfolds from his first tentative steps into verse: "And he thought to himself, perhaps if I were to add lines that I heard during prayer and verses I remembered by heart and throw in a few words that popped into my head, I too would be able to write something in the form of a poem and call it my own" (43). At the core of Ḥezkel's ruminations on the creative process is the question of what constitutes Hebrew poetry and where improvisation, memorization, meter, and the Arabic tonal system might fit into the equation. In one of the most poignant reflections on the linguistic predicament of the post-Arabic generation, Behar invites the reader into Ḥezkel's process of becoming a poet: "And Hezkel started to write bilingual poetry, in Hebrew and in Silence" (46).

On his way back from a disheartening session with the rabbi, Ḥezkel notices posters advertising "an authentic Iraqi *ḥafla*" featuring the repertoire of Salima Pasha and Nazem Al-Ghazali (240). Lured by the promise of "old and familiar" Iraqi songs and curious about the star performer whose last name matches his own, Ḥezkel convinces Tchachla to join him for the performance. In their best Sabbath clothes, they travel by bus to Talpiot and enter a hall normally reserved for weddings. When the music starts, Tchachla suspects that Ḥezkel is enacting a sort of mimicry. He is familiar with the melodies, but he parrots the lyrics "as if they were mere sounds devoid of meaning rather than words that you had to understand before singing them out loud in a concert in order to exalt them" (242). This realization throws her into a rage, but she ultimately consoles herself with the thought that she could teach him what she recalls of Baghdadi Judeo-Arabic. In a rare moment of tenderness and intimacy, Tchachla continues to explain the lyrics to Ḥezkel, and he imagines the Arabic letters joining together to form words in his mind's eye. Though his family left Iraq before he had learned the alphabet, Ḥezkel imagines that the very presence of his father's library had endowed him with a certain literary predisposition, a means of intuiting Arabic. "Poetry is the register of the Arabs," he recalls his father saying with reverence (243).[21] Not only does the *ḥalfa* awaken in Ḥezkel an innate desire to unearth the "words hiding in his soul," but the scene represents the moment in which *diwan al-'arab* makes itself legible in the Israeli context (244). Through the character of Ḥezkel, Behar paints a thought-provoking portrait of a new Israeli literature simultaneously inflected with a centuries-old Arabic poetic register and innovating its own syncretic symbolic lexicon.

The evocation of an ancient line of cultural poetics is curiously juxtaposed in *Tchachla veḤezkel* with the commercialized nature of the advertised event. Behar models his fictional *ḥafla* after a real-life collaboration between Etti Levi and Yaacov Nashawi.[22] In the novel, Ḥezkel picks up a recording of Nashawi, the type of recording that you might expect to find at one of the many kiosks in the central bus station. Though the performance in Talpiot has none of the gravitas associated with the epic *ḥafalāt* of the 1950s and '60s, Ḥezkel experiences a profound transfiguration, as if Salima Pasha herself had taken the stage and coaxed his "mute" Arabic out of him. Seemingly buried in the silt of historical memory, her legacy makes a marked return in *Tchachla veḤezkel*. The new Israeli poetry emerging alongside this return, not unlike the poetry of Behar himself, celebrates the long history of Jewish participation in the Arabic *diwān*. Behar does not shy away from use of Arabic that could potentially confuse or alienate the monolingual Israeli reader. During the *ḥafla*, Ḥezkel sings along to a folk song, *fawq al-nakhl fawq* (Above the Palm Tree). Behar offers a boldface Hebrew transliteration with vowel markings to signal an Arabic song, but he does not include a Hebrew translation as Amir typically does with songs in Arabic. The passage follows Ḥezkel's interior monologue as he shifts from transliterated Arabic to a repetition of the song in Arabic script with no Hebrew gloss. As he reflects on his father's mention of *diwān al-'arab*, Ḥezkel thinks to himself that he ought to read more in Arabic if he is to become a [Hebrew] poet. To reiterate an earlier point, Ḥezkel typifies the post-Arabic generation in the sense that he is a monolingual speaker of Hebrew with limited access to a patchwork of colloquial Arabic phrases. Though he cannot speak or read Arabic, language seems to operate under a different set of parameters in the context of a *ḥafla*. Song and poetry emerge from a deep affective residue. Though

Ḥezkel has no memory of Arabic, he *sees* the folk song in his mind's eye, rendered in Arabic script, with no Hebrew translation: "And [Ḥezkel] *remembered* and the Arabic letters filled his mind" (ibid.; emphasis mine).

Conclusion

As a poetic reservoir in its own right, the *ḥafla* facilitates a creative tension between past, present, and future temporalities. When considered in the context of contemporary Mizrachi literature, the elasticity of time and place characteristic of *ḥafla* poetics allows for a profound meditation on the arc of an exodus *to* Israel and the return to poetry in exile. My comparative analysis of Amir's Iraq Trilogy and Behar's *Tchachla veḤezkel* identifies Psalm 137 as a lingering topos reframed as a reverse exodus to Israel. Amir and Behar orient themselves differently vis-à-vis the resounding question of *how* poetry (extended in this essay to include literary production at large) can continue to thrive in exile. By reading these works along a continuum from the *ma'abarah* novel to the post-Arabic novel, I am asking what avenues of expression emerge when Mizrachi authors employ the *ḥafla* trope, an Arabic literary idiom couched in musical affect. The connection between an Arab Jewish past, a Mizrachi present, and the possibility of an Arab Jewish future is far from obvious in mainstream Israeli literary frames of reference. My analysis illuminates a cross-section of a burgeoning Mizrachi literature that contests and stretches the boundaries of the printed Hebrew word. Through a thematic emphasis on *ḥafla* poetics, these works probe pockets of silence deemed opaque and culturally untranslatable. From Ars Poetika's loud and brazen busting open of the silences, to Amir's selective translations of the melancholia of no return, to Behar's bilingualism of Hebrew and Silence, *ḥafla* poetics in Israeli literature signal a sounding of the Mizrachi voice.

Notes

1. Eli Amir, *Mafriach hayonim* (Tel Aviv: Am Oved, 1992); *Tarnegol kaparot* (Tel Aviv: Am Oved, 1983); *Yasmin* (Tel Aviv: Am Oved, 2005). Almog Behar *Tschachla veḤezkel* (Jerusalem: Keter, 2010).

2. Given the relative dearth of contemporary Israeli literature translated into Arabic, it is noteworthy that both Amir and Behar have seen their novels

translated into Arabic in Cairo: Amir's *Yasmin* was translated by Hussein Sarag and released as a limited edition through Ibn Laqmān Publishing House (2007). Behar's *Tchachla veHezkel* was translated by Nael El-Toukhy and released to wide critical acclaim by Kotob Al-Khan (2016). In a rare exception to the taboo on normalization with Israeli authors and institutions, *Tchachla veHezkel* has appeared in international book festivals from Cairo to Beirut to Abu Dhabi.

3. I am using the phrase "rupture and return" in reference to Ella Shohat's article, "Rupture and Return: Zionist Discourse and the Study of Arab Jews," *Social Text* 21, no. 2 (2003).

4. For an in-depth discussion of the interface between ontologies of place and ideologies of space in Hebrew literature, see Karen Grumberg's *Place and Ideology in Contemporary Hebrew Literature* (Syracuse: Syracuse University Press, 2011).

5. My use of the terms *Mizrachi* and *Arab Jew* vary throughout this essay depending on my frame of reference at a given moment. Broadly speaking, I use the term *Mizrachi* to describe cultural production and demographic trends in Israel. My use of the term *Arab Jew* acknowledges a connection between Iraqi Israeli representations of the *hafla* and the Arabic-language poetic tradition to which such representations owe their symbolic vocabulary, even, and perhaps especially, if they are composed in Hebrew.

6. Prashanth Ramakrishna, "Ars Poetika: Poeticizing Mizrahi Inequality in Israel," *The Believer Logger*, March 16, 2017.

7. Behar describes his role as an activist/poet in the following terms: "The activism with which I've been involved (through, among other movements, the group Cultural Guerilla) is to an extent connected to poetry and literature. Our aim is to connect identity, culture, and class politics and create a community of both Hebrew and Arabic writers. One of our goals is to introduce economics into literature, and bring literature into the economy. . . . The goal is to explode these dichotomies, to transgress the boundaries and cross-contaminate the two domains so that they are no longer self-contained." Shoshana Olidort, "The Language We Inherit Is Not One: A Conversation with Almog Behar," *Los Angeles Review of Books*, May 1, 2017.

8. Nancy Berg, *Exile from Exile: Israeli Writers from Iraq* (Albany: State University of New York Press, 1996).

9. Lital Levy, *Poetic Trespass: Writing Between Hebrew and Arabic in Israel/Palestine* (Princeton: Princeton University Press, 2014).

10. Michal Raizen, "Cairo as Borderland: Of Disruption and Love in Arabic Translations of Hebrew Literature." Paper presented at the National Association of Professors of Hebrew, Los Angeles, 2012.

11. Dudu Tassa and A-WA have produced albums in Iraqi and Yemeni dialect respectively. See the 2011 documentary *Iraq n' Roll* by Gili Gaon (Station Films Ltd.) and Gaar Adams, "Sick Beats and Sikes Picot," *Foreign Policy* (2015).

12. In *New Babylonians: A History of Jews in Modern Iraq* (Stanford: Stanford University Press, 2012), Orit Bashkin elaborates on the 1950 denationalization law that ultimately served as the death knell of the embattled Iraqi Jewish community. Drafted through a hurried series of negotiations between Zionist emissaries and the newly appointed Iraqi prime minister, Tawfik al-Suwaydi, the law framed the opportunity to emigrate in terms of a benevolent gesture on the part of the Iraqi government.

13. All translations are my own unless otherwise noted.

14. Salima Pasha, a Jewish Iraqi singer, was one of the most cherished performers of Arabic song in the first half of the twentieth century. Together with the Kuwaiti Brothers, she was one of the great innovators of Iraqi music. The Kuwaiti Brothers emigrated to Israel in the 1950s whereas Salima Pasha stayed behind in Iraq and ultimately converted to Islam. Her repertoire continues to be popular until this day.

15. Abu Kabi (the father of Kabi) follows the Arabic convention of a parent assuming the name of their first born.

The Hebrew word *yetsi'ah* has accrued myriad associations, among them *hayetsi'ah miMitsrayim* (the Biblical exodus from Egypt) and *yetsi'at eiropa tav-shin-zayin* (Exodus 1947, the immigrant ship transporting Jewish refugees out of Europe and forced by the British to return).

The categorization of Arab Jews as migrants or refugees would have major ramifications in terms of population exchange. Yehuda Shenhav discusses this point at length in "Arab-Jews, Population Exchange, and the Palestinian Right of Return," in *Exile and Return: Predicaments of Palestinians and Jews*, ed. Ann M. Lesch and Ian S. Lustick (Philadelphia: University of Pennsylvania Press, 2005). The film adaptation of *Mafriach hayonim* emphasizes this point with the scene of Palestinian refugees moving into the homes of Jewish emigrants.

16. In his groundbreaking study *After Jews and Arabs: The Remaking of Levantine Culture* (Minneapolis: University of Minnesota Press, 1993), Ammiel Alcalay builds on ethnographer and historian S. D. Goitein's concept of "Jewish-Arab symbiosis" and sheds light on a continuum of syncretic cultural production spanning the centuries from Dunash Ben Labrat's tenth-century wine song to the Yemeni poetry of lamentation born of the transit camps in the 1950s.

17. I am using the term *Arab noise* in reference to the article "Arab Noise and Ramadan Nights: Rai, Rap, and Franco-Maghrebi Identity," by Joan Gross, David McMurray, and Ted Swedenburg, *Diaspora: A Journal of Transnational Studies* 3, no. 1 (1994): 3–39.

18. These lyrics come from the 1964 song, *inta 'umri* ("You are my life").

19. Laudan Nooshin, ed., *Music and the Play of Power in the Middle East, North Africa, and Central Asia* (London: Ashgate, 2009), 55–73.

20. The *muṭrib* (fem. *muṭriba*) was an artist with a distinct gift for facilitating ecstatic transcendence. These artists held a special status and were categorically

different from sentimentalists or folkloric singers. Umm Kulthum and Salima Pasha both fell under this category. Boris Mafatsir, *Ṭarab: A Search of Memory and Identity in Two Parts* (Zvi Shefi Productions, 2009).

21. Behar includes this phrase first in Hebrew (*hashirah hi sefer hatoladot shel ha'aravim*) and then in transliterated Arabic (*al-sh'ir diwān al-'arab*). Commonly translated as "poetry is the register of the Arabs," this phrase belongs to a vast hermeneutic tradition.

22. Levi and Nashawi have produced a series of compact discs titled "Oriental, Iraqian, and Middle Eastern Hafla"; http://www.israel-music.com/yaakov_nashawi/.

Anthological Poetics
Reading Amichai and Halfi in Liberal Prayerbooks

WENDY I. ZIERLER

Ever since the assassination of Prime Minister Yitzhak Rabin on November 4, 1995, an effort has been underway to infuse secular Israeli identity and Zionist Hebrew culture with a new connection to classical Jewish texts and Jewish religious expression. If the secular kibbutz community had previously ceded critical Jewish, textual and religious ground to the *haredi* and religious Zionist camps, and if Rabin's religious Zionist assassin, Yigal Amir, had justified his heinous act on the basis of Jewish religious principle, a new determination took root among kibbutz and other liberal Israeli educators and community leaders to reclaim Jewish texts, values and religious practices on their own terms.[1] The result of all of this, seventy years after the establishment of the state, has been a secular Jewish religious renaissance of sorts, one that since the early 2000s has extended to synagogue life as well, giving rise to a number of vibrant and experimental secular Israeli prayer communities, including the Kehilat Niggun Halev in the Jezreel Valley, Kehilat *Achva Bekerem* in Ein Kerem, Nava Tehila also in Jerusalem, and most notably, Beit Tefilah Israeli in Tel Aviv, which celebrated its bar mitzvah year last summer (2017).[2] This renaissance been accompanied by liturgical innovation, including the production of innovative *siddurim* that revise the traditional liturgy with contemporary values in mind and make broad use of secular Hebrew poetry and folksongs (many with lyrics by noted Israeli poets). So extensive is the use in these *siddurim* of contemporary Israeli poetry that they might be considered important Hebrew poetry anthologies in their own right, with modern Hebrew poems functioning as new sources of interpretation of classical Jewish texts and classic texts shedding new light on the contemporary Israeli condition.

This paper delves into the powers of anthologizing and intertextuality to counter the rigid silos of religiosity and secularism in Israeli Judaism.[3] Specifically, it examines the use of Hebrew poetry by Yehuda Amichai (1924–2000) and Avraham Halfi (1904–1980) in the recently published Israeli prayer book *Siddur 'erev shabbat umo'ed*. In terms of the poets chosen, Yehuda Amichai enjoys a super-canonical status, his poetry serving the function for many as *"me'ein tachlif lasiddur,"* as a kind of substitute prayer book.[4] Halfi is beloved among secular Israelis because of the setting of several of his poems to music by beloved folk/rock singer Arik Einstein (1939–2013), though the use of his poetry in a synagogue context is a distinct innovation. Halfi's yoking together of unrelenting theological skepticism with prayerful seeking makes him a particularly provocative and important poetic voice for discussion of the contemporary use of poetry in prayer. More and more in Israel, as Adina B. Newberg observes, "the old labels of 'secular' and 'religious' no longer work";[5] Amichai and Halfi's hybrid, secular-religious poetry underscores the attenuated meaning of these binary labels. Juxtaposed with traditional prayers, their poems produce new liturgical tones especially fitting for the current moment. At the end of the essay, I examine poetry by Amichai in *Mishkan Hanefesh*, the new (American) Reform Yom Kippur Machzor. Despite being produced in two different hemispheres, this prayer book and *Siddur 'erev shabbat umo'ed* happen to include overlapping selections and so provide evidence of consultation and collaboration between their editors as well as an indication of the impact that Israeli spiritual trends are having on American Liberal Judaism.[6]

The intellectual and aesthetic value of reading the poetry of Amichai, Halfi, and others within the context of Jewish prayer finds theoretical support in the work of such scholars of intertextuality as Louise M. Rosenblatt and more recently, Jahan Ramazani, who insist on the ways in which poetry acquires meanings within specific times and contexts and in relation to other textual genres. According to Rosenblatt's transactional theory of literature, a poem should be "thought of as an event in time. It is not an object or an ideal entity. It happens during a coming-together, a compenetration of a reader and a text. The reader brings to the text his past experience and present personality."[7] Rosenblatt's transactional theory highlights the role of context and reader in creating a new text, while Ramazani advocates a dialogical approach that emphasizes the influence of other genres on the otherwise unique and idiosyncratic features of poetry.[8] If for Rosenblatt the meaning of the poem is formed anew with each readerly transaction with the text, for Ramazani the meaning of a poem is also "born and shaped in the process of interaction and struggle with other discourses, other genres, other kinds of utterance. Poems come into being partly by echoing, playing on, reshaping, refining, heightening, deforming, inverting, combating, hybridizing, and compressing extrapoetic forms of language."[9]

What I would like to add to this intertextual framework is the effect on the production of poetic meaning which results from *anthologizing*—that is, the editorial placement of a poem within a body of other texts or poems. When, after all, does a poem ever truly stand alone? If declaimed or performed in the context of a ceremony or poetry slam, it takes its meaning in relation to that performative event. If a poem is published in a newspaper or magazine, it gains significance in light of the events of the day or through the theme and arrangement of the particular publication. If published in a collection of other poems by the same poet, it assumes meaning in relation to the other poems in the collection. Likewise, if placed together in an anthology with poems by other authors and time periods, it participates in the meanings and messages that are coaxed out by the editor of the anthology. Often editors will preface anthologies with titles and introductions that assert a particular poetic or thematic argument, and they will order and arrange poems in such a way as to highlight a tradition or a set of textual affinities that unite disparate authors. The *siddur*, of course is also an anthology, combining prose and poetic texts from different periods, and as such participates in an anthological argument with attendant, new interpretive consequences.[10]

In a volume entitled *The Anthology in Jewish Literature*, editor David Stern discusses the central role of the anthology as a medium both for the transmission and innovation of Jewish tradition, noting how "the very act of selection can be a powerful instrument for innovation; juxtaposition and recombination of discrete passages in new contexts and combinations can radically alter their original meaning." Stern also highlights the role of the anthology in re-creating or imagining "new communities of readers and audiences,"[11] a notion that is especially relevant to the activity of creating new liberal *siddurim* that feature contemporary poems, many of which are the product of experimentation within an ever-changing synagogue community context.

It is important to note that not all scholars welcome the liturgical appropriation of secular Israeli poetry. In her recent study *The Full Severity of Compassion* (2016), Amichai scholar and translator Chana Kronfeld trenchantly critiques this phenomenon. She attributes Amichai's popularity in the United States to readerly obtuseness: a lack of sensitivity to his iconoclastic allusions to sacred texts.

> All too frequently . . . I have seen his poetry embraced by American readers who, knowing very little about the sacred texts he takes apart, remain unaware of—and uninterested in—his resistant, anticlerical poetics and are lulled into complacency by the apparent simplicity of his poems' surface. The mere reference to prayers, God, and the Bible in his poetry has qualified him for the role of a religious Jewish poet laureate for the American Jewish community. Thus, Amichai's poetry is not infrequently used to provide readers in the United States with something textual to hold onto, either as a marker of some fuzzy feel-good Jewish identity or, more generally, for its pleasantly vague sense of Old World tradition.[12]

To be sure, not all recent experiments in using modern Israeli poetry as liturgy are successful or represent the best readings of the poetic works. That said, liturgical uses of Amichai and other modern poets do not necessarily entail ignorance, censorship or simplification of the poetry at hand.[13] To read the meaning of Amichai's poetry in particular as so God-skeptical and anti-institutional as to be incompatible with prayer indirectly simplifies Amichai's poetry, not to mention that it underestimates the complexities of contemporary prayer. I do not believe, as Boaz Arpaly suggests, that Amichai's poetry teaches in some ultimate sense that "there is no God in this world" and that "there is no point in searching for him, or for any other entity that may possess the qualities attributed to God in the religious tradition."[14] In contrast to David Averbach, I also do not view Amichai's poetry as "littered with cynical traces of abandoned beliefs,"[15] thereby making them unsuitable for a liberal prayer context. On the contrary, like Yosef Milman, I maintain that Amichai's sacrilegious "use of concepts from sacred sources to undermine and replace these same concepts is to be understood as an act which is, at one and the same time, deconstructive-reconstructive,"[16] reflecting an ongoing effort to continue a dialogue with God despite or in light of skepticism and a loss of faith.[17] Especially in the Israeli context, *siddurim* are being produced that highlight rather than blunt the iconoclastic effects of the poetry of Amichai, Halfi, and many others. This poetry does the work of contemporary prayer because, originating from avowedly and recognizably secular or atheistic poets, it nevertheless engages seriously, provocatively, and artistically with the notion of God and the act of prayer. And it has a renewed impact as poetry, not despite but because of its appearance alongside traditional prayers and *piyyutim*, the disparate but nevertheless related texts provoking mutual rereading and reinterpretation.

I would argue, then, that rather than affording a pleasant but ill-founded, warm feeling of Old World nostalgia, secular Hebrew poetry placed in the context of Jewish prayer provokes a multilayered sense of nostalgia. I refer to nostalgia here in the more literal sense of the term, as homesickness or a painful desire to return to an irretrievable state or place, and I say multilayered, because statutory rabbinic prayer is at its root a nostalgic substitution for the lost temple service.[18] Furthermore, in the context of Zionist return to Israel, modern Hebrew poetry, set to music and sung at kibbutz sing-alongs and other ʿ*arvei shirah*, often substituted for traditional public prayer; these songs served as a nostalgic "remnant of synagogue culture."[19] More recently, revived interest in the *piyyut* form[20]—itself a post-Talmudic effort to restore fluidity and creativity to fixed, statutory prayer[21]—has come to substitute doubly nostalgically for a waning Labor Zionist pioneer sing-along culture and traditional, statutory prayer.[22] The result of these experiential and print concurrences, which juxtapose very different kinds of prayer texts, exposing profound connections as well as gaps between traditional and contemporary mindsets, is a textured, fractured, many-layered experience of both pain and comfort, an appreciation of the universal, ever-renewed "drive to create and the drive to know a creator,"[23] set within the particular, vexed, and ironic contemporary Jewish and Hebraic moment.

Rereading the Siddur with Amichai and Halfi

I turn now to specific poem inclusions by Yehuda Amichai and Abraham Halfi in *Siddur ʿerev shabbat umoʿed*. Bearing in mind Rosenblatt's notion of a poem "as an event in time" or as an "element of the environment to which the individual responds,"[24] I aim to show how the textual/anthological environments of these *siddurim*, in which traditional liturgical and poetic texts are placed side by side, serve to complicate one's notions of traditional prayer and modern poetry, as well as the categories of religious and secular in Israeli culture.

Siddur 'erev shabbat umo'ed was compiled and published by the leaders of Beit Tefilah Yisraeli, a Tel Aviv–based Liberal congregation created with secular Israelis in mind, most famous for its summer Kabbalat Shabbat services on the Tel Aviv beach that attract hundreds of secular and traditional worshippers on a summer Friday evening.[25] Under the rabbinic leadership of Esteban Gottfried, the congregation has been ideologically shaped both by the Jewish cultural agenda of Haim Nahman Bialik and the theological writings of Abraham Heschel, itself evidence of an Israeli/American synergy.[26] The congregation's Shabbat *siddur*, which began as a privately published pamphlet, has gone through several published editions since the founding of the congregation in 2004. This fact testifies to the leaders' commitment to experimentation and to learning from experience what works best in facilitating meaningful prayer. Foundational to this experience is the bringing together of traditional and modern forms of prayer and song in a meaningful interchange, an orientation reflected in the typographical/editorial arrangement of *siddur*. The layout features the traditional liturgical text in a more traditional prayer book font against a blue background on the right side of the open prayer book page and the alternative modern text in a more modern-looking font against a white background on the left side of the page. Next to one another but set apart by typeface, background color, and the inner fold of the page, the juxtaposed texts converse with, comment upon, and quarrel with one another in the mind of the attentive reader.

As seen in the figure on the opposite page, the first text that we shall examine is a poem by Amichai that accompanies Psalm 95, "*Lekhu neranenah*," the first psalm in the traditional Kabbalat Shabbat liturgy. "*Lekhu neranenah*" is a collective call to sing and genuflect before God: Come, let us bow down and bend the knee . . . before YHVH our Maker."[27] The biblical psalm divides into two parts, the first offering songs of praise to God the Creator, the second part warning the community against rebellious behavior like that of the Israelites at Merivah. (Numbers 20). Set to the immediate left of this psalm is Amichai's "Shir leil shabbat"[28] (Sabbath Eve Song), widely known in its musical setting by Moshe Vilensky, and hauntingly performed by Chava Alberstein.[29]

Anthological Poetics

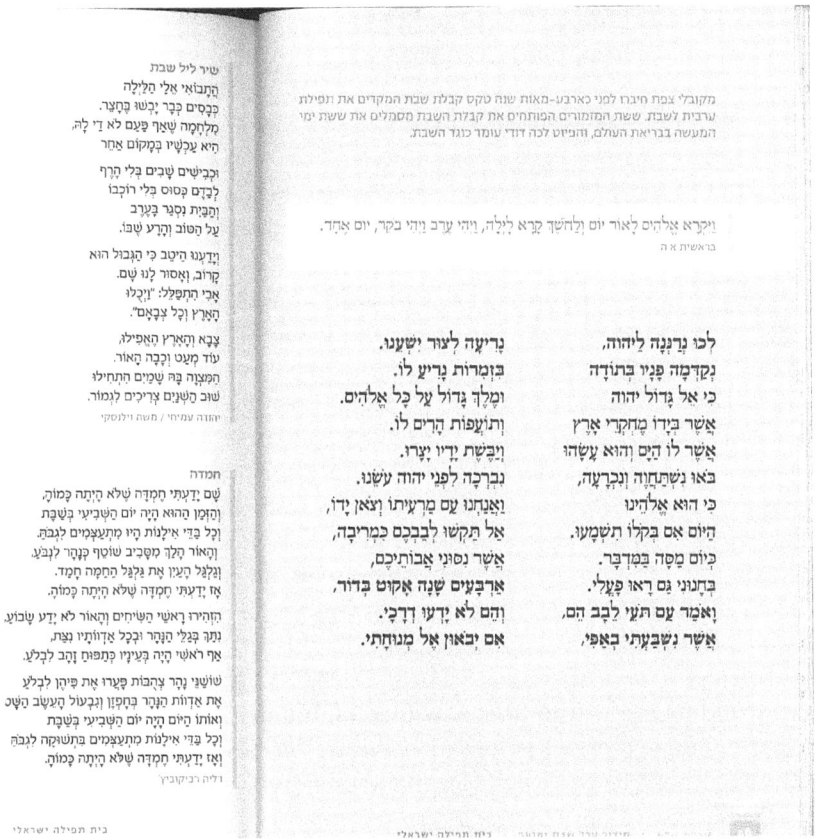

Figure 3.1. Psalm 95 and Yehuda Amichai, "Shir shel shabbat."

Will you come to me tonight
The laundry has already dried on the line.
The war that never gets enough
For now is out of mind.

And the roads return alone unceasing
Like a horse without a rider bestride
And the house is sealed up at evening
Upon the good and the evil inside.

And we know well that the border is
Near, and for us it is barred away.

My father prayed, "Thus the heavens and the earth
Were completed in their vast array."

The earth and array have darkened
Before long the light will be through.
The commandment which the skies had begun
Must be done by the other two. [My translation]

There is no intertextual marker clearly linking the poem with the juxtaposed liturgical text. The reference to the Sabbath liturgy, which appears in the third stanza of the poem, refers not to Psalm 95 but to the speaker's childhood image of his father praying the Sabbath evening Amidah/Kiddush (*Avi hitpallel vayekhulu/ ha'arets vekhol tseva'am*). Nevertheless, the anthological/juxtapositional placement of the poem in this liturgical context coaxes out new meanings from the poem that might not arise otherwise. Indeed, common words and motifs help forge a link between the texts. In the same way that the psalm exhorts the people *to come* genuflect before God (*bo'u venishtachaveh venikhra'ah*, let us bow down and bend the knee; let us kneel before the LORD), the speaker asks his beloved, a kind of secular Sabbath Bride,[30] *if she will come* (*hatavo'i*) and spend the night with him, now that the laundry is drying on the line and the theater of war has moved elsewhere for now. One imagines the scenario of a soldier on a leave for the weekend, an impression reinforced by the successive appearance in lines 13 and 14 of the biblical words "*tsva'am*" (the hosts thereof or the vast array, as translated above, Gen. 2:1) and "*tsava*" (the modern word for army), suggesting a provocative mixing of modern and ancient resonances.

Whereas the psalm issues its call to the community in the first person plural, Amichai's poem issues its invitation in the intimate, second personal singular, but each ends on a portentous note. The joyous tone of the psalm is interrupted by the references in the second part to the rebellion of the Israelites at Meribah (Numbers 20), and a swearing in wrath that these rebels "shall not come to My resting place [*menuchati*]," a reference to the Promised Land[31] that also brings to mind a notion of thwarted Sabbath rest. In the Amichai poem, the expectation of Sabbath evening peace is even more seriously imperiled by the image of lonely roads returning like riderless horses, hinting at those who have fallen in battle and thus will never again return home for Sabbath leave. The childhood memory of the speaker's father praying/reciting Kiddush on Friday night offers only faint consolation in the face of such stark realities.

Here we have a poem in which the conventions of rhyme serve to highlight, ironically, the disruption of conventional assurances, bringing together such words as *"lailah"* (night) and *lo dai lah* (she, femininely personified war, is not satisfied); *'erev*, the evening time that ushers in the Sabbath, and *bli heref,* without pause or incessantly, all undercutting the notion of Sabbath rest. The enjambment of *ki hagevul / hu* (the border is), which rhymes with *vayekhulu* (and they were finished, Gen. 2:1), underscores the notion of a temporary, all-too-fleeting pause to an unending war. On the one hand the biblical/liturgical keyword *vayekhulu* calls to mind the notion of Divine rest as a pretext for the Sabbath; on the other hand, the cyclical nature of the work week presages the inevitable ending of such restorative moments, and predicts an ongoing cycle of ceasefire and war.

As already intimated, "Shir leil shabbat" includes a number of intertextual references to the Genesis creation narratives, including the *"vayekhulu"* reference mentioned above. Recalling Adam's disapproved of loneliness in Genesis 2:18 (*lo tov heyot Adam levado,* it is not good for the human to be alone), the returning, riderless roads are described as *levadam* (lonely), implying something less than good about their incessant return. Line 8 describes a house that is closed off to *hatov vehara shebo,* to the good and the evil inside, recalling the fruit of the tree of knowledge of *tov vara,* of good and evil, (Genesis 2:9, 2:17), and by extension, the twin notions of moral discrimination and carnal knowledge. Indeed, the last two stanzas of the poem seem to play out a series of double/triple meanings, referring at once to the dangers of armies (*tsava* and *tseva'am*) lurking at forbidden borders, and the transgression of forbidden borders in the form of sexual relations and consummation. If the divine heavens initiate the creation of the world, the other two partners in creation, the earth and its array (army) must complete the work. By analogy, *hashenayim,* the two, the speaker and his partner here on this earth, need to complete/consummate their love. But do they, actually? Does the beloved addressee ever come? Does the last line referring to the two needing to end (*ligmor*) refer to the consummation of the sexual act or the end of their love relationship? Does the whole stanza refer to the two warring parties in the Arab Israeli wars and the need somehow to bring an end (*ligmor*) to the conflict? Either way, this poem adds a doubtful, searching chorus to the Sabbath evening prayers, a meaning that comes to the fore more clearly as a result of *siddur* anthologizing.

The same might be said of "*Eineni yode'a*,"[32] a poem by actor and poet Avraham Halfi (1904–1980), a contemporary of Natan Alterman and Avraham Shlonsky, whose poetry differed conspicuously from his famous pre-statehood contemporaries in its "intensive religious quest."[33] The particular poem by Halfi that I'd like to examine appears alongside "Mizmor shir leyom hashabbat," (Psalm 92) in *Siddur 'erev shabbat umo'ed*:

The themes of Psalm 92, designated in the Bible as a Sabbath day "*mizmor shir*" (hymn), are well known. It is good, declares the Psalmist, to thank God and recount God's lovingkindness and faithfulness in the morning and at night. God's work and the greatness of God's deeds make the Psalmist glad; only fools fail to recognize this. The notion of the fool calls to mind those evildoers who sprout like grass, enemies of the Psalmist and of God, whom God will eventually bring to ruin. It is with all this that the Psalmist looks out at his adversaries (*vatabbet 'einai beshurai*), knowing that it is righteousness rather than evil that eventually triumphs. The psalm culminates with the spiritually confident image of the

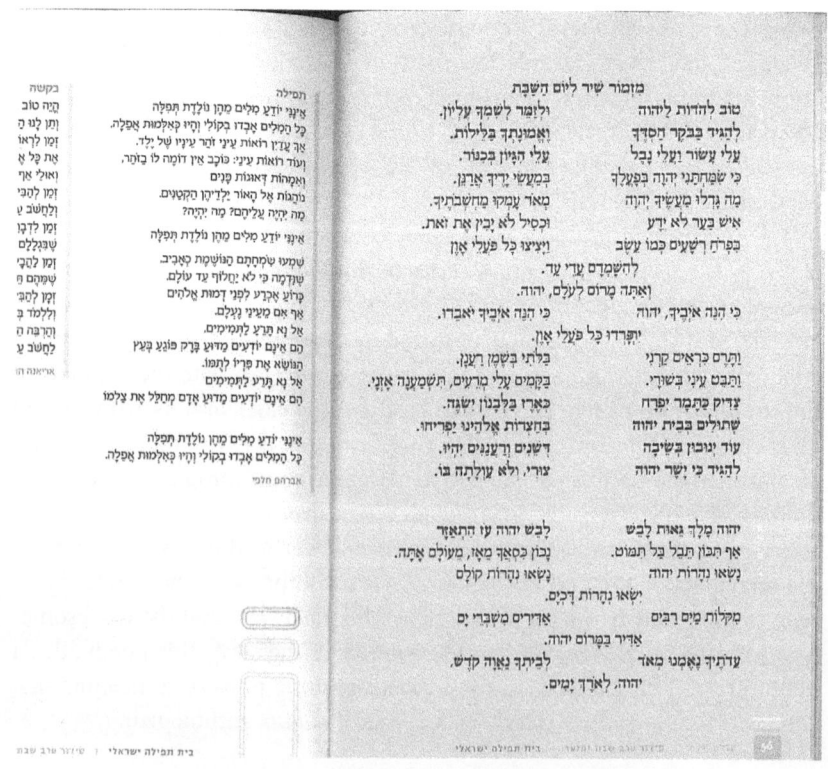

Figure 3.2. Psalm 92 and Avraham Halfi, "*Tefilah*."

righteous person flourishing like a date palm and a cedar tree, planted in the house of God unto old age. In his commentary on Psalm 92, Benjamin Segal calls attention to the sevenfold repetition of the name of God in the psalm, evoking the seven days of Creation as well as the repetition of the verb *lehaggid* (to declare), bracketing and filling the psalm with a sense of confident utterance and reassurance.[34]

The Avraham Halfi poem that is placed to left of Psalm 92 in *Siddur 'erev shabbat umo'ed* offers a sharp contrast, thereby drawing out provocative, juxtapositional meanings.[35]

> I know not the words from which prayer is born.
> All the words have been lost in my voice and become a dark
>   muteness.
> But my eyes still see the radiance in the eyes of a child.
> And my eyes still see: a star with no peer in its radiance.
> And worried-faced mothers   5
> Guide their small children toward the light.
> What will be over them? What will be?
>
> I know not the words from which prayer is born.
>
> Hear their joy breathing like a springtime,
> Which will never ever pass away.   10
> Surely I shall kneel before an image of God
> Even if that God has disappeared from my eyes.
> Harm not the innocents, please.
> They know not why lightning strikes a tree
> That naively bears its fruit. [That bears its fruit to its
>   conclusion]   15
> Harm not the innocents.
> They know not why a human being profanes his image
>
> I know not the words from which prayer is born.
> All the words have been lost in my voice and become a dark
>   muteness. [My translation]

As in case of the previously discussed poem by Amichai, Halfi's poem includes neither an epigraph nor an outright reference to Psalm 92; the dialogue that is carried out in the mind of the reader is an event in time catalyzed by editorial/anthological arrangement and juxtaposition. The result: a skeptical challenge to all the Psalmist's positive assertions about the merits of speaking God's praise. If the psalm is bracketed at its beginning and its end (verses 3 and 16) with confident declaration (*lehaggid baboker chasdekha / lehaggid ki yashar Adonai*), Halfi's poem begins and ends and is peppered in the middle with the rhymed assertion (*tefilah*, prayer, rhyming with *afeilah*, darkness) that the poet speaker knows not how to pray or praise. In marked contrast to the Psalmist's determination to praise God day and night, the poem paradoxically refrains with dark muteness. If the Psalmist marshals the imagery of the palm and the cedar as similes for righteous prosperity, Halfi adduces the image of an innocent tree struck by lightning as proof of random, undeserved victimization by nature despite the tree's persistent and naive (one possible meaning of *letumo*) determination to carry its fruit to term (another possible meaning of *letumo*). Where is God, and what is God's role in nature? The poem remains radically agnostic with regard to these theological issues.

Set in this context, the repeated images of sight in Halfi's poem also converse and comment upon Psalm 92. The vision reference in the psalm, "*vatabbet 'einai beshurai*,"[36] is an empirically based declaration of victory on the part of the Psalmist, commonly translated as "my eyes behold my foes' defeat."[37] Halfi's poem similarly employs motifs of sight as the basis for empirically based optimism: the speaker still sees "the radiance in the eyes of a child" and the peerless radiance (at night) of a star, itself a kind of naive reference, evocative of the children's nursery rhyme, "Twinkle, Twinkle little Star." The choice of the word *zohar* for radiance or light adds a potential mystical element to this notion of light, given that the Zohar is the foundational Jewish mystical text.[38]

Immediately following these images of reassuring radiance, however, comes a description of worried mothers trying to conduct their children in the direction of this light, along with the phrase "*ma yihyeh 'aleihem*," an expression of the speaker's worry for these innocents and for their future innocence. What abides above them? What providential power will there be to protect them from harm and cynicism? Looking forward, what obligations *'aleihem*—upon them—will bear down on them, force them out of their prior naiveté? "In his great worry, [the speaker] is not bothered by the paradox of kneeling before a God that may not actually exist," observes critic Zvi Luz. "The key is that the children are happy right now and are breathing like springtime, deluding themselves that their joy will never pass away, while the speaker recognizes the danger in change and fears that this will harm the innocents."[39] Whereas the Psalmist turns to what he sees for reassurance of God's role in the world, Halfi's speaker sees the tenuousness of innocence and kneels in great fear before the uncertain future. Not just that: implied in these lines is that there is something in the divine order of things that threatens innocence or wholeness, compelling the poet, paradoxically, to petition this same God not to harm (*al na tera'*) those *temimim* who have no knowledge of the fundamental division at the root of human knowledge.[40]

The specific references to the image of God (*demut Elohim*, line 11),[41] "*tsalmo*," (his [human image], God's image, line 17),[42] and the figure of a tree (of innocence), once again recall Genesis 1–3, the notion of human creation in the image of God, of primordial human innocence in the Garden of Eden, and the attempts by an all-knowing Creator God to thwart human knowledge of good and evil. Genesis 3 suggests that with the transgressive eating of the fruit of the tree of knowledge, primordial humans came to know: intellectually, morally, and sexually. Halfi's poem, however, suggests abiding human ignorance and perplexity, a notion accentuated by the repetition at the poem's opening and closing of the words *Eineni yode'a* (I know not) as well as by the repeated description of the *temimim* (innocents) as *einam yod'im* (they know not).

Whereas the psalm ends with an assertion of the uprightness of God (*ki yashar*, an inverting play on the earlier reference to the enemies who lie in wait as *shurai*), the image of lightning striking an innocent tree casts doubt upon God's righteousness and upon the assertion that righteous men are destined to flourish like cedars or palms on this earth. In fact, the poem suggests, human beings repeatedly choose to profane God or the godliness (*tsalmo*) within themselves.

In sum, the bringing together of these two texts acknowledges but also complicates traditional liturgical theology, making room in contemporary worship for those who continue to search for God despite disillusionment, who seek a place in communal prayer in the face of skepticism and doubt. "Prayer," write Zvi Luz, "is essentially a yoking together of opposites: the acknowledgement of an absent presence, a hidden existence, a perceptible nothingness."[43] The provocative juxtaposition or yoking together on the page of this *siddur* of Halfi's poem with Psalms 92 serves, in a sense, to acknowledge and highlight this feature of contemporary prayer, in general, and contemporary Israeli prayer, in particular.

Amichai in American Reform Liturgy

Current secular Israeli spiritual trends have had a distinct impact on American Liberal Judaism as well, with Israeli leaders, rabbis, and educators such as Ruth Calderon and Esteban Gottfried frequently visiting and teaching in the United States and with American rabbinic students and liturgical innovators studying, consulting, and collaborating with colleagues in Israel. And while Reconstructionist and Reform *siddurim* have long shown an interest in incorporating modern poetry, the most recent Reform prayer books include more poems in the original Hebrew and in the kind of juxtapositional format featured in *Siddur 'erev shabbat umo'ed* as well as in the recently published *siddurim* of the Israeli Reform movement.⁴⁴ With this in mind, I'd like to examine a provocative liturgical pairing, which occurs in *Mishkan Hanefesh*, the new American Reform Yom Kippur Machzor,⁴⁵ a prayer book that includes a fine array of modern Hebrew poems in the original and in English translation juxtaposed with traditional texts, further evidence of the ways in which *siddurim* are becoming important new vehicles for the dissemination and reconsideration of Israeli poetry.

The particular juxtaposition I explore is Yehuda Amichai's famous poem "*Beterem*," which appears in *Mishkan Hanefesh* to the left of the Ne'ilah *piyyut*, "*Petach lanu sha'ar*," a liturgical text that also figures prominently in Amichai's 1963 novel, *Lo me'akhshav, lo mikkan* (*Not of This Time, Not of This Place*):⁴⁶

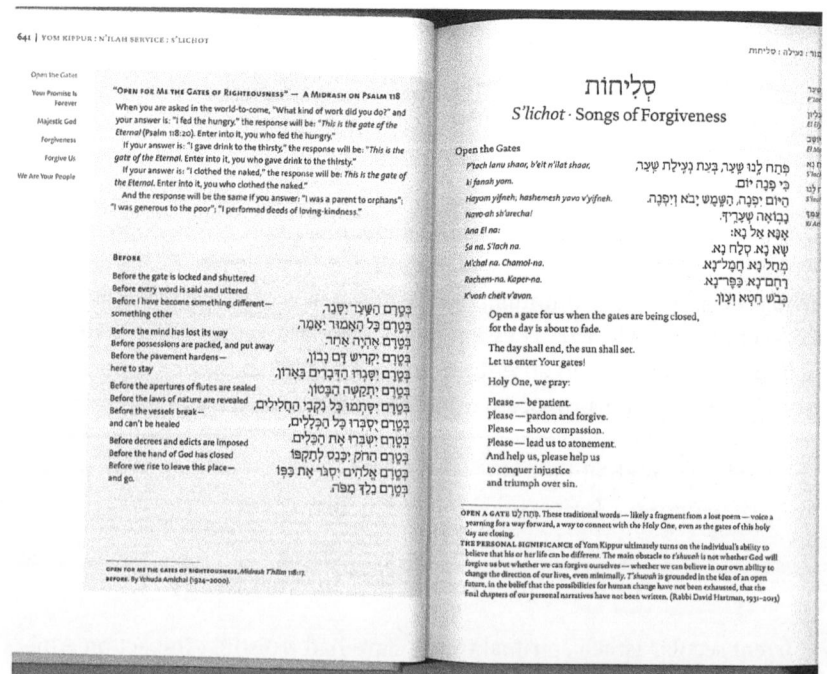

Figure 3.3. S'lichot and Yehuda Amichai, "*Beterem*."

In contrast to the poems discussed previously that do not overtly allude to the liturgical text with which they are paired, Amichai's "*Beterem*" overtly references its traditional companion text in the very first line ("Before the gate is locked and shuttered").[47]

In his book-length study of Amichai's structure, thematics, and poetics, Boaz Arpaly analyzes "*Beterem*" as a catalogue poem, a list of time descriptions, subordinate clauses without the accompanying independent clauses, the common principle of which the reader is left to deduce. Arpaly adduces two opposing ways of bringing the parts together into an interpretive whole. On the one hand, he sees the list of "befores" as representing an optimistic call to do as you see fit before the rules are set, before frozenness or death set in. On the other, he sees a multipartite, pessimistic declaration about the inevitability of mortality.[48] In keeping with his reading of Amichai's staunch, uncompromising secularism, Arpaly makes no attempt in his reading to offer a liturgical context or interpretation.

But as Arpaly himself notes, Amichai's catalogue in "*Beterem*" includes elements that differ as well as converge, making it difficult to come to one unified, overarching (secular) understanding.[49] Chana Kronfeld refers to the liminal time period invoked anaphorically in the poem—*beterem* (before)—in the context of a discussion of what she calls Amichai's poetics of "*beinayim*" or in-betweenness. "Rhetorically," Kronfeld argues, "this principle of an in-between existence motivates the interpenetrations of opposing genres (sonnet and ode, elegy and joke), of literal and figurative, and of poetry and non-poetry."[50] This idea finds expression in "*Beterem*," I would argue, in the stringing together of elements that are concrete, literal, and secular with those that are abstract and liturgical. Some of the elements embody both aspects simultaneously, such as the gate in the first line of the poem, which belongs to the world of the concrete architecture as well as the liturgical invocation of God's mercy in the evenings, particularly at the end of Yom Kippur. Likewise, the reference in line 2 to things being said reads as both prosaic and liturgical, resonant of God's speaking the world into existence in Genesis 1 and of the uttering of prayers in a synagogue on Yom Kippur. A similar mix of everyday, ultimate, and abstract appears in line 3 in the expression *ehyeh acher*, which can be simply translated as I shall become different, at the same time evoking both faith and apostasy, with *ehyeh* (I shall be), recalling God's self-naming in Exodus 3:14 as *ehyeh asher ehyeh* (I shall be who I shall be), and *acher* calling to mind *Acher*, the moniker assigned in the Talmud to the heretic Elishah ben Abuyah.[51] The *aron* in line 5 can be seen simultaneously as referring to a closet, the ark in a synagogue, or a coffin. Likewise, the reference in line 7 to the stopped-up openings of flutes (*nikvei chalilim*) can be interpreted as alluding to the *asher yatsar* blessing (traditionally said both in the morning prayers and after going to the bathroom), which praises God for fashioning our bodies with wisdom and creating *nekavim, nekavim, chalulim, chalulim* (many openings and cavities). At the same time, the expression *nikvei chalilim* brings to mind the Hebrew word *challal*, which connotes both empty space and a slain person, a fallen, victim of war, perforated (*nakuv*) by bullets and shells. The next line, which refers to the moment before the law takes effect (*yikanes letokpo*), explicitly returns the poem back to the Yom Kippur context, and to the radical binaries of fate outlined in the high holiday *Unetaneh tokef* prayer, in which God is seen as deciding who shall live, who shall die, who by fire, and who by water. As Kronfeld observes, "According to Jewish tradition, heaven's gates are most wide open and most receptive to human prayers at twilight, yet this is also an hour when life comes precipitously close to death. The in-between state is thus both precious and dangerous."[52] Almost every line in this poem occupies this interpretive middle-ground or zone of liminal meaning, suggesting both resignation and possibility.

The editors of *Mishkan Hanefesh* who have inserted Amichai's "*Beterem*" into the Ne'ilah service build on and heighten this sense of the poem's many meanings. What additional interpretive effect results from juxtaposing Amichai's well-known but cryptic poem that has several pop musical settings[53] with a similarly famous, oft-sung Yom Kippur *piyyut*? To what extent does this apposition provide an opportunity to complete the unfinished sentence that constitutes Amichai's poem with the petitionary words of the *piyyut*? Before all that is enumerated in Amichai's poem plays out, will God actually open the gates? Note the interplay in the poem of inactive and active verbs: while passive verbs such as "shuttered" and "uttered" suggest a fated inevitability, countervailing active constructions (*dam navon yakrish*: wise blood will congeal / *Elohim yisgor et kappo* / God will close his palm / *neilekh mi po*, we shall leave), hold out the possibility of activity and agency, while *yishberu et hakeilim* (they will break the vessels), calls to mind the Lurianic Creation myth, with the Divine emanation shattering the vessels, leading to an ongoing human need to gather the many broken shards and to repair the word (*tikkun 'olam*).[54] One can always choose to mobilize, decide, and initiate a change, as intimated by the reference in the third line to becoming other or different (*ehyeh acher*). The poem ends with *neilekh mippo*, which can be understood simultaneously as a reference to the time limit imposed by the end of the *Ne'ilah* service, that time when people leave synagogue and go home to eat, and the ultimate leaving of this world that is death, when all choices and actions are forever foreclosed.

Conclusion

"*Ani bikhlal choshev shehamilim shel shirah hem kemo tefilah*"—"I generally think," Yehuda Amichai declared in his last, filmed interview, "that the words of poetry are like prayer."[55] It is the argument of this paper that liturgical uses of the poetry of secular poets such as Amichai, Halfi, and others bring to light and shadow the complexity of such a statement. While it is certainly true that Amichai and Halfi "no longer possess[ed] traditional faith in an ordered universe or in divine love and protection,"[56] this did not prevent them from seeking out this faith and love and returning to the traditional context and construct of prayer to imagine the universe as they wished it to be. As such, the inclusion of these poems in these *siddurim* helps bring this paradoxical process to light, complicates the very notion of contemporary Jewish religiosity, and deepens the meanings, for an attentive reader, of both poetry and prayer.

These are timely sources of meaning, offered at a historical moment when secular Israelis are increasingly ripe and ready for such insights. A recent survey conducted by the Dialogue Company, one of Israeli leaders' public opinion consultants, shows higher rates of self-identification with Liberal Judaism than ever before in Israel, with 56 percent of secular Israeli Jews saying that they have attended a life-cyle or religious event led by a Reform or Conservative rabbi, a significant increase from the 10 percent found in 2010. According to another survey conducted by the Midgam Polling agency nearly two-thirds of Israeli Jewish respondents surveyed said that Reform Judaism deserves rights equal to those afforded to Orthodox Judaism.[57] The new *siddurim* that are being produced by Liberal Jews are contributing to and reflecting this evolving sociological picture. As Israeli attitudes change, the juxtaposition of poems and prayers in the new *siddurim* is generating new understandings of and conversations about poetry once assumed to be purely secular and rejecting of religion. They speak to a larger trend in Israeli Judaism that is expanding and giving nuance to the definition of Jewish religious life, text, and liturgy.

Notes

1. See the web sites of such organizations as BINA, https://bina.org.il/en/about-bina/ and Alma, http://www.alma.org.il/content.asp?lang=en&pageid=8 and the Midrasha at Oranim http://www.hamidrasha-israel.org/about-us/; accessed June 5, 2018.

2. "Over two hundred representatives from various communities in Israel participated in May of 2008 in a conference organized by the "Network of Independent Israeli Communities." As of 2010, close to fifty such communities existed in Israel, and more were being established. See Yaron Kapitulnik, "The Liturgy and Ritual of Independent Congregations in Israel," Rabbinic Thesis, HUC-JIR, Jan. 2010, 19, 6. http://library.huc.edu/pdf/theses/Kapitulnik%20Yaron-NY-Rab-2010%20rdf.pdf; accessed Feb. 2, 2018.

3. For more on the need to redefine the terms *secular* and *religious* in light of recent interest on the part of secular Israeli Jews to reclaim Jewish identity and practice, see Kapitulnik, 13–18. See also Charles Liebman and Yaacov Yadger, "Secular-Jewish Identity and the Condition of Secular Judaism in Israel," in *Religion or Ethnicity? Jewish Identities in Evolution*, ed. Zvi Gitelman (New Brunswick, NJ: Rutgers University Press, 2009), 149–70. For earlier studies that look at prayer themes in secular Hebrew poetry see, David Jacobson, *Creator, Are You Listening?: Israeli Poets on God and Prayer* (Bloomington: Indiana University Press, 2007) and Avi Sagi, *Prayer After the Death of God: A Phenomenological Study of Hebrew Literature*, trans. Batya Stein (Boston: Academic Studies Press, 2016), 91. Originally published in Hebrew as *Petsu'ei tefilah* (Jerusalem: Bar Ilan Press/Mechon Shalom Hartman, 2011).

4. Eilat Escozido, "Mah lechiloni ulesiddur tefilah," *Ynet*. https://www.ynet.co.il/articles/0,7340,L-3717743,00.html; accessed Jan. 27, 2018.

5. Adina B. Newberg, "New Prayers, Here and Now: Reconnecting to Israel Through Engaging in Prayer, Poetry and Song," *Israel Studies Forum* 23, no. 2 (Winter 2008): 78.

6. In a visit to my Hebrew Poetry and Prayer Seminar on Nov. 8, 2017, CCAR editor Rabbi Hara Person confirmed that she is in regular contact with such Israeli prayer book editors as Dalia Marx and that in some instances, new Israeli *siddurim* have been influenced by selections made by American editors.

7. Louise M. Rosenblatt, *The Reader, The Text, The Poem: The Transactional Theory of the Literary Work* (Carbondale and Edwardsville: Southern Illinois University Press, 1978), 12.

8. Jahan Ramazani, *Poetry and Its Others: News, Prayer, Song and the Dialogue of Genres* (Chicago: University of Chicago Press, 2014), 15. Kronfeld herself refers to the notion of dialogism in her discussion of intertextual agency in Amichai's poetry. See pp. 163–70.

9. Ibid., 6.

10. For more on the prayer book as anthology see Joseph Tabory, "The Prayerbook (Siddur) as Anthology of Judaism," in *The Anthology in Jewish Literature*, ed. David Stern (Oxford: Oxford University Press, 2004), 143–58.

11. David Stern, "The Anthology in Jewish Literature: An Introduction," in *The Anthology in Jewish Literature*, ed. David Stern, 7.

12. Chana Kronfeld, *The Full Severity of Compassion* (Stanford: Stanford University Press, 2016), 3. Kronfeld buttresses her point by reference to a particularly infelicitous use in the Reconstructionist High Holiday Machzor (*Kol haneshamah: Machzor layamim hanora'im* [Elkins Park, PA: The Reconstructionist Press, 1999], 899–900) of Amichai's "Shehar Hazikaron yizkor" ("Let the Memorial Hill Remember"), poem 34 in Amichai's 1974 poem-cycle, *Shirei erets tsiyon yerushalayim* (Jerusalem: Schocken, 1974), 26. Amichai's poem-cycle was written as a sardonic response to the Yom Kippur War and is meant to undermine the obsession in Israeli culture with memorialization. According to Kronfeld, in placing the poem as part of the "Eleh ezkereh" martyrology, the *Kol Haneshamah* props up that very culture of memorialization and "performs an outright act of political censorship." See Kronfeld, 63.

13. For an early consideration of prayer references and potential liturgical uses of Amichai's poetry, see Craig H. Axler, *Liturgical Aspects in the Poetry of Yehuda Amichai*, Rabbinical Thesis, Hebrew Union College-Jewish Institute of Religion, Feb. 28, 2003.

14. Boaz Arpaly, "On the Political Significance of Amichai's Poetry," in *The Experienced Soul*, ed. Glenda Abramson (Boulder: Westview, 1997), 41.

15. David Averbach, "Religious Metaphor and Its Denial in the Poetry of Yehuda Amichai," *Judaism* 53, no. 3–4 (Summer/Fall 2004): 289.

16. Yosef Milman, "Sacrilegious Imagery in Yehuda Amichai's Poetry," *AJS Review* 20, no. 1 (1995): 101.

17. Sidra DeKoven Ezrahi makes a related point in an article about Amichai as poet of the "everyday." According to Ezrahi, "In Amichai's poetry God still survives—as a familiar Other, as a source of ethical norms, as an elderly legislator of law or ceremony, and most of all as address for human prayers" (my translation). See Sidra Ezrahi, "Yehuda Amichai: Paytan shel hayom yom," *Mikkan* 14 (2014): 157.

18. See the statement of R. Joshua ben Levi in BT Brachot 26b.

19. Oz Almog, *The Sabra: The Creation of the New Jew* (Berkeley: University of California Press, 2000), 236. For a discussion of sing-alongs in the context of Israeli emigrants to New York, see Moshe Shokeid, "The People of the Song," in *Children of Circumstances: Israeli Emigrants in New York* (Ithaca: Cornell University Press, 1988), 104–25.

20. For information on Israeli and American cultural/synagogue projects see *Hazmanah lepiyyut*, http://web.nli.org.il/sites/nlis/he/song and and *Kehillot sharot,* http://kehilotsharot.org.il/הקהילות-המשתתפות/.

21. For more on this see "The Fixed and The Fluid in Jewish Prayer," in *Prayer in Judaism: Continuity and Change*, ed. Gabriel H Cohn and Harold Fisch (Northvale NJ: Jason Aronson, 1996), 45–52.

22. According to Esteban Gottfried, the rabbi of Beit Tefilah Yisraeli, he and his prayer-leading colleagues are continually trying new things, and therefore continue to revise and reissue their community *siddur*, based on what has worked or does not work within the prayer service. From my phone interview with Esteban Gottfried, Nov. 2016.

23. Jay Hopler, "Editor's Preface," in *Before the Door of God* (New Haven: Yale University Press, 2013), xxii. For philosophical exploration of this phenomenon in Israeli culture see Avi Sagi, *Prayer After the Death of God: A Phenomenological Study of Hebrew Literature*, trans. Batya Stein (Boston: Academic Studies Press, 2016).

24. Rosenblatt, 18.

25. Beit Tefilah Israeli was founded by Esteban Gottfried and Rani Jaeger, with early support from Yoav Rosenberg, Ezri Tarazi, and the late Elisheva Greenbaum. For more information see http://btfila.org/english/about-beit-tefilah-israeli/.

26. For more on the ideological underpinnings and vision for the congregation, see Esteban Gottfried, *Heschel pinat Bialik: Hats'ah levniyat tashtit ruchanit tarbutit lechayim yehudi'im beyisra'el*, Rabbinic Thesis, HUC-JIR, Jerusalem (Sept. 2012). http://library.huc.edu/pdf/theses/Gottfried%20Esteban-JS-Rab-2012%20rdf.pdf; accessed June 13, 2018.

27. Psalms 95:6.

28. Yehuda Amichai, *Shirim 1948–1962* (Jerusalem: Shocken, 1963), 111. See *Siddur 'erev shabbat umo'ed*, 40–41. Though this is the one published *siddur* that I found that makes this particular juxtaposition, Amichai's *"Shir shel shabbat"* is also included in other liberal Israeli Kabbalat Shabbat services, such as that at the Masorti Tiferet Shalom congregation in Tel Aviv. See Einat Libel-Hass, *The Development of Liberal (Reform/Mitkademet and Conservative/Masorti Judaism in Tel Aviv: Organizational Patterns and Identities in the Congregations Beit Daniel and Tiferet Shalom (1991–2015)*, PhD thesis, Department of Jewish History and Contemporary Jewry, Bar-Ilan University (Sept. 2015), 152.

29. See https://www.youtube.com/watch?v=f9pm1AsV9mE.

30. The "Lekha dodi" prayer, which comes toward the end of the traditional Kabbalat Shabbat service, culminates with the line, "*Bo'i khallah*," Come my Bride.

31. *The Hebrew Bible: Volume 3, The Writings*, trans. Robert Alter (New York: W. W. Norton, 2019), 228.

32. Avraham Halfi, *Ke'almonim bageshem* (Tel Aviv: Kibbutz Hameuchad, 1958), 8–9.

33. Haim O. Rechnitzer, "To See God in His Beauty: Avraham Chalfi and the Mystical Quest for the Evasive God," *Journal of Modern Jewish Studies* 10, no. 3 (Nov. 2011): 383. For more on the differences between Halfi and his better-known contemporaries, see Tzvi Luz, *Shirat Avraham Halfi* (Tel Aviv: Hakibbutz Hameuchad, 1994).

34. Benjamin Segal, *A New Psalm* (Geffen: Jerusalem, 2013), 439–43.

35. Avraham Halfi, *Ke'almonim bageshem* (*Like the Anonymous in the Rain*) (Tel Aviv: Hakibbutz Hameuchad, 1958), 8–9. The title "*Tefilah*" is an addition to the poem as it appears in the *siddur*; it does not appear in the original. Halfi's poem has been set to music by Shelomo Bar. See https://www.youtube.com/watch?v=iWFC9ezlBnE.

36. Punning because the word here for adversaries or foes *(shurai)* derives from a verb meaning to see or foresee.

37. Alter translation, 22.

38. The Zohar first appeared in Spain in the thirteenth century, and was published by a Jewish writer named Moses de León (1240–1305). For more on mystical elements in the poetry of Avraham Halfi, see Haim O. Rechnitzer, "'To See God in His Beauty': Abraham Chalfi and the Mystical Quest for the Evasive God," *Journal of Modern Jewish Studies* 10, no. 2 (2012): 383–400.

39. Zvi Luz, *Shirat Avraham Halfi* (Tel Aviv: Hakibbutz Hameuchad, 1994), 160.

40. The poet's twice-uttered plea of *al na tera* also calls to mind two biblical episodes in which that same plea occurs, Genesis 9:7 and Judges 9:23, both of which featured the threat of or actual grisly sexual violence. For more on this as a key to understanding Halfi's poem see Wendy Zierler, "On Sacrifices and Life: Wholeness Dismembered but Remembered," https://www.thetorah.com/article/on-sacrifices-and-life-wholeness-dismembered-but-re-membered.

41. See Genesis 5:1.

42. וַיִּבְרָא אֱלֹהִים אֶת-הָאָדָם בְּצַלְמוֹ Gen. 1:27).

43. Luz, 22.

44. See for example, *Siddur leil shabbat*, ed. Dalia Marx (Jerusalem: Mo'etset harabanim hamitkadmim beyisra'el, 2016) and *Shacharit lechol*, ed. Dalia Marx (Jerusalem: Mo'etset harabanim hamitkadmim beyisra'el, 2018).

45. *Mishkan Hanefesh* (New York: CCAR Press, 2015–16).

46. Yehuda Amichai, *Lo me'akhshav lo mikkan* (Jerusalem: Schocken, 1963) / Yehuda Amichai, *Not of This Time, Not of This Place*, trans. Shlomo Katz (London: Valentine Mitchell, 1973). For an excellent recent analysis of the novel, see Nitza Ben Dov, *Chayei milchamah* (Jerusalem: Schocken, 2016), 113–32.

47. Yehuda Amichai, "*Beterem*," in *Shirim 1948–1962* (Jerusalem: Schocken, 1963), 201. Translation by Sheldon Marder, included in *Mishkan Hanefesh*, Yom Kippur, 641. This translation, like others, takes liberties with literal meaning for the sake of replicating Amichai's rhyming triplets.

48. Boaz Arpaly, *Haperachim veha'agartal: Shirat Amichai: mivneh, mashama'ut, poetikah* (Tel Aviv: Hakibbutz Hameuchad, 1986), 105–106.

49. Ibid., 108. For another article that examines the mixing of elements from the "superior and the humble" in Amichai's poetry see Naomi Sokoloff, "Amichai's El Maleh Rahamim," *Prooftexts* 4 (1984):127–40.

50. Kronfeld, 110.

51. See for example, BT Chagigah 15b.

52. Ibid., 110.

53. I have identified at least three different musical settings of this poem beginning with Hanan Yuval's 1974 setting. See https://www.youtube.com/watch?v=oWyw2HIQw3U. See also Maureen Nehedar's setting https://www.youtube.com/watch?v=4WKb-KyUwQU and that of Karni Postal, https://www.youtube.com/watch?v=ppIMK33LFHA.

54. On the Lurianic notion of the breaking of the vessels see Gershom Scholem, *Major Trends in Jewish Mysticism* (New York: Schocken, 1995), 244–86.

55. See https://www.youtube.com/watch?v=9BoF_nqh_WU; accessed Sept. 27, 2017.

56. Glenda Abramson, "Amichai's God," *Prooftexts* (May 1984): 112.

57. For more information on these sociological surveys see for example, https://www.ynetnews.com/articles/0,7340,L-5048733,00.html; https://urj.org/blog/2017/11/29/urj-releases-preliminary-findings-2-important-surveys-demonstrating-effectiveness; https://www.jta.org/2016/05/27/israel/survey-third-of-israeli-jews-identify-with-reform-movement.

Part Two

Across Language and Territory: Literature and Identity

When Yiddish Was Young in Israel

Shachar Pinsker

In the 1980s, the bilingual writer Yossl Birshteyn wrote a collection of short stories published in Hebrew with the title *Ketem shel sheket* ("A Drop of Silence"), and in Yiddish with the title *Dayne geslakh, Yerushalaym* ("Your Streets, Jerusalem"). One of these stories starts with the following reflection by the autobiographical narrator:

> I've been told that I belong in the past. I speak about old people, and after many years in Israel, I still continue to write Yiddish, a silent (deaf-mute) language which no one speaks or hears anymore. No one told me this directly. I overheard people when they spoke about me, and I agreed with them. I could have added that I'm upset when I'm not statisfied with a page I wrote in Yiddish. But what there is here to be upset about; words that no one will read or hear? But anyway, I continue to sweat and work on things that don't exist anymore. So I guess I really belong in the past. In order not to be lonely there, in the past, I went to look for other people like me.[1]

This passage expresses the qualms of Birshteyn's narrator, but it also seems to illustrate well the predicament of Yiddish in Israeli literature. Yiddish is seen as the language of the past, associated not only with old people, but also with exile, destruction, and death. This leads the narrator to present Yiddish as a silent, or "deaf-mute language" (*safah chereshet ilemet*), because no one speaks or hears it. However, this is also a highly ironic text with multiple levels of meaning. From a historical perspective, the assertion that Yiddish is a silent language is a reversal of the long-term status of Yiddish as a widespread Jewish vernacular, spoken by around 80 percent of the world's Jewish population at the beginning of the twentieth century. After the Holocaust, Yiddish began to be transformed into a language preserved in books, anthologies, libraries and archives.[2] But Birshteyn's text seems to undermine itself precisely because it is expressed by his autobiographical narrator. It raises a number of questions: Is it true that in Israel Yiddish was a silent language? Did Birshteyn not know that Yiddish was the mother tongue of many of Israel's founding fathers, one that was still used in the 1950s and 1960s, and even 1980s?[3] After all, many characters in his stories and novels are speakers of Yiddish. They are far from being silent. In fact, Birshteyn's stories are full of the "noise" of spoken Yiddish. If this is the case, what makes Yiddish silent? Is it that mainstream Israeli culture erased, repressed, and ignored Yiddish, and very few are able to "hear" it? Does Birshteyn adopt, or ironically expose the common perception of Yiddish in Israeli culture? Furthermore, what conclusion does Birshteyn infer from the assertion that Yiddish is a "silent language"? He writes with more than a pinch of irony that he cannot stop writing it because "he really belongs in the past." His solution is to enter the past and find "others like him." But when is "the past"? What does it mean to be *there*? How far in time and place does Birshteyn need to go in order to find Yiddish?

In some sense, Birshteyn needed to go very far, but also very near. Not only did he speak and write Yiddish, but he also attempted to create a Yiddish literary and cultural center in Israel in the 1950s and early 1960s. For the rest of his life, Birshteyn continued to write and publish both in Yiddish and in Hebrew, to be active on the border/zone between the languages. Even when he became a popular Hebrew writer, one could identify the Yiddish that lurks behind his Hebrew texts on every level.[4]

At first glance, the questions that Birshteyn's story and work raise might seem peculiar, even idiosyncratic to a bilingual, Yiddish-Hebrew Israeli writer. Nevertheless, I argue that they are central not only to discussions of Yiddish language, literature, and culture in the period after the Holocaust, but also to issues of multilingualism, literary history, ethnicity, nationality, and cultural hegemony, which are at the heart of the notion of "Israeliness" and "Israeli literature." As Shai Ginsburg claims in his survey of the topic, the question of what constitutes "Israeli literature" is not only a literary or cultural question, but a political one as well. Since Statist ideology has privileged Hebrew, the language most associated with Zionist nationalism, scholars have mostly assumed Israeli literature to be monolingual, and thus conflated Israeli literature with Hebrew prose and poetry from the late 1940s onward. This is problematic for at least two reasons: one, it assumes a continuity between the transnational Hebrew literature written in Eastern and Central Europe, America, and the Middle East from the eighteenth century onward, and the literature written in the sovereign state in Israel; and two, it elides the complex multilingual literary reality in Israel.[5]

Only in recent years have scholars turned their attention to the multiplicity of languages in which literature was and still is written and read in Israel, as well as Hebrew literature written outside the state. They have explored literature written in Arabic, Russian, German, English, French, Polish, and others, as well as the relations between these languages and Hebrew.[6] My work contributes to this growing field by examining the role of Yiddish in Israeli literature, a topic that, for a number of reasons, has not attracted much scholarly attention until now.[7] The study of Yiddish in Israeli literature includes a large corpus of texts written in Yiddish from the establishment of Israel until today, as well as many translations from Yiddish into Hebrew. There is also a significant body of literature created in Hebrew by important and well-known writers such as Avot Yeshurun, Aharon Appelfeld, Yaakov Shabtai, Aharon Megged, Haim Be'er, David Grossman, Yoel Hoffman, and others, in which Yiddish plays an explicit or implicit role.[8] Due to the historical circumstances of Yiddish after the Holocaust, writing in or about Yiddish involves questions about what Jeffery Shandler identified as "post-vernacular culture," a situation in which symbolic significance is carried by the language apart from the semantic content of utterances.[9] Not surprisingly, Israeli-Yiddish writers were preoccupied with the relations between Yiddish and Hebrew, and dealt with images of Yiddish as *mame-loshn* ("mother tongue"). They challenged what Yasemin Yildiz called the "monolingual paradigm"—in which individuals are imagined to possess "one 'true' language only, their 'mother tongue,' and through this possession to be organically linked to an exclusive, clearly demarcated ethnicity, culture, and nation"—and showed that to write in Yiddish (or on the border/zone between Yiddish and Hebrew) in Israel is to be part of a "postmonolingual condition."[10]

So where and when should such a project begin? Locating a point of origin is always difficult and somewhat arbitrary, but let me suggest this: Avrom Sutzkever's poem "Yiddish."[11] This is a good starting point not only because it was written in 1948 in the first book Sutzkever published after he arrived in Israel (*In Fayer-vogn* ["In the Chariot of Fire"]), but also because it interrogates and thematizes the very question of beginning in the context of Yiddish and Israel.

„ייִדיש"/ אברהם סוצקעווער

זאָל איך אָנהייבן פֿון אָנהייב?
זאָל איך ווי אברהם
אויס ברודערשאַפֿט צעהאַקן אַלע געצן?
זאָל איך זיך אַ לעבעדיקן לאָזן איבערזעצן?
זאָל איך אײַנפֿלאַנצן מײַן צונג
און וואַרטן ביז פֿאַרוואַנדלען
וועט זי זיך אין אבֿותדיקע
ראָזשינקעס מיט מאַנדלען?
וואָס פֿאַר אַ קאַטאָוועסדיקע
וויצן
דאַרשנט מײַן פּאָעזיע־ברודער מיט די באַקנבאָרדן,
אַז מײַן מאַמע־לשון גייט באַלד אונטער?
מיר וועלן נאָך אין הונדערט יאָר אַרום דאָ קעגנטיק זיצן
און פֿירן די דיסקוסיע בײַ דעם ירדן.
ווײַל אַ שאלה נאָגט און נאָגלט:
אויב ער ווייס גענוי ווו
די תּפֿילה פֿון בערדיטשעווער,
יהואשעס ליד
און קולבאַקס
וואַגלט
צו דעם אונטערגאַנג —
טאָ זאָל ער מיר, אַ שטייגער,
אָנווײַזן וווּהין די שפּראַך גייט־אונטער?
אפֿשר בײַ דעם כּותל־מערבֿי?
אויב אַזוי, וועל איך דאָרט קומען, קומען,
עפֿענען דאָס מויל,
און ווי אַ לייב,
אָנגעטאָן אין פֿײַערדיקן צונטער,
אײַנשלינגען דעם לשון וואָס גייט־אונטער.
אײַנשלינגען און אַלע דורות וועקן מיט מײַן ברומען!

1948

Yiddish

Shall I start from the beginning?
Shall I, a brother,
Like Abraham
Smash all the idols?
Shall I let myself be translated alive?
Shall I plant my tongue
And wait
Till it transforms
Into our forefathers'
Raisins and almonds?
What kind of joke
Preaches
My poetry brother with whiskers,
That soon, my mother tongue will set forever?
A hundred years from now, we still may sit here
On the Jordan, and carry on this argument.
For a question
Gnaws and paws at me:
If he knows exactly in what regions
Levi Yitzhok's prayer,
Yehoash's poem,
Kulbak's song,
Are straying
To their sunset—
Could he please show me
Where the language will go down?
May be at the Wailing Wall?
If so, I shall come there, come,
Open my mouth,
And like a lion
Garbed in fiery scarlet,
I shall swallow the language as it sets.
And wake all the generations with my roar!
(1948; English translation: Benjamin and Barbara Harshav)[12]

As should be evident even in a superficial reading, this is a poem full of questions written in a tense dialogue with an addressee, a Hebrew-speaking

Israeli, perhaps even an established Hebrew poet who has posed to a Yiddish poet, newly arrived in the country, the question of why: Why write in Yiddish? Why in Israel? Is there any future for Yiddish in Israel? When the speaker-poet gives an answer, in typical Jewish mode of answering with a question, he begins with Genesis. This is hardly surprising because Sutzkever often employed a network of images derived from the Bible—as well as from the landscape of Israel and Jewish mythology—to deal with his major themes: issues of traumatic memory, how to come to terms with the Holocaust, how to achieve continuity and renewal.[13]

But we should be attuned to the subtle ways in which Sutzkever invokes Genesis. He insists on using the Yiddish word *onheyb* and not *bereshis*, the Hebrew word (or the alternative Yiddish word *onhoyb*). *Onheyb* was widely used in the early twentieth century as a title for Yiddish modernist journals, books and publishing houses: In August 1928, a group of writers published *Onheyb*, the first Palestinian collection of Yiddish literature, and the poet and translator Yehoash (Solomon Bloomgarden) used the same spelling (*Onheyb*) to begin his Yiddish translation of the Bible from the same time. The word and its spelling connect the Land of Israel and the Bible with Yiddish itself. The word *Onheyb* also indicates the existence of a significant body of Palestinian literature in Yiddish before 1948, explored in details by Yael Chaver and Aryeh Pilowsky.[14] In this context, it is important to note that 1948 might be the starting point for the State of Israel, but from the point of view of Sutzkever and of Yiddish in Palestine/Israel, 1948 is a moment of continuity as much as rupture.

In light of the questions about beginnings and the difficulty in locating a point of origin in the poem, it is not surprising that the next line moves not to the biblical Adam, the first human being, but to Abraham, the father of the nation (as well as the poet's first name). When God commands Abraham: "Get thee out of thy country" (Genesis 12:1) he is asked to make a clear break with the past, and a fresh start in the new land. According to the Midrash, to which the poem alludes, Abraham not only crosses the Jordan and leaves his father's house behind him, but also smashes the idols; not merely departing but destroying his father's past. Thus, I understand the lines: "Shall I, Like Abraham/out of brotherhood smash all the idols"? as referring to the Israeli ideology of *Shlilat-hagalut*, the "negation of exile," or cutting off the relations with the Jewish diaspora, and ostensibly with Yiddish, the Ashkenazi diasporic language. So, the speaker asks, is Yiddish considered "an idol" that one needs to smash in order to become an Israeli? This rhetorical question shows Sutzkever's defiance of monolingualism as a prerogative of Israeli cultural identity.

The tone of questioning and defiance of cultural norms continues in the following line: *Zol ikh zikh a lebedikn lozn?* ("Shall I let myself be translated alive"?). This question seems quite surprising at first, because of the implied equation of translation with death. But why? What is wrong with being translated? After all, most writers and poets are delighted to be translated due to the opportunity to reach new audiences in new languages. But here the tension between Hebrew and Yiddish, and the place of Yiddish in the new State of Israel, makes translation a thorny issue. For Sutzkever in 1948—as for other Yiddish writers —the danger of "being alive" only through translation is all too real, as is evident from responses to attempts (by Sutzkever and others) to publish new works and new forums of Yiddish literature in the young State of Israel. For example, the Hebrew writer and critic Sh. Y. Pnueli wrote that he didn't understand the need for a Yiddish journal in Israel. "Yiddish," he wrote, "is one language of one Jewish diaspora, not the golden chain of our culture." "The poems of H. Leyvik and Leyeles," he exclaimed, "belong in New York . . . and if they should be published in Israel at all, it should be done in Hebrew translation for the Hebrew, Israeli reader."[15] In light of such responses, it is clear that the anxiety about translation and about the relevance of Yiddish in a monolingual Israeli culture hostile to diasporic languages was justified. This anxiety, and the refusal to exist only in translation are linked to the question of Yiddish as a viable language of communication and culture and to the danger that after the deaths of so many Yiddish speakers in the Holocaust, Yiddish will become a kind of hallowed monument to the past.

Thus, when the poet-speaker asks: "Shall I plant my tongue/and wait till it transforms into our forefathers' Raisins and almonds?/What kind of joke/ Preaches my poetry brother with whiskers,/That soon, my mother tongue will set forever?" he struggles again with the place of Yiddish in Israel, and with how his own poetic tongue could be preserved and understood in this environment. Is it a *mame-loshn*, a "mother tongue," that is about to disappear? Is it going to turn into the "forefathers' Raisins and almonds?" Sutzkever illustrates various perceptions of Yiddish in Israel: either as the *mame-loshn*, with its gender assumptions of Yiddish as a "maternal language," that must be suppressed and forgotten, as a language suited only for nostalgic songs like *Rozhinkes mit mandlen*, or as a humorous language that is being used for jokes, a comic relief, like "whiskers" added to a portrait.[16] For the poet-speaker, Yiddish is neither funny nor nostalgic. It is also not going to disappear so fast, despite the murder of its native speakers in Europe and its suppression in Israel. He predicts that even "a hundred years from now" Yiddish will not die. Instead "we" (the Jewish collective) will continue to sit on the Jordan, the liminal site of the river that separates the Land of Israel and the Diaspora and carry on the discussions and heated debates about Jewish (national) languages.

What is most significant for the speaker as a Yiddish poet in this discussion is not whether Yiddish would enjoy a national status in the state. Rather, the issue is a literary lineage and its continuation. This is a lineage of "poetic fathers," which links the Hassidic rabbi Levy Itzkhok of Berdichev to Yehoash, the Yiddish American master of impressionist poetry, whose translation of the Bible gave it a new lease on life among modern Yiddish readers. From here, he moves to Moyshe Kulbak, the modernist Yiddish poet, novelist, and dramatist, who was born in Smorgon, the same town near Vilna where Sutzkever himself was born, and who was an inspiration to the "Yung Vilna" group, in which the young Sutzkever began his literary career.[17] Where, the speaker-poet asks, will this tradition of modern Yiddish literature go when the Yiddish language itself is in danger of decline? "Maybe to the Wailing Wall"? כותל מערבי the site most associated with traditional Jewish memory, but one that became part of Jordanian Jerusalem after the 1948 war? If this is where Yiddish will go, then: "I shall come there, come,/Open my mouth,/And like a lion/ Garbed in fiery scarlet,/I shall swallow the language as it sets./And wake all the generations with my roar!"

At the end of this powerful poem, the speaker-poet hijacks many devices of the prophetic mode, associated with the Hebrew/national poetry of Hayim Nahman Bialik and Uri Zvi Greenberg: the roaring lion, the fiery scarlet garment, and the language itself, which he devours and swallows like Jeremiah the prophet.[18] Unlike the prophet, however, the speaker-poet does not seek fire to devour the people, but rather he himself seeks to devour the Yiddish word. The meaning of this is a symbiosis between the speaker-poet and the language, *his* language and the language of his people.

It became a commonplace to refer to Sutzkever as (in the words of Ruth Wisse, the eminent scholar of Yiddish literature) "the last great Yiddish poet."[19] However, we should think of Sutzkever not as the last, but also as the first great Israeli Yiddish poet. As he declared so powerfully in the poem, Sutzkever became an embodiment of Yiddish, its literature and culture in Israel. He did so by writing and publishing Yiddish poetry, and by establishing and editing, in 1949, the journal *Di goldene keyt* ("The Golden Chain"), which became the most important post-Holocaust literary and culture forum in the world. Against all odds, *Di goldene keyt* was published not in New York, Montreal, or Buenos Aires (the centers of Yiddish culture after 1945), but in Tel Aviv. Sutzkever even managed to get the support of the *Histadrut* ("General Organization of Workers in the Land of Israel").[20]

No less important, Sutzkever embodied Yiddish literature and culture by being a father figure to a new generation of Yiddish Israeli writers, which came to life in the literary group Yung Yisroel. Yung Yisroel was established in 1951 in Kibbutz Yagur, by young Yiddish writers, mostly refugees and Holocaust survivors, who arrived in Israel after 1948, and by and large began their Yiddish literary activities in the country. Among them were Yossl Birshteyn, Tzvi Eisenman, Mendel Mann, Rivka Basman, Avrom Rintsler, H. Binyomin (Binyamin Hrushovski-Harshav), Rukhl Fishman, Avrom Karpinowitz, and Moshe Yungman.

The writers Leib Rochman, Yankev Friedman, Yishayahu Shpigel, Malasha Mali, and the artist Yosl Bergner did not belong to the group, but participated in their activities and published works with them. At first, members of the group published their work in *Di goldene keyt*, under a special rubric of "young Yiddish literature in Israel," and later in their own journal and book series. The group existed, in one way or another, until the mid-1960s.

Group members, and people associated with the group and its publications, produced what I consider the most interesting Yiddish literary texts written in and about Israel. In their meetings, and on the pages of journals and newspapers, they debated vigorously the reasons to write (or continue to write) in Yiddish in Israel, and the directions which Israeli Yiddish writing should take. Thus, the examination of *Yung Yisroel*—the journal and the book series they published, the literary texts

Figure 4.1. Photograph of Yung Yisroel Members (courtesy of Tzvi Eisenman).

Figure 4.2. Cover of the journal *Yung Yisroel*, December 1954.

they produced, the ways in which they understood their project, and how they were received, as well as its impact—touches on the primary issues surrounding Yiddish literature in Israel.[21]

The story of Yung Yisroel, a highly dynamic group that was very active, and produced original Israeli Yiddish literature in the 1950s and 1960, illustrates well the fact that Yiddish literature has effectively been silenced from the historiography of Israeli literature. The necessary task of bringing these voices back to the consciousness of readers begs the question: How do we read the Israeli literature in a different way when we take into account what was written in Yiddish by members of Yung Yisroel and other writers who were active in Israel and wrote about Israel? I would like to offer two short examples of prevalent concerns, themes, and styles in Yiddish Israeli literature of the 1950s and 1960 toward answering this question.

One is the trope of "Israeli snow," common in a number of Yiddish poems and stories written the early years of the state by Avrom Sutzkever, Avrom Rintsler, Rivka Basman, H. Binyomin, Rukhl Fishman, Yankev Friedman, Tzvi Eisenman, and Yossl Birshteyn.[22] Writing about snow is just one example of how Israeli Yiddish writers portrayed the Israeli landscape in a way that represented their unique encounter. This encounter was informed by the landscape of Europe before and during World War II, as well as by the Yiddish literary vocabulary and motifs that were rooted in the East European shtetl, and the European and American metropolises (New York, Warsaw) and cities. Of course, snow—a common phenomenon and familiar part of East European life— is a rare occurrence in Israel, limited to a small area of the country (Mt. Hermon), or to unusual winter storms, like the one that took place in the winter of 1950.[23] It is hardly surprising that snow was employed as a trope by European and American immigrant Hebrew writers from Leah Goldberg to T. Carmi.

In the hands of Yiddish writers, "Israeli snow" emerges as a productive, albeit paradoxical, discordant trope for Israeli Yiddish literature. It shows the continuities and ruptures between past and present, between the Middle East and Europe, between the Jewish diaspora and a new Israeli society in the making, as well as the various textual traditions that mostly clash with each other, and occasionally enable writers to find moments of commonality.

This can be seen, for example, in H. Binyomin's poem *Shney in Yerusholoayim* ("Snow in Jerusalem") from 1950.[24]

שניי אין ירושלים
ווייסט, שניי, גוט וואָס ביסט געקומען !
כ'וואָלט דאָך אויסגעגאַנגען פאַר אומעט
נאָך דײַן זאַפטיקן ייִדישן לשון.
מײַנע שכנים, די נאָדלדיקע ברושן,
האָבן שוין לאַנג צום הימל געשפיצט מיט דער טענה :
די שנייען, די פוכיקע שנייען ווו זײַנען ?

— און אָט ביסטו אונדזערער ווידער.

You know snow, it's good that you've come
I'd melted from longing
for your succulent Yiddish language.
My neighbors, the pointy cypresses
have long been pleading with the sky:
The shows, the downy snows, where are they?
—And here you're ours again.

The longed-for snow is equated here with "the succulent Yiddish language" and then rhymed with the Israeli Hebrew trees, but in their Yiddish plural suffix "*broshn.*" The famously sharp Mediterranean Cyprus trees are waiting, like the speaker, for the soft, down-like snow. The three-way analogy the poem makes between the speaker, the snow, and Yiddish becomes by the end of the poem an intimate encounter between them.²⁵

(– ווייסט, שניי, – מיר זײַנען דאָך ביידע אויף דו,
אַז ס'וועט די היץ דיר ניט לאָזן צו רו
אין דער הייליקער שטאָט –
איז איידער מיר צעגייען ווידער,
לאָמיר זיך פֿאַרקלײַבן זאַלבעצווייט אין אַ סוד,
וווּ קיינער זעט אונדז ניט, –
און כ'וועל דיר לייענען מײַנע לידער...)
ווינטער תש״י

(You can tell, snow—yes, the two of us are already on familiar
 terms—
that the heat won't let you rest
in the holy city—
so before we melt away,
let's escape together to some secret corner,
where no one will see us,
where no one will follow us—
and I will read to you my poems . . .)²⁶
Winter, 1950

The speaker chooses the intimate language of Yiddish since the snow is so reminiscent of other, older places in the speaker's childhood. He speaks with the snow in a familiar grammatical form as if they were close relatives or friends, rather than mere acquaintances and reads to him from the Yiddish poems that he wrote. But this reading can only take place in "hiding," in a place that no one would discover and ruin by ridicule. Mockery and derision of Yiddish, together with the fear of its widespread influence, was the common attitude toward the "language that must be forgotten," to use Yael Chaver's apt term. And yet, H. Binyomin and his fellow writers of Yung-Yisroel not only wrote Israeli poetry in Yiddish, but also used Yiddish in order to renew Israeli literature in

Hebrew, for example in the group *Likrat* that created what is known as the Statehood Generation of Israeli poetry. The hidden, submerged links between Yiddish poetry in America and Europe and Israeli poetry of the 1950s were bridged and moderated by the explorations of young Yiddish writers in Israel, H. Binyomin among them.[27]

The second example I would like to touch on is a significant, but largely unexplored corpus of stories, poems, and novels written by members of *Yung Yisroel* that depict, and wrestle with difficult, sometimes traumatic events that took place in Israel during the tumultuous period of its establishment, the 1948 War, and the mass migration of the 1950s. A number of texts focus on the uprooting of local Palestinian Arabs from their villages and neighborhoods, and the repopulation of these "abandoned" spaces with Jewish refugees following 1948. We can think in this context of Mendel Mann's novel *In a farvorloztn dorf* ("In a Deserted Village," 1954).[28] The novel tells the story of newly arrived Jewish immigrants who were put in the transit camp Azur, built hastily on top of the Palestinian town of Yazur, southeast of Jaffa.[29]

The plot of Mann's novel goes back and forth between the present (1949–50) and the period before World War II and the 1948 War. It does it by focusing on the character Monye—a refugee who was forced to flee his Polish small town at the time of the Nazi occupation of Poland—and his attempt to find a new place in the village and in Israel. What is unique about Mann's Yiddish novel is the extent to which the encounter with the deserted village and with the former inhabitants is built on an analogy with the trauma of the Holocaust and the Palestinian Nakba. The daily life of Monye and the other refugees is being interrupted when they meet a Palestinian man who returns to the village one day. The reaction of the Yiddish-speaking Jewish refugees to his appearance ranges between confusion, suspicion, and the clear understanding that they might be living in a house that belonged to the Palestinian not long ago. The narrator also employs the character of a "yellow dog" who goes back and forth into the village. Through the dog's eyes, readers can follow the life of the Palestinian inhabitants before and after the traumatic moment of the occupation of their village, in which they lost their home. This is parallel to Monye's memory of his Polish life before the war, and his attempts to imagine what life in Poland could be after the Holocaust.

The story *Tsvishn ailbertn* ("Between the Olive Trees," 1954) by Yossl Birshteyn is closely related, as Adi Mahalel has shown, to the events of the 1953 Qibya massacre ("Operation Shoshana"), in which at least sixty-nine

Figure 4.3. Cover of Mendel Mann, *In a farvorloztn dorf.*

Palestinian villagers were killed by the Israeli army.[30] The story relates the appearance of an old Palestinian farmer, Hassan Abu-Thnoa, and his unexpected interaction with the Israeli Army. It is told largely from the point of view of Hassan, who walks out with his donkey one early morning and meets an Israeli soldier, who "stood . . . there, where there were no trees, only the bright light from the sky" (74–75). The soldier stops Hassan and asserts his authority as part of the armed forces. While Hassan collects the oranges that fell from the donkey "on all four," the Israeli soldier is high above him and their glances meet for a few seconds. In this brief meeting, the Jewish soldier hears the long shriek by the submissive Arab and is "bewildered" by it. The bewilderment is due to his waking consciousness and his memory of his own very recent experience of Jewish persecution and destruction in World War II. Thus, the story presents both characters, the Palestinian Arab and the Israeli Jew, as figures who repress their recent painful, traumatic pasts and can have only fleeting moment of mutual understanding. It depicts a new kind of armed Jew as someone who must deny his connection to the recent past, although his trauma persists on a deeper level.

Another good example of the ways in which Yiddish writers depicted the shock of migration, life as refugees, and encounters with Palestinian Arabs and their experience of 1948 War, is Tzvi Eisenman's short story *Vu der himel mitl yam* ("Where the Sky and the Sea Meet," 1966).[31]

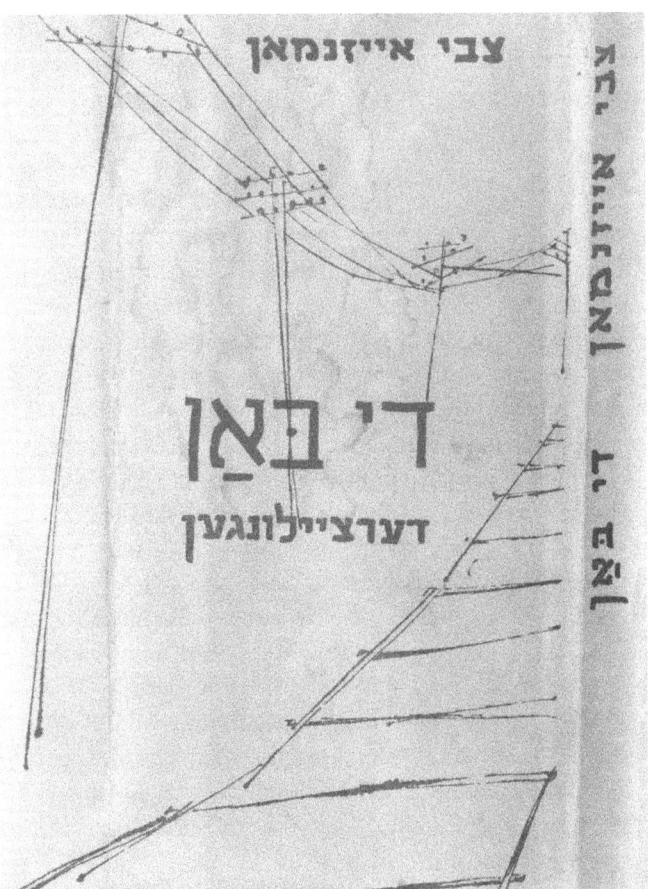

Figure 4.4. Cover of Tzvi Eisenman, *Di ban: dertseylungen.*

The story does not provide a specific location, but depicts a family of Jewish refugees south of Jaffa, most likely in Jabaliya, the location of a number of Yiddish stories and novels.[32] Jabaliya was captured by the Etzel militia in 1948, and was quickly renamed *Givat Aliya*.[33] In this neighborhood, many Holocaust survivors who came to Israel from DP camps lived side by side with the few Arab families that remained there and with Jewish families who had just arrived from North Africa in houses that clearly still carried the traces of their former Arab inhabitants.[34]

In Eisenman's short story, while the father of the family joins his fellow Jews and Arabs to play cards and backgammon in a shack that received the highly ironic name "Café Moledet" [Homeland Café] the child, Mendel, imagines the house being carried by the waves of the Mediterranean to the horizon, the "place where the sky and sea meet." The story beautifully captures the precarious existence of Yiddish-speaking Holocaust survivors in the new environment that was supposed to be a new "homeland," but is haunted by the violence and experience of uprooting of both World War II and the 1948 War.

While this article only touches on a few examples of Yiddish literature written in the 1950s and 1960s, it is quite clear that it must be taken into account to understand the Israeli literature taking shape, with the prose fiction of S. Yizhar and Moshe Shamir, the poetry of Nathan Zach and Yehuda Amichai. Studying them and comparing them to what was written in Hebrew, Arabic, and other languages will supply us with a better and fuller understanding of a multilingual literature that was developed in Israel at the same time. We also must remember that Israeli Yiddish literature was transnational by definition: Yiddish journals and books produced in Israel were read not just by Israelis, but by Jews all over the world. We could learn much from comparing post-Holocaust Yiddish in Israel to America, Europe, and Australia.[35] Yiddish writers in Israel fused Israeli landscape and characters with those of other places and times. When Israeli Hebrew writers invoked Yiddish, they were also summoning the Jewish (and non-Jewish) world outside Israel, as well as the past. Finally, Yiddish was crucial to all attempts to deal with the memory of the Holocaust, and especially of the survivors, in Israeli literature.

Rethinking Israeli literature in these terms might be something that we can only grasp now, seventy years after the establishment of the state. This is evident, perhaps, in a recent documentary film about Sutzkever, produced as part of the prestigious "Ha'ivrim" series, as well as by recent publications such as a bilingual volume of Binyamin Harshav/H. Binyomin's

Yiddish-Hebrew poetry, new anthologies of Yiddish Israeli stories and poetry, and a volume of the journal *Ho!*, which is dedicated to "Arabic and Yiddish, the two sisters of modern Hebrew culture."[36]

Notes

1. Yossl Birshteyn, *Ketem shel sheket* (Tel Aviv: Hakibbutz Hameuchad, 1986), 173. In Yiddish, the short story was published under the title *Altmodish* ("Old Fashion") in *Dayne geslakh—Yerushalayim* (Tel Aviv, Sifrey Siman Kria, 1989).

2. Anita Norich, "Yiddish Literary Studies: The Future of the Past," *Modern Judaism* 10, no. 3 (1990): 297–309.

3. For a discussion of and information about multilingualism in Israel, see Bernard Spolsky and Elana Goldberg Shohamy, *The Languages of Israel: Policy, Ideology, and Practice* (Clevedon, UK: Multilingual Matters, 1999).

4. See Avraham Novershtern, "The Multicolored Patchwork on the Coat of a Prince: On Yossl Birstein's Work," *Modern Hebrew Literature* 8–9 (1992): 56–59; David Roskies, *A Bridge of Longing: The Lost Art of Yiddish Storytelling* (Cambridge: Harvard University Press, 1995), 329–39.

5. Shai Ginsburg, "Israeli Literature," in *Oxford Bibliographies in Jewish Studies*, 2016, DOI: 10.1093/OBO/9780199840731-0130. See also Adia Mendelson-Maoz, *Multiculturalism in Israel: Literary Perspectives* (West Lafayette, IN: Purdue University Press, 2014); Liora Halperin, *Babel in Zion: Jews, Nationalism, and Language Diversity in Palestine 1920–1948* (New Haven: Yale University Press, 2015).

6. Lital Levy, *Poetic Trespass: Writing between Hebrew and Arabic in Israel/Palestine* (Princeton: Princeton University Press, 2014); Na'ama Rokem, "German-Hebrew Encounters in the Poetry and Correspondence of Yehuda Amichai and Paul Celan," *Prooftexts* 30, no. 1 (2010): 97–127; Rachel Seelig, "The Middleman: Ludwig Strauss's German-Hebrew Bilingualism," *Prooftexts* 33, no. 1 (Winter 2013); Maya Barzilai, "S. Y. Agnon's German Consecration and the 'Miracle' of Hebrew Letters," *Prooftexts* 33, no. 1 (2013): 48–75; Melissa Weininger, "Hebrew in English: The New Transnational Hebrew Literature," *Shofar* 33, no. 4 (2015): 15–35; Anna Ronell, "Russian Israeli Literature through the Lens of Immigrant Humor," *Journal of Jewish Identities* 4, no. 1 (2011): 147–69; Alex Moshkin, "The Fourth Wave: Israeli-Russian Literature and Film 1989–2016," PhD Dissertation, University of Pennsylvania.

7. Rachel Rojanski, "The Status of Yiddish in Israel, 1948–1951: An Overview," in *Yiddish after the Holocaust*, ed. Joseph Sherman (Oxford: Boulevard Press, 2004), 46–59; Gali Drucker Bar-Am, "Bekolam uvisfatam: Yisra'el bir'i siporet yidish shenikhteva bimedinat Yisra'el biyedey 'olei she'erit hapleta," in *Yisra'el be'eynei sordei hasho'ah venitsoleha*, ed. Dalia Ofer (Jerusalem: Yad Vashem, 2014), 353–82.

8. See Shachar Pinsker, "That Yiddish Has Spoken to Me: Yiddish in Early Israeli Literature," *Poetics Today* 35, no. 1 (2014): 325–56.

9. Jeffery Shandler, *Adventures in Yiddishland: Postvernacular Language and Culture* (Berkeley: University of California Press, 2006).

10. Yasemin Yildiz, *Beyond the Mother Tongue: The Postmonolingual Condition* (New York: Fordham University Press, 2011).

11. Avrom Sutzkever, *In Fayer-vogn* (Tel Aviv: Goldene Kayt, 1952), 34.

12. A. *Sutzkever: Selected Poetry and Prose* (Berkeley: University of California Press, 1991), 214.

13. On Sutzkever's poems of this period, see Dan Miron, *Sheleg 'al knaf hayonah: pegishot 'im shirato shel Avraham Sutskever* (Tel Aviv: Kehshev, 1999); Justin Cammy, "Vision and Redemption: Abraham Sutzkever's Poems of Zion(ism)," in *Yiddish after the Holocaust*, 240–65; Hannah Pollin-Galay, "The Epic Demands of Postwar Yiddish: Avrom Sutzkever's Geheymshtot (1948)," *East European Jewish Affairs* 48, no. 3 (2018): 331–53.

14. Aryeh L. Pilowsky, *Tsvishn yo un neyn: Yidish un yidish-literatur in Erets-Yisroel, 1907–1948* (Tel Aviv: Veltrat far yidish un yidisher kultur, 1986); Yael Chaver, *What Must Be Forgotten: The Survival of Yiddish in Zionist Palestine* (Syracuse: Syracuse University Press, 2004).

15. Sh. Y. Pnueli, "Shalshelet Hazahav," *Gilyonot* 22, no. 12–13 (1948): 179–84.

16. As Dan Miron has observed: "One of the *implicit* assumptions of the young Israeli culture was that that the Yiddish that the East European immigrants brought with them is a comic 'funny" language. Saying something in Yiddish in the right circumstances—always in public—would be funny almost independently of its content. . . . This very 'fact' was exploited by many actors, comedians and other people who needed a kind of 'comic relief.'" Dan Miron, "Hem tsochakim, ani bokheh," *Haaretz Literary Supplement*, July 16, 2004. Reprinted in *Hatsad ha'afel bitzhoko shel Shalom Aleichem* (Tel Aviv: Am Oved, 2004), 9.

17. Justin Cammy, "Tsevorfene bleter: The Emergence of Yung-Vilne," *Polin* 14 (2001): 170–91.

18. Dan Miron, *The Prophetic Mode in Modern Hebrew Poetry* (New Milford, CT: Toby Press, 2010).

19. Ruth Wisse, "The Last Great Yiddish Poet?" *Commentary* 76, no. 5 (1983): 41–48.

20. Rachel Rojanski, "The Final Chapter in the Struggle for Cultural Autonomy: Palestine, Israel, and Yiddish Writers in the Diaspora, 1946–1951," *Journal of Modern Jewish Studies* 6, no. 2 (2007): 185–204.

21. For studies of the group see, David Roskies, "Di shrayber-grupe Yung Yisroel," *Yugntruf* 28–29 (Sept. 1973): 7–12, 33; *Yugntruf* 33 (July 1975): 7–8, 24; *Yugntruf* 34 (Feb. 1976): 4–7, 12. Shachar Pinsker, "Choosing Yiddish in Israel: Yung Yisroel between Home and Exile, the Margin and the Center," in *Choosing*

Yiddish: Studies on Yiddish Literature, Culture, and History, ed. Shiri Goren, Hannah Pressman, and Lara Rabinovitch (Detroit: Wayne State University Press, 2012).

22. See Shachar Pinsker, *Sheleg yisra'eli, Haaretz tarbut vesifrut*, October 19, 2011.

23. For an analysis of this snowstorm and how different elements in Israeli society responded to it, see Anat Helman, *Becoming Israeli: National Ideals and Everyday Life in the 1950s* (Waltham: Brandeis University Press, 2014), 1–19.

24. The poem was published in *Di goldene keyt* 7 (1951): 152.

25. For an extensive reading of the poem in the context of H. Binyomin's Yiddish and Hebrew poetry see Chana Kronfeld, "Hakdamah," in Binyamin Harshav, *Kol hashirim* (Jerusalem: Carmel, 2017), 49–52. See also Shachar Pinsker, "How to Build Bridges to People? Benjamin Harshav and Yiddish," *In geveb* (Aug. 2015).

26. English translation by Saul Noam Zarrit and Shachar Pinsker.

27. Kronfeld, "Hakdamah"; Pinsker, *That Yiddish Has Spoken to Me.*

28. Mendel Mann, *In a farvorloztn dorf: roman* (Buenos Aires: Ḳiyem, 1954).

29. Arnon Golan, "Redistribution and Resistance: Urban Conflicts During and Following the 1948 War," *Journal of Modern Jewish Studies* 1, no. 2 (2002): 117–30. See also, Zochrot's page on Yazur: https://zochrot.org/en/village/49209.

30. Yossl Birshteyn, *Tsvishn Aylberten*, *Yung Yisroel* 1 (1954), 6–10. See Adi Mahalel, "Yiddish, Israel, and the Palestinians: Yosl Birshteyn's 'Between the Olive Trees,'" *Israel Studies Review* 30, no. 2 (Winter 2015): 71–91.

31. Tzvi Eisenman, *Mazoles* (Tel Aviv: Farlag Y. L. Peretz, 1965), 20–32.

32. See Rachel Rojanski, "A Yiddish Shtetl near Tel Aviv," in *Yiddish Cities: Montreal, Melbourne, Tel Aviv*, ed. Shlomo Berger (Amsterdam: Menasseh ben Israel Institute, 2013).

33. See Haim Bereshit, Givat Aliya Kemashsal, *Teoria uvikoret* 16 (2000): 233–38; Arnon Golan, "The Battle for Jaffa, 1948," *Middle Eastern Studies* 48, no. 6 (2012): 997–1011.

34. On Holocaust survivors in the early years of the state in transit camps and "abandoned" houses, see Hanna Yablonka, *Survivors of the Holocaust: Israel after the War* (New York: New York University Press, 1999); Gali Druker Bar-Am, "May the Makom Comfort You."

35. Indeed, most Yiddish writers in Israel were Holocaust survivors (or lost their families in the Holocaust). At the same time, I am trying to get away from the notion that Yiddish literature in Israel can only be read (or is only worth reading) as "Holocaust Literature," in the way this term is understood in the Israeli context.

36. Uri Barabash et al., *Dvash shachor: shirat chayav shel Avraham Sutskever* (Israel: Ya'ir Ḳedar yerashut hashidur, 2018); Harshav, *Kol hashirim*; Shachar Pinsker, ed., *Bamakom bo shamayim noshkim layam: sipurei Yiddish beYisra'el* (Jerusalem: Magnes, forthcoming); *Ho!: ketav 'et lesifrut* 17 (2018).

A Canaanite Story

Language, National Identity, and the 1948 War

YAEL DEKEL

Hebrew literature consists of texts written in the Hebrew language. Israeli literature has commonly been defined by geography and citizenship: as literature written in the State of Israel. Jewish literature, though hard to define, has often been considered as literature written by Jews, as literature written in a Jewish language, and/or as literature pertaining to topics that concern Judaism. However, these terms often overlap. They get defined and redefined; they effect and get effected by ideology, nationalism, and by political discourse and its vicissitudes.

In this essay I address these topics by focusing on a literary product of a marginal political-artistic group: the story "Hashevach le'elohim" ("Praise be to God," 1950), written by Eitan Notev (pseudonym of Shraga Gafni). At the time the story appeared, he was a member of the Young Hebrews (known as the Canaanite group). As I explain, the story published in the group's magazine, *Alef*, calls into question the then widely accepted equation of Hebrew literature with Jewish literature, as well as the equation of the Hebrew language with Jewish Israeli identity.

Critical of the mainstream narrative of Zionism and dissociating itself in various ways from Zionist fiction, Canaanite fiction has remained on the margins of the canon of Israeli literature.[1] Despite its marginal position, and because of it, the fiction published in *Alef* raises important questions from which we stand to gain new insights about hegemony and its margins alike. Following Deleuze and Guattari's notion of a "minor literature" and of its subversive powers, I suggest that Notev's story contests the affinity between language and national identity, is highly political, and ultimately reterritorializes language.

Canaanite Ideology, Canaanite Fiction

The Canaanite movement was an Israelite non-Zionist movement that emerged in Palestine in the late 1930s made up largely of young men, artists, authors, and thinkers who identified with its ideological/cultural values. The movement was active originally under the name "The Council for the Coalition of Hebrew Youth" (or more concisely, "The Young Hebrews").[2] The movement was launched with the work of two Revisionist Zionists: the poet and activist Uriel Shelach (born Uriel Halperin and better known as Yonatan Ratosh), and the historian and philologist Adia Gur Horon (born Adolphe Gourevitch). In their writings, they advocated for a nonapologetic, confident Hebrew identity based on ancient Hebrew culture. They found cultural inspiration and mythological sources in newly discovered archeological sites. Dissociated from Zionism as well as from pan-Arabism, they aspired to establish a Hebrew nation in the broad region that was considered to be the ancient land of Canaan. In their writings, the Canaanites insisted on calling it "The Land of the Euphrates," stressing what they perceived as the specifically Hebrew nature of the region.[3]

Canaanite ideology is based on an idea connecting geography and culture, an "environmental determinism." Thus, according to their ideology, human identity is seen as shaped by the physical factors of its environment. In contrast to the Zionist understanding of Jewishness, the Canaanites maintained that national identity is not determined by biology, race, and genealogical descent. Rather, nativism, manifested in one's connection to the land, is the crucial factor in determining national affiliation and identity. The Canaanites believed that this identity is fostered by language and literature; thus, they insisted on using exclusively the Hebrew language—especially biblical Hebrew—in their poetry and prose.[4]

In the movement's 1944 ideological manifesto *Masah hapetichah* ("The opening speech"), Ratosh offered, among other axiomatic ideas, the following message regarding the need to embrace Hebraism and abandon Judaism:

> As long as the land of the Hebrews is not cleansed of Zionism and the hearts of the Hebrews made pure of Judaism, all efforts will be in vain and every sacrifice a wasted one . . . ; as long as the Hebrews will not fully recognize that they are the direct descendants of their forefathers in the Golden Age of the Hebrew splendour, from the days of the Judges and the Kings . . . ; as long as the Hebrews will not fully recognize that Jewish history is a foreign history for us . . . ; as long as they are not able to draw necessary conclusions concerning Judaism through the ages and Zionism with all its trends and all of its personages . . . then the Hebrew splendour will remain locked away, and the road to the Hebrew future will remain a desolate one.[5]

Here, as in others of his Canaanite political writings, Ratosh uses anti-Semitic rhetoric to fashion the myth of the native Hebrew. The text expresses its author's revulsion against anything "Jewish" and "Zionist" while advocating the new "Hebrew" identity. Canaanite ideology was widely criticized in the main newspapers of the time, and although it directly influenced only the small circle that surrounded Ratosh, it raised deep concerns over the younger generation's anti-Jewish tendencies.[6]

Canaanite ideology was essentially paradoxical: it was belligerent, anti-Zionist, and anti-Jewish; yet it wanted to embrace all of the land's native residents and to form a secular nation. This new and progressive nation was inspired by ancient Hebrew heritage, and was designed to be a Hebrew—neither Jewish nor Arab—nation. Together with their national vision, the Canaanites had territorial aspirations. Concomitantly, they longed for a magnificent Hebraic past, manifested especially in the biblical times of the kings and the judges. They exalted war and rejected weakness. In addition, the members in the movement were skillful authors and gifted artists who, although developing their talents individually, nevertheless made detailed and specific demands on literature and art.

Their political marginality and ideological inconsistencies notwithstanding, the Canaanites have had an effect on the course of Israeli literature and art since their heyday in the 1940s. When expressed in their art, Canaanite ideology focused mainly on notions of nativism in various ways. Because of Zionism's embrace of nativism, Canaanite art became accepted into mainstream Israeli culture and had an impact well beyond extremist circles. By and by, Canaanite art—notably the works of the sculptor Yitzhak Danziger, who holds a major place in the canon of Israeli art—has received substantial scholarly attention. Danziger's famous sculpture "Nimrod," portraying the biblical leader and mighty hunter featured in Genesis 10, has become both a Canaanite symbol of nativism and power and one of the most acclaimed pieces of Israeli art.[7] Likewise, Ratosh's poetry, with its lexical as well as rhythmical innovations, influenced the course of Israeli poetry, and it has also been the subject of numerous studies in different disciplines, including linguistics, poetry, and history.[8]

In addition to its extensive cultural influence, Canaanism as an ideological and political movement has been broadly studied in terms of its critique of the State of Israel, its position toward Judaism, and its dismissive attitude toward the diaspora and the Holocaust.[9] Indeed, Liat Steir-Livny and Yaacov Shavit have argued that the Canaanites' harsh rejection of diasporic Jews and their demonizing attitude toward Holocaust survivors contributed to the marginalization of the group's ideology.[10] More recently, the Canaanite stance toward the Palestinians has also received scholarly attention.[11] As presented by Roman Vater, the Canaanites maintained that Palestinians, like Jews, are but an ethno-religious community, rather than a nation.[12] In their writings, they advanced the idea that both Jews and Palestinians are of ancient Hebrew origin, and therefore both should be incorporated into the large unifying nation—a Hebrew nation.

Even when we take this state of research into account, Canaanite fiction remains a relatively neglected area in literary scholarship. The works themselves were never reprinted, and many of them can be read solely in the issues of the movement's magazine, *Alef*. An essay by Nurit Gertz serves as an introduction to the topic, mapping the fiction of the Canaanites vis-à-vis both Zionist and Canaanite ideology.[13] An essay by Hanan Hever exposes the inconsistencies within the movement's principles, pointing out the contradictory images of the Arabs and of the 1948 war in several Canaanite stories and arguing that the Canaanites were appropriated by Zionism as both "native" and as "Other," thus conveniently replacing the Palestinians.[14] Other than these accounts, there is very little exploration and analysis of the rich material that Canaanite fiction contains. In addition, there is very little research in English written on Canaanite fiction.[15] Thus, the present article is a gateway to Canaanite fiction, available also for English-language readers.

Canaanite fiction was written by authors such as Shraga Gafni (that is, Eitan Notev), Yaakov Ashman, Benjamin Tammuz, Aharon Amir, and

Amos Keinan. These stories address the 1948 war critically, through parody ("Romantika kushit," by Ashman), direct criticism ("Haboker hechadash," by Amir), and the acting out of trauma ("Hamishte," by Keinan). They provide a glimpse into the Canaanite worldview as well as into one of the ways in which the 1948 war was perceived in the Israeli discourse after the war.

The Canaanite response to the 1948 war represents one of the group's deviations from mainstream Zionist ideology. Members of the group opposed the war's conduct and denounced its results, contending that the territory occupied was too narrow and that the people—soldiers who carry within them the tradition of the diaspora—did not believe in what they were fighting for. They protested the fact that the defining policy of the state was of an ethno-religious community—Jewish. Moreover, the 1948 war actually hindered the Canaanites' main national and territorial goal—a large Hebraic state. Many of them expressed their frustration at having fought in a war that they felt had been appropriated by the Zionists.

So, for example, Yoram Nimshi (pseudonym of Yaakov Ashman) lamented the loss of life in the war, caused in his view by the values of Zionism, for which he and his comrades had ostensibly fought in 1948: "The truth should be told: we were alone in our death. We were sent to fight with a strange set of values. Hollow values—like scarecrows we were. . . . As we attacked, none of us shouted 'For Zionism' . . . 'For Defense.'"[16] Nimshi also accused Hebrew wartime literature of concealing the true stories of those who returned from the front, thereby indirectly supporting the Zionist project and, in particular, its silencing of voices that deviated from what was deemed appropriate from the national perspective:

> We appear to have war-fiction. A monthly military novel, bon appetit! A monthly war play, bon appetit! . . . But within all of this, did you ever hear the cry of those who fought? Did you ever hear their piercing questions? Did you ever hear their terrible doubts, the sound the values made as they collapsed?[17]

In their fiction published in *Alef*, members of the Canaanite movement attempted to sound these voices, voices of Jewish fighters as well as those of Palestinians. The latter were regarded by Canaanite ideology as allies, natives of the Fertile Crescent and therefore rightful members of the Hebrew Nation. In his "Opening Discourse," Ratosh addresses this issue when he refers to: "this population, which nobody knows how much Hebrew blood flows through its veins . . . we the Hebrews, released from the barriers of religiousness and communality, will be able to accept anyone among them [the Arabs] who would wish to assimilate . . . and become one of us, with all the duties and the rights."[18] This statement makes clear the wish to change the Arabs and to assimilate them into the Canaanite/Hebrew culture. How did Canaanite authors deal with this paradox of embracing the Palestinians as fellow citizens yet negating their separate nationality? Dissociated as they were from Zionism yet striving for a new and exclusively Hebraic nation, how, in particular, did they depict Palestinian characters? Commenting on a few short stories, Hever suggests that Canaanite fiction contains "contradictory" representations of Palestinians insofar as they mix negative stereotypes with identification and sympathy. Reflecting on similar questions with respect to the story "Hakrav al mivtsar Williams" ("The Battle of Fort Williams," Notev, 1950), Hever argues that the story, which is located mainly in the imagination of the fighters and in their childhood memories, displaces the historical context of the actual Jewish Arab war, distancing it to faraway battles and landscapes. In this way, Hever maintains, the narrative obscures the actual, specific war, reducing it to mere territorial and spatial relations that inevitably repeat over time. In this sense the story unwittingly supports—rather than undermines—Zionism.[19]

Another story published in *Alef*, "Romantika kushit" by Yaakov Ashman ("Black Romance," unknown date of publication), shifts focus inward to Israeli society and is devoted solely to criticism of Zionist culture.[20] The story is a parody of famous 1948 songs, plays, symbols, and Zionist clichés—cultural postulations that within the mainstream of Israeli culture quickly became national myths. Through comic realizations of these symbols, the story is able to void them of their familiar cultural meaning and thereby to deride Zionist culture, standing here also for Zionist ideology. Ashman's story does not include Palestinian characters, and it offers no insights regarding the actual historical context of the war or its aftermath. It undermines Zionism without suggesting an alternative and, indeed, without acknowledging the actual war that the symbols parodied in the story serve to justify.

In view of the above, "Hashevach le'elohim" stands out not only against the backdrop of canonical writings on the 1948 war, but also in comparison to other stories written by members of the Canaanite group. In addition, the biography and political views of Gafni demonstrate the complexity—and also, in a way, the totality—of his connection to Zionist discourse.

"Hashevach le'elohim" is an early work by an author who later on became renowned for his cultural nationalistic efforts in support of Zionism. Gafni, who had joined the Zionist paramilitary group The Stern Gang (Lehi) at the age of fourteen, went on to become a military historian, specializing in the semihistorical documentation of battles. His books were published mainly by the Ministry of Defense press as well as by "Ma'archot," the IDF press. In addition, Gafni was one of the most popular and prolific writers for youth in the first decades of the state. His books for youth—including the iconic *Dani-Din the Invisible Boy*—featured child characters who are patriotic heroes, risking their lives to save the nation; many of Gafni's books and characters went on to become a part of Israeli collective memory.

In 1950, and after the Stern Gang had disassembled, Gafni joined the Canaanite movement. This was not necessarily a digression from his previous, as well as future political views. Rather, it could be understood as an attempt to continue his zealous and active devotion to the land of Israel. Following the Canaanite episode, Gafni joined in—as well as actively created—mainstream Zionist discourse in Israel, and particularly in its militaristic aspects.

"Hashevach le'elohim," though, is not a militaristic account; neither does it suggest its author's extreme devotion to the land. Moreover, it differs from other Canaanite fiction in that it directly engages with descriptions of Palestinians as well as of Jews, of war and death, and it is located in the specific historical context of the Jewish-Arab war of 1948. Throughout my reading of the story, I refer to the categories of language, translation, and territory, and argue that the story contests the national, Zionist appropriation of Hebrew literature.

"Everything as it was a long time ago"— Language and Translation

"Hashevach le'elohim" is one of only two cases—in those years—of a story written in Hebrew that advances a Palestinian perspective by focalizing the entire narrative through a Palestinian character.[21] Through this perspective, the story allows the reader to become part of the characters' reflections from within, thereby changing the entire identification matrix of self and other available to Hebrew readers of the time. The following segment from "Hashevach le'elohim" helps in discerning the main character of the story, as well as its style of narration:

> Every morning, when Dawud took the sheep and goats down the slope and into the valley, to pasture, he would picture the goats as the fleeing *yahud* and himself as the one ruling over them, herding them. His fists gripped the whip vigorously. His black eyes shone in his dark, soft face. But all these things were just a colorful addition to that which was and remained the unchanging essence of their lives. The boys continued to herd the sheep and goats. The women descended into the valleys to harvest with a sickle and at dusk carried home a jug of water on their heads. When the season came, the men hitched camels to the plows, tilling the earth seeded with stones. At night the hyena laughed and the jackals answered with a howl. Everything as it was a long time ago. . . .
>
> But now things have changed. Now the *yahud* were here. The village was filled with them and with their deeds. Their patronizing strolling about in the alleys. They walked into yards and houses, behaving as if they belonged to them. Their cars were parked in the square and the mukhtar's house was their kitchen. From the balcony of the mosque, one of their scouts would keep watch. And at the summit of the sheikh's graveyard, young prisoners of war dug military positions for them. They terrorized man and animal. The enduring things that should never change faded away, to be replaced by the dread of war. It happened overnight.[22]

The story—narrated in the third person by an omniscient narrator—is oriented to the viewpoint of Dawud. The Palestinian perspective is evident in the nostalgic, close description of life in the village prior to the occupation and in the detailed description of the soldiers' behavior following the occupation. In itself, this perspective is worth noting insofar as it can raise questions of authenticity, of the appropriation of voices, and of the power dynamics embedded in any act of narrating a text from the perspective of a character cast as an "Other" relative to the author's group of reference.

Fiction by the acclaimed and canonical Israeli author S. Yizhar was also perceived as a challenge to the Zionist discourse circa 1948, and the similarities between Yizhar's and Notev's stories are noteworthy: most prominently, like Yizhar's "Khirbet Khizeh" (1949), "Hashevach le'elohim" portrays the occupation of a Palestinian village. However, Yizhar's stories, though criticizing the war and the expulsion of the Palestinian people from their land, in effect deal primarily with the moral uncertainties of their Israeli narrators. Unlike "Khirbet Khizeh," Notev's story is told from the point of view of a Palestinian boy who experiences the invasion and occupation of his village. Like the prisoner in Yizhar's "Hashavuy" (1948), Dawud is an innocent Palestinian who, later on in the story, is caught by an Israeli soldier. However, unlike "Hashavuy," which deals primarily with the consciousness of the Jewish soldier, "Hashevach le'elohim" focuses solely on the experience of the Palestinian.

In his discussion of Hebrew literature of the 1960s, Hever defines the literary phenomenon of canonical stories written, like "Hashevach le'elohim," in the language of the majority [Hebrew] from the viewpoint of the national minority [Arab] as a "minority discourse of national majority."[23] Notev's story carries this notion one step farther. Since the story is written in Hebrew but the Palestinian character presumably thinks in Arabic, the text presents itself almost as a translation. This presumption is strengthened by a number of conversations quoted in the story that, as the narrator indicates, take place in Arabic. Yet the story is brought to the reader not in its original language, Arabic, but rather in Hebrew.

This view of "Hashevach le'elohim" as a translation is further supported by the variety of linguistic registers used in the story. The narrative is generally written in literary Hebrew, but includes several other linguistic registers. One of those is a biblical Hebrew used in dialogue. For instance, following the occupation of the village the story records conversations between the Palestinian prisoners and their Jewish captors and also among the prisoners themselves, Palestinians and foreign fighters. These exchanges clearly take place in Arabic—though they are recorded in their Hebrew "translation."

The higher register of Hebrew in which these dialogues are delivered fashions the Arabs—in the eyes of the Hebrew reader—as eloquent interlocutors, contra their common characterization in Hebrew literature of the time. The very inclusion of such dialogues is rare in Hebrew literature, which—both then and for several decades later—hardly ever recorded a Palestinian speaking in full sentences. Thus, Hebrew literature, from Moshe Smilansky's "Hawaja Nazar" (1911) to A. B Yehoshua's "Facing the Forests" (1968), is filled with stammering, dumb, and mute figures of Arabs. Against the backdrop of the Orientalist descriptions of the Arab in Hebrew literature, as well as its many depictions of Arabs as animals, the dialogues in "Hashevach le'elohim" stand out for their portrayal of the Arab characters as complex human beings, partners in a dialogue, and not as enemies who, for the sake of perpetuating war, have to be seen as speechless animals.

Consider the following dialogue between a Jewish guard and a Palestinian prisoner, which features both speaking in a high, archaic register of language, decidedly not the language used in contemporaneous day-to-day communication.

> "You, the elder! Could you count thine years?" the dark skinned one turned to another venerable man. It was Abu-Hasan, a senior wealthy man in his village.
>
> "Should I know, sir? It may be sixty, perhaps ninety, or more than one hundred. Indeed I am very old." . . .
>
> "And are the members of thine family here? Close by you?"
>
> "They are not here, sir. They ran away, but I remained here, as I knew that the *yahud* are good-hearted and merciful. Thou art good people. You will not do any harm. Righteous, noble thou art . . . !"[24]

The formal Hebrew underscores the story's nature as a translation. It is a technique for representing Standard Literary Arabic used in writing and in formal speech. As the standardized version of Arabic, Literary Arabic is also the common language of Arabic speakers from different regions. Thus, the Jewish guard—who knows Arabic and whose own origin is presumably in an Arab country—and the Palestinian prisoner Abu-Hasan can communicate only in Standard Arabic, represented in the story by biblical Hebrew.

The story's title, "Hashevach le'elohim," similarly emphasizes the story as translation. Over the course of the story, Dawud has two encounters with a Jewish soldier (different from the soldier quoted above, speaking with Abu-Hasan). Their dialogue is repeated twice, word-for-word. The title of the story is taken from Dawud's reply to questions he is asked by the soldier that seem inappropriate insofar as they blur the line between an investigation and a personal conversation:

> "What is your name?" asked the red head in Arabic.
>
> "Dawud Ibn Mahmud," he answered quickly.

"And how are you?" continued the red head, his face becoming serious.

"Praise be to God," said Dawud.

"Content?" asked his interrogator.

"Praise be to God," answered Dawud.[25]

In its first appearance, this dialogue occurs roughly midway through the story, following the occupation of the village, as the Jewish soldier discovers the boy hiding. Following this conversation, the soldier takes him prisoner. The second appearance of the dialogue is at the very end of the story, after Dawud has escaped and been recaptured by the same red-headed soldier. Dawud's words contribute to the ambivalent note on which the narrative concludes: when he notices Dawud for the second time, the soldier is prepared to use his weapon, but it remains unclear whether he indeed shoots the boy.

The soldier's questions are clearly ironic: he is neither an acquaintance of Dawud's, inquiring casually about how he is doing, nor in any way interested in Dawud's actual condition. Still, he asks this question and receives an answer, the answer he expected to hear. This answer is ironic as well—nothing in Dawud's current situation calls for such a mundane answer.

The repetition of this scene is noteworthy. It offers the reader an understanding that the conversation is not a real dialogue: there is no development, thus there is no future. Rather, it is a mock dialogue. Since it is probably limited to the only words in Arabic that the red-headed soldier knows, the content of the dialogue is but an empty gesture; nothing can come out of it. Therefore, the story perhaps ends ambivalently, yet still with one certainty: the lack of hope for relationship (dialogue, conversation, give-and-take) between Jews and Arabs.

The words "praise be to God," yet again support the argument for seeing the story as a translation. The phrase is a word-for-word rendition of the Arabic expression *Alhamdulillah*, a common answer in Arabic to questions concerning individual as well as collective well-being. The Hebrew version of the same expression, however, is rarely used in everyday communication. Translating the mundane Arabic phrase *Alhamdulillah* into the flowery, ceremonial and heavily religious "Hashevach le'elohim" is therefore a significant choice. Standing out as an overly ornate response to mundane questions, and given the context in which these words are repeated, the phrase "Hashevach le'elohim" is charged with irony. It seems doubly unfitting here: once, for the scene (as Dawud faces a life-threatening experience), and then again for the character who speaks it (because his language is Arabic and thus he clearly used the more mundane *Alhamdulillah*).

In the framework of translation theory and following the distinctions first suggested by Friedrich Schleiermacher, this choice of words can be seen as a method that aims to domesticate (rather than foreignize) the translation (Schleiermacher 2012).[26] The domesticating method of translation attempts to bridge the gap between the original language of the text and that of the readers by assimilating the foreign text into the target language. In the dialogues quoted in "Hashevach le'elohim," as well as in the story's title, Standard Arabic is assimilated into the Hebrew through its translation into a biblical register. It should be noted that this particular manner of domesticating translation seems somewhat artificial, as the characters speaking in biblical Hebrew are precisely Arabs. Thus, beyond the technical act of translation, biblical Hebrew spoken by Palestinians renders them (as well as their Jewish interlocutors) almost biblical figures.

In keeping with Canaanite ideology, the dialogues here stress the Hebrew language as an adequate replacement for Arabic. In so doing, the dialogues in "Hashevach le'elohim" echo the seemingly inclusive objective of Canaanite ideology—to unify Jews and Arabs under the Canaanite common denominator, i.e., the Hebrew language, and to anchor both to their shared biblical past.

"Now the *yahud* were here"

Every word in "Hashevach le'elohim" is in Hebrew, with only one exception: the word *yahud* [Jews], which is left untranslated—appearing instead in Arabic transliterated into Hebrew letters. Whereas "Hashevach le'elohim" was described above as a translation aimed at domesticating, the word *yahud*, left in Arabic, conversely stresses the aspects of the story as a foreignizing translation, one that makes the readers acknowledge the original language of the character and forces readers to take a step toward that language, toward the people who use it and especially toward their worldview. Arabic words appear occasionally in Hebrew literature of the time that features Palestinian characters (for example in Yizhar's "Hashavuy"). But typically these words are much more mundane, recording rudimentary and casual conversations between Jews and Palestinians, and they do not serve to enhance the conversation.

The word that Notev chooses to leave untranslated encapsulates the crux of his story. *Yahud*, the Arabic word for "Jews," invokes negative connotations in the minds of the Jewish Israeli readers of this story, who most likely did not (and today still do not) have everyday encounters with the Arabic language. Their scarce encounters with Arabic are during times of war and tension, in which the word *yahud* is often spoken in a negative, violent context. It is a word that creates estrangement, or a "de-familiarization" in the terminology of Victor Shklovsky, who writes: "The purpose of art is to impart the sensation of things as they are perceived and not as they are known. The technique of art is to make objects 'unfamiliar,' to make forms difficult, to increase the difficulty and length of perception."[27] The estrangement created in Notev's story is not just poetic or aesthetic; nor does it entail the same ethical and holistic purpose that Shklovsky assigned to it, to rehabilitate the perception of life and to retain life's value. The word *yahud* creates estrangement because it instantly generates a de-automatization of the reading process. Thereby, as I argue, it has direct political implications: it forces another perspective on the Hebrew-speaking Jews who are the natural readers of this story, and it forces this perspective specifically on their own view of themselves. They are not called Jews, nor are they called *yehudim*. They are referred to neither as Zionists nor as *Zionim*. Rather, in a text brought to them in their own language, a text that they wish to fully comprehend as "their own," and moreover in a text published within the State of Israel, they become essentially foreigners, even enemies, in the eyes of the dominant perspective (the perspective of the national minority) through which the story is narrated.

Why does the author-"translator" of "Hashevach le'elohim" deliberately attempt to foreignize his translation, and why does he do so through this particular word? Notev could have left several words in Arabic (*Alhamdulillah* being one example) without disrupting the story's smooth transition into Hebrew. Yet he chooses to translate every Arabic word except one, which from a linguistic perspective, could easily have been translated into *yehudim*. The reason for this choice is found in Notev's affiliation with the Canaanite movement and his alignment with the Canaanite principles articulated by the movement's spokesman, Ratosh.

Ratosh, as mentioned earlier, held a negative image of the "Jew" and an idealized image of the "Hebrew" person, whose identity, in Ratosh's view, constituted the central pillar of the new nation to be founded. In his numerous articles he delineates the difference between "Jewish" and "Hebrew," emphasizing especially the difference in the distinct cultural products of these two groups

In his famous essay "Sifrut yehudit belashon 'ivrit" ("Jewish Literature in the Hebrew Language"), Ratosh defines his literary ideology, calling for a break from the Jewish culture that centralizes the Jewish—rather than the Hebrew—present, and for a literary use of Hebrew symbols, language, and landscapes as a way to start a new Hebrew culture. This Hebrew culture, he argues, should be based on the archaic period that "preceded Judaism."[28] Moreover, Ratosh lists the faults of the Hebrew literature written up to that time, describing it as merely "Jewish literature in the Hebrew language" written in the diaspora but also in Palestine. As explained by Shavit, insofar as he centralizes the experience of the immigrants the author of such literature is barred from being considered a "Hebrew writer."[29]

As a member of the Canaanite movement, Notev was inclined to embrace its ideology and reject the "Jewish" identity; as a Canaanite author, if he followed Ratosh's literary demands Notev was to advance the Hebrew (rather than the Jewish) national affiliation in his fiction. His use of the word *yahud* addresses this aim in a sophisticated way. First, the word is placed in the mind of the story's protagonist; hence, it is the Palestinian character—rather than the biographical author—who is presented as owning this worldview, which regards the Jews as a remote group. Yet the very choice to distance his narrator from the Jews implies the author's own set of values, which includes embracing the "Hebrew" and rejecting the "Jewish." In this story, published soon after the 1948 war, Notev shares the Palestinians' viewpoint of the Jews; for him as for the other members of the Canaanite ideology and also for the Palestinians depicted in his story, the Jew is the enemy.

Second, by making the readers perform the word *yahud* through their act of reading, the implied author acts to align them with subjects of this text.[30] As Catherine Belsey writes, literature "interpellates the reader, addresses itself to him or her directly, offering the reader as the position from which the text is most 'obviously' intelligible, the position of the *subject in (and of) ideology*."[31] Notev's story does not perform the same direct "hailing" of the Althusserian interpellation, the call "Hey, you there!" as exclaimed by the policeman in Althusser's famous example, which transforms the individual who turns around into a subject.[32] Instead, as I argue, since the word *yahud* becomes conflated with the readers' sense of

"I am," it offers a more subtle form of interpellation that creates a shift in the readers' sense of subjectivity.

"Hashevach le'elohim" was never canonized; like many stories first published in *Alef*, it has remained on the margins of Hebrew literature. Through the process of interpellation that takes place in this story, the reader is changed into a subject in (and of) a marginal ideology that was neither endorsed nor promulgated by the establishment in the State of Israel. So, through the repetition of the word *yahud*, the readers acknowledge in themselves an ideology that opposes Zionism and Judaism, and thereby one that de facto opposes their own group of reference. In other words, the word *yahud* serves to subvert Zionism, to undermine national hegemony, and to shift the readers' sense of subjectivity, collective as well as individual.[33]

Re-Territorializing the Hebrew Language

Gilles Deleuze and Felix Guattari famously define minor literature as literature that is composed by a minority in the major language, is subversive, and is connected immediately to politics and to a collective experience.[34] The definition of minor literature can aid in commenting on Canaanite fiction: it was written in Hebrew by authors who created themselves as a minority group, it has a clear relation to politics and collectivity, and, as I argue below, it complicates the relations of language and territory.

Minor literature detaches language from its territory and from its "natural users"; in it, "language is affected with a high coefficient of deterritorialization."[35] As Deleuze and Guattari maintain, minor literature locates the major language elsewhere, appropriating it from the margins. Moreover, as the literary scholar Roland Bogue writes, "Only by becoming 'other,' by passing between the poles of binary oppositions and blurring clear categories can new possibilities for social interaction be created. Such a process of becoming other is central to minor literature."[36]

"Hashevach le'elohim" complicates the seemingly natural connection between the language and its users; it detaches Hebrew from them (from Jews, Zionists), and blurs the clear categories of "self" and "other," "Jew" and "Palestinian." In a sense, "Hashevach le'elohim" de-territorializes Hebrew. After detaching Hebrew from its users and from the common understanding of its usage, the story locates the language precisely in the territory, in the land, in the mouths of its dwellers. In this sense, the story re-territorializes the Hebrew language—turning it into the language of the territory.[37]

The de-territorialization and re-territorialization of Hebrew in Notev's story can be seen as part of the history of Modern Hebrew literature. The Zionist aspiration—which materialized over the course of the nineteenth and twentieth centuries—was to reconnect the Hebrew language and the Jewish people (for whom Hebrew had been substituted in everyday use by various vernacular languages), thereby turning Hebrew into a national (rather than a sacred) language, and the Jews into a nation (rather than a religious group). To buttress this agenda, the cultural products of Zionism maintained the overlap between Hebrew literature and Jewish literature. This essentialist perspective dominated the understanding of what constitutes Hebrew literature at least until the 1980s, when Hebrew literary works by the Palestinian Israeli author Anton Shammas shook the canon of Hebrew as well as Israeli literature. Especially his novel *Arabesques* (1986) destabilized the assumptions underlying the term *Hebrew literature*.[38]

"Hashevach le'elohim" was published decades before that. Furthermore, Notev's story appeared just after the foundation of the State of Israel, an important moment in the history of Modern Hebrew literature. Whereas in the nineteenth century and the beginning of the twentieth century Hebrew literature was written in multiple Jewish intellectual centers located mainly in Europe, by the 1920s the Yishuv had become a nascent intellectual center in Palestine; then the foundation of the state of Israel cemented this shift. The result was to replace multiplicity with a more unified understanding of Hebrew literature and culture.[39] In 1948, then, Hebrew literature had come to overlap with Israeli literature, maintaining a similar premise that equates it with Jewish literature.

"Hashevach le'elohim" appeared at this critical moment that transformed Israel into the undisputed center of Hebrew literature.[40] At this important moment, though, the story questions the seemingly "natural" connection between Hebrew literature, Israeli literature, and Jewish literature. By severing the automatic link between Hebrew, Israeli, and Jewish, it undermines the dogma of Zionism. In its translational aspects and estrangements, in its effect on the reader, and lastly in its re-territorialization of Hebrew, "Hashevach le'elohim" maintains that Hebrew literature is not necessarily Zionist, nor is it necessarily Jewish. Hebrew is the language of the land, rather than the language of the State of Israel; and Hebrew literature is a vehicle to promote this notion.

Notes

1. *The Oxford Dictionary of Literary Terms* defines *canon* as "A body of writings recognized by authority.... The canon of a national literature is a body of writings especially approved by critics or anthologists and deemed suitable for academic study." When referring to the canon of Israeli literature, and when pointing to the social place and the effect of a literary work, I accept this definition and follow its criteria. See: "canon," in *The Oxford Dictionary of Literary Terms*, ed. Chris Baldick (Oxford: Oxford University Press, 2008). Oxford Reference Online, Oxford University Press, Fordham University, August 2008; http://www.oxfordreference.com/views/ENTRY.html?subview=Main&entry=t56.e163.

2. The pejorative title *Canaanite* was coined by poet Avraham Shlonsky. It was later on adopted by the members of the group as well as by their opponents, *inter alia* literary critic Baruch Kurzweil who, in his 1953 essay, regarded with great concern the emergence of this intellectual movement and its possible effect on Jewish life in the State of Israel. See: Baruch Kurtzweil, "Mahutah umekoroteihah shel tenu'at 'ha'ivrim hatse'irim' ('Kenaanim')," in *Sifrutenu hechadashah: Hemshekh o mahapekhah?* (Tel-Aviv: Shocken, 1953 [1971]), 270–300.

3. In a column published in *Alef*, Ratosh presents this idea straightforwardly. See: "Hasaharon haporeh," *Alef* (April 1949). Published also in *Reshit hayamin: Petichot 'ivriyot* (Tel-Aviv: Hadar, 1982 [1944]), 133–34).

4. Their demands from painting and sculpture were similar: they called for the use of natural materials taken from their local natural habitat: Nubian sandstone, wood, iron.

5. Yonatan Ratosh, "Masah hapetichah," *Reshit hayamin*, 149–204. Translated in Yaacov Shavit, *The New Hebrew Nation: A Study in Israeli Heresy and Fantasy* (London: Routledge, 1987), 63; my added emphasis.

6. Dan Laor analyzes the polemic responses to Canaanite ideology and especially Kurzweil's criticism of the group. Dan Laor, "Kurtzweil vehakena'anim: bein tovanah lema'avak," *Hama'avak al hazikaron* (Tel Aviv: Am Oved, 2009).

7. An extensive genealogy and analysis of Danziger's sculpture "Nimrod" and of the myth encapsulated in it and fostered by it is found in David Ohana, *Modernism and Zionism* (England, Palgrave Macmillan, 2012), 122–78.

8. See, *inter alia*, Dan Miron, *Arb'a panim basifrut ha'ivrit* (Tel Aviv: Shocken, 1975), 195-203; Ziva Shamir, *Lehatchil me'Alef: Shirat Ratosh: Makoriyut umekoroteha* (Tel-Aviv: Hakibbutz Hameuhad, 1993); Michal Ephratt, *Hamilim hamitbakshot: tachdishav shel Yonatan Ratosh* (Ramat-Gan: Bar Ilan University, 2010); as well as collections of essays: Michal Ephratt, ed., *Shirat Ratosh uleshono* (Haifa: Haifa University, 2002); and Laor, *Yonatan Ratosh*.

9. In the 1980s the movement received the scholarly attention of two historians, each devoting a book to the Canaanites. See: Yaacov Shavit, *The New*

Hebrew Nation; J. S. Diamond, *Homeland or Holy Land? The "Canaanite" Critique of Israel* (Bloomington: Indiana University Press, 1986).

10. Liat Steir-Livny and Yaacov Shavit, "Yonatan Ratosh, hakna'anim veyachasam lasho'ah," *Sho'ah mimerchak tavo* (Jerusalem: Ben-Zvi, 2009), 85–99.

11. Roman Vater, "Beyond bi-nationalism? The Young Hebrews Versus the Palestinian Issue," *Journal of Political Ideologies* 21, no. 1 (2015): 45–60.

12. Ibid.

13. Nurit Gertz, "Hakvutsah hakna'anit: bein idiologiyah lesifrut," *Hakvutsah hakena'anit: Sifrut ve'idiologiyah* (Tel Aviv: Open University, 1986), 214–31.

14. Hanan Hever, "Teritoriyaliyut kena'aniyut ve'acherut besifrut milchemet ha'atsma'ut," in *Hasipur vehale'om: kriyot bikortiyot bekanon hasiporet ha'ivrit* (Tel-Aviv: Resling, 2007), 175–209.

15. Hever's article mentioned above appeared also in English: Hanan Hever, "Territoriality and Otherness in Hebrew Literature of the War of Independence," in *The Other in Jewish Thought and History: Constructions of Jewish Culture and Identity*, ed. Laurence J. Silberstein and Robert L. Cohn (New York and London: New York University Press, 1994), 236–57. Moreover, it is worth noting that Diamond's English book aforementioned, while dealing with ideology, politics, and the figure of Ratosh, and while pointing to the influence of Canaanism on the course of Israeli art, does not discuss the fiction published in *Alef*.

16. Yoram Nimshi, "Lamut, aval—head mah?" *Hakvutsah hakena'anit: Sifrut ve'idiologiyah* (Tel Aviv: Open University, 1986 [Original date missing]), 44–47; my translation.

17. Ibid. Amos Keinan, too, questions the Zionist ideology through harsh criticism of the literary accounts of the time. Amos Keinan, " 'Ivrim velo tsabarim," in *Hakvutsah hakena'anit: Sifrut ve'idiologiyah* (Tel Aviv: Open University, 1986 [1949], 42–43.

18. Ratosh, "Masah hapetichah." Translated in Vater, "Beyond bi-nationalism?," 48.

19. Hever, "Teritoriyaliyut kena'aniyut ve'acherut besifrut milchemet ha'atsma'ut."

20. Yaakov Ashman, "Romantika kushit," *Hakvutsah hakena'anit: Sifrut ve'idiologiyah* (Tel Aviv: Open University, 1986 [original date missing]), 186–88.

21. The other case I know of is in Aharon Megged's short story "Hamatmon" ["The Treasure," 1949]. I thank Omri Asscher for this reference.

22. Eitan Notev, 1986 [1950], "Hashevach le'elohim," in *Hakvutsah hakena'anit: Sifrut ve'idiologiyah* (Tel Aviv: 1986 [1950]), 179; my translation.

23. Hanan Hever, "Minority Discourse of a National Majority: Israeli Fiction of the Early Sixties," in *Producing the Modern Hebrew Canon: Nation Building and Minority Discourse* (New York and London: New York University Press, 2002), 140–75.

24. Notev, "Hashevach le'elohim," 181.

25. Ibid., 180.

26. Friedrich Schleiermacher, "On the Different Methods of Translating," in *The Translation Studies Reader* (London: Routledge, 2012 [1813], 43–63.
27. Victor Shklovsky, "Art as Technique," in *The Critical Tradition: Classic Texts and Contemporary Trends* (London and New York, 2007 [1917]), 778. Shklovsky's use of "estrangement," as delineated in his essay "Art as Technique," is broad, referring to poetic language that has the ability—through estrangements—to redeem life. However, as pointed out by Svetlana Boym, the idea of national language is central to the very etymology of this concept. Boym writes: "Tracing the genealogy of estrangement, Shklovsky also questions the autonomy and unity of the 'national language.' Ostranenie [Russian for 'estrangement'] means more than distancing and making strange; it is also dislocation, depaysement." Svetlaana Boym,"Estrangement as a Lifestyle: Shklovsky and Brodsky," *Poetics Today* 17, no. 4 (1996): 515.
28. Yonatan Ratosh, *Sifrut yehudit belashon 'ivrit* (Tel-Aviv: Hadar, 1982), 41.
29. Shavit, *The New Hebrew Nation*, 113–14.
30. Louis Althusser, "Ideology and Ideological State Apparatuses," *Lenin and Philosophy, and Other Essays*, trans. Ben Brewster (New York and London: Monthly Review Press, 1971), 127–86.
31. Catherine Belsey, "Addressing the Subject," in *Critical Practice* (New York: Methuen, 1980), 57; original emphasis.
32. Althusser, "Ideology and Ideological State Apparatuses," 174.
33. On the duality of the term *subject* and its connection to the power of the state, see Michel Foucault, "The Subject and Power," *Critical Inquiry* (1982): 777–95; and Etienne Balibar, "The Nation Form: History and Ideology," in *Becoming National* (New York: Oxford University Press, 1996), 132–51.
34. Gilles Deleuze and Felix Guattari, *Kafka: Toward a Minor Literature* (Minneapolis and London: University of Minnesota Press, 1986).
35. Deleuze and Guattari, "What Is a Minor Literature," 16.
36. Roland Bogue, "Minoritarian + Literature," in *The Deleuze Dictionary*. (Edenborough: Edenborough University press, 2005), 168–69.
37. Deterritorialization is described in the works of Deleuze and Guattari in a variety of ways. I focus here on the way in which the term appears in "What Is Minor Literature?" where the deterritorilized language is seen as a language appropriate for strange and minor uses (e.g., disconnect between the language and what is seen as "its natural users").
38. For more on this debate, see, *inter alia*, Hanan Hever, "'ivrit be'eto shel 'aravi," *Teoria uvikoret* 1 (1991): 23–38; Rachel Feldhay Brenner, "In Search of Identity: The Israeli Arab Artist in Anton Shammas's *Arabesques*," *PMLA* 108, no. 3 (May 1993): 431–45; "Postcolonial Memory, Postmodern Intertextuality: Anton Shammas's *Arabesques* Revisited," *PMLA* 114, no. 3 (May 1999): 373–89.
39. This collection of essays addresses this process: Avner Holtzman, ed., *Perspectives on Modern Hebrew Literature* (Tel Aviv: Tel Aviv University, 2005).

40. This premise was recently challenged with the publication of *Mikan Ve'eilakh: Journal for Diasporic Hebrew* (first issue published in Berlin and Paris in 2016), which aims to renew the Hebrew intellectual and literary activity in the diaspora, that is, outside of its seemingly natural center in Israel.

Hebrew Unbound

Alternative Homelands in the New World

MELISSA WEININGER

Transnational Hebrew literature is not new. Rather, the history of the development of modern Hebrew literature is a fundamentally diasporic, transnational story, rooted in the capitals and cafés of Europe, borrowing from the languages and literatures of the continent.[1] Likewise, many pioneering works of modern Hebrew literature unfolded their plots in the streets of Berlin and Odessa, the protagonists studying at the great universities of Germany or Switzerland, finding themselves in the mountains of the Alps and the forests of Poland. However, with the rise of Jewish settlement in Palestine and the establishment of the state of Israel in 1948, the transnational history of Hebrew literature began to be overwritten with a Zionist narrative that privileged *Yisraeliut*, Israeliness, which associated Hebrew with the land of Israel and Hebrew literature with its landscapes. The norms and aesthetics of Hebrew literature shifted toward an Israeli center.

The diaspora as the site of formulation of both Hebrew literature and the (largely male) Jewish subject became slowly obsolete, as the focus of Zionist nationalism pivoted toward the settlement of Palestine and the land of Israel as the site of homeland. Eric Zakim has detailed the way that Zionism and its adherents articulated an understanding of the modern Jewish subject as tied specifically to that setting.[2] An integral part of the creation and articulation of this new Jew was Hebrew literature. As Motti Regev describes it, "Zionism, as a set of cultural practices, evolved around

123

two interrelated themes: the rejection of diaspora culture (the *galut*) and the invention of a 'new Jew,' the Israeli. . . . [T]his logic resulted in the successful invention and public imposition of a dominant cultural package known as 'Hebrew culture' (*tarbut ivrit*), or *ivriut*—Hebrewism."³

However, as we mark the seventieth anniversary of statehood, it is clear that this process of Israelification of Hebrew literature has taken a new turn. Partially as a result of globalization and the internet, along with the circulation of both bodies and ideas that these phenomena have engendered, Hebrew literature is once again exploring, even embracing, its transnational history and origins. Israeli writers living both in Israel and outside of it have begun to push back against the narrow definition of Hebrew literature as exclusively Israeli and Israeli literature as exclusively Hebrew. In the last ten years or so there has been a rise in the creation of what I have called "diaspora Israeli literature": always transcultural, sometimes translingual, it locates itself in what Homi Bhabha has called the "in-between" space of culture, contesting hegemonic national narratives through an insistence on crossing, blurring, or questioning the cultural, linguistic, and national boundaries that have defined Hebrew literature for the last seventy years or more.

Some of this literature has been written in languages other than Hebrew, such as the work of Ayelet Tsabari and Shani Boianjiu in English, or Tomer Gardi in German.⁴ And some of this literature has been written in Hebrew, by Israeli expatriates living in the United States and Europe, such as Maya Arad and Mati Shmuelof.⁵ Previously, I have written about the way that translingual Israeli literature challenges the singular association between Hebrew and Israeliness, while also questioning some Zionist tropes and assumptions central to the history of Israeli literature.⁶ In this essay, I will discuss two works of diaspora Israeli fiction that are not translingual, Ruby Namdar's *Habayit asher nechrav* (*The Ruined House*, 2013) and Nava Semel's *E-srael* (*Isra Isle*, 2005). These are novels by respected and award-winning Israeli writers, very much at the center of Israeli culture, written in Hebrew about and from diasporic spaces. Unlike translingual Israeli literature, whose language of composition places it consciously and conspicuously in a diasporic or intermediate cultural space, these novels bring those diasporic spaces into Hebrew literature, and use their very liminality to unravel the naturalness of the identification of Hebrew literature with Israel and a unitary, monolithic homeland. In doing so they open space for reconsidering the very category of Israeli literature, after seventy years of statehood, as inextricably tied to the land of Israel and the Hebrew language, by recalling the transnational roots of Hebrew literature at a time when Hebrew literature circulated across national boundaries and diasporic spaces.[7]

Semel's and Namdar's novels work to challenge both the imbrication of Hebrew literature with the land and landscapes of Israel, and the equation of Hebrew with Israeli literature. The transnational setting and focus of these works reconceive Zionist notions of homeland and exile, undoing binary modes of thinking about Israel and diaspora. Both novels are set in and around New York City during the period leading up to September 11, 2001, and use techniques of magical realism or speculative history to explore the possibilities inherent in liberating Hebrew culture and Jewish identity from the bonds of a monolithic Zionist ideology.

Both *Isra Isle* and *The Ruined House* focus on American Jewish identity and its connection to the idea of homeland. The plots of these narratives are deeply rooted in diaspora landscapes, histories, and mythologies, both Jewish and not. At the same time, they are both written in Hebrew, using the language to record dialogue, thoughts, and action that is intended to have occurred in English (as well as a bit of Yiddish and some Native American languages).[8] Very different in form, language, and even genre, these novels decentralize the idea of homeland, blurring national and ideological boundaries and suggesting a return to the transnational character of Hebrew literature. In discussing the consequences of transcultural literature, Arianna Dagnino notes that it has the tendency to transcend "the borders of a single culture and nation, but . . . also promote and engage with a wider global and literary perspective and, possibly, a new way of imagining and living identity."[9] These novels both turn from strict realism in an attempt to envision a transnational conception of homeland that exists beyond geographical boundaries and points on a map. Unlike the early Hebrew writers writing from the very diaspora locales that they described, or contemporary Jewish writers in the diaspora imagining Israel and alternative homelands, these novels offer a window into the Israeli imagination of alternative homelands and diaspora Jewish identity. Zionism conceives of Israel as the home of the Jewish people, but this work explores what it means to look out from the vantage point of homeland and see other homes. It envisions a specifically Israeli encounter with multiple homelands that challenges the boundaries of Zionist ideology.

This transnational movement is most apparent in *The Ruined House* in its orientation toward its setting, Manhattan. New York City is not just the backdrop to the events of the book, but is, in a sense, a character itself. The title of the book refers to the destroyed Temple in Jerusalem. In Hebrew, the dual meaning of *bayit* (house), which can refer both to an everyday home as well as to the central location for worship in Judaism, makes the title a kind of double-entendre. Not only does it conjure up the origins of Jewish diaspora, which began with the destruction of the first Temple in 586 BCE, it also suggests a more quotidian type of ruin, the deterioration of the very idea of home. In contrast to this image of a destroyed home (or homeland), it presents a vital, dynamic portrait of contemporary New York in the months leading up to September 11 (which brought with it another kind of ruin).

The terms in which New York is described and discussed in the novel verge on an almost liturgical glorification. The second chapter begins with a lofty homage to the city: "O Manhattan, isle of the gods, home to great happenings of metal, glass, and energy, island of sharp angles, summit of the world! Have not we all—rich and poor, producers and consumers, providers and provided for—been laboring for generations with all our might, under the direction of an unseen Engineer, to build the most magnificent city ever known to humankind?"[10] The passage continues with specific references to the landmarks and landscapes of Manhattan: the Empire State Building, the Hudson River, Wall Street, and the like. It celebrates, with possessive language such as "our island," the grand beauty and accomplishments of New York, identifying the place as belonging to both speaker and readers. This focus on New York as a celebrated locale establishes the city not just as a setting for the novel but as a character in it, the place (or at least one place) to which the *bayit* of the title refers.

This apostrophic ode to New York also recalls the work of Walt Whitman, an iconic poet of the landscapes of New York. In his poem "Manahatta," Whitman writes of "Numberless crowded streets, high growths of iron, slender, strong, light, splendidly uprising toward clear skies" and "[t]he mechanics of the city, the masters, well-form'd, beautiful-faced, looking you straight in the eyes."[11] Namdar's celebration of the landscape describes, like Whitman's, an almost religious admiration for the craft and construction of such a massive city, finding beauty in its buildings and streets. But the beginning and end of Whitman's poem may provide an even clearer reading of the specifically transnational character of Namdar's New York. The first line of "Mannahatta" begins, "I was asking for something specific and perfect for my city,/Whereupon lo! upsprang the aboriginal name." Whitman begins from an acknowledgment of the city's origins as a native space, adopted (or stolen) by those who built it into its current incarnation. After recounting its many wonders, Whitman ends, "City nested in bays! my city!" In the course of the poem, New York has gone from its "aboriginal," native roots to becoming the possession of the poet, the white settler. The original name, that "word from of old," is now "the word of *my* city" (emphasis added). Likewise, Namdar's ode to New York, echoing Whitman's poem in Hebrew, suggests that through this linguistic transformation and appropriation he, too, takes possession of the city, bringing it into the Hebrew literary tradition, according it the position of a linguistic homeland.

The permeability of homelands and the linguistic connection with Hebrew is evident from the very opening of the novel, which describes in visionary, mystical terms the possibility of communication and exchange across cultures, time periods, and places. The opening scene, written in an elevated, precise style, describes the opening of "the gates of heaven above the great city of New York, and behold: all seven celestial spheres were revealed, right above the 4th Street subway station, layered one on top of another like the rungs of a ladder reaching skyward from earth" (H 11, E 3). The Temple in Jerusalem was imagined by the Israelites as the place where the *Shekhinah*, the presence of God, resided, a gateway into heaven much like the one described in the opening of the novel. Here, the same honor is bestowed on the 4th Street subway station, a quintessentially New York space.

The image of the ladder in this scene also recalls the biblical story of Jacob's flight from his own home in the land of Israel, an individual exile. On his journey, Jacob dreams of "a ladder set up on the earth, and the top of it reached to heaven; and behold the angels of God ascending and descending on it" (Gen. 28:12). The novel borrows language verbatim from this passage, inserting in the middle of the biblical language the passage that locates the event in the middle of Manhattan:

וַיַּחֲלֹם, וְהִנֵּה סֻלָּם מֻצָּב אַרְצָה, וְרֹאשׁוֹ, מַגִּיעַ הַשָּׁמָיְמָה; וְהִנֵּה מַלְאֲכֵי אֱלֹהִים, עֹלִים וְיֹרְדִים בּוֹ. (Gen. 28:12)

...סולם הניצב ארצה, ממש מעל תחנת הרכבת התחתית של הרחוב הרביעי, וראשו מגיע השמימה. (11)

a ladder planted on the ground, precisely above the 4th Street subway station, with its top reaching the heavens.

This passage, in language typical of the novel's mixed style, which itself recalls the heterogenous roots of Hebrew, quite literally inserts New York itself into the Hebrew canon by placing the 4th Street subway station in the middle of Jacob's biblical dream.

This placement also has meaning for the relationship between Israel and diaspora; a midrash in Bereshit Rabbah connects the dream metaphorically to the Temple:

> "That there was a ladder": refers to the ramp to the altar. ". . . Set up on the earth": that is the altar, "An altar of dirt you will make for me" (Ex. 20:24). ". . . And the top of it reached to heaven": these are the offerings, for their fragrance goes up to heaven. ". . . And behold, the angels of God": these are the high priests. ". . . Were ascending and descending on it": for they go up and go down on the ramp. "And behold, the Lord stood above it": "I saw the Lord standing by the altar" (Amos 9:1). (Gen. Rabbah 68:12)[12]

In this interpretation, the elements of Jacob's dream represent elements of the Temple and its sacrificial cult. The image of the ladder, here extending from the 4th Street subway station into the heavens, relocates the center of Jewish life, Jerusalem, squarely in the midst of New York City. Thus, not only is New York relocated into the central text of the Hebrew canon, but Jerusalem, and by extension the Jewish homeland, is relocated into the space of the diaspora.

These reconfigurations of space offer a fluid conception of the relationship between center and periphery, homeland and diaspora, that challenges the binarization of these concepts and locations. Likewise, the content of the Jacob's dream, in which he sees angels ascending and descending a ladder to heaven, offers a conception of the relationship between homeland and exile as one of exchange rather than separation. In another midrash, the rabbis claimed that the angels ascending the ladder—notably, the ascent comes before the descent—were those who accompanied Jacob inside the land and those who descended were a separate set of angels meant to accompany him in exile (Gen. Rabbah 68:12). Again, here we have a dichotomy between the land of Israel and the diaspora, but again that binary is bridged by the image of the ladder and the angels who move from earth to heaven and back. This movement suggests exchange rather than separation, and the association of New

York with a direct line to the divine—whether through angelic exchange or access to the Temple—anoints the city as a center, or homeland, much like Jerusalem. And like the ladder, the novel itself, as a Hebrew novel written in and about New York, acts as a bridge between Israel and diaspora, moving freely between them like the angels in a way that suggests closeness or dependence rather than a distinction.

The permeability of worlds both ancient and modern, the ideas of homeland and diaspora, the cities Jerusalem and New York, also suggest the instability of the idea of a fixed and permanent center. The novel, divided into seven books, contains an epigraph at the beginning of each book. The epigraph of the sixth book is a translated excerpt of William Butler Yeats's 1919 poem "The Second Coming," which contains the well-known line, "Things fall apart; the center cannot hold."[13] This epigraph signals one of the novel's main themes: the suggestion that no one "center" can, for all eternity, function as the fulcrum for a diverse, rich, heterogeneous Jewish life and culture. By privileging New York as a Jewish homeland, while at the same time acknowledging the historical primacy of Jerusalem, the novel repudiates the binarism of homeland and diaspora that underlies Zionist ideology and, by extension, Israeli culture. At the same time, as a Hebrew novel deeply tied to the landscape of New York, it breaks the possessive hold of Israel over Hebrew and Hebrew literature. In doing so, the novel carves out space for an Israeli understanding of homeland that does not distinguish itself from diaspora but integrates both into a more multivalent understanding of home.

Isra Isle similarly instates New York as a point on the fluctuating map of Jewish homelands, although in this case it is the hinterlands, specifically Grand Island, New York, once imagined by the American statesman Mordecai Manuel Noah as a potential Jewish autonomous state. The novel is divided into three parts, loosely connected: the first part is set in September 2001 and tells the fairly straightforward story of a New York City police detective of Native American ancestry, Simon T. Lenox, who has been tasked with searching for a missing Israeli national who turns out to be a descendant of Mordecai Manuel Noah, the American journalist, diplomat, and visionary who imagined a Jewish state on Grand Island, New York; the second part of the novel, set in September 1825, recounts an alternative history of Mordecai Manuel Noah, in which he travels to Grand Island with a young Native woman, whose family has been violently driven from their homes there, as his guide; the third part of the novel is pointedly set in an alternative September 2001 and tells the tale of a world in which Isra Isle, a Jewish state on Grand Island, has become the homeland of the Jews, and the state of Israel does not exist.

Isra Isle, like *The Ruined House*, engages with the questions of homeland and language through a focus on its diasporic setting. The novel also presents a recurring metaphor for the idea of home as unfixed through the concept of the *boydem*, which is a feature of the first and last sections, bracketing the narrative. *Boydem* is a Yiddish word referring to an attic or garret. It has entered modern Hebrew to refer to a small storage space in a house or apartment, hidden and extraneous. Interestingly, this term itself reveals the heterogenous, diasporic history of Hebrew, which, despite claims to purity and ancient authenticity, absorbed many terms, expressions, and grammatical constructions from the languages of Europe, especially from Yiddish, the diaspora "jargon" of the Jews denigrated by early Zionists and Hebraists. Yet the *boydem* also becomes, in the story, a powerful image of a shelter that can exist in any place, a moveable refuge that is not itself home but in which home can be kept. As Simon T. Lenox remarks in the first section of the novel, "Maybe Israel is the Jews' *boydem*?"[14] Like the *bayit* (whether home or Temple) that moves through space and time in *The Ruined House*, the *boydem* is a metaphor for a moveable center, a homeland that follows the Jews wherever they go.

Each section of the novel takes up the question of homeland in its own way, and these multifarious conceptions are loosely connected primarily through the shared locale of Grand Island.[15] Tracing the way that the landscape of the island and America itself operate in the three sections of the novel reveals the way that the concept of the *boydem* is translated into an alternative space, a traveling home, one that again, like Jacob's ladder, forms a bridge between Jewish homelands. The novel uses the landscapes of America—the wilderness and eventual megastate of Grand Island, the landmarks of New York City—as the touchstone for Jewish identity and belonging. Indeed, the novel freely mixes Native American and Jewish mythology, religion, and culture in a way that deeply roots Jewish existence in American soil. Like the mystical invasion of Jerusalem and the Temple into New York City in *The Ruined House*, in *Isra Isle* the American setting is freely mixed with Jewish narratives of redemption, producing various models and shifting notions of home that preclude a single definition.

Part One of the novel, titled "Grand Island," in a nod to the centrality of that location, begins not in that place but in Manhattan. The New York City police detective Simon T. Lenox, who is of Native American ancestry, has just been assigned to locate a missing Israeli national, Liam

Emanuel, against his own protestations. As part of the assignment, his office is relocated to the 84th floor of the North Tower of the World Trade Center, where he feels "stuck in a place where he doesn't belong. . . . He has better conditions here, ample space—an office designed to win him over, furnished with an executive leather chair and state-of-the-art laptop. But all these props serve only to underscore how foreign he is in this new domain" (H 8–9, E 5).

The irony of Lenox's relocation to the World Trade Center and the somewhat mocking nod to the history of Native American displacement in the United States parallels the novel's challenge to fixed ideas of homeland and nation. The World Trade Center, particularly for the post-9/11 reader, has become synonymous with American nationalism. As Neil Leach has documented, buildings like the WTC can become points in a symbolic structure that enable the fantasy of national identity through materiality, much as a flag might: "[Buildings] may become the visible embodiment of the invisible, the vehicle through which the fantasy structure of the homeland is represented."[16] After 9/11, American national identity was consolidated around the symbol of the WTC.

Thus, Lenox's forced move into the WTC building can be seen as an echo of the genocide and displacement of native peoples on which the United States was built. However, it is also an inversion of that historical narrative, because in this instance Lenox is moved into the iconic symbol of American nationalism—drawn into, not pushed out of, the nation. Lenox himself voices the centrality of Americanness to his own identity when he muses, "American—that's what he was. If he were to yield to superstition, he would be undermining the ideal of one nation" (H 33, E 43). Through Lenox's relocation to the WTC, the novel introduces the complexity and interpenetration of homeland and nation that is at its heart: America as a Native American homeland, now appropriated by a nationalism symbolized in the WTC, and by extension assimilating natives into this settler colonial nation.

The reference to American colonialism, land expropriation, and Native American genocide raises the specter of the Israel-Palestine conflict, perhaps suggesting the victimization of Native Americans as parallel to that of Palestinians. At the same time the example of American colonization of Native lands shows that national conflict, like that in Israel, is not unique but rather reflects problems endemic to any national project. As Adam Rovner has suggested, "The paradoxical messages underlying Semel's alternate history help expose a fundamental ambivalence at the root of Zionism itself: the simultaneous desires to be a nation apart and to be a nation like all other nations."[17] This example demonstrates the way that the novel negotiates this nationalist dilemma through a parallel with American history. The oppression of native or preexisting populations is presented as a fundamental problem at the root of nationalist expansion and sovereignty. Yet this parallel is also in conflict with Zionist representations of Israel as a uniquely ethical, egalitarian, and democratic nation, one whose army, for example, is routinely represented by the state as the most moral in the world. By bringing American nationalism into symbolic contact with Zionism, *Isra Isle* exposes this ambivalence about the morality of nationalism and the desire to be both special and ordinary. This ambivalence is thus amplified and reflected through the imagination of an alternative homeland.

The novel continues to engage with this dilemma through the plot, in which an Israeli descendant of Mordecai Manuel Noah comes with deed of ownership to claim Grand Island as his patrimony. As Lenox's and Emmanuel's narratives converge, and the two meet at Grand Island, these two modern national narratives also come together. Lenox wonders, "How can the Native American investigator explain to the Israeli that land is not property and no one can own it? It was given to both the creators and the creatures to guard. We are all temporary guests, and land cannot be inherited" (H 65, E 90). As in *The Ruined House*, Semel also takes recourse to the biblical text in order to bring the alternative homeland in New York literally into Jewish tradition, rewriting Psalm 137, the iconic song of diasporic lament:

"עַל נַהֲרוֹת בָּבֶל/שָׁם יָשַׁבְנוּ/גַּם-בָּכִינוּ/בְּזָכְרֵנוּ אֶת-צִיּוֹן" (Ps. 137:1)

"By the rivers of Babylon,/there we sat,/sat and wept,/as we thought of Zion."

Semel's version inverts the formula, substituting remembrance for forgetting and the first person for the collective voice:

בשוכחי את אררט, שם ישבתי גם בכיתי, על נהר הניאגרה (71).

"By the rivers of Niagara I sat and wept when I forgot Ararat" (100).

The text also transposes the iconic warning, "אִם אֶשְׁכָּחֵךְ יְרוּשָׁלָ͏ִם" (Ps. 137:5), into its opposite: אִם אזכרך ירושלים. "If I remember thee Jerusalem on the Niagara.... If I remember thee Tel-Aviv on the Niagara" (H 71, E 100). This mashup of homelands, holy centers, languages, and foundational texts muddles the boundaries between these spaces both geographically and symbolically, forming a complex web of interconnections rather than a linear one. The transposition of these lines reflects the unusual perspective of the novel, which, like *The Ruined House* and unlike the Psalm, looks out from the perspective of the homeland, of one already "at home," to consider what that means in light of other possible homelands. In this case, those homelands are not constructed as oppositional, but rather as enmeshed; thus, the psalm becomes not a lament, but a celebration of the imaginative possibilities of diaspora.

This transformation of the American landscape into an element of Jewish, and Hebrew literary, tradition continues in the Part Two, "Ararat," titled after the name Noah gave to the putative Jewish homeland on Grand Island. In this section, a first-person narrative told from the perspective of a young Native American woman whose community on Grand Island was violently expelled by American forces, the landscapes of America are constructed as a touchstone for Jewish identity and belonging. The narrator has been taken in as a servant (although she appears to be treated essentially as a slave) by a white couple on the mainland, and when Mordecai Manuel Noah comes to stay with them she offers to be his guide to the island he has just purchased. As she rows him to the island she reflects on the concept of homeland and the island itself:

> There are other islands in the world besides this small strip of earth that juts out of the water.... Nevertheless, this island is my home. For me it is the whole world. And for the Jewish chief? Nothing. A tiny patch scratched with a nail on the scrolls of paper the white people call "maps."... Except that their maps do not show the traces scattered around this land, nor even the downy meadows that turn golden in summer, or the rustling canopy of foliage that comes in winter. The coyotes, the raccoons, the doves, and the ravens all move in their circles with the maple and elm trees. Everything in its place, as though there were no Buffalo, no America, only this island alone. (H 83, E117–18)

This narrative, centered in between the two contemporary stories, grounds her observations about the American landscape and the Native and Jewish relationship to the island. The admixture of these two cultures and the land itself is literally embodied in the novel when the narrator and Noah have a sexual encounter that, it is implied, impregnates her. This ancestral connection is the link that binds the other characters in the book both to their Jewish identities and to the American landscape they call home.

Nonetheless, the novel does not indicate that this home is bounded by the borders of Grand Island, Isra Isle, or the United States. Rather, as the narrator of the second section says, "If land is not property, then anywhere may be considered a homeland, and the Jewish tribe may therefore adopt the island even without a deed of ownership. The Jew is free to settle in whichever land he desires" (H 94, E 136). She asks, "Why, then, does he insist on drawing borders for himself?" Part Three of the novel, "Isra Isle," confronts this question through the device of an alternative history in which Noah's dream of a Jewish state on Grand Island has been realized. In this story, a candidate from Isra Isle, a female descendant of Mordecai Manuel Noah, has won the nomination of an unspecified political party for the presidential race. The narrative takes the form of a long diary entry or letter from a black American photographer also named Simon to his Jewish boyfriend Jake, who was born on Isra Isle but has lived for many years in self-exile on the mainland. In this alternative history the state of Israel does not exist, and the ancestral land of Israel is part of a political entity called Grand Palestine, largely Arab, in which only a small community of Jews lives.

Isra Isle, however, now one of the United States, is a thriving independent metropolis on Grand Island. Its existence as a city of refuge has prevented the Jewish genocide of the Holocaust although not the Nazi persecution and murder of the disabled, homosexuals, Roma and Sinti, and others. The Jewish culture that has developed there is also deeply imbricated in the American, and particularly Native American, history of the place. Isra-Islander culture has appropriated, in not entirely comfortable ways, certain elements of Native culture in the form of a bar mitzvah ritual involving a vision quest, the javelin throw as the island's most competitive sport, and various ritual objects incorporated and adapted into Jewish culture: peace pipes, wampum belts, moccasins embroidered in Hebrew. Isra-Islanders even worship a deity known as Yehowakan Tanka, a mix of Yahweh, the God of the Hebrew Bible, and Wakan Tanka, the God of the local native tribe. In this synthesis of cultures the text again embeds the landscapes, histories, and mythologies of America into Judaism and the hybrid Isra-Isle Jewish culture. It also demonstrates the extent to which Jewish culture has been dependent on local cultures for its development, never remaining one fixed mode of religious expression, but constantly evolving. This dependence on local cultures again recalls the diasporic roots of Hebrew and even Zionism itself, projecting this history into a speculative future. As Adam Rovner has noted, "Semel's text rewrites history, representing the real-world Israel not as the promised land but as a land premised on contingencies."[18] In the real world these contingencies produced the modern state of Israel, but in *Isra Isle*'s alternative world they have produced another variant of Jewish national culture, strongly linked to place.

At the same time, the novel carefully preserves the shadow of Israel's existence, playing somewhat humorously with its own knowledge of its fictionality, nodding to real-life places and events as a way of underscoring the status of Isra Isle as alternative homeland while at the same time recalling the state of Israel within the text. For example, there is an area of Isra Isle known as the West Bank, in this case the west bank of the Niagara River, an upscale area "with all the yachts docked in the private marinas" (H 124, E 184). In a more overt comparison to the contested landscapes of the state of Israel, as well as the integration into the American landscape, Simon reflects on the way that Isra Isle has accommodated its increasing population into a tiny territory by "pack[ing] them all in vertically, turning Isra Isle into an imitation of Manhattan. Of course it also emulates Gaza in Grand Palestine, the most tower-laden metropolis in the world" (H 156, E 231). In these nods to the disputed spaces of modern-day Israel/Palestine, the novel gestures at what might have been—a peaceful marina called the West Bank, innovative housing for all of Gaza's residents that becomes an example to the world—while troubling the alternative homeland of the text with a shadow of today's reality.

But perhaps the most interesting reference to the ghost of a sovereign Israel within the world of *Isra Isle* is the name of the neighborhood where Winona Emanuela Noah lives: Spring Hill. The name Spring Hill, which sounds just like what it designates in the book, an upscale suburban neighborhood, is also a direct translation of Tel Aviv. Although even in the Hebrew version of the text, it is written phonetically as "spring hill" (H 135, E 200), it cannot be mistaken for anything other than a reference to the city that is a symbol of Israel's modernity and cosmopolitanism, a city established by Zionist pioneers as a sign of Jewish progress and advancement. But in transliterating the name of the city into Hebrew, the text in this case imports its own alternate homeland into the language that has been constructed as synonymous with Israel, and with Israeli identity and culture. Nonetheless, the appearance of this name in the text is also a reminder that Israel does, in fact, exist, that this diasporic imaginary is a mere fantasy.

Most interesting is Simon's reflection on the name, not fully translated into the English version of the novel. As he watches the candidate arrive at her estate, he thinks, "Spring Hill. Home. The more I repeat these words to myself, which were meaningless last night, the more loaded they sound. A sort of whispered spell *that was intended to build the diaspora (galut), but strangles the place to death.*"[19] Something about the conjunction between the place name, Spring Hill, and the concept of home is suffocating. Given the shadowy presence of Tel Aviv contained within the transliterated English, this suggests the potential danger in calling any one place home. Making a homeland out of diaspora has strangled that place, and the implication is that the same might be true for its shadow parallel. The concept of a fixed and immovable center, a singular home, suggests constriction of Jewish life and culture rather than vitality.

The land and landscapes of Israel do make one appearance in the novel, in what appears also to be a movement between various possible ideas of home and homeland. The end of the novel revisits the territory of Grand Palestine, describing the pilgrimage of Simon's boyfriend Jake to scatter the ashes of his grandmother in the land of Israel, according to her final wishes, combined with soil taken from the ruins of the Twin Towers as an homage to Simon. The ritual is not a familiar Jewish one, because Judaism demands burial, and represents, like the mixture of the ashes themselves, another hybrid form of religion and culture. Here, this amalgam is relocated to a homeland unrealized, described as "a desolate place, which has sunken into blessed oblivion" (H 164, E 243). Again, the unbounded movement of the narrative between the locations and landscapes of various homelands, real and imagined, and the imbrication of local and imported cultures suggests a more multivalent, dynamic, and transnational conception of home.

Both *Isra Isle* and *The Ruined House* destabilize established conceptions of home as a fixed location and monolithic conceptions of a Jewish identity tied to homeland through a revaluation of diasporic spaces and places. Through imaginative rewritings of history and the present, they suggest that more than one narrative of identity and belonging is possible—

and that, sometimes, these competing narratives may even be temporally coexistent, as when visions of Jerusalem invade New York or a moment in time recurs in different circumstances. Their attention to and use of the landscapes of New York and Grand Island foreground these places with an almost loving admiration, linking the stories and identities of the characters, to the contemporary diasporic spaces of Jewish life. That they do so in Hebrew marks a conscious return to the origins of Hebrew literature as a transnational form of culture, free to cross political and ideological borders. Yet their very language also reminds us of the existence of the state of Israel, as does the appearance, in various ways, of signs and symbols that recall the shadow of Israel within the text. Thus, rather than placing themselves squarely within the tradition of diaspora Hebrew literature, these novels offer a perspective on diaspora and homeland from the vantage point of what is ostensibly a singular and privileged home. In doing so, they destabilize Israel's status as a monolithic homeland, while at the same time arguing for Israel's place in the community of homes that have nourished and sustained Jewish culture.

Notes

1. For more on the transnational history of Hebrew literature, see Shachar M. Pinsker, *Literary Passports* (Stanford: Stanford University Press, 2011); and Allison Shachter, *Diasporic Modernisms: Hebrew and Yiddish Literature in the Twentieth Century* (New York: Oxford University Press, 2012). For the role of café culture in the creation of modern Hebrew literature, see Shachar M. Pinsker, *A Rich Brew: How Cafés Created Modern Jewish Culture* (New York: New York University Press, 2018).

2. Eric Zakim, *To Build and Be Built: Landscape, Literature, and the Construction of Zionist Identity* (Philadelphia: The University of Pennsylvania Press, 2006), 3.

3. Motti Regev, "To Have a Culture of Our Own: On Israeliness and Its Variants," *Ethnic and Racial Studies* 23 (2000): 227.

4. Shani Boianjiu, *The People of Forever Are not Afraid* (New York: Hogarth, 2012); Ayelet Tsabari, *The Best Place on Earth* (Toronto: HarperCollins, 2013); Tomer Gardi, *Broken German* (Graz, Austria: Droschl, 2016).

5. Maya Arad's novels about expatriate Israelis include *Me'achorei hahar* (Tel Aviv: Xargol, 2016) and *Hamorah le'ivrit* (Tel Aviv: Xargol, 2016); Mati Shmuelof, who is at the center of a multicultural poetry scene in Berlin, which includes some Israeli writers, most recently published the poetry chapbook '*Ivrit mechutz le'ivreha hametukim* (Tel Aviv: Pardes, 2017).

6. See Melissa Weininger, "Hebrew in English: The New Transnational Hebrew Literature," *Shofar* 33, no. 4 (Summer 2015): 15–35; and "Language Politics: The Boundaries of Homeland and Translingual Israeli Literature," *Studies in the Novel* 48, no. 4 (Winter 2016): 477–93.

7. Diaspora settings were a central feature of the development of modern Hebrew literature. The figure of the "talush," the deracinated, young, Jewish man searching for his place in modern Europe linked modern Hebrew literature with various European landscapes. Elimelech, the lovelorn protagonist of Micah Yosef Berdyczewski's novella *Urva parach*, leaves behind the *shtetl* and the world of traditional Judaism for the big city, studying first in a large unnamed metropolis that is probably Berlin and later moving to what appears to be Bern, Switzerland. Here the lush European landscape is described in detail: "In this land there were thousands of mountains and sloping hills, rivers and streams flowing through them, refreshing trees and bushes and flowers, all quiet and peaceful and speaking to us in their language." Indeed, the landscape is integral to his understanding of himself as a modern man and a type of New Jew, and as Elimelech walks home from the university he feels "all the land is my place, the whole world is my place." Micha Yosef Berdyczewski, *Urva parach, Kol sipurei Micha-Yosef Bin Gorion (Berdyczewski)* (Tel Aviv: Am Oved, 1950), 38.

8. Adam Rovner has noted that there is really no theoretical term to describe novels such as these, which record language supposed to have been spoken or thought in one language in another. See his article, "Alternate History: The Case of Nava Semel's *IsraIsland* and Michael Chabon's *The Yiddish Policemen's Union*," *Partial Answers: Journal of Literature and the History of Ideas* 9, no. 1 (Jan. 2011): 138.

9. Arianna Dagnino, *Transcultural Writers and Novels in the Age of Global Mobility* (West Lafayette, IN: Purdue University Press, 2015), 2.

10. Reuven Namdar, *Habayit asher nechrav* (Or Yehuda: Dvir, 2013), 15. Translation adapted from Ruby Namdar, *The Ruined House*, trans. Hillel Halkin (New York: Harper, 2017), 7. Future citations in text. On occasion I have made modifications to the published translation.

11. Walt Whitman, "Mannahatta," https://www.poets.org/poetsorg/poem/mannahatta; accessed May 14, 2018.

12. This translation is taken from *Genesis Rabbah: The Judaic Commentary to the Book of Genesis: A New American Translation*, vol. III, trans. Jacob Neusner (Atlanta: Scholars Press, 1985).

13. This appears on page 329 of the Hebrew edition; the epigraphs were not included in the English translation.

14. Nava Semel, *E-srael* (Tel Aviv: Yediot Aharonot, 2005), 40. English taken from *Isra Isle*, trans. Jessica Cohen (Simsbury, CT: Mandel Vilar Press, 2016), 54. Future citations in text.

15. There are also other connections unrelated to geography: names that have special significance, which occur in various combinations attached to different characters in each section; timeline, in that the events of the first and last section are both set in September 2001 and involve the September 11 attacks in their plots; genetics and "blood," in that each section focuses on characters who have familial ties to Noah, to the land, or, it is implied, to characters from other sections.

16. Neil Leach, "9/11," *Diacritics* 33, nos. 3/4 (Autumn-Winter 2003): 84.

17. Rovner, "Alternate History," 141.

18. Ibid., 139.

19. This section can be found on page 202 of the English edition, up to the italicized portion. The italicized text is my translation of an extra line included in the Hebrew edition, found on page 136.

PART THREE

BETWEEN THE LINES: RETHINKING GENRES

From Here to Elsewhere and Back in Israeli-Hebrew Children's Literature

SHAI GINSBURG

Fantasy occupies an uneasy place in Hebrew children's literature.[1] Conceived as an instrument of nationalist pedagogy, Hebrew children's literature struggled to reconcile the dictate to serve the acquisition of a national territory with the acclaim of make-believe as central to happy childhood. On the face of it, make-believe marks a disengagement from the political, social, and economic forces that inform the *hic et nunc*. Imaginary spaces in European and American children's literature are accordingly often read as "escapes from 'real,'" experience.[2] However, in what follows I suggest that in Israeli Hebrew children's literature, transitions between real and imaginary spaces are employed to reflect on the politics of the Israeli here and now and to engage with Israeli rhetoric of territory and history.[3]

1

The best-known imaginary space in Israeli Hebrew children's literature is arguably Hasamba's electric cave. The forty-four books of Yigal Mossinsohn's series *Hasamba* (an acronym of *An Absolutely Absolute Secret Group*), which appeared between 1950 and 1994, achieved great popularity and became a staple of Israeli culture to such an extent that their protagonist, Yaron Zehavi, has become the best-recognized depiction of the Israeli mythical new Jew.[4] The first volume of the series, *"Hasamba" o: chavurat sod muchlat behechlet* (*Hasamba, or: The Absolutely Absolute Secret Group-*),[5] was serialized in the children's magazine *Mishmar liyeladim* starting June 23, 1949, just as the Israeli "War of Independence" (1947–49) was brought to an end. It relates the exploits of a group of young adults from Tel Aviv who band together to aid the pre-State Jewish militias in their struggle against British mandatory authorities, then in rule of Palestine.

Hasamba's first installment was published against the backdrop of daily reports in the Israeli press on the Lausanne Conference and on the ongoing negotiations between Israel and Syria on a ceasefire agreement.[6] The latter officially concluded the 1948 War. Three main issues emerged out of the war: the fate of Palestinian refugees, Israel's territorial gains, and the status of Jerusalem. The conference, however, failed to settle any of these issues and the parties disbanded without any agreement. Both the (successful) negotiations with Israel's Arab neighbors on a (temporary) cease fire and the (failed) attempts at Lausanne to resolve (permanently) the Israeli-Arab conflict raised the questions that continue to haunt Israeli politics to the present: What are the geographical, historical, and demographic boundaries of the state? Are these boundaries permanent or temporary? Do they mark an irreparable rift or could the ruptures of conflict and war be mended? *Hasamba* was conceived, then, during a summer of great uncertainty about the territorial, temporal, and demographic scope of the State of Israel.

Mossinsohn's book reflects these uncertainties.[7] The latter are embodied, for instance, by the antagonists of choice in the different books of the series. Whereas in subsequent volumes an ever-larger gallery of Arabs and Palestinians play the role of Hasamba's adversaries, the first two volumes of the series assign the role to British Mandatory security forces.[8] The immediate past of conflict and war is thus portrayed as between native Jews and foreign British colonial/imperial authorities rather than between the local residents and political entities of the region, who are not mentioned even once. One could trace this particular rendition of the 1948 War to the publication platform of the stories: *Mishmar liyeladim* was published by the daily newspaper *'Al ha-Mishmar*, the organ of the Zionist Marxist *Mapam*. The children's magazine consistently pointed at Western imperialism as the true threat to the new state and played down the significance of hostilities between Jews and Arabs.[9] Hasamba, then, gives expression to *Mapam*'s vision of past, present, and future.

The electric cave, a cave where the Hasamba crew gathers and stores guns and which came to epitomize the series as a whole, similarly embodies this vision. Rather than a refuge and a break from "reality," a realm of children's sovereignty that is constructed over and against adults' sovereignty—as imaginary spaces are commonly conceived in European and American children's literature—the cave is but an extension of reality. It is the parents' bequest to their children: the parents, all members of a Jewish militia fighting the British mandatory forces, who use the cave for their clandestine activities, pass it on to their children as a reward for willingly joining the struggle. The children then turn the cave into a base from which they emerge as a "Special Operation Team" to secure Israeli territory and history and, in the process, reaffirm Israeli sovereignty. As Yael Darr suggests, the series as a whole and, I would add, the electric cave in particular, serves as a site of mobilization of children and their recruitment to the Israeli security forces as worthy heirs to their parents.[10] It can do so, however, only at the expense of the imaginary, which becomes but a thinly veiled rendition of the real.

2

In 1957, Avraham Shlonsky published *Ani veTali o, sefer me'erets halamah* (*Me and Tali, or Book of the Land of Why*), his second children's book, and his first since the establishment of the state.[11] The book features a series of humorous dialogues between the adult poet and a young child of four or five, Tali. When Tali first asks the poet to write her a poem, he responds with the following:

סֶלַע פֶּרֶא. הַר קֵרֵחַ.
כּוֹן, הַכּוֹנָה, חַלָּמִישׁ!
בְּמַקֶּבֶת וּבְמַקְדֵּחַ
נְפוֹצֵץ סְלָעִים לַכְּבִישׁ.[12]

Wild rock, bald mountain.
Get ready, flint!
With sledgehammer and with drill
We will blow up rocks for a road.

Shlonsky opens with what could be read easily as stereotypical Labor poetry, or a sly reference to his poem "'Amal" ("Toil").[13] Tali, however, rejects this poem outright:

"הֵן הַשִּׁיר—אָמְרָה לִי—שַׁטְיָא
כְּבָר נִדְפַּס בַּכְּרֶסְטוֹמַטְיָה
[. . .]
שֵׁב וּכְתוֹב לִי שִׁיר חָדָשׁ:
רְצִינִי, אַךְ מְקֻשְׁקָשׁ.[14]

Fool—she told me—the poem
Was already printed in a schoolbook
. . .
Sit down and write me a new poem:
Serious, but scribbled.

Tali's response reveals the poem to be but a parody of what is commonly deemed to be proper for children.[15] Instead of such stereotypical, pedagogic poetry, she asks for something else, both serious and scribbled. Scholars commonly underscore the "scribbled" (or nonserious) aspect of Shlonsky's poetry for children, but neglect to explore its seriousness. The latter lies, I shall suggest, precisely in the turn between the two poetics Tali calls on the poet to effect.

The said turn from serious, pedagogic poetry to poetry that is, paradoxically, both serious and nonserious is a turn from assertion to disputation. It is one from unquestioning adherence to ideological edicts as marked by Labor poetry to a carnivalesque doubt and challenge to authority (including the poetic authority of the poet himself). The regulating principle of the book is, accordingly, the query *why*:

טַלִי אוֹהֶבֶת לָדַעַת הַכֹּל,
טַלִי אוֹהֶבֶת לִשְׁאוֹל וְלִשְׁאוֹל
[. . .]
טַלִי שׁוֹאֶלֶת בְּלִי הֶרֶף: אָז לָמָה?
אָז לָמָה זֶה הֵנָּה?
וְלָמָה זֶה שָׁמָּה?
וְלָמָה זֶה כָּכָה?
וְלָמָה זֶה כָּךְ?
אֲנַחְנוּ בְּלָמָה שֶׁל טַלִי נִפְתַּח.[16]

Tali loves to know everything
Tali loves to ask and ask
. . .
Tali asks why? all the time:
So why is it here?
And why is it there?
And why is it so?
And why is it thus?
We shall begin with Tali's why.

Poems in the book are thus spawned out of such Whys: why is the *ḥamsin* (dry, hot, sandy wind) called *ḥamsin*? Why does the pond laugh? Why are fish called fish? Why do fish not talk? Why does the crane stand on one leg? And so on. The logic that drives the poems of *Me and Tali* is one of language, as the poet tries to decipher the meaning of words.

In his writing, Shlonsky advocated a modernist aesthetics that employs complex lexical and rhythmic patterns and sophisticated wordplays.[17] On the face of it, Shlonsky's immersion in language—in puns, witticism, quips, and the like—appears to have little to do with the political and social reality of the day and could be easily construed as an escapist attempt designed to avoid these. Indeed, Shlonsky's modernist poetics in general and his children's poetry in particular are commonly read as a protest against the politicization of poetry, privileging the aesthetic qualities of poems over ideology. Yet, in the "Land of Why," space of doubt and questioning, can we not see a challenge to official language?

Shlonsky published *Me and Tali* at a moment in history in which the notion of Israeli territory and history was explicitly tested. In late October 1956, Israel joined forces with France and the United Kingdom in a military campaign, whose aims were to topple the Egyptian president Gamal Abdel Nasser, destroy the Egyptian army, and seize control of the Suez Canal. Within days, the Israeli military took over the Sinai Peninsula. In elevated, hyperbolic rhetoric, Ben-Gurion staked Israel's claim to the new territories by alluding to Exodus and the conquest of Canaan: "Once more will Eilat be the chief southern Hebrew port . . . and Yotvat . . . part of the Third Kingdom of Israel."[18] Still, under international pressure led jointly by the United States and the USSR, Israel was forced to withdraw from all occupied areas.

Shlonsky's *Me and Tali* appears to react to grandiloquence such as Ben-Gurion's. The theme of space and territory is most explicitly broached in one of the poems concluding this book:

הַרְבֵּה אֲרָצוֹת בָּעוֹלָם שֶׁגָּדוֹל הוּא, –
הָעוֹלָם הַגָּדוֹל שֶׁל הַטַּף הַקָּטָן,
אֶל כָּל מֶרְחַקָּיו לְהַגִּיעַ יָכֹלְנוּ
רַק שְׁנַיִם מֵאֶלֶף: תִּינוֹק וּפַיְטָן.
רַק שְׁנַיִם מֵאֶלֶף: כָּמוֹנִי וְטָלִי
וְכָל חַבְרֶיהָ בְּגַן וְגָנוֹן.
שָׁאַלְתִּי: "אֵיךְ עַפְנוּ לְשָׁם?"–וְעָנְתָה לִי:
"הִמְרֵאנוּ לְשָׁם עַל כַּנְפֵי-הַדִּמְיוֹן".
כֵּן, יֵשׁ לְאָדָם מִין כְּנָפַיִם כָּאֵלֶּה,
צָרִיךְ רַק לָדַעַת אֵיפֹה לְחַפֵּשׂ:
הַתְחִילוּ לָשִׁיר—וְתִרְאוּ אֶת הַפֶּלֶא!
הַצְהִילוּ מִשְׂחָק—וְיוֹפִיעַ הַנֵּס![19]

> Many lands are in the world, for it is wide,—
> The wide world of young kids,
> We could reach its furthest distances
> Only two of a thousand: an infant and a poet.
> Only two of a thousand: such as Tali and myself
> And all of her friends in nurseries and day cares.
> I asked: "how did we get there?"—and she answered:
> "We took off and flew on the wings of imagination."
> Yes, humans have such wings,
> One has only to know where to look:
> Start singing—and you'll see the wonder.
> Start playing—and a marvel will come into view.

In these verses, it appears as if the poet sets out to undo the premier's rhetoric. In effect, Shlonsky sketches a poetic vision to counter Ben-Gurion's militaristic, imperialist vision. Over and against army columns, tanks, and fighter aircraft, which cut across enemy territory, Shlonsky poses the imagination, which traverses far greater distances, real and unreal alike. And over and against generals, politicians, and their overwrought rhetoric he calls into action children and childlike adults in the discovery and recovery of the treasures and joys of language. In the exchange between the adult/poet and the child, the *why* becomes a new credo, which seeks to redefine not only rhetoric, but one's relationship to territory and to history as well. In that, Shlonsky imagines (in the most positive sense of the word) new politics whose prime agent, as he declares time and again, are children.

3

Devorah Omer's 1970 children's novel *Kol mah shehayah (ulai), vekol mah shekarah (kim'at) leKarashindo veli* (*Everything That Happened [Maybe and Almost] to Karashindo and Me*)[20] marks a departure from the realistic narratives immersed in contemporary everyday life in Israel and the historical, often heroic fiction that gained her both critical acclaim and commercial success.[21] Its protagonist, the seven-year-old Hannah'le, relates her adventures with Karashindo the Dwarf as they journey together in a barrel-made spaceship from her kibbutz to the Dream Star, Spandoza-Mardimon. As we shall see, Omer's knowing turn to fantasy is a deliberate reaction to the anxieties of the here and now.

From its very beginning, *Everything That Happened* offers a harsh censure of the kibbutz. The daydreamer Hannah'le cannot find her place within a close-knit community preoccupied with practicality and self-abnegation. Her imagined journey to her Dream Star expresses her protestation against the mores of the kibbutz and allows her to indulge in shunned pleasures such as daydreaming. Whereas critical portrayals of the kibbutz were not unusual in adult Hebrew fiction of the time it was, in fact, extraordinary in children's literature.[22] Yet, Omer's critical engagement with Israeli reality does not stop with the kibbutz.

Hannah'le's tale is generated by anxieties brought about not only by her immediate community, but also by the circumstances that informed life in Israel of the time at large. Indeed, the story quite explicitly refers to these circumstances, of a lingering war. The first day of the tale sees Hannah'le's father, a soldier, returning to military duty. To comfort Hannah'le and reassure her, her dad leaves her with Karashindo the Dwarf who, in an endeavor to divert her attention from her father's absence, proposes the space journey. *Everything That Happened* does not minimize or displace the strains and stresses that inform the Israeli Jewish experience of the time. On the contrary, the story acknowledges explicitly the toll imposed by military duty and death on everyday life. Just as importantly, it portrays the effects of the emotional restraint in the face of pain and loss that is core to the communal ethos in the story. The journey to Spandoza-Mardimon is, then, not only a journey away from war and death, but also a reaction to the stoicism demanded by the community during war.

Omer published *Everything That Happened* at the apex of the War of Attrition between Israel on the one side, and Egypt, Jordan, Syria, and Palestinian militias, as well as Soviet forces, on the other side. Erupting in the immediate aftermath of the 1967 War and lasting for more than three years, daily clashes along the borders resulted in thousands of civilian and military casualties. While much of the Israeli Jewish public supported the security measures taken by the government, the protracted bloodshed took its toll, and pessimism grew over the prospects for peace. The target of much protest was the adoration of death in battle, a figure central to the Israeli ethos (to the present) as epitomized, for instance, in Shmuel "Gorodish" Gonen's address to his brigade in the summer of 1967.[23] In his address, Gonen transubstantiated the gore of battle and death into a vision of national glory and eternity; one of his phrases in particular, "We looked straight at death, and death lowered its eyes," became a well-known motto. As it became clear that the conclusion of the brief war of the summer of 1967 marked merely the launch of another, protracted war, critics began, however, to question both the portrayal of death and the logic used to justify it.

Omer's *Everything That Happened* is "a child of its time" and takes part in such questioning. Hanna'le's journey serves, quite explicitly to challenge the Israeli fixation with death. It is a figure of averting the gaze elsewhere. Omer turns her eyes to the stars in an endeavor to assert the significance of the here and now. In her historical fiction, Omer portrays characters who willingly sacrifice their well-being and even life for nationalist ideals. *Everything That Happened*, on the contrary, seeks to elude the demands of these ideals and to assert alternative values, of the individual, his or her dreams and pleasures.[24]

Hannah'le makes it to Spandoza-Mardimon and spends there a couple of happy days. Yet, one night she dreams of her family back in the kibbutz:

> I saw the room at Kibbutz Ma'ayan and there were Dad and Mom. What's that? Is Dad on leave again? Or maybe there's no more war and no soldier would be needed ever again? . . . They seemed to me completely happy and entirely not sad that I had disappeared and I am no more for them. I didn't feel they were missing me. They looked like, as if they do not feel my absence.[25]

Wishing to be with her family, she finds herself immediately in her old bed:

> By the light of the moon that peeped though the window I saw that I was dressed in my old pajamas . . . the one with

a stain from a chocolate I once ate in bed and did not come off. . . . So what? Now, that I know that there is such a thing as a Dream-Star, I can go back every time. I could dream, I could tell myself. Always. Everybody says I dream too much. Maybe. But I do like to dream and to make up stories for myself.[26]

The turn to fantasy allows Hannah'le to look back home and examine her relationship toward it. Yet, in the end, what she sees is not comforting. Whereas Keren-Yaar reads Omer's fiction as bringing together the personal and the collective realms and reconciling between individual desires and state ideology, I would suggest that *Everything That Happened* pits the two against each other and concludes that reconciliation is indeed possible yet uneasy and unsatisfying. The fantasy of an imaginary space that would transform the way Hannah'le is perceived and cared for in the here and now is superseded by a vision of the here and now without her (in other words, of her own death; she notes, "I am no more for them"). Whereas at first the turn to fantasy provides Hannah'le with a sense of liberation and freedom, she quickly realizes she cannot stay there and retain her grip over life in the here and now. And whereas Omer ends her fantasy narrative on a conciliatory tone, the strains and anxieties that have generated the tale in the first place do not disappear.[27] Hannah'le sets out on the journey to Spandoza-Mardimon as a mode of intervention in a reality she finds unbearable, yet the turn to fantasy fails to effect a change and the story concludes with no hope for a real change. For Hannah'le, real political agency is revealed to be imaginary. The only agency available to her is that of the teller of fantastical tales.

4

No discussion such as this can pass over Nurit Zarchi's poetry and prose for children, arguably the principal rendition of fantasy in Israeli Hebrew children's literature. Whereas her fantastical narratives seem altogether removed from the Israeli circumstances, she nevertheless repeatedly insists that her works in general and those for children in particular are political through and through.[28] Consider, for instance, her 1992 *Amori Asig Atusa*.[29] This short story reverses the problem posed by the other texts in this chapter: rather than a turn from the realm of reality to the realm of fantasy, the protagonist has to find her way from the realm of fantasy to the realm of reality.³⁰ Concluding the course of her studies at a school for young witches, Amori faces the headmaster, who examines her to determine whether she is ready to go out to the real world. To pass the exam, he insists, she has to produce "something strong, something fast, something barreled, something marketable."³¹ That is, she has to reproduce the logics of reality and yield to its physical, military and economic violence and, in effect, reinforce it.³² Yet, hard as she tries, she fails: she first produces two roses, then glass balls, seashells and finally, cockroaches. The abhorred headmaster determines she would never go out to the realm of reality and expels her from school. What commentary, then, does *Amori* offer on the Israeli rhetoric of territory and history of the time?

Zarchi published her book during the final stages of the First Intifada, the Palestinian revolt against the Israeli rule in the West Bank and the Gaza Strip between December 1987 and September 1993. In part, the revolt was instigated by worsening economic conditions in the Territories, the result of repressive policies and exploitation of Palestinian resources. Israeli politicians and generals repeatedly gave expression to their ruthless and self-serving treatment of Palestinians. One example that was circulated widely and informed the Israeli public discourse on the Territories and the Occupation should suffice here. In a meeting of the Knesset Foreign Affairs and Defense Committee in April 1983, Rafael Eitan, concluding his command as the IDF chief of staff, opined that the response to Palestinian stone throwing should be the establishment of new settlements; Palestinians would then "run in circles like cockroaches in a bottle."³³ Eitan's turn of phrase quickly became a widely used figure in popular portrayal of Palestinians, and is still used today.

Amori seems to address, then, the logic that welds together ruthless militarism and consumerism and that posits cockroaches (or Palestinians, for that matter) as its abject, negligible subjects-victims. Initially repulsed by the two roaches, Amori tries to get rid of them, but they insist that she is responsible for them. They further demand that she compliment and, in fact, love them. Finally, Amori yields and shouts:

> "You are the most wonderful, pleasant cockroaches in the world."
> There was a moment of silence . . . right before Amori's eyes they . . . turned into two wonderful white horses . . . a carriage appeared [and the two horses, S.G.] harnessed themselves to it. . . .

The two horses each stomped . . . , neighed, and launched on their way.
"Fly Amori Asig Atusa, now fly into the world. Onward, fly on something wonderful, something exciting, something gallopable, something lovable."³⁴

Quite clearly, Zarchi seeks to challenge the Israeli discourse of cockroaches and transform it. Initially the two cockroaches appear like a pest that—notwithstanding Amori's pleas—will not go away. Yet, once Amori acknowledges her responsibility not only to take care of them but to love them, they transform and, in the process, transform the relationship between the realm of fantasy and the realm of reality. Not only do they allow Amori to move to the real world, but they also provide her with a new perspective of what is possible in that world, supplanting the images of military and economic violence with excitement, wonder, and love. In this, Zarchi's story appears to put forward a counterimage to Omer's utter powerlessness of fantasy and of the child-agent in the face of reality. *Amori Asig Atusa* suggests, in contradistinction, that fantasy, inasmuch as it allows one to imagine alternative logics to the ones that inform reality, holds the promise to transform reality, a promise pinned on the child-witch.

5

In 2007, Yanetz Levi published the first of what would become an international success, *Harpatka'ot Dod Ariyeh* (*The Adventures of Uncle Arieh*).³⁵ The six books of the series have been critically acclaimed and commercially successful not only in Israel, but—unlike the other texts under discussion—internationally as well. Books of the series have thus far been translated into Chinese, Korean, Japanese, Czech, Hungarian, Macedonian, Arabic, and English (in India but not in the United States, the United Kingdom, or Australia) as *Uncle Leo's Adventures*.³⁶ The first book in the series, *Uncle Arieh's Adventures in the Romanian Steppes*, opens thus:

> You would probably not believe a word I say. You'd say I'm a liar. You might even laugh at me. But I swear that everything I'm about to tell you really happened. Nothing is a lie. I didn't make up anything. And if I am lying, then . . . then . . . may

my ears fall off, 'cause everything I'm about to tell you I heard with my very own ears from my uncle, Uncle Arieh.

Uncle Arieh visits us every Wednesday. Uncle Arieh is not an ordinary uncle. My dad once said: "Uncle Arieh is not an uncle you can find in any shop. He is a 'special order' uncle."

My big brother, on the other hand, doesn't believe a single word of Uncle Arieh. It's all just baloney, he always says. . . . But what does my brother know? He thinks stories are only for little kids and that he's no longer a kid.[37]

Uncle Arieh reveals the changes in language and narrative norms in Hebrew children's literature from the 1950s to the present. Whereas Shlonsky's poems are driven by his exploration of language and Omer's plot by Hannah'le's emotional struggles, Levi's narrative is action- and object-driven. Each chapter in the book begins and ends in the middle-class apartment of the child narrator and his family. Mundane strife of family life prompts Uncle Arieh to spin his stories; they are designed to bolster the child narrator's confidence and provide him with ammunition in his ongoing squabbles with his brother, mother, and father. They elaborate the everyday experiences into farcical tales.

One example must suffice here: an argument over whether the child narrator should get a haircut or not leads to a story about Uncle Arieh's time in the circus, where he worked as a human cannonball. When one day, by mistake, he is shot to a far greater distance than intended, the only four hairs on his head get entangled in a tree and save his life. The child appeals to his parents, pointing at the story, but to no avail, and he is forced to cut his hair with the argument that he does not work in a circus.

One can easily trace Uncle Arieh's literary ancestors to well-known uncles and aunts in Israeli Hebrew children's literature who disrupt the social order and challenge its norms. Leah Goldberg's Nobody's Aunt in *Miracles and Wonders* and Uncle Simcha in Ayin Hillel's eponymic rhymed stories, as well as Shlonsky's narrator in *Me and Tali* immediately come to mind.[38] Yet, Levi's primary sources of inspiration, as the blurb on the back cover of the book states, are two primary texts of "World Literature," which have become staples of Israeli Hebrew children's literature (as they have also in other languages): Jonathan Swift's 1726 *Gulliver's Travels* and, particularly, Rudolf Erich Raspe's 1785 *Surprising Adventures of Baron Munchausen* (as well as Gottfried August Bürger's 1786 German rendition of Raspe's text).[39] One can thus read Levi's *Adventures of Uncle Arieh* as a scion of the tradition that parodies serious travel literature.

Squarely within the framework of parodic travel literature, Levi charts a fanciful geography in which he traces Uncle Arieh's humorous and preposterous travels. The titles of his books make the cartographic urge explicit: The Romanian Steppes, Siberian Jungle, Swiss Desert, West Pole, Sahara Forests, and Tibetan Ocean. Levi's books thus open up vistas of imaginary spaces for their readers and offer them a parody of the *Wanderlust* of the contemporary Israeli middle class (or rather, as the international success of Levi's books evinces, of a certain global middle class), and of its obsession with trips abroad. He guides his readers into strange places made up of absurd conflations of disparate travel tropes and incongruous welding of geographic features and names—like the Swiss Desert or the Sahara Forests—and supplants the boring mandatory sightseeing tours from one exhibit of treasured "cultural heritage" to the next with outlandish objects and exciting adventures. Notwithstanding, however, their exotic locations, little do the stories explore the fantastical geography in which they are set. They focus almost exclusively on action, of which the most important is the telling of stories itself. *Uncle Arieh* does not merely take pleasure in the very act of telling whimsical tales and in fantastical adventures but privileges these as sufficient in and of themselves. Yet, both *Gulliver* and *Munchausen* also poke fun at social and political mores of their time and satirize them.[40] Levi, in contradistinction, appears to do his utmost to avoid any allusion to the Israeli reality of the present.

The first volume of *The Adventures of Uncle Arieh* appeared when Israel was still reeling from the Second, "Al Aksa," Palestinian Intifada (September 2000–February 2005), the Disengagement Plan (summer 2005), and Operation Summer Rains (June-November 2006). The difficulties the Israeli military had in asserting its control over a hostile Palestinian population and in defending Jewish settlers led the Israeli prime minister, Ariel Sharon, to propose in 2003 a unilateral Israeli withdrawal from the Gaza Strip and the removal of the block of Jewish settlement there, known as Gush Katif, as well as of isolated settlements in Samaria (the northern West Bank) region. The implementation of the Disengagement Plan was concluded in September 2005 after a heated public debate and mass public protest. In his address to the joint U.S. Congress shortly afterward, then-Israeli prime minister Ehud Olmert elaborated on the rationale for the plan. He sought to differentiate the realm of dreams from the realm of pragmatism, a distinction between "our forefathers" and "us," between thousand years of history and the present moment, between the greater promised land and part of it, between war and peace. In the name of the latter, Olmert submitted, Israel was willing to compromise the biblical promise and to relinquish territory saturated with historical and transcendental significance.[41]

On the face of it, Levi seems to endeavor to depoliticize his stories and to muffle their critical potential. The absurdity of the stories allows the middle-class family to contain and offset whatever critical energy they might have. Indeed, in their portrayal of family squabbles—trivial and nonthreatening as they are—*Uncle Arieh* sees no urgent need for critique. Consequently, then, the stories matter little and have little impact over the middle-class life that brackets them:

> Over the dinner table, I asked my brother, Yinon: "Do you know Uncle Arieh really got stuck on a cloud once?"
> "Oh, what kind of nonsense does he tell you? You can't get stuck on a cloud," said my brother. . . .
> "Why do you have to believe everything Uncle Arieh tells you?" he asked.
> "Why shouldn't we believe Uncle Arieh?" asked mom. "Uncle Arieh told me lots of wonderful stories when I was little. I wish I had the time to sit and listen to all his stories these days."
> "Yes, but these are just stories," said Yinon.
> "So what?" said mom.[42]

Simultaneously, however, the very move to imagine space and time relieved of any demand, territory and history divested of transcendental significance, Levi recapitulates the terms of Olmert's address and mounts a protest (albeit muted) against the deadliness of such significance.

As these characters ponder the relationship between the realm of fantasy and the realm of reality, Levi's story reflects the yearning for an unburdened time, unburdened space, unburdened action.[43]

In this chapter, I sought to read texts that explore the turn to and from imaginary spaces, suggesting that such turns are used to reflect on the

Israeli *hic and nunc*. Scholars have commonly argued that from the 1960s on, Israeli Hebrew children's literature increasingly disengaged itself from politics, seeking to move away from the demand to represent and promote collective national tasks.[44] Such contention, however, conflates all too simplistically politics, partisanship, and conservative attitudes, suggesting that whereas the commitment to collective endeavors and ideals is political, the turn to personal themes, individual concerns and so-called universal values is not. It likewise perceives the turn from the public sphere to the domestic sphere of family and home as the relinquishing of political engagement.[45] Indeed, over the years, political parties lost their grip over Israeli Hebrew children's literature, which allowed it to divert from dictates of politicians and ideologues. Yet, by and large, as John Traugott comments vis-à-vis *Gulliver's Travels*, that literature features "a figurative relation between child play and the terrifying games of politics."[46] Even as it increasingly turns to fantasy, a genre commonly read as an attempt to chart an escape from the *here and now*, its exploration of imaginary spaces remains committed to comment on Israeli political discourse. As Olmert's speech noted above evinces, negotiating the relationship between the realm of reality and the realm of fantasy is anything but apolitical. Ultimately, I would suggest, literature, and children's literature included, is always topical and, as such, political, even if its topicality is often overlooked in the search for values that transcend the here and now.

Notes

1. Indeed, until the late 1990s, fantasy had been marginal to Hebrew children's literature as well as to canonical literature in general; on fantasy in Hebrew literature, see the essays collected in Danielle Gurevitch, Elana Gomel, and Rani Graff, eds., *With Both Feet on the Clouds: Fantasy in Israeli Literature* (Brighton, MA: Academic Studies Press, 2013).

2. See, among others, Susan E. Honeyman, "Childhood Bound: In Gardens, Maps, and Pictures," *Mosaic: A Journal for the Interdisciplinary Study of Literature* 34, no. 2 (June 2001): 117. See also Jon C. Stott and Christine Doyle Francis, "'Home' and 'Not Home' in Children's Stories: Getting There—and Being Worth It," *Children's Literature in Education* 24, no. 3 (1993): 223–33; and Peter Hunt, "Landscapes and Journeys, Metaphors and Maps: The Distinctive Feature of English Fantasy," *Children's Literature Association Quarterly* 12, no. 1 (1987): 11–14.

3. See, for instance, Menahem Regev, *Bedarkhei hasifrut liyeladim* (Tel Aviv: Hakibbutz Hameuchad, Sirfriyat Po'alim, 1985), 77; and Charles Sarland,

"The Impossibility of Innocence: Ideology, Politics, and Children's Literature," in *Understanding Children's Literature: Key Essays from the International Companion Encyclopedia of Children's Literature*, ed. Peter Hunt (London: Routledge, 1999), 39–55.

4. In 2003, it was estimated that the series sold more than one million copies (Yehuda Koren, "Hari poter 'adayin lo 'avar et hata.na.kh," *Ynet*, March 26, 2003; https://www.ynet.co.il/articles/0,7340,L-2670518,00.html; retrieved Aug. 7, 2018. For a review of the series and for the plots of the different volumes, see Eli Eshed, *miTarzan ve'ad Zbeng: hasipur shel hasifrut hapopularit ha'ivrit* (Tel Aviv: Bavel, 2002), 84–103.

5. Yigal Mossinsohn, *"Hasamba" o: chavurat sod muchlat behechlet* (Tel Aviv: N. Twersky, 1950).

6. The literature on the Israeli-Arab conflict is extensive. I limit my references here to two general surveys, Benny Morris, *Righteous Victims: A History of the Zionist-Arab Conflict, 1881–2001* (New York: Knopf, 2001) and Ahron Bregman, *Israel's Wars: A History Since 1947* (Milton Park: Routledge, 2016), and to analysis of political and public debates offered by Gad Barzilai, *Wars, Internal Conflicts, and Political Order: A Jewish Democracy in the Middle East* (Albany: State University of New York Press, 1996).

7. Zohar Shavit provides a detailed analysis of the norms in the *Hasamba* series and underscores the conservative character of the text, as affirming accepted values. See Shavit, *Ma'aseh yaldut: mavo lepo'etika shel sifrut yeladim* (Tel Aviv: 'Am 'Oved, 1996), ch. 10.

8. See also Eitan Bar-Yosef, "Bonding with the British: Colonial Nostalgia and the Idealization of Mandatory Palestine in Israeli Literature and Culture after 1967," *Jewish Social Studies* 22, no. 3 (2017): 1–37, on the perception of the British Mandate and on "colonial nostalgia" in Israeli culture, and on the first two volumes of *Hasamba* in this context, pp. 5–7.

9. On *Mishmar liyeladim* during the late 1940s and 1950s, see Rima Shikhmanter, *Chaver miniyar: 'itonut yeladim yisre'elit be'asor harishon lamedinah* (Jerusalem: Yad Izhak Ben-Zvi, 2014).

10. Yael Darr, "Nation Building and War Narratives for Children: War and Militarism in Hebrew 1940s and 1950s Children's Literature," *Paedagogica Historica* 48, no. 4 (2012): 604.

11. Avraham Shlonsky, *Ani veTali, o sefer me'erets halamah* (Merhavya: Sifriyat Poalim, 1957).

12. Ibid., 20. Here and throughout, all translations from the Hebrew are mine. Given the untranslatability of Shlonsky's puns, I provide here the original alongside my literal translation.

13. On Hebrew labor poetry see Hanan Hever, "Hashir beshirat 'ha'avodah' ha'erets yisre'elit," *Mechkarei Yerushalayim besifrut 'ivrit* 20 (2006): 53–86.

14. Shlonsky, *Ani veTali*, 21.

15. See also Yael Darr, *Kanon bekhamah kolot: sifrut hayeladim shel tnu'at hapo'alim 1930-1950* (Jerusalem: Yad Izhak Ben-Zvi, 2013a), 119-22.

16. Shlonsky *Ani veTali*, 24-25.

17. Shlonsky gave expression to his views on literature for children and its poetics in a series of manifestos collected in *Yalkut eshel: tsror ma'amarim vede'ot* (Merhavya: Sifriyat Po'alim, 1960), 154-63. On Shlonsky's modernist poetics in his writing for children and the way it informs *Me and Tali* see, among others, Darr, *Kanon bekhamah kolot*, 69-73, 117-34; Shlomo Har'el, *Kol me'emek, kol mehar: panim, tachanot umahalakhim, basifrut ha'ivrit liyeladim* (Kefar Sava: Merkaz Yemima, 1993), ch. 2; Lea Hovav, *Bitslil vatsev'a: 'iyun vecheker besifrut liyeladim* (Jerusalem: Akademon, 1997), 57-72; Dana Keren-Yaar, *Sofrot kotvot liyeladim: kri'ah post-kolonyalit ufeministit besifrut yeladim 'ivrit* (Tel Aviv: Resling, 2007), 89-92; Menahem Regev, "'Harei ted'u ki echad mikem ani, ish ta'alulim vameri': 'al kama hebetim besifrei hayeladim shel Avraham Shlonsky," *Moznayim* 8 (2000): 16-19; Yehezkel Tzoref, "Shirat hayeladim shel Avraham Shlonsky," *Ma'agalei kri'ah* 1 (1977): 29-50.

18. Yisrael Paz and Amnon Lev, "Ben-Guryon: Yotvat tehe chelek Yisra'el," *Davar*, Nov. 7, 1956.

19. Shlonsky, *Ani veTali*, 82.

20. Devorah Omer, *Kol mah shehayah (ulai) vekhol mah shekarah (kim'at) leKarashindo veli* (Tel Aviv: Yossef Sreberk, 1970).

21. Dana Keren-Yaar unpacks the ideological patterns of both of these genres in Omer's writing (2007, 147-77).

22. Keren-Yaar traces criticism of the kibbutz in Omer's fiction to the early 1980s (2007, 160) but, in fact, it appears already in the late 1960s.

23. On the adoration of death in Israeli literature and criticism, see Shai Ginsburg, *Rhetoric and Nation: The Formation of Hebrew National Culture, 1880-1990* (Syracuse: Syracuse University Press, 2014), 240-51.

24. Rima Shikhmanter contends that even Omer's historical fiction manifests criticism of the traditional nationalist narrative. See "Heroes of Our Time: The Historical-Political Context of Devorah Omer's Novels," *Israel Studies Review* 32, no. 2 (2017): 110-25. On the way Israeli children's literature of the time reflected the political and public discourse, see Na'ama Sheffi, "Shifting Boundaries: The 1967 War in Israeli Children's Magazines," *Journal of Israeli History* 28, no. 2 (2009): 137-54.

25. Omer, *Kol mah shehayah (ulai) vekhol mah shekarah (kim'at) leKarashindo veli*, 153.

26. Ibid., 158.

27. Keren-Yaar reads Omer's fiction as reaffirming collective national norms (2007, 157). Shikhmanter, on the contrary, contends that it "portray[s] a process by which protagonists, who come from the social periphery, become part of the social center" (2015, 180). *Everything that Happens* fits neither mold

and the critique it phrases appears much more radical than Omer is commonly allowed. It should be noted that this particular book has received little attention if any from scholars and critics, perhaps precisely because it does not fit the mold.

28. See, for instance, Nurit Zarchi, "'Ani lo ba'olam, ratsiti lihiyot ba'olam'— re'ayon 'im Nurit Zarchi," *Hasafranim*, Aug. 3, 2017. http://blog.nli.org.il/mussach_9_panim/; retrieved Oct. 14, 2018.

29. Nurit Zarchi *Amori Asig Atusa* (Tel Aviv: Hakibbutz Hameuchad, Sirfriyat Po'alim, 1992).

30. For the centrality of childhood, loss, and alienation in Zarchi's poetics, see Nurit Zarchi, *Machshavot meyutarot shel gveret: masot* (Tel Aviv: Hakibbutz Hameuchad, 1982). For the roles fantasy plays in Zarchi's fiction and poetry as well as her explicit feminist challenge to the patriarchal order see, among others, Elkad-Lehman 2006; Keren-Yaar, *Sofrot kotvot liyeladim*, 2007, 178–202; Noa Manheim, "The Grand High Witch of Dreams," in *With Both Feet on the Clouds: Fantasy in Israeli Literature*, ed. Danielle Gurevitch, Elana Gomel, and Rani Graff (Brighton, MA: Academic Studies Press, 2013), 163–69; Menahem Regev, "Hakesem hu be'eyn hamitbonen ('al metsi'ut vedimyon biyetsirot Nurit Zarchi)," *Sifrut yeladim vano'ar* 22, no. 4 (1996): 14–22.

31. Zarchi, *Amori Asig Atusa*, 5.

32. See also Ilana Elkad-Lehman, *Levadah hi oreget: kri'ah biyetsirat Nurit Zarchi* (Jerusalem: Karmel, 2006), 135–37; Keren-Yaar, *Sofrot kotvot liyeladim*, 197–198. Whereas scholars are quick to identify Zarchi's challenge to established orders and norms, they refrain from reading her texts topically, within the partisan discourse of the day, as I do in what follows.

33. See, for instance, Haggai Eshed, "Avira pru'ah beve'adat chuts uvitachon," *Davar*, April 13, 1983.

34. Zarchi, *Amori Asig Atusa*.

35. Yanetz Levi, *Harpatka'ot Dod Aryeh be'arvot Romaniyah* (Or Yehuda: Kinneret, Zmora Bitan, Dvir, 2007).

36. See, for instance, Maya Sela, "Harpatka'ot Dod Aryeh be'arvot Romaniyah nivchar lesefer hayeladim hameturgam hatov beyoter biDrom Kore'a le-2013," *Haaretz*, Feb. 12, 2014; Itamar Eichner, "Hadod Aryeh kavash et Sin," *Ynet*, May 17, 2016. https://www.yediot.co.il/articles/0,7340,L-4804432,00.html; retrieved June 9, 2018.

37. Levi, *Harpatka'ot Dod Aryeh be'arvot Romaniyah*, 9–10.

38. Leah Goldberg, *Nisim venifla'ot* (Merhavya: Sifriyat Po'alim, 1954); Ayin Hillel, *Dodi Simchah* (Tel Aviv, Hakibbutz Hameuchad, 1964). See, for instance, Adina Bar-El, "Dod Simchah me'Argentina vedodim nosafim," *Sifrut yeladim vano'ar* 130 (2009): 4–14.

39. Uri Hollander elaborates on Levi's indebtedness to Raspe's *Baron Munchausen*; see "Harpatka'ot Dod Aryeh be'arvot Romaniyah: tismonet minkh'hauzen," *Haaretz*, Dec. 17, 2008. For many decades, the bookshelf of

children's literature in Hebrew was predominated by translations from European languages. A full account of Israeli Hebrew children's literature would, then, address the reception of children's world literature and its relation to literature written in Hebrew. On Hebrew adaptations for children of Swift's *Gulliver Travels*, see Zohar Shavit, *Ma'aseh yaldut: mavo lepo'etika shel sifrut yeladim*, ch. 12. Like *Gulliver's Travels*, *The Adventures of Baron Munchausen* was translated into Hebrew and adapted for children very early on. The catalogue of the Hebrew National Library lists at least fifteen different translations/adaptations (both of the English and of the German text), with the first one dating from 1909.

40. See, for instance, Ian Higgins, *Swift's Politics: A Study in Disaffection* (Cambridge: Cambridge University Press, 1994); Ronald Knowles, *Gulliver's Travels: The Politics of Satire* (New York: Twayne, 1996); Sarah Tindal Kareem, "Fictions, Lies, and Baron Munchausen's Narrative," *Modern Philology* 109, no. 4 (2012): 483–509. On satire in Hebrew children's literature in general and in the work of Ephraim Sidon in particular, see Yaakova Sacerdoti, *Beyachad vekhol echad lechud: 'al nim'an mevugar venim'an yeled besiyach hasifrut liyeladim* (Tel Aviv: Hakibbutz Hameuchad, 2000), ch. 3.

41. On the ambivalence of space in the Jewish, and subsequently Israeli, tradition see Zali Gurevich and Gideon Aran, "The Land of Israel: Myth and Phenomenon," *Studies in Contemporary Jewry* 10 (1994): 195–210.

42. Yanetz Levi, *Harpatka'ot Dod Aryeh be'arvot Romaniyah* (Or Yehuda: Kinneret, Zmora Bitan, Dvir, 2007), 24–25.

43. In this, Levi goes against the tradition represented by Baron Munchausen, at least as Sarah Tindal Kareem reads the latter, as the personification of anxieties about the nature of the real and "the delusional conflation of fantasy and reality," 485.

44. See, for instance, Zohar Shavit, "Sifrut yeladim 'ivrit," *'Olam katan: ktav 'et lesifrut yeladim vano'ar* 1 (2000): 11–21, and "Hebrew Children's Literature," *Modern Hebrew Literature* (New Series) no. 5 (2009–10), 29–35; Shikhmanter, *Chaver miniyar*, and "Homogeneity vs. Heterogeneity in the Young Adult and Children's Literature of Devorah Omer," *Israel Studies* 20, no. 1 (2015): 180–94.

45. See, for instance, Yael Darr, *Kanon bekhamah kolot*, and "Heading Home: The Domestication of Israeli Children's literature in the 1960s as Reflected in Am Oved's Shafan ha-Sofer Series," *Journal of Israeli History* 32, no. 1 (2013): 127–39. Naomi B. Sokoloff critiques this school of thought along similar lines in "From *Shir hashirim* to *Sir hasirim*: Hebrew Children's Literature and Its Critics," *Prooftexts* 12, no. 3 (1992): 278.

46. John Traugott, "The Yahoo in the Doll's House: 'Gulliver's Travels' the Children's Classic," *The Yearbook of English Studies* 14 (1984): 128.

"The pigs were my best friends"
Animals and the Holocaust in Alona Frankel's Memoirs

NAOMI B. SOKOLOFF

In the early part of the twenty-first century, renowned Israeli children's author Alona Frankel turned to memoir writing. She published a trio of narratives aimed not at young audiences, but at grown-up readers. *Yaldah* (*Girl*, 2004) recounts Frankel's childhood years in Poland (1937–1949), where she survived the Holocaust in hiding. *Na'arah* (*Teen Years*, 2009) reports on her adolescent experience as a new immigrant in Israel. *Ishah: chayim uva'alei chayim* (*Woman: Life and Living Creatures*, 2012) presents aspects of adulthood.[1] This last volume, curiously, pays little attention to Frankel's career as an author; there is no mention that she wrote and illustrated dozens of books, some of which have been translated into multiple languages. Instead, as its title suggests, the final installment in her autobiographical series focuses to large extent on animals and animal welfare. That point turns out to be revelatory. It can alert the reader to ideas that first emerge from the opening pages of *Girl*. Observations about animals there prove to be central to the author's concerns throughout the trilogy.

These memoirs, which have also been called "biographical novels," constituted a new genre of creative expression for Frankel and they brought her new prominence.[2] The trilogy merits close examination, because it illustrates significant development in this author's work and also because it is indicative of wider trends in Hebrew culture—including a recent surge of autobiographical writing and renewed focus on the Holocaust. Since the late 1990s, memoirs by Israeli authors have proliferated. Previously, major writers gravitated more toward fiction, but in the last two decades Israeli autobiographical writing has flourished.[3] Frankel's work joins those developments even as it accords with the Zeitgeist in its attention to the Shoah. At the turn of the millennium, any number of aging survivors stepped forward to record their memories, and writers of the second and third generation were delving into family histories. Frankel contributes to another literary phenomenon as well. Her emphasis on living creatures puts into relief a longstanding, though little remarked subgenre of Hebrew writing that combines animal themes with responses to the Holocaust. Like quite a few other high-profile Israeli authors, Frankel approaches the topic of catastrophe by blurring boundaries between human and nonhuman characters. She tells of her time in hiding, living on a farm and occupying an ambiguous position between human and animal. By way of comparison, consider Yoram Kaniuk's *Adam ben kelev* (*Adam Resurrected,* 1969). That novel presents two Holocaust survivors in a psychiatric hospital who bark, growl, howl, and crawl on all fours, thus expressing the trauma they sustained during the war when they were treated like dogs. Think, too, of David Grossman's '*Ayen 'erekh ahavah* (*See Under: Love,* 1986). There, Polish Jewish author Bruno Schulz transforms into a fish, joins a school of salmon, and learns their language as he attempts to escape from Nazi pursuers. Nava Semel's *Tschok shel akhbarosh* (*And the Rat Laughed,* 2001) similarly obscures dividing lines between humans and nonhumans. It features a talking rodent along with a human who morphs into animal guise.[4] A precursor for all of these texts can be found, too, in S. Y. Agnon's *Temol shilshom* (*Only Yesterday*), a novel from before the establishment of the State of Israel. Agnon creates a canine narrator, Balak, who suffers discrimination, stigma, and displacement. Published in 1945 in the shadow of the Holocaust, the dog's soliloquies against the unfair treatment he receives inevitably serve at some level as reflections on antisemitism. All the titles mentioned in this list respond to Nazi views of Jews as subhuman and to anti-Semitic comparisons of Jews to dogs, apes, and vermin.[5] Sometimes Israeli writing internalizes such imagery, sometimes it subverts it, and sometimes it speaks back boldly in defiance of it. Frankel's memoir, to varying degrees, adopts all three strategies.

While the texts by Agnon, Kaniuk, Grossman, Semel, and Frankel are canonical works, scholarly debate has offered scant consideration of them through the lens of critical animal studies—a field that has been gaining momentum since the year 2000 and that has found application in connection with Holocaust studies.[6] An animal studies framework can reveal compelling artistic tensions in Hebrew narratives that pair the treatment of animal imagery with innovative storytelling and that stretch the limits of representation. I argue that, by challenging and dismantling the notion of the "dumb" animal,[7] these narratives signal their attempt to venture into a realm beyond ordinary human language. Engagement with the vantage point of the nonhuman animal helps authors critique, abjure, or repudiate the atrocities of the human world, sound suppressed voices and counteract silence surrounding Holocaust victims and survivors, or enter into previously unspoken territory. All of these writers eschew plausibility and verisimilitude as they aim to grapple with extremes of experience. Agnon's enigmatic talking dog offers ironic commentary on human folly;[8] Kaniuk incorporates absurdity and tragicomic grotesquerie; Grossman experiments with wildly phantasmagoric excess; Semel deploys elements of science fiction to imagine a posthumanist world that undermines truth and memory. Frankel, invoking and building on conventions of children's literature, fable, and fairy tale, creates a distinctive narrative art to convey a traumatic childhood.

With its easy-to-read narrative surfaces, her prose directly connects attention to animals with issues of voice and suppressed or repressed memory. As such, her trilogy can put a spotlight on the confluence of animal themes and Holocaust themes in literature, thereby inviting reevaluation of other Israeli texts that deal with similar matters. Furthermore, because Frankel's memoirs prima facie are not so demanding, they invite readers in; they make stories about tough issues more accessible. And, not unlike Art Spiegelman's *Maus*, Frankel's narratives make horrific tales more approachable through the use of animal characters.[9] Still, what may at first glance seem simple in Frankel's writing ultimately reveals complicated relationships with nonhuman beings and difficulties with processing and expressing a painful past. In this essay, I assess Frankel's accomplishment by looking at several aspects of her trilogy: (1) how the self, as portrayed there, moves from a childhood of unvoiced trauma to mature self-discovery, and how, along the way, the narrative "I" connects the child's survival to animals; (2) how the author's own creative work, in its shift from storytelling for children to adult memoir, moves from animal fable and techniques of writing for children to a new stage in her narrative art; and (3) how the author links the suffering she endured as a Jew in an inhumane world to her empathy for nonhuman creatures and for the underdogs in human communities. The ethical dilemmas Frankel confronts in her third memoir suggest that her early experience during the Holocaust has not just given rise to a unique set of artistic qualities in her work, but has also shaped her values and her views of Israeli society.

"They were always with me. The lice, my lice. . . ."

With these words, Frankel begins her memoir, *Girl*. The opening lines of the book merge human and nonhuman realms of life, introducing a self that is inseparable from vermin. The narrator makes a simple statement of fact: they live together, with a close and personal connection. No prefatory explanation sets the scene. Indeed, the word *lice* appears like an afterthought to the word *they*—as if the reference of the pronoun were self-evident, something taken for granted. Only subsequently does the narrator provide context. Frankel, at age five, has lived in a ghetto, been sent away by her parents to escape the Nazis, and is passing as a Christian in the Polish countryside. The girl doesn't question this arrangement; on the contrary, she knows no other reality. With this information, the reader is offered insight into the mode of storytelling at hand. It becomes apparent that a child's perspective dominates in the text, and matter-of-fact prose expresses the little girl's unquestioning acceptance of her awful circumstance. Frankel draws attention to the child's assumptions by remarking explicitly,

> When I was in the village, the lice never bothered me. They swarmed all over me, and of course I scratched constantly. I thought that's how it was in the world. (1)

The child's point of view normalizes an extreme situation[10] and naturalizes incongruities; (although she is constantly scratching, she does not feel "bothered"). The emphasis here on incomprehension and on the girl's limited grasp of her plight serves as the point of departure for the entire memoir and then becomes a recurring element of the narrative.

Take, for example, this passage, in which Frankel recounts that she identified with the animals she met in the village, rather than with people:

> The pigs lived in a pen. The pen had a low door, and only a little girl like me, about six years old, could crawl inside. I spent many happy hours in that pigpen, on the straw that was sometimes fresh but usually damp, packed tightly and probably smelly. I loved straw. The coffin I slept in was lined with straw,

too. The pigpen was my hiding place, my most private place, and the pigs were my best friends. I thought that's how it was in the world. (21)

Reinforcing the impressions created in the opening paragraph of the book, the text notes that everything about her abnormal conditions seemed natural to the child. Accordingly, the prose moves seamlessly from mention of "happy hours" to mention of a coffin, with a description of straw connecting the two ideas. Both pigs and child sleep in straw. And yet, at the same time, the segue serves as non sequitur. What seemed a smooth transition abruptly becomes disjunct and gives the reader pause. How can a coffin be acceptable bedding for a child? Only on the next page does it become clear that the girl actually slept inside a piece of furniture, deep and narrow, which served as a bench by day and a bed by night (22). The use of the word *coffin* indicates that an adult narrator is crafting a metaphor for a dreadful situation. (In the Hebrew original the phrase "*aron hametim*" renders the transition from happiness to horror at once more natural and more shocking. The word *aron* may in fact refer to a piece of furniture, an armoire or closet, but suddenly it connects with *hametim*, the dead, and so conjures up a crude casket.) This imagery effectively conveys the multilayered reaction Frankel had to her situation: as a little girl, separated from family and living in constant danger, she seemed on the surface unperturbed, but at a deep level she experienced severe distress which she only later came to recognize.

What the girl herself is keenly aware of at an early age is her interaction with animals. In the village she meets chickens, roosters, geese, goats, and insects. She emphasizes that she loved the pigs especially, noting:

> Their sweet little faces, with their flat pug noses and round, wide nostrils that looked at me like a pair of eyes that always seemed to express amused understanding. Their curly tails were especially merry. I didn't like their ears. They were flawed. All sorts of shapes had been cut out of them. The pigs were my best friends. They would make snorting sounds, and I'd answer them. We talked. (21)

The border between human and other creatures dissolves here, much as it did in the opening lines of *Girl*, and so the text touches on the kind of question that has been fundamental in animal studies' approaches to fiction: how to reassess the scope of the human and rethink ideas about personhood, to reconsider hierarchies of values "premised on the centrality of the human" being.[11] In Frankel's text, the child's perceptions place humans and nonhumans on the same plane. One result is that the girl's resilient response to her situation puts into critical light the dehumanizing logic of Nazi ideology. In anti-Semitic propaganda, comparing Jews to animals was meant to degrade; here, the Jewish girl does not see playing in a pigsty as something degrading. Rather, she finds joy in it and she perceives the world with wonder and affection. The scene portrayed is especially notable given traditional Jewish aversion to pigs. The child lives a reality in which such conventions—and disparaging stereotypes of animals, more generally—do not prevail. The pigs even become interlocutors, and cross-species communication is not an oddity but a given. "We talked," Frankel remarks with utmost simplicity.

In the subsequent volume of her trilogy, *Na'arah*, Frankel returns to this memory, reflecting upon and articulating her early experience from a more mature point of view. There, an adult narrator more explicitly rejects derogatory views of pigs.

> People say "he eats like a pig." That's not fair. I know pigs. Pigs are intelligent and pleasant creatures. Once, when the war was in the world, they were my best friends They eat like they eat; after all, they don't have hands. (112)[12]

Animal studies scholars, similarly, have argued against what they condemn as speciesism: "Wolves do not philander like the human 'wolf'" and "[c]hickens are not 'chicken,'" nor do pigs "make pigs of themselves."[13] The child in *Girl* is as yet unspoiled by the prejudice embedded in such expressions, and the narrative style of the text conveys her innocence. The prose is neither preachy nor explanatory. In contrast, *Teen Years* takes on more of an analytic stance. In that book, the voice of the adult narrator clearly asserts itself and forcefully adopts an advocacy position. The earlier memoir, in contrast, simply proffers concrete details: the pigs are "[p]ink, plump, round." (21). This condensed style, a "poetics of minutiae" and tangible particulars, has won the author considerable critical praise.[14] By avoiding a dissonant narrator—that is, by doing without a mature, cognizant, speaking self who might explain the confusions of youth— *Girl* forefronts the child's observations. The result is a kind of witnessing that minimizes sentimentality and historicity. Even though it displays accuracy, the text offers little by way of summary or panoramic views; it never uses the word *Shoah* and refers instead only to a time when war was in the world. The result is vivid immediacy, rather than pathos. Frankel's writing offers a vibrant, ahistorical present much as is often found in children's stories. To be sure, irony emerges from the description of the pigsty, but only thanks to the reader's previous knowledge. Again, to appreciate resonances implied but unstated by the text, the reader must be aware of Jewish revulsion toward pigs, of Nazi references to Jews as subhuman, and, most centrally, of assumptions that nonhuman animals are lesser than people. These points remain unstated on the page itself. Aiming to present the child's view, as much as can be filtered through adult prose, *Girl* offers both a text and a subtext—one for those in the know, one for those who are not—much as is true in many examples of children's literature.

Still, the narrative does not just register the child's perceptions; it also insists on the child's mind as creative, resourceful, capable of providing a kind of resistance to oppression. In the pigsty, the little girl fashions herself a doll from an apple and a stick. While in hiding in a narrow bunker with her father and mother in Lvov, she sculpts bread into bird shapes to appeal to some mice she has befriended (32). As one review concluded,

> [I]n the face of it all, she builds a world that is entirely hers, an alternative world. In this world are dreams, games, painting, tiny creatures that may be recruited as playmates, and an abundance of inventions, imagination, and even amusing situations. . . . In these moments of grace Frankel's girl, for the very reason that she is a child, emerges triumphant.[15]

The childish capacity for unconventional perception yields an inspiring picture of unspoiled and spirited imagination.

At times, the child's innocence does lead to grotesque clashes between her point of view and that of the adult reader. For example, her first pet after the war is a dead rat that she finds next to a pile of garbage. For a full day she plays with it happily, and the text even remarks that she was proud of her "soft, adorable, furry treasure" (57). Readers may feel admiration, pity, or affection for a child who experiences such joy, but they will likely feel disquiet, anguish, and revulsion as well. Further disquieting is Frankel's account of a slaughterhouse and a tannery where her father works for a time during the war and where a kind German manager shelters him and his family. Frankel comments, "It was a paradise compared to where we lived in the ghetto," but readers no doubt recoil when she goes on to describe what seemed like paradise to her in her childhood:

> My father helped save many Jews from hunger by hiding entrails and keeping pails of blood from the slaughterhouse for them. They drank the blood on the spot. The entrails they wrapped around their bodies and smuggled into the ghetto in the hope that the Germans wouldn't catch them. (28)

The imagery here is striking, because it shows by means of a few concrete details how dire were the circumstances of the ghetto residents. For readers familiar with Jewish custom, this report makes even more of an impact. Drinking blood is forbidden by the laws of kashrut. The passage is also distinctive in the context of animal studies. In that field, slaughterhouses have become a fraught topic, particularly with regard to the Holocaust. For example, philosophers and literary critics have analyzed the ways in which highly controversial public campaigns for animal rights have compared the meat industry to Nazi genocide. Historians, for their part, have noted that Himmler and other Nazi leaders worked in agribusiness and adopted practices from slaughterhouses into the running of death camps.[16] In *Girl*, Alona Frankel looks at the butchering of animals in a different way. While aware of the violence she witnessed as a child, she neither denounces nor elaborates on the cruelty that animals suffer, nor does she make facile analogies.[17] Instead, she simply acknowledges her reality, in a manner that is at once gruesome and calmly life-affirming.

This stance is not the same as equanimity. Evidence of how traumatic the slaughterhouse episode really was, and how lasting its impact, surfaces in the multiple repetitions of the story that are scattered throughout the memoir. One time, when the author revisits the scene, she insists over and over on the word *blood*. The understatement characteristic of her prose evolves into an intensity that reaches a furious pitch:

> My father stole entrails and pails full of *blood* from the slaughterhouse.
> The Jews who arrived from the ghetto every dawn would slip into our tiny room and my mother would give them *blood* from the pails and wreaths of entrails.
> They would break away from the line of slaves for a second, get some clotted *blood* that they drank on the spot

and wreaths of entrails that they wrapped around their waists or hid in their inner pockets, in the hope that there wouldn't be any searches, that they would manage to sneak the food of life into the ghetto for the children, the wife, the mother, the little sister.

Bone-weary people, dead tired after long hours of hard labor.

Those entrails and that *blood*, the *blood* of dead animals, was the source of life. That *blood* saved people from starving to death. They drank that *blood*. The fact that my mother and father endangered themselves to help those people and even save their lives fills me with pride.

My mother, my father, and I also drank that *blood*. (66; emphasis added)

It is unclear exactly what emotions Frankel expresses here. She says that she feels pride, but something more complicated emerges as well. Repugnance? Horror? Anger? Grief? Guilt? If nothing else, this passage bristles with irony. The people drinking blood are not bloodthirsty, they are the victims of bloodthirsty oppressors. Significantly, in the Hebrew Frankel uses the word *le'ekhol* (to eat) and not *lishtot* (to drink), thereby underscoring that blood for the ghetto Jews was sustenance and not indulgence. Again, the irony emerging from the text depends mostly on the reader's previous knowledge. For those in the know, Frankel's choice of words resonates profoundly. It calls to mind the long history of anti-Semitic discourse that associated Jews with bloodthirstiness and that for centuries led to accusations of ritual murder. Historian David Biale remarks that Jews in Europe for many years were seen as uncanny creatures that, "vampire-like, suck the blood out of Christians for their religious rites" and "suck the wealth out" of non-Jews.[18] Frankel, using elementary vocabulary, dispels such negative stereotypes with seemingly artless ease, denying the beastliness of Jews even while expressing gratitude to animals and raising questions about how much she does or does not identify with the beasts brought to slaughter.

From Animal Fable to "How Could Such Things Happen?"

Frankel's childhood relationship with animals was far from simple. Though she identified with animals, she depended on killing them for food. She saw pigs as companions, but she also maintained a sense of mastery over a flock of geese she herded, a horse she tended, and mice she trained (whom she refers to as "my friends"). Furthermore, the idyllic early memories of human/nonhuman symbiosis in country life eventually gave way to a more mediated relationship with animals, one that involved storytelling. In the memoir, animal stories shape the child's grasp of her world.[19] Of special note is a fable her mother told while they were in hiding together. In this tale some goats survive attack by a wolf. Six kids are eaten, but a seventh one hides in a clock and lives. When she was little, Frankel drew strength from this story, imagining herself the survivor. The talking animals in this case differ from the pigs with whom she conversed in the village. They represent not a partner, but a didactic device. The adults in Frankel's life turn to anthropomorphized characters in order to explain human behavior and help their child cope with trauma. Frankel's memoir thus moves out of the realm where no binary opposition exists between human and nonhuman animals and into a sphere of understanding where animals serve as instruments for human purposes.

Significantly, mention of the goat fable comes up various times in *Girl*; only toward the end of the volume does Frankel recount the story in full. That narrative move marks an important transition. By telling the goat story, by becoming the storyteller herself, the adult narrator in a self-conscious way separates from her younger, experiencing self, and she decisively acknowledges her early responses to fable as a waystation on the road to maturation. In this way she recognizes how stories have mediated her struggle to understand what animals mean to her—as companions, as cultural constructs, and as food.

This is not to say that Frankel's writing depends on clear linear progression or plot development. On the contrary, in the memoirs her recollections unfold in fits and starts, and the texts often repeat anecdotes. Such repetition indicates how difficult it is to make sense of the past and piece together a coherent story. The narrator is stuck with the same recurring scenes over and over. Sometimes, as with the accounts of the slaughterhouse, the later versions of events do provide greater detail and so indicate an increasing willingness to confront and come to terms with the suffering in her youth. Significantly, when Frankel finally tells the story of the goats at length (almost three full pages), she places that tale in the midst of an account about a very narrow escape that came to pass in Lvov. There, the little girl was concealed in a closet with her mother, who clutched cyanide to take in the event of being captured. The Gestapo entered the building, but the family went undiscovered. In Frankel's memoir, the moment of narrating this experience is a moment of adult reckoning with the past. *Girl* has previously presented a number of memories from the same hiding place (such as the one about befriending mice), but it is only at this point in the narration that a detailed description of the Nazi raid arises. Apparently, the narrator now feels strong enough to contend with what for long had gone unexamined. It is also at this the point that the text puts the goat story into words. That is to say, at long last, the book states what before had not yet been fully articulated—both the fable and the emotions associated with it. At this juncture the perspective of the adult narrator establishes itself clearly, superseding the perspective of the child character so dominant in the narrative thus far.

It is precisely now, too, that the adult narrator reveals new aspects of the child's past, noting:

> I didn't cry then. I never cried. Everything seemed natural to me.
> That's how it was, and maybe it was then that I started to dream of myself being the color of asphalt, or the color of crumbled bricks—the color of clotted blood. (239)

What does the text uncover here? For starters, it asserts yet again that the child remained impervious; her circumstances seemed self-evident to her. The passage acknowledges, though, that on a subconscious level the girl was deeply troubled. In her dreams she associated herself with blood. Permeating her self-definition is an image at once forceful and ambivalent. The blood in the dream, after all, is not healthy and circulating, but rather clotted—a word at one and the same time indicative of a wound and of a life-sustaining function that stems bleeding from a wound. The mention of clotting therefore accentuates stoppage. Frankel's younger self held her emotions in. Containing them was no doubt a psychological defense necessary for self-preservation, but over time it became a terrible burden which expressed itself in the kind of recurrent dreams typical of post-traumatic reaction. Keep in mind, too, that a blood clot at times may be life-threatening, and so the text reverberates with intimations that unexpressed trauma can be profoundly damaging. Frankel, as adult author, produces further resonance by creating a parallel between this scene and the scene at the slaughterhouse. There, clotted blood was the source of life but also horror. By the same token, at the time of her narrow escape the little girl held onto life yet was filled with horrifying memories. Furthermore, since the girl incorporates the color of blood into her self-image, the dream creates an equivalence between the slaughtered animals and the child who was designated for slaughter but escaped. The text never spells out a connection between the Gestapo raid and the slaughterhouse, but the choice of words in these separate scenes invites the reader to understand the comments on page 239 as a reference back to, and a kind of repetition of, the episodes recounted on pages 22 and 66.

The repetition in question here comes with a difference, of course; it enriches and reinterprets what came before. Such reiteration, with various functions, is a hallmark of Frankel's memoir—one that builds on her narrative style in children's books. In her picture books, repetition is paramount. Recurring words present plot actions and central ideas, thereby conveying a toddler's propensity to practice the same tasks repeatedly until mastery. In addition, as a storytelling technique, repetition has great appeal for young children; they delight in hearing the same story over and over. Frankel's most famous book, *Once Upon a Potty* (*Sir hasirim*, 1975), keenly incorporates these principles. The child character in this tale learns to use the potty only after sitting and sitting and sitting and sitting. The word *sat* appears dozens of times, filling up several full pages of text. In Frankel's adult narrative, restatement also appears insistently and one of its functions is to intensify. While presenting the scene with the Gestapo in *Girl*, Frankel writes three times in a row, "And the way they had come in—they went out" (238). This simple sentence, multiplied, suggests how difficult it is for the author to process a danger so narrowly averted. Again, restatement contributes to the effort of working through emotions. Moreover, repetition in this case comprises a kind of homage to and complaint against the mother. Frankel points out that her mother often told the story of the close call in Lvov ("My mother told me, told me, and told me, she told me until the end of her long life," 240). Frankel imitates her, through repetitious wording of her own as well as through frequent return to the topic of her mother's obsessions. Each time, the mimicry suggests both deference and increasing anger, an insistent carping that reveals Frankel's simultaneous devotion to and resentment of her mother. All told, Frankel has taken an element of her own childhood, made it into a signature move in her writing for children, and then adapted it in her memoir for adult audiences in a way that echoes yet transforms the same material for new artistic purposes.[20]

The uses of repetition, together with starts and stops, contribute to an artistic style at times concise and choppy, at times lyrical, at times grotesque. This is writing that has the effect of conveying inchoate realities.

It de-familiarizes by offering haunting explorations of a child's perceptions. Frankel is not alone in trying to convey the incomprehensibility of the Holocaust via a young person's incomprehension. Maintaining a young focalizer with a grown-up narrator (double-voicing), emphasizing detail at the expense of context, and foregrounding loss of affect are qualities common to many memoirs and fictional works that present a child's experience of the Holocaust. To these techniques, however, Frankel also adds her own touches. Importantly, she cultivates elements of fairy tale. She introduces animal companions to a setting that seems imaginary, where anything can happen and where unlikely helpers and adversaries may materialize at any time: for example, a wicked peasant woman plucks the child from the safety of the village and delivers her to almost certain death in the city; a kind carpenter and his wife turn away the Gestapo, almost magically, with some laconic remarks and a calm demeanor; fortunes rise and fall instantaneously. Together with Frankel's poetics of minutiae, with narrative that proceeds in spurts, with vivid immediacy and lack of historicity, with charm-like (quasi-incantatory) repetitions, and with animal characters, the implausible turns of plot work toward expressing what had been unspoken trauma and what, eventually, became Frankel's ongoing effort to speak up and tell her personal story.

These characteristics of her writing foster a pervasive sense of astonishment. In an interview Frankel noted,

> I think that the repeating motif spread throughout all the pages of the book is the motif of amazement (*hihsta'ut*), of "I don't understand anything." As a little girl this is natural, and there's hope that when you grow up you'll understand. Today I still don't understand, I understand less. How could such things happen?[21]

The author's comments here are telling, because they directly articulate challenges faced by memoirists who lived through the Holocaust and attempt to speak the unspeakable. Indeed, Frankel's remarks call to mind the radical amazement that readers have seen as central to Aharon Appelfeld's art.[22] His memoir *The Story of a Life* (1999), for instance, relies on understatement, repetition, and muted expressions of bafflement and wonder to recount his childhood experiences during World War II.[23] Like Frankel, Appelfeld survived in part by taking refuge in the countryside, and significant parallels between his memoir and hers emerge in conjunction with unspoken emotions and reference to animals. Confronted with unfathomable human cruelty, Appelfeld found communion more with farm animals than with people. He remarks, "The hours I spent with puppies, cats, and sheep were the best of the war years. I would blend in with them until I was part of them, until forgetfulness came, until I fell asleep alongside them (101-102).[24] Frankel in much the same way calls the pigpen "my hiding place, my most private place" (21). Although she walked freely around the village passing as a Gentile, the pigpen was a place where she could maintain a more private self, an intimate self not to be mentioned to people, a place where she could play happily with the pigs.[25] As an adult author, Frankel—like Appelfeld—attempts to convert into verbal art the early memories of having lived an astonishing experience, an experience from a realm beyond words.

Wounded Crows and "Prisoners of Zion"

In the second and third books of her trilogy, Frankel further explores her relationship to animals as well as her feelings about survival and fraught family relationships. Her mother (repeatedly referred to as "mother bird") protected her and saved her during the war, but the daughter sees her afterward as overbearing and as a constant reminder of a world best forgotten. *Na'arah* recounts how, in Israel and now an adolescent, Alona wants desperately to fit in, to be more like a sabra, to wear clothes that look fashionable and not so reminiscent of Poland. She resents her family's friendships with survivors, who strike her as shameful and pathetic, and she only slowly recognizes herself as one of them. Nonetheless, they haunt her thoughts and, once she becomes an adult writer, she fills her memoir with vignettes of them. She also develops strong sensitivity to the suffering of nonhuman creatures—any and all kinds—and she pairs anecdotes about vulnerable animals with troubling stories of Holocaust victims and vulnerable survivors. Her empathy then extends from helpless animals to underdogs of Israeli society, including new immigrants, Sephardim, and Arabs. Similarly, in a chapter called "Prisoners of Zion," she focuses on a wounded crow abandoned on a highway while also offering remarks on the Jews from the Soviet Union and how they felt abandoned politically.[26]

In the third book in her trilogy, Frankel wrestles most explicitly with ethical dilemmas related to the treatment of animals. She repeatedly saves hurt or abandoned creatures. She abruptly stops a bus driver in the middle of his route in order to rescue a turtle from the road; she bursts into a stranger's apartment in order to save a wounded bird on the roof. Likewise, she takes numerous small animals in need into her apartment, at great inconvenience, ceasing only when her children's health might be compromised. She includes several chapters describing how conflicted she feels about cooking meat or fish. Nowhere, though, does she endorse vegetarianism with the ideological zeal of an I. B. Singer, who famously compared the Holocaust to the suffering of farm animals and called the meat industry an "Eternal Treblinka."[27] Instead, she reflects on the cruelties of the food chain in the natural world. She remarks, for instance, that saving a hurt bird may deprive a cat of a meal. The narrative avoids overt comparisons between animal suffering and the Holocaust, and it never indulges in self-righteousness. Rather, it brings a refreshingly candid and confused look at human love for animals. The narrator reveals that she often bumbles and fails: for instance, she sets some pet turtles loose, trying to respect their freedom, but she subsequently realizes—with humor and self-deprecation—that she has done this in a way that has ruined the ecosystem of a park and damaged other species. The memoir also avoids sanctimony as the narrator openly reports the mixed feelings she has had, particularly her history of feeling ashamed of survivors and oppressed by their neediness.

These second and third volumes in Frankel's trilogy thus offer thematic freshness. However, the narration itself moves away from some of the innovative qualities found in *Girl*. The prose becomes more expository and sheds some of the double-voicing, the loss of affect, and the fairy tale twists of fate that so effectively foster expression of childhood experience. At the same time, the later volumes do retain striking detail, an atmosphere of immediacy, repetitions, and humor, even as they highlight the adult Frankel's efforts to live compassionately and to be humane. This combination of elements in her writing comes to showcase her own individual voice, in its process of emerging out of the pain she experienced at a young age. *Yaldah*, *Na'arah*, and *Ishah* trace how the girl grew from trauma to mature recollection, and they document her efforts to grapple with a painful past. The narrative voice, weaving a story of how that growth took place in relation to animals, evolves into the distinctive styles of volume one and then volumes two and three. All three of these autobiographical texts draw on hallmark features of the author's picture books for children.

These aspects of Frankel's art spring from the formative experience she had of being treated inhumanely. Her memoirs turn repeatedly to a focus on animals while struggling with what it means to be human in an inhuman world. In this regard, her work is not unlike and so can call attention to texts by other Israel authors who wrestle with similar issues. Kaniuk's antic and bizarre plot actions in *Adam ben kelev* blur boundaries between species in order to show the effects of abuse on survivors who, mistreated and animalized, no longer seem quite human. Grossman, with a superabundance of imaginative abandon, leads his characters in *See Under: Love* to escape the bounds of a human-centered world. This novel asks, is humanism still possible after the Holocaust? Semel's *And the Rat Laughed*, with a kaleidoscopic mixing of genres, showcases a digital world that confuses human and nonhuman categories. This author ponders what a posthumanist world will look like and what place the individual might hold in it. Frankel, for her part, identifies with animals and expresses solidarity with them, not so much to reflect on humanity broadly conceived, but—in keeping with the memoir genre—simply to wonder, What kind of person have I been?

Like these other writers, Frankel speaks back against the Nazi view of her as less than human. She nonetheless also deeply internalizes an identification with animals. And, like the child she was (as portrayed in *Girl*)—who provided a kind of resistance against her enemies by exerting imagination and humor, who talked with the pigs—the adult author has developed a personal, imaginative, creative nonfiction, with childlike qualities and with features of children's literature. All of these facets of her writing allow her own voice to be heard and long untold stories to be told.

Notes

1. *Yaldah* (Tel Aviv: Mapa: 2004), *Na'arah* (Tel Aviv: Xargol, Am Oved: 2009), *Ishah* (Tel Aviv: Xargol, Am Oved: 2012). So far, only *Girl* has been published in English, with translation by Sondra Silverstone (Bloomington: Indiana University Press, 2016).

2. *Girl* won the Sapir prize in 2005 and garnered wide acclaim. Dan Laor refers to *Yaldah* as a "biographical novel" in a lecture delivered at the University of Illinois, March 4, 2012, "Writing the Holocaust: Is It Still Relevant?" https://mediaspace.illinois.edu/media/t/0_1xx666hq/19889991.

3. Tamar Hess, *Self as Nation: Contemporary Hebrew Autobiography* (Waltham, MA: Brandeis University Press, 2016), 5–7. Hess notes work by Dan Tsalka, Yoram Kaniuk, Amos Oz, and others, including Frankel, as evidence of this

phenomenon. For foundational scholarship on Israeli autobiography, see work by Yael S. Feldman, such as "In Pursuit of Things Past: David Shahar and the Autobiography in Current Israeli Fiction," *Hebrew Studies* 24 (Jan. 1, 1983): 99–105; "Ideology and Self-Representation: The Case of Israeli Women Writers," in *Redefining Autobiography in Twentieth-Century Women's Fiction: An Essay Collection*, ed. Janice Morgan, Colette T. Hall, Carol L. Snyder (New York: Garland, 1991), 281–301.

4. A rodent who voices a wish to laugh finds he cannot, for he inhabits a world—a hiding place where a small girl endures repeated sexual assault—that leaves no room for laughter. The man who finally rescues the child returns her to human communication, even laughter, but only by mimicking a rat. Alan L. Berger outlines these plot turns in his review, "The Holocaust Novel from Israel that Americans Can't Handle," *The Forward*, Oc. 26, 2009. https://forward.com/culture/117704/the-holocaust-novel-from-israel-that-america-can/.

5. In young adult fiction, Asher Kravitz's *Hakelev hayehudi* (Tel Aviv: Yedi'ot Aharonot, Sifrei Hemed, 2007) features a talking dog who recounts his life in Nazi Europe. This character clearly speaks back against negative stereotypes; he is articulate and clever and champions the Jewish people. An English version of the novel has appeared as *The Jewish Dog*, trans. Michal Kessler (Brooklyn: Penlight, 2015), and as a film version, "Shepherd: The Story of a Jewish Dog" in 2019. https://www.imdb.com/title/tt3278810/.

6. In her essay "'We are Story Animals': Aesopics in Holocaust Literature by Art Spiegelman and Yann Martel," Laura Petersen provides a concise overview of animal studies in the field of Holocaust literature along with her take on *Maus*, a text that has received a lot of critical attention related to cultural representations of animals. In *Aesopic Voices: Re-Framing Truth through Concealed Ways of Presentation in the 20th and 21st Centuries*, ed. Gert Reifarth, and Philip Morrissey (Newcastle upon Tyne: Cambridge Scholars, 2011), 174–207.

Animal Studies scholars have begun to engage with the field of Modern Hebrew literature. For comment specifically on Holocaust themes and Israeli literature, see Naomi Sokoloff, "The Nazi Beast at the Warsaw Zoo: Animal Studies, The Holocaust, *The Zookeeper's Wife*, and *See Under: Love*," in *Palgrave Handbook of Holocaust Literature and Culture*, ed. Victoria Aarons and Phyllis Lassner (London: Palgrave Macmillan, 2019). Iftah Birah's psychoanalytic reading of Kaniuk's *Adam ben Kelev* does not come from an animal studies perspective, but it has a lot to say about animal themes in that novel. Birah also observes in an endnote that Kaniuk deserves analysis in comparison with Kravitz's *Hakelev hayehudi*, Agnon's Balak, and the motif of the Nazi beast in the Momik section of Grossman's *See Under: Love*. For topics other than the Holocaust, see also Uri Cohen, "Only Yesterday: A Hebrew Dog and the Colonial Dynamics in Pre-Mandate Palestine," in *A Jew's Best Friend? The Image of the Dog throughout Jewish History*, ed. Philip Ackerman-Lieberman and Rakefet Zalashik (Portland, OR: Sussex Academic

Press, 2013), 156–78 and "Hachayah hatsionit [The Zionist Animal]," *Mechkarei Yerushalayim besifrut 'ivrit* (2013–14), 167–217; Gideon Nevo, "*Hereg chayot basifrut ha'ivrit hamodernit: gilgulo shel motiv*," in *Rega' shel huledet: mechkarim besifrut 'Ivrit uvesifrut Yidish likhvod Dan Miron*," ed. Hanan Hever (Jerusalem: Mossad Bialik, 2007), 448–66; Noam Pines, *The Infrahuman: Animality in Modern Jewish Literature* (Albany: State University of New York Press, 2018); and Na'ama Harel, "Woman into Cow: The Animalization of Victimized Women in Devorah Baron's Fiction," *Prooftexts* 37, no. 2 (2018): 243–74. In *The Zionist Paradox* (Waltham, MA: Brandeis University Press, 2014), 63–66, Yigal Schwartz discusses images of animals in narrative by a range of Hebrew writers to gauge their attachments to the Land of Israel. For instance, examining fauna in *Altneuland* becomes a way to discern fundamental features of Theodore Herzl's worldview.

7. In Western discourse the idea of animals as being without language stretches back at least to Aristotle's *Politics*, which holds that man alone is "the speaking animal" with the gift of speech and a sense of good and evil.

8. While Agnon's masterpiece creates an original character and a dense tissue of symbolism and allusion with Balak, this novel inserts also itself into a long literary tradition centered on talking dogs, from Cervantes's *Colloquio de los perros* to Kafka's "Investigations of a Dog," and more. See Theodore Ziolkowski, *Varieties of Literary Thematics* (Princeton, NJ: Princeton University Press, 1983) for history of that tradition. The commentary on Balak and his possible significations is vast.

9. For comments on *Maus* in this regard see Laura Petersen, "We Are Story Animals," 2011.

10. On narrative that presents a child's eye view of the Holocaust, see Naomi Sokoloff, *Imagining the Child in Modern Jewish Fiction* (Baltimore: Johns Hopkins University Press, 1992), and Sue Vice, *Children Writing the Holocaust* (New York: Palgrave MacMillan, 2004).

11. David Herman, "Animal Worlds in Modern Fiction: An Introduction," *Modern Fiction Studies* 60, no. 3 (2014): 421–43.

12. My translation.

13. Joan Dunayer, "Sexist Words; Speciesist Roots," in *Animals and Women*, ed. Carol J. Adams (Durham: Duke University Press, 1995), 29–30.

14. This point was noted in the speech presenting Frankel with the Buchman Award on behalf of Yad Vashem. The members of the award committee included David Bankir, Yisrael Gutman, Bella Gutterman, Dan Laor, Iris Milner, Dan Michman, Tikva Fatal, and Avner Shalev. They also remarked, "The text itself is highly condensed and overflowing with details. . . . There are no summaries whatsoever, no generalizations." http://www.alonafrankel.com/girl21.html.

15. Again, from the speech awarding Frankel the Buchman Prize by Yad Vashem.

16. For discussion of this history, see for instance Boria Sax, *Animals in the Third Reich: Pets, Scapegoats, and the Holocaust* (New York: Continuum, 2000) and Charles Patterson, *Eternal Treblinka: Our Treatment of Animals and*

the Holocaust (New York: Lantern Books, 2002). Both comment on the ironies of Hitler's vegetarianism and of movements for the prevention of cruelty to animals that flourished in Nazi Germany.

17. Debate about the ethics of such analogies has figured prominently in scholarly discussion about writers J. M. Coetzee and I. B. Singer and their fiction. See, for instance, Emily Miller Budick's "Holocaust, Apartheid, and the Slaughter of Animals," the epilogue to her book *The Subject of the Holocaust* (Bloomington: Indiana University Press, 2015), 228–37. The animal rights organization PETA famously launched an ad campaign called "Holocaust on a Plate"—for which they eventually apologized.

18. David Biale, *Blood and Belief: The Circulation of a Symbol between Jews and Christians* (Berkeley: University of California Press, 2007).

19. Frankel writes fondly of the many creatures "that weren't people" that she got to know during the war, but she also wonders if maybe she remembers these animals "only from stories" (14).

20. For excellent discussion of repetition as an element of Frankel's style in *Girl*, see Liraz Axelrod, *Ketz hayaldut*, from *Yedi'ot acharonot*, June 6, 2005. תפילה. בחזרה העקשנית הזאת יש מהדואליות של מי שרוצה לספר החזרה היא גם מונוטונית וגם או מנטרה של מוזיקה לטקסט נותנת היא משתנה. רוצה לא גם אבל. https://www.ynet.co.il/articles/0,7340,L-3095479,00.html.

21. Cited by Or Barnea, "Alona Frankel Has Won the Sapir Prize," *Yedi'ot acharonot*, June 22, 2005. https://www.ynet.co.il/articles/0,7340,L-3102399,00.html#n.

22. Alan Mintz uses the phrase "noninterpretive amazement" to indicate this basic quality of Aharon Appelfeld's writing, particularly in his novel *The Age of Wonders*. See *Hurban; Responses to Catastrophe in Hebrew Literature* (New York: Columbia University Press, 1984), 219.

23. Aharon Appelfeld, *Sipur chayim* (Jerusalem: Keter, 1999). This passage appeared in English in Aloma Halters's translation, *The Story of a Life* (New York: Schocken Books, 2004), vii. Compare Frankel's comments on astonishment to these by Appelfeld, describing his boyhood hiding in the woods: "Thoughts and feelings were greatly constricted. In truth, sometimes there swelled up within me a painful sense of astonishment at why I had been left alone. But these reflections would fade with the mists of the forest, and the animal within me would return and wrap me in its fur" (vii).

24. Even more intimately, he reveals: "During the war I was not myself, but like a small creature that has a burrow." *Story of a Life*, vii.

25. Strikingly, Appelfeld and Frankel both write in their memoirs about terrible struggles with learning Hebrew. Both met harsh discouragement from teachers and readers who doubted their ability ever to write in this new language. Both then went on to turn silences and struggles with language into a vital part of their narrative art, and to write fondly of the animals they met in their youth with whom they communicated easily.

26. She is referring specifically to abandonment by the chancellor of Austria, Bruno Kreisky.

27. The phrase appears as the words of a character in the story "The Letter Writer," in *The Séance and Other Stories* (New York: Farrar, Straus, Giroux, 1968), and the author himself frequently made comments endorsing the sentiment. Singer's story is alluded to directly in the title of Charles Patterson's book, *Eternal Treblinka* (2002).

Stalagim

At the Limits of Israeli Literature

Eric Zakim

Eighteen minutes into the 1978 Israeli teen comedy *Eskimo limon* (*Lemon Popsicle*), the adolescent (and naturally sex-crazed) protagonist, Benzi, briefly lounges in the family bathtub, until his overbearing mother screams in to him to hurry up and get out. The bathroom, we are to understand, is his only possible, fleeting retreat into privacy—just like his literary American cousin, Alexander Portnoy, who shares with Benzi an adolescent penchant for the bathroom as his preferred site for masturbation. But unlike Philip Roth's declarative verbal bluntness in describing Portnoy's bathroom forays, Benzi's sexual agenda is conveyed by a more nuanced, if nonetheless explicit, *visual* marker: the small pocketbook he is reading in the tub, a book that would have been easily recognized by the 1978 film audience or within the depicted scene of the early 1960s: *Kalbato shel Schultz* (*Schultz's Bitch*).

To be fair, the audience may not have been familiar with this particular title, but the genre to which *Kalbato shel Schultz* belonged—a genre of pulp fiction called "stalagim"— would have been well known and easily recognizable in its physical form, especially among adolescent boys attuned to secretive sexual codes. Familiar too would have been Benzi's shame at being caught; he quickly and anxiously dispatches the book at the acousmatic sound of his mother's voice. Masturbation, for an adolescent like Benzi, entwines both shame and desire, a reaction hardly specific to a particular time and place. But the pulp title, *Kalbato shel Schultz*, speaks as well to the broad cultural setting and the specific history of Israel, and raises myriad questions about the exact nature of Benzi's anxiety over his choice of titillating material. In brief, the stalagim, a repressed erotic genre, pushed Hebrew writing to the very limits of what could be considered Israeli literature. These books did not merely constitute a noncanonical genre; rather, they were a group of popular novels so far beyond the pale of acceptability that their entire existence was suppressed and their history all but expunged from any account or definition of national culture. As a recent commentary captures an enduring understanding of the stalagim, they were for much of the country "the most disgusting [books] ever to appear in Hebrew literature."[1]

Beginning in 1961, just weeks after Adolf Eichmann went on trial in Jerusalem, the kiosks and bookstalls throughout Israel began selling these new books: short, soft-covered novels (of about 180 pages), all of similar size (11.5 x 16.5 cm.), printed on thick, high-acid paper, whose plots take place primarily in Nazi prisoner of war camps (*stalagim*), and that in most cases tell the story of American or British prisoners-of-war guarded and dominated by female Nazi soldiers. Foreign exoticism pervades these books. Non-Israeli-sounding pseudonyms hide authorial origin, and in a similar way cover images plucked from American men's magazines conceal a genre of Hebrew writing, promising explicit sexual and violent content, which these books actually rarely supply. Inside, the texts themselves try to speak with a foreign accent, as if translated into Hebrew and thus fulfilling the covers' promises of exoticism. In their plots, the novels are suffused with erotic overtones that regularly erupt on the page into soft-core descriptions of sexual desire, aggression, and assault against men, including rape. The books sold themselves in these terms: the back cover of *Stalag 217*, an early example, promises a "real and cruel" story about male prison life at the hands of "sadistic young women, mad with sick and twisted passion."[2] In this, the sexual domination of Anglo-American male prisoners by their female Nazi guards treads an ambiguous (and clearly ambivalent) line between torture (the books and their female characters are almost always described as "sadistic" and "monstrous") and prurient—even perverse—desire.

The stalagim have always been understood as pornographic and transgressive, the object of attack by several national institutions in the country, including the army, which actively worked to keep them out of the hands of young soldiers. Ironically, *Kalbato shel Schultz* was one of the least explicit of the stalagim when it came to sexual description. The book, as it turns out, has no explicit sexual description, since it appeared in reaction to the eponymous novel, *Hayiti kalbato hapratit shel kolonel Schultz* (*I Was Colonel Schultz's Private Bitch*), the only stalag title ever officially censored by the government. After the courts censored the book and police removed it from bookstalls, copycats, including *Kalbato shel Schultz*, capitalized on the novel's notoriety with titles referencing this mistress of a fictional Colonel Schultz[3]—but without the offending content. In fact, the "bitch" of *Kalbato shel Schultz* is his "wolf" dog, Cleo, who saves the colonel's life during the Battle of the Bulge. Thus, authorship, cultural significance, and even sexual content are all displaced from *Kalbato shel Schultz*, whose significance (in *Eskimo limon* and beyond) lies in the way it refers not to its own content but toward the absent progenitor and, indeed, the very *idea* of titillation signified by the genre. What then, exactly, was transgressive—and enjoyable—in these books? What was the challenge they offered to Israeli society, especially since pornography of a more visually explicit sort was already available in the country, even in native form?[4] How does transgression indicate and tease out the limits of acceptable literature, especially within the historical context and continuum of Israeli literary development?

I want to suggest a significant, *critical* place for this body of work in the history of Israeli literature, a significance for which eroticism and pornography act as a cipher. I do not mean to downplay the erotic function of the stalagim, especially for a younger generation of readers in the early 1960s. Far from it, I want to ask how desire and enjoyment can become so transgressive within Israeli society that the very inclusion of this literature in the national life of the country seems impossible. Beyond the vague sociological explanations that dominate the limited scholarship on the stalagim—Holocaust plots as a way for a generation experiencing the Eichmann trial to "come to terms" with these events; eroticism as rebellion in a puritanical society—the stalagim hint at *how an aesthetic enactment of desire* could become so un-assimilable by Israeli culture. At a point of vast change in Israeli society and culture in the early 1960s, from ostensibly the collectivism of the Palmach Generation of the 1940s and '50s, to the individualism in the 1960s of the Statehood Generation, the prism of the stalagim reflects on the very nature and limits of that change.

Those limits might best be teased out by feminist criticism of American pornographic cinema, which offers perhaps the most powerful perspective for understanding the challenge that the stalagim represent. Feminist readings of pornography have never been monolithic in deriving a singular meaning in pornographic aesthetics. Rather, feminist debates, from the pioneering anti-porn writing of Andrea Dworkin in the late 1970s and early 1980s,[5] to the critical readings of pornography by Linda Williams in the late 1990s,[6] map out a wide field of critical assessment, but one that consistently focuses on two particular questions of subjective fluidity and identification in the pornographic scene: the position of the female subject (within a heteronormative pornographic cinema) and the subject position of the (primarily male) audience in that scene. Dworkin and Williams describe, each in her own way, an aesthetic field of dynamic subjects and shifting identifications with the various roles and perspectives of pornography.

The history of Israeli literature has never asked the same questions of the Hebrew text, even at those crucial junctures, such as the early 1960s, when the dynamism of change seemed wholly dependent on the transforming relations between collective and individual. Indeed, much of Israeli literary criticism has been predicated on a well-established structural opposition between collective and individual, without ever calling into question the stability and decidability of these very terms.[7] The stalagim, *if read critically*, disrupt the very foundation of Israeli literary and social stability by constructing a different sort of literary subject to what dominated Hebrew writing and Israeli culture at this moment of social and cultural transformation, thereby calling into question some of the certainties of Israeli literature. The history of Israeli literature—in parallel to social histories of individualism in Israeli society—has generally followed a strict teleological movement from the collectivism of the early state (the Palmach Generation) to a reimagining of the individual in various Zionist and post-Zionist forms.[8] In one narrow sense, the challenge and suppression of the stalagim fit a well-worn story: the teleological narrative of a puritanical collective repressing individual desire, before individualism erupts in a younger generation's rebellion. However, that type of reading cannot explain the success of certain writings (the Statehood Generation, for example) and the complete suppression and virtual erasure of another (the stalagim). I want to propose a reading of the stalagim that would resist teleological orthodoxy and see in the genre an important challenge to the very ways that the Israeli subject was reformulated within a generation of writing that began to emerge in the country.

The transgression of the stalagim serves as an important prooftext of the limits of what might be permissible within a new-found individualism and what might *not* be. In this, the stalagim represent a counterpath to the inevitable development of a concept of individualism in Israeli culture and society, a thwarted path that would disrupt the certitude within which the move from collectivism to individualism has always been viewed. Rather, the stalagim offer a complex, dialectical model of Israeli subjectivity. The countersubjects constructed within the stalagim, with their overlapping and layered ideas of identification, desire, and ethnic/national alliances, proffered a very different notion of how literature conveyed the individual, different, that is, from the normative models of subjectivity in the Statehood Generation and in almost every subsequent literary movement in the country. In that sense, the radicalness of Holocaust pornography as it is expressed in the stalagim might indeed have been the least assimilable form—the most "disgusting," as we've already noted—within the history of Israeli—and perhaps Hebrew—literature.[9]

The publishers of the stalagim well understood the boundaries these books were transgressing. They deployed a strategy of foreignness in order to efface and dissemble the genre's origins and identity to make it palatable. Even today, more than fifty years later, the hoax of the books' authorship is still encoded in the digital catalogue of the National Library of Israel, which lists these titles under the subject heading, "Fiction—Translations into Hebrew."[10] Leaving aside obvious internal evidence of origin in the texts themselves, the hoax was lying in plain sight: readers of the popular literary gossip magazine *Ha'olam hazeh* would have read about the question of authorship in the stalagim as early as February 1962, soon after *Hayiti kalbato hapratit shel kolonel Schultz* was officially removed from book stalls.[11] Later that spring, in a broad critical exposé on the stalagim, *Ha'olam hazeh* reported, "On their covers, the stalagim display catchy names like Joe Hagen, Mike Baden, Victor Bolder, Kim Rockman, and Heinrich Distal. But behind these pure Aryan names are hidden Israeli authors with sabra names like Eli Keydar, Yosef Safra, Mordechai Ronen, and others."[12] Keydar indeed penned the very first appearance of the genre, *Stalag 13*, but his name appears nowhere in the book itself. Instead, "Mike Baden" is listed as the author, who, we are to infer, composed the story in a language other than Hebrew, since printed opposite the title page, alone in a box on the recto side, is the vague note, "Appearing for the first time in unabridged Hebrew translation—a superb translation."[13]

All the titles were published with similar pseudonyms implying foreign authorship, usually of Anglo-American origin. There was no necessary correlation between pseudonym and ghostwriter, or, for that matter, with made-up translators. Sometimes the name of a translator actually appears on the copyright page. "I. Eshkoli," for instance, "translated" Victor Bolder's *Stalag 10*, as well as Monique de-la-Tour's *Kalbato shel Schultz*. The catalogue of the National Library, along with the subject heading of translated fiction, dutifully and un-ironically lists translators when available.

Claims for an international provenance might characterize much of Israeli cultural production in the 1960s, as economic and political segments in the country began looking outward. Throughout the decade, both literature and politics focused ever more on relations with the West, and with the United States in particular, especially after 1967 and the beginning of political isolation in the international arena.[14] In literature, Statehood Generation writers consistently distinguished themselves from prior generations by looking self-consciously to the West—especially toward Anglo-American and German modernism—for models of literary forbears. Natan Zach had made claims since the mid-1950s for Statehood Generation poetry as shifting poetic allegiances away from the maximalism of Eastern Europe and toward the restrained poetics of German Expressionism and American Imagism. In prose, A. B. Yehoshua, who began writing and publishing, alongside Amos Oz, in parallel to the phenomenon of the stalagim, was never reticent about his admiration for William Faulkner's modernist renderings of consciousness as a potent model for Hebrew writing.

The stalagim went even farther and reconceived of foreignness altogether by inverting the dominant models of adaptation and adoption that had always characterized Hebrew literature's relation to foreignness. In a way, their claims of foreign provenance were over the top, a joke, a wink (like the facetious tone of the articles in *Ha'olam hazeh*) at an older generation that would never countenance foreignness in the midst of reinvention through the land and through Hebrew.[15] In a more serious way, the stalagim react to the endurance of Ahad Ha-am's admonition during the poesy debates at the turn of the twentieth century to divide strictly between personal/foreign and collective/Hebrew writing.

The symbolic tensions, then, of inside and outside, of foreign and native (the foreign pseudonym hiding an Israeli author) were further exacerbated and emblematized by the covers of these books. The covers—sexually provocative, oftentimes misogynistic images, usually of men tortured or otherwise dominated by buxom, blond women in Nazi uniforms—were lifted wholesale from American magazines and by themselves reinforce the generic plot outline, as it was taken from the same American sources. But then, in the deployment of the cover images to support the Hebrew adaptations of the plots, something strange happens: the covers of the stalagim rarely reference much, if any, of the textual content, suggesting ambivalence in the appropriation of the American model—as if the cover announces its Americanness, even as the content speaks a different language altogether. In a particularly egregious example of the disconnect between cover and novelistic content, *Stalag Stalingrad* tells the story of three German soldiers navigating the world of Red Army prisoner of war camps after the surrender of the German 6th Army outside of Stalingrad in 1943. However, the cover depicts a completely different scene: a scantily clad, buxom blond woman with her hands tied high above her head to the

Figure 9.1. Cover of Ivan Spasky, *Stalag Stalingrad*.

top of a large gong, about to be tortured by a thick, bare-chested Chinese man, while a suspiciously (and thus anachronistically) Maoist-looking army officer watches from the side. Not a single element of the visual scene reflects the text, which tells a much more sanguine tale, where sexual titillation and prurient description play no role.

The divergence between cover and text in this example seems particularly telling, since *Stalag Stalingrad*, in its plot, represents perhaps the farthest distance from generic norm and American sources—and might be the most Hebrew and Jewish of the stalagim. Its author has an atypical name, Ivan Spasky; there's nothing "Aryan" about it. "Spasky" sounds Russian and Jewish, which is what the book claims for the author: a Jewish doctor in the Red Army who befriends one of the German prisoners and either witnesses or retells the events depicted. Like other authors of the stalagim, Spasky is part of the story he tells, but *not* as a protagonist. Rather, Spasky inhabits the margins of the story and tells the tale in a strange mixture of distanced observer and ventriloquist for the thoughts, feelings, and even dialogue of the German prisoners themselves.

In many instances, the Anglo-American pseudonymous writers are both author *and* protagonist of their stories—an odd sort of narrative role in novels that generally eschew a first-person voice; instead, the figuration of authorial consciousness is enfolded within multiple layers of narrative obfuscation. Mike Baden, for instance, is not simply an "author"; he's also the protagonist of his own tale, but not in a conventional first-person retelling. Like other author-protagonists in the stalagim, Baden liberally employs free indirect discourse in the narrative in order to punctuate experience in the novel. The same is true for Roy Adams, the author-protagonist in *Stalag banot hasatan* (*Devil Girls Stalag*), where the narrative (ostensibly the character's own voice) presents the author's consciousness at critical moments of narrated monologue.

There are no other significant models in Hebrew literature of this sort of figuration of voice, despite the fact that literature of both the Palmach Generation and the Statehood Generation was rife with literary depictions of interiority. The interior dialogues of S. Yizhar, in "The Prisoner," say, and Yigal Mossinsohn, in a novel such as *Derekh gever*[16]—let alone almost the entire *oeuvre* of Oz and Yehoshua—might come closest to dissembling the unity of individual consciousness and collectivity. Yet, canonical literature from both generations maintains the structuralist opposition of interior and collective expression *within* narration, and within a closely disciplined narrative.

In contrast, the effect of the unusual narrative device within the stalagim is a middle-voice reconstitution of the author-protagonist as both an actor in the scene and completely determined by it. As Barthes writes, "[I]n the modern verb of middle voice to write, the subject is constituted as immediately contemporary with the writing, being effected and affected by it."[17] The historian Hayden White then takes this idea from Barthes and makes it into a principle for a type of encounter with history (a phenomenology of history) that resounds with the sort of dialectical subjectivity described in the stalagim for these author-protagonists: "Discourse and figurality, knowledge and power, the chiasmic intertwining of desire and its objects—all this calls into question the possibility of a middle voice that overcomes all dichotomies."[18] The stalagim play on these suspended dichotomies of the middle voice and never attempt to resolve them. Indeed, the lack of resolution between "desire and its objects" might be the way that titillation and eroticism are tamed, or at least made presentable, within the anxiety of writing these stories in Hebrew.

The unresolved tension, then, of a subject enveloped within middle-voice narration, on one hand, and a narrative distancing itself from it, on the other, seems to predominate in the stalagim. For instance, in *Stalag banot hasatan*,[19] Roy Adams's seduction at the hands of the Nazi "devil girl" Grete Weber plays on the dialectical pulls of passive objectivity in the face of the sadistic monster, on one hand, and subjective reverie, when confronted by interior desire, on the other:

> "Hungry, Amerikaner?"
>
> "And what if I'm not hungry, Oberscharführer?" he answered.
>
> "Oberscharführer! Excellent, Amerikaner, excellent!" exclaimed the monster with obvious pleasure at hearing him pronounce her Nazi rank. "But let's leave that aside tonight, Captain," she added as she came closer and placed her hands on his shoulders. "By the way, do you have a nickname?"
>
> Damn was she gorgeous! A blond bombshell who could capture any man's heart. Her blue eyes, whose evil and savagery were completely undetectable, caressed with their gaze. And her face—the face of a young girl, pure and innocent. Her hands that she laid on his shoulders penetrated with a warmth that spread throughout his limbs and in a little bit, in a little bit he might have lost all self-control and pulled this wonderful

feminine body tightly against his. But just then his gaze fell on the whip that she had set down on the chair just before and immediately he was back in reality. (95–96)

Barthes's "moment of writing," in this case, is the moment of dreamlike memory and seduction by the beautiful object of Grete—a moment of temporal suspension (against the inexorable context of history itself), which is broken by the metonymic "whip" that pulls the narrative back into a normative division between a subject capable of acting (Grete) and the passive object of being acted upon (Roy Adams).

Figure 9.2. Cover of Roy Adams, *Stalag banot hasatan* (*Devil Girls Stalag*).

The dialectics of this sort of middle-voice writing—of subject and object enfolded within the same figure, holding in unresolved tension the contradictions of desire and victimhood—differentiates the stalagim significantly from the American magazines that provided the cover images and, too, the genre's urtext of male sexual submission. In America, the story of masculine anxiety in the face of changing social conditions seems constructed of an existential fear of inevitable passivity, of losing position within a modern world that has overtaken and suppressed male subjectivity, especially within a sexual setting.

The mode of reading itself enacted an important difference between the American and Israeli versions of this new masculine subject and his desires. The eyes of American magazine readers could dart and scan from article to advertisement, from text to photo to illustration, from the Wild West to Nazi Germany. Stalagim, however, demanded a very different reading, more distant from a simple identification with the kinetic action of the implied male subject of the magazine. The American male subject *was* the reader, who would improve himself—intellectually, physically, *sexually*—with the tools the magazine had to offer, available for him to pick and choose. The Israeli reader, on the other hand, was less active as a willful subject or as a subject that could identify within the world depicted in the stalag, where Jews were barely present and the Holocaust as such was never mentioned. Of course, there *was* some sort of thematic identification with the historical setting in the stalagim. Eichmann was brought to Jerusalem to stand trial certainly because Israel needed to assert its ownership of this history, its control over the Nazi past.[20]

However simple the Eichmann trial meant to present the moral issues of Nazism for the Israeli public, in the stalagim, identification with the subject of the novels was more complex and conflicted—"anxious" because of the "lack" always present in identification. Action and intention suffused the Israeli experience with Eichmann—of capture, of putting on trial, of executing—just as it did the American reader of the magazine tales. *True Men Stories*, perhaps the tamest of the American magazines that depict torture, sex, and violence,[21] subtitled itself: "The Action Magazine for Men." The irony of *Kalbato shel Schultz*, the sex book without the sex (it was not the only one), speaks to the way that pornographic meaning in the genre needs to be understood in terms of the figuration of a conflicted, anxious subject. If, as Barthes writes, the middle voice describes an "interior" and not an "anterior" writing—and thus a compromised subject in relation to the stability of the writing subject in Romantic literature—then Roy

Adams's experience of the enfolding of "activity and passivity," as Hayden White calls it, would be typical.

In this context, *Stalag Stalingrad* seems both exceptional and completely generic, in ways that speak to the dialectical instability of identification in the genre. There is nothing prurient about the sexual descriptions in the novel. Sexual desire, in all its forms and complexity, reflects onto a figuration of identity and identification that is fluid, unstable, and completely fungible. Indeed, the refusal in the book of pornographic sexual description challenges much of the way that the genre has been critically understood. In 2002, for instance, Eshed both reinvigorated an awareness of the stalagim decades after they had receded into obscurity *and* established a restricted reading of the novels that did little to move beyond the original outcry when they first appeared. In his reading, the stalagim signify sex and torture, beginning with *Stalag 13* and moving linearly to a complete exhaustion of the genre by 1965. According to Eshed, the progression of generic development from rise and apotheosis to degeneration is not only inexorable but teleological, as novelty demands ever greater radicalization in the primary elements of generic conformity.[22]

Stalag Stalingrad challenges the intuitive logic of both Eshed's study and Ari Libsker's 2007 documentary *Stalagim*, by highlighting the figuration of the subject and not descriptions of sex. *Stalag Stalingrad*[23] derives from an expansion of the genre well beyond the original generic story, but does not degrade into mannerism. Rather, in a way, this novel deconstructs the entire genre. In *Stalag Stalingrad* the camp becomes several different *Soviet* facilities set up for *German* prisoners, as the novel follows three German soldiers, Adolph Braunmann, Wilhelm Junger, and Fritz Fritzental. While all three eventually end up in Stalag Stalingrad, a special camp for incorrigible prisoners, their peregrinations through the Soviet camp system first has them split up and experiencing less severe conditions: Adolph at a work farm run by women (the strongest gesture to generic norms), and Wilhelm and Fritz at a work detail clearing a forest. Eventually all three reunite at Stalag Stalingrad, where, it seems, no one is meant to survive.

Many of the genre's conventions are ostensibly present in the novel: disease (typhus and lice, specifically); women guards (at the work farm); and eventual escape (but only for Wilhelm). Of greatest interest is the role of sex and sexual description in the narrative. And here the novel begins to deviate significantly from the expectations of Eshed, Libsker, or any number of critical assessments. Normative heterosexual desire applies only to Adolph Braunmann, the least sympathetic of the three Germans. We read of Adolph's fantasies of his girlfriend back home while he despairs during the encirclement of the Germans outside of Stalingrad. Then, at the work farm Adolph becomes the lover of the female commandant. However, she is anything but the generic ideal of young, blond, and svelte, in contrast to the seductively buxom vixen, Ludmilla, who repeatedly refuses Adolph's sexual advances. Instead, sex with the older, zaftig commandant becomes merely instrumental and devoid of desire, a moral and strategic transgression, according to the text, that ends badly for all involved, both Russian and German. Finally, when Adolph and Wilhelm eventually escape Stalag Stalingrad and scavenge through the countryside, Adolph meets his demise attempting to rape a Russian farm girl. Her mother fatally stabs him with a kitchen knife while Wilhelm looks on, morally and physically paralyzed and dumbstruck. Intentionality and willfulness consistently get the better of Adolph and, indeed, lead to his death. Wilhelm and Fritz, on the other hand, have no sexual experiences, save for the homosexual intimacy that builds between them, reflecting their identity fluidity, which would be contingent on any present experience. Their relationship is depicted as unintentional, supportive, and authentically tender, in contrast to much of the brutality that accompanies the depravations of war, disease, desperation, and heterosexual union.

Possibly, the inversion of the story—German prisoners in an ostensibly allied camp—allows for a different treatment of sexuality and torture. The German-ness of the three men certainly permits a moral fungibility in how readers will react to them, and because of this, identification shifts radically throughout the book, based on very narrow contexts. Subjects float freely, untethered to large, national networks of signification, as the narrative focalizes on a surfeit of moral actors performing in ever-shifting, local contexts. In other words, the narrative does not rely on discursive or national distinction to formulate moral and emotional identification with, or distance from, characters. Moral judgment depends on the dialectical interplay of action on the surface of a present-time only mildly inflected by German-ness or Russian-ness. Indeed, it can be difficult—and for a young Israeli in the early 1960s in the midst of the Eichmann trial, probably dizzying—to follow the narrative's shifting sympathies and identifications. *Stalag Stalingrad* shows the expressive possibilities of a dialectics of anxiety where desire (the world of fantasy) plays out amid the overwhelming events of history. Rather than degenerating into the rawest forms of aggression and violent rape, *Stalag Stalingrad* is a complex excursus on questions of perspective and literary identity within a moral setting whose strength has always been the absence of a moral compass.

The figure of the Jew partially fills a moral gap in *Stalag Stalingrad* (and in the stalagim more generally). While few Jews appear in these books and are rarely named, the Jew fulfills a significant function in the dialectics of anxiety that drive the genre.[24] *Stalag Stalingrad*, in this sense, represents something of an outlier with its Jewish doctor/author, Ivan Spasky. But Spasky's position in the construction of the book typifies a certain function for the Jew throughout the genre. He acts as the passive, distanced observer, a moral corrective to the scenes he observes and describes. In the economies of desire within the genre, sutured identification with the German characters is not easily avoided. Thus, at moments of danger, when the fantasy of the reader's experience threatens to fall into a specific mode of character identification, the narrative pulls back (reverses, really) into the cultural imaginary of the world outside the book and the real "bears down," as Lacan would say,[25] to create the anxious dialectics at work between identification and disgust. The result is a constantly shifting narrative point of view that reflects the instability of the genre's moral force. As Wilhelm and Fritz, for instance, enter Stalag Stalingrad and begin to understand the extent to which their chances of survival have declined, we both approach Junger's consciousness and recoil from a moral corrective:

> [Junger's] thoughts at that moment had turned to a particular picture that he remembered at that time—an image of civilians, Polish Jews, as they were being moved to a concentration camp.
> "Someone sees all and everyone pays according to his actions," he said to himself bitterly.
> "What?" asked Fritzental. "What did you say?"
> "Nothing, Fritzi. Nothing."
> After a few minutes Fritz Fritzental asked again:
> "But why did they send us to a penal camp for prisoners of war? What was our crime? Yours and mine, at least?"
> "And what crime did the Jews commit?" Junger answered in a continuation of his prior thoughts.
> "What?" said Fritz astonished, "I don't understand."
> "Nothing, Fritzi, nothing. Try to get some sleep!" (135–36)

Stalag banot hasatan, as Eshed notes, contains even more explicit reference to the Holocaust; the prisoner-of-war camp where Roy Adams finds himself imprisoned sits adjacent to a concentration camp filled with

Jews. Through the brief appearances of Jewish figures, the text constructs a moral corrective to desire run amok. Pornographic eroticism in the text always already is mediated through Jewish experience. Just as subject and object dialectically refer to their opposites within the complex signifying logic of the stalagim, so too the terms of individual and collective lose any ideational stability. As the text delves further into one side of this opposition, the more the other side imposes itself. The constant complaining of the American officer, Roy Adams, subjected nightly to the sexual exploitations of Grete Weber—even as he lusts after her during the day—seems comical. Indeed, prurient content in the novel exists only in the complaint of sexual *excess*—not in the idea that sex might be happening, but that it might be too much; pleasure spills over from the insatiability of the sexualized woman.

At two critical junctures, where desire and lust *for* Grete might seem to overwhelm any understanding of her political and sexual dominance over the story, the Jew—and really, the Holocaust—intrudes on free interchanges of that desire. We already encountered above one of the expressions of middle-voice desire, when Roy Adams's consciousness elides with the narration and notices Grete's beauty. The scene unleashes desire, even as the glimpse of the whip makes the "real" press onto the moment of seduction. But excess desire hovers in the air unsatisfied after this erotic turn with Grete. And so, a few pages later, the text retreats into a determined description of Grete's inherent evil and savagery, which might have been earlier obfuscated by her lovely blue eyes. Grete's true nature—or the complementary evil to erotic arousal—reveals itself in violence against the Jew, in full sight of Roy Adams's gaze. What the metonym of the whip only implied, the image of the suffering Jew metaphorically fulfills:

> At Grete Weber's command the blond monsters lined up along the fence with submachine guns drawn. . . .
>
> The Jew . . . stood standing in the middle of the yard with his back to the hut and facing Grete, when suddenly the monster shouted:
>
> "Come here, Jew!"
>
> According to the rules of the "game," which had been explained to the Jew beforehand, the Jew jumped from his place at the sound of her voice and ran as quickly as he could to within two paces of Grete. There he stopped and fell to his knees.
>
> "You love me, don't you?" Grete directed in mockery to the Jew. (105–106)

After two more pages of humiliations, Grete finally unleashes an attack dog, who kills both the Jew and the rest of Roy Adams's fantasized desire. The Jew in the stalagim thus corrects an identification that would confuse desire and "the real," reminding the reader of the dialectical negotiation taking place, and the horrors of excess enjoyment.

It might *not* be that sex in the stalagim only acts as a metaphoric cover story—a cipher—to a more profound encounter with experience in the camps. Sex might just be sex. And the stalagim might best be remembered for the arousal they allowed in a closed, inward-looking, and puritanical society that was Israel in the 1950s and early 1960s. But the setting is so overdetermined within a Jewish world that books like *Stalag Stalingrad* and *Stalag banot hasatan* seem unthinkable in any other form or genre of Israeli canonical or popular literature of the time—and well beyond. For these reasons, we might conclude, the genre *must* be suffused by its own foreignness. The subjectivity of the author-protagonist of the stalagim, and the way these novels pull their implied readers into an identification with the anxious tensions of lust, desire, and violence in the books, marks a uniqueness in the genre—and a challenge to other figures of Israeli individualism that emerged at the same time.

Libsker's documentary film, *Stalagim*, seems typical in following Eshed's reading of the genre and thus draws a direct connection between the stalagim and the earlier work of Ka-tzetnik's sexualized descriptions of Jewish experience in Nazi ghettos and camps in his 1953 novel, *Beit habubot* (*The House of Dolls*).[26] The connection between Ka-tzetnik and the stalagim runs, according to Libsker, directly through the Eichmann trial, when Yehiel Dinur took the stand and finally revealed his identity as the infamous author of tales of Holocaust sexual depravation, Ka-tzetnik.

A comparison of the stalagim and Ka-tzetnik's story of a concentration camp "pleasure house," staffed by Jewish women for the pleasure of Nazi officers, however, might better be seen for the contrasts that emerge between the books. Whatever similarity might exist in the sexual perversions implied by these books, an important question of difference persists, first posed in Merav Kristal's article on Libsker's film: If the sexual-aesthetic mechanisms they both counted on are similar, why did Dinur remain a part of Israeli culture, while the stalagim disappeared?[27] Dinur's writings may have fallen out of favor by the 1990s, but after his collapse on the witness stand at Eichmann's trial he became something of a minor celebrity in the country, and *Beit habubot* entered the Israeli school curriculum for some years. In a way, the strength of Kristal's question might lie in its flawed assumption of equivalence between *Beit habubot* and the stalagim, that the perversions, taboos, and implied descriptions of sexual experience work within a significatory mechanism that is the same across these works.

A certain historical coincidence does triangulate both the stalagim and Ka-Tzetnik within the Eichmann trial. As Pinchevski and Brand aptly conclude, "The Stalags testify to the nascent Holocaust consciousness among the Israeli young generation: early articulations of things previously unspoken—new speech for sex and at the same time new speech for *trauma*." But historical coincidence also downplays the significance of the stalagim as a critical reaction to the time. While trauma accounts for much of the Israeli reaction to the Holocaust, the stalagim actually seem quite unaffected by trauma—and this small fact might account for much of their irreverent strength. Rather, the stalagim display an anxiety of desire looking outward, through the *autre* of a Holocaust experience that dialectically outlines a subject struggling with the confines of a statist identity, not "a generation's coming to power, coming to terms."[28] The trauma that Dinur figures does little to subvert an ideological construction of literature and culture in Israel. Trauma in *Beit habubot* reinforces the intactness of Jewish subjectivity; desire plays no role in Dinur's construction of identity within the camps. Dinur's writing, in *Beit habubot* and well beyond, looks completely inward, into a self-contained, completely stable, and intentional subject. Dinur's figures stand in contrast both to a subjectivity forged by the stalagim that is *nonidentical* to itself (to borrow from Adorno)[29] and to the ways that writers such as Jean Amery or Primo Levi saw the breakdown of a Cartesian intactness in the individual's experience of the camps.[30] For Amery and Levi, like the stalagim, identity is mediated through a complex network of imposing forces, and is primarily defined by a lack of ability to fulfill desire. Dinur's protagonist, Daniella, on the other hand, is a willful subject, even as a victim; for her, consciousness remains intentional.

The dialectical subject of the stalagim can never envision or imagine the possibility of willed action that drives Dinur's characterization of Daniella, for whom fantasy is neatly organized through time and is always nostalgic, as it is in so many Holocaust representations: desire yearns for what was, for the life that preceded the horrors of the narrative present. In contrast, the hero of the stalagim exists in the nonidentity of the present, a *Jetztzeit*, as Benjamin would call it,[31] which sees in history perhaps not absolute nonidentity, but an intersubjectivity that is dynamic and changing in relation to structures outside of the self. In that, the stalagim are built around a pornographic scene of indeterminable identification and open up a critique of the dominant structures of Israeli stability by revealing the complex, dialectical tensions that bind the individual within the collective. These books stood far outside of a normative Israeli discursive apparatus, and for that reason could never be appropriated or assimilated into any conception of Israeli or Hebrew literature.

In the end, the stalagim may not deserve to enter the literary canon of Hebrew letters. They are, after all, pulp fiction. But a *critical* reading of how they figure a type of dialectical subjectivity and nonidentity for their Hebrew audience certainly leads to a counter-reading of the development of normative Israeli individualism within the sanctioned literature of their day and thus moves the stalagim—if only for critical purposes—to the very center of that cultural moment.

Notes

1. Eli Eshed, *MiTarzan ve'ad zbeng: hasipur shel hasifrut hapopularit ha'ivrit (From Tarzan to Zbeng: The Story of Hebrew Pop Fiction)* (Tel Aviv: Bavel, 2002), 239.

2. "Victor Bolder" (Meron Oriel), *Stalag 217*, "translated by A. Rosen" (Tel Aviv: Yam Suf, 1961), back cover. Quoted in Eshed, 243.

3. In addition to *Kalbato shel Schultz*, there was also "Victor Bolder's" *Fraulein Schultz* (Tel Aviv: Yam Suf, 1962). *Hayiti kalbato hapratit shel kolonel Schultz*'s focus on a woman's narrative voice almost certainly led to the book's suppression. While none of the stalagim were much tolerated by Israeli officialdom, *Hayiti kalbato hapratit shel kolonel Schultz* indicates the limits of legal tolerance. On the question of acceptable and unacceptable transgression in Israeli pornographic literature of the 1960s, see Ofer Aderet, "Ahavah lesbit lo, iskei znut ken: kakh ishru ufaslu sifrei porno bishnot ha-60," *Haaretz* 21, no. 6 (2018).

4. The Israeli magazine *Gamad*, which published nude photographs, pornographic stories, and sexual humor, began publishing in 1960.

5. See, for instance, Andrea Dworkin, *Pornography: Men Possessing Women* (New York: Perigee Books, 1981).

6. See, for instance, Williams's *Hard Core: Power, Pleasure, and the "Frenzy of the Visible"* (Berkeley: University of California Press, 1999).

7. The oppositional structure of collective and individual has defined a great deal of scholarship on Israel across several disciplines. See, for instance, Yaron Ezrahi's analysis of Israeli political culture in *Rubber Bullets: Power and Conscience in Modern Israel* (New York: Farrar, Straus, and Giroux, 1997). Shabtai Teveth's

popular account of tank warfare in the Sinai during the Six-Day War in 1967 (*Hasufim batsariach*) begins with perhaps one of the most insightful accounts of the difference between individualism in the Palmach Generation and individualism in the Statehood Generation, in an analysis of the transformation of the army into a mechanized fighting force between 1962 and 1967. *Hasufim batsariach* (Jerusalem: Shoken, 1968); translated as *The Tanks of Tammuz* (New York: Viking Press, 1969). Recently, in literary history, Oded Nir, in *Signatures of Struggle: The Figuration of Collectivity in Israeli Fiction* (Albany: State University of New York Press, 2018), cogently reads the work of Gershon Shaked, Hanan Hever, and Shai Ginsburg as dependent as well on a structuralist opposition between collective and individual. Nir attempts to offer a counter-reading to the dominant model of Shaked, Hever, and Ginsburg, but oddly refuses to question the very terms of opposition, namely, individual and collective. Even in Nir's critical reading of his Israeli literary historical precursors, he is unable to rethink the stability of the terms deployed, let alone criticize the way that stability—or totality, as he might write, borrowing from Lukacs—always already depends on a stultifying lack of critical flexibility. My own work, as will become apparent below, relies on Adorno's ideas of negative dialectics and nonidentity, in contradistinction to any totalized decidability of aesthetic meaning and terms.

8. Recent social histories that take up the question of the development of the individual in 1950s Israel include: Orit Rozin, *The Rise of the Individual in 1950s Israel: A Challenge to Collectivism* (Waltham, MA: Brandeis University Press, 2011); and Anat Helman, *Becoming Israeli: National Ideals and Everyday Life in the 1950s* (Waltham, MA: Brandeis University Press, 2014).

9. "Gratuitous violence," a phrase Ohad Fischof uses to describe Uri Katzenstein's extreme performance art of the 1990s, might be the inheritor of the stalagim's effort to rework Israeli subjectivity (*Missive—patshegen* (Jerusalem: Israel Museum, 1993), 10). The literary equivalent of Katzenstein's deployment of disgust as an expressive mode of radical resistance in the 1990s might be Ronit Matalon's depictions of violence in "Little Brother" ("Ach katan," in *Zarim babayit* [Tel Aviv: Hakibutz Hameuchad, 1992]).

10. A simple key word search of "stalag" in Hebrew in the library's catalogue (http://merhav.nli.org.il/primo-explore/search?sortby=rank&vid=NLI&lang=iw_IL) will return these results.

11. "Kalbah lelo ba'alim" ("A Bitch with No Owner"), *Ha'olam hazeh* 1276 (Feb. 21, 1962): 18. See also Eshed, 251.

12. *Ha'olam hazeh* 1289 (May 23, 1962): 13.

13. Tel Aviv: Yam Suf, 1961.

14. For a history of these changes, see Warren Bass, *Support Any Friend: Kennedy's Middle East and the Making of the U.S.-Israel Alliance* (Oxford: Oxford University Press, 2003). See also Shabtai Teveth's account of the mechanization of the tank corps of the IDF in *Hasufim batsariach*.

15. For a wonderful expression of the clash between foreignness and Zionist purity in the 1950s and 1960s, see Meir Shalev's childhood memoir about his grandmother and the sudden arrival of an American vacuum cleaner into the sanctified grounds of the canonical pioneering settlement, Nahalal: *Hadavar hayah kakhah* (Tel Aviv: Am Oved, 2009), translated as *My Russian Grandmother and Her American Vacuum Cleaner: A Memoir* (New York: Schocken Books, 2011). The Hebrew title embeds within it the almost comical (and nearly untranslatable) obstinacy and haughtiness of the grandmother's pioneering generation, where "things" (*hadavar*) were "just so." In Hebrew, "thing" (*davar*) doubles as "word" in one of the language's greatest and most revealing ambiguities.

16. Tel Aviv: N. Twerski, 1953.

17. Roland Barthes, "To Write: An Intransitive Verb?" in *The Rustle of Language* (New York: Hill and Wang, 1986), 19.

18. Quoted in Martin Jay, "Of Plots, Witnesses, and Judgments," in *Probing the Limits of Representation: Nazism and the "Final Solution,"* ed. Saul Friedlander (Cambridge: Harvard University Press, 1992), 110–11.

19. "Roy Adams," *Stalag banot hasatan* (Tel Aviv: Hermash, 1963).

20. See Gideon Hausner, *Justice in Jerusalem* (New York: Schocken, 1968) and Hannah Arendt, *Eichmann in Jerusalem: A Report on the Banality of Evil* (New York: Penguin, 1963).

21. Images and stories from magazines such as *Man's Story, Man's Action, Men Today, All Man, Wildcat Adventures, Men in Conflict, Man's Adventures, Real Men, Man's Best, Man to Man,* and *Man's Daring* predominantly feature torture of women when their stories depict Nazis. As opposed to the covers of the stalagim, in these magazines the body, especially the woman's body, bears the mark of torture. Particularly prominent are tattoos on women's bodies: either prisoner numbers on arms or Nazi swastikas in various places. The cover of *Wildcat Adventures*, for instance, from April 1962, features a buxom blonde, Nazi woman terrorizing two half-naked, female inmates bearing camp tattoos just above their ample right bosoms: K-53 and K-68, perhaps a model for Ka-tzetnik. The cover for the American mass-market paperback edition of his *The House of Dolls* (New York: Pyramid Books, 1958) draws on this graphic trend of tattooing the breasts of women.

22. Eshed, 238–55.

23. The catalogue at Arizona State University lists the publication date as 1962, but there is no date indicated in the book.

24. Eshed reads the stalagim as completely absent of references to Jews and the Holocaust, with a single exception: *Stalag banot hasatan*. Amit Pinchevski and Roy Brand also minimize Jewish content in the stalagim, even though they discuss oblique references to the Holocaust in several of the novels and the direct mention of Jewish experience in *Stalag 33*. Amit Pinchevski and Roy Brand, "Holocaust Perversions: The Stalags, Pulp Fiction, and the Eichmann Trial," *Critical Studies in Media Communication* 24, no. 5 (2007): 398.

25. Jacques Lacan, *Anxiety: The Seminar of Jacques Lacan* (Cambridge, UK: Polity Press, 2016), 116.
26. Tel Aviv: Dvir, 1953.
27. Merav Kristol, "Porno bemachanei harikuz," *Ynet*, Oct. 26, 07.
28. Both quotations from Pinchevski and Brand, 403; emphasis added.
29. Throughout this chapter, I have employed the terms *nonidentity* and *dialectical subject* somewhat interchangeably, as informed by the writings of Theodor Adorno, especially his early essay, "The Idea of Natural History," *Telos* 60 (1984): 111–24, and his later works, *Negative Dialectics* (New York: Continuum, 1992) and *Aesthetic Theory* (Minneapolis: University of Minnesota Press, 1997). My understanding of these concepts is greatly informed by Martin Jay's study of the Frankfurt School, *The Dialectical Imagination* (Boston: Little, Brown, 1973), and by Alain Badiou's study of the later writings of Adorno, *Five Lessons on Wagner* (London; New York: Verso, 2010). See also Lane Kauffman's review of Jay and the Frankfurt School, which makes an important distinction in how these two terms, *nonidentity* and *dialectical subject,* intersect in Adorno and in Jay's understanding of the history of Frankfurt School ideas: "Critical Theory: The Nonidentity Crisis," *Diacritics* 6, no. 1, (1976): 16–22.
30. See, for instance, Jean Amery, *At the Mind's Limits* (Bloomington: Indiana University Press, 1980), especially his essay on torture; and Primo Levi, *The Periodic Table* (New York: Schocken, 1984), especially the essay on carbon.
31. From "Theses on the Philosophy of History," No. IX, in *Illuminations* (New York: Schocken Books, 1969), 261.

PART FOUR

CONCERNING CANONS

Disruptive Nativity
The Poetry of Rina Shani and the Sixties in Israel

RIKI TRAUM

אֵשׁ נִפְתְּחָה מִשָּׂדֶה, נֶפֶשׁ עֲיֵפָה נֶחְבֶּטֶת
לְקִיר עָפָר, לְקַו יָרֹק, קַו אָדֹם, קַו
אֵשׁ נִפְתְּחָה מִצָּפוֹן, רָעָה חוֹלָה מִמִּזְרָח,
מְזִמָּה קָשָׁה מִדָּרוֹם, נֶפֶשׁ כָּלְתָה,, לֵב
נִתַּז לְשַׂק חוֹל, רֶגֶל נֶעֶקְרָה מִבֵּיתָה . . .

A fire was opened from a field, a tired soul stricken
towards a wall of dust, a green borderline, red line, line of
fire was opened from north, sick evil from east,
harsh task from south, a soul extinguished, a heart
was sprayed over a sandbag, a leg was torn from its home . . .[1]

—*Shalom le'adoni hamelekh*, 1970

Reading Rina Shani's book *Shalom le'adoni hamelekh* (*Farewell to a King*, 1970) in present-day Israel clarifies both the strength of her poetry and the development of what she was fearing at the end of the 1960s. In this book, Shani expresses her anguish following the war of 1967 and issues an apocalyptic prediction about its irreversible outcomes. This book radicalizes a poetic course established in her two previous books, *'Ir zarah* (*Foreign City*, 1961) and *Yam na'ul* (*Locked Sea*, 1963) in which she describes the unbearable burden imposed by a birthplace on its devoted female subject, and in which she situates herself within a torment of existential loneliness and alienation.² After the Six-Day War, however, her existential distress found poignant poetic expression with deep roots in the war and its consequences. The lines above, taken from the poem "I Am in the East and My Heart Is in the East," offer explicit and expressive images of Shani's political agony and helplessness in the wake of the war: she depicts the violent and bloody new reality of her "expanded" land through a clear allusion to Yehuda Halevi's well-known twelfth-century poem, "Libi bamizrach" ("My Heart Is in the East") in which he expresses his yearning for Eretz-Yisrael and which opens with the now-hackneyed line, "My heart is in the east, and I in the uttermost west." The ill, exhausted subject of Shani's poem assures her reader that, unlike Halevi, her mental and physical beings overlap.

The title, "I Am in the East and My Heart Is in the East," draws attention to the painful abyss between the medieval Spanish Jewish poet and the Israeli-born Shani, who distances herself from the tradition of yearning for and romanticizing the land of Israel. Shani renounces the phantasmatic diction of the medieval poet and portrays the brutality of war in brief but violent images that turn her poem into a space of despair. Yet, the use of the word *beytah* (her house), referring to the severed leg, immediately evokes another space, neglected but always emotionally charged in times of war: home. Home and battlefield are incompatible spaces, and Shani places herself squarely in the abyss between them. This abyss is a point of departure in many of her poems and central in comprehending her ethical and aesthetic choices. Shani's conflictual and multifaceted dialogue with her birthplace, in all its existential-cum-political significance, is emblematic of her poetics from its early stages.

Shani's arrival on Tel Aviv's poetic scene in the early 1960s produced a corpus of writing that would span two decades, several genres, and many audiences. Born in Hadera, Rina Shani (1937–1983) started writing poetry as a young adult, sharing her complex, rather mature poems only with a few trusted confidantes. As a student at Hebrew University, she showed her poems to Leah Goldberg, who mentored her and encouraged her to publish her work. Shani's early poems carry a strong sense of alienation and the detachment of a young poet who constantly negotiates with her birthplace and is highly troubled by her position and vocation within it. Her despair is sociopolitical and associated with her geography, while her metaphysical hope that occasionally reveals itself, transcends geography and defies any relation between her location and her sense of belonging.³ That despair intensifies over time and generates an expressive voice of dissent and opposition—far different from that of Leah Goldberg, her mentor and a foundational figure in Israel's literary and academic establishment. Shani formed poetic language and aesthetics that rejected and undermined the poetic establishment and expressed the conflictual mentality of her literary group. Her idiosyncratic patterns not only shed new light on the Israeli poetics of the 1960s, but also reveal a poetic network that constitutes an important stage in the formation of counterculture identity.

In what follows, I examine Shani's modes of resistance to the concept of belonging. I am interested in the tropes, metaphors, and poetic strategies she uses to convey her rejection and defiance, and I explore the spatial figurations she uses to express her audacious positions. I start with the aesthetic ideas she shared with contemporary artists and her good friends, the playwright and translator Nissim Aloni (1926–1998) and the painter Yosl Bergner (1920–2017). Both played a significant role in her life and poetry. Their desire to undermine and challenge their relationship with their homeland is not only intriguing, but also discloses a distinctive group of artists who felt and acted as outsiders in their "home." Although the "young poets" of the 1960s, Meir Wieseltier, Yair Hurwitz, and Yona Wallach were better known, Shani's group was no less significant and left an indelible impression on Israel's cultural and literary circles during that decade and after. In the second part of my essay, I discuss Shani's poetic (and personal) relationship with Leah Goldberg, with whom she shared a strong sense of foreignness and existential concerns. Her lifelong affinity for Goldberg's poetry, as expressed in her personal notes and diaries, has much to do with the fact that they both were translators who could relocate themselves in other traditions and reterritorialize a sense of belonging unbounded by geography. A thorough examination of Shani's poems shows that early on her poetic self-consciousness had been formed in relation to her birthplace, whose presence constitutes a major stratum even in her first poems. When she met Goldberg, Shani already had a solid and clear sense of who she was as a poet. Her poems carried linguistic constructs and elements from her poignant dialogue with her contemporaries, but they drew from Goldberg's imagery that transforms the female biographical experience "to forms of multiple existence in her historical chronotopus."[4] Goldberg's and Shani's temporal and spatial configurations enact modes of belonging and nonbelonging, but they depart from different poetic stances and visions anchored, among others, in different generational circumstances. A better grasp of Shani's writing, however, requires a consideration of her work in relation to other artistic forms and expressions of the 1960s.

Committed and Nomadic:
The Counterculture of the 1960s

To understand Shani's poetic and ideological stances, it's important to consider the sociopolitical climate of the 1960s in Israel, the United States, and Europe. Charles Altieri describes the poetry scene of that decade: "Poetry sought to be 'experience in capital letters,' . . . because poets felt that intense poetic experience might serve as witness and proof of the power of mind to recover numinous values trampled underfoot by the assumptions of liberal industrial society."[5] Indeed, in its simplest terms, the 1960s were synonymous with female liberation, the Black Panthers, sexual freedom, rock and roll, and protest; however, the social changes were not simple. The transformation started in the family, spilled into the streets, and affected political life. Resistance was built by the young generation in the United States and students who protested on the campuses of Paris in 1968. The "Angry Young Men" in England and the Beat poets in the United States were two groups of working and middle-class artists and writers who had paved their artistic road in the 1950s, and then marked, inspired, and led the change in the 1960s. The postwar years, however, seemed to generate the need for what Allen Ginsberg called "Secret Heroes," who had been rejected by the canon and the mainstream.[6] Poetry anthologies that were published in Greenwich Village reveal the authentic desire for a revolutionary change that stirred young hearts. This desire is also found in Shani's poetry and personal notes.

Shani was surrounded by friends who had returned from revolutionary Paris, and since she translated from Italian, French, Spanish, and English into Hebrew, she could keep abreast of global events. At the time, Israel was on the verge of the Six-Day War. Israeli society was undergoing a radical change, since sociopolitical reality had shattered the myth of the collective. Concepts such as place, territory, and land became semantically multilayered and complex, ambiguous and questionable. In this fraught political atmosphere, the traveler-artist carried a major responsibility of witnessing and mobilizing ideas.[7] Shani's circle consisted of such artists whose linguistic sensitivity affected their poetic perceptions. Like her, Aloni was a translator and a traveler who constantly challenged his Israeli identity; Bergner had immigrated to Israel and, unlike most newcomers, renounced Hebrew and insisted instead on speaking Yiddish and English.

Shani published *'Ir zarah* (*Foreign City*) in 1961. In this book, she relies on biblical linguistic constructs while presenting a disturbing stance of rootlessness and estrangement. As '*Ir zarah* attests, she targeted the city as the major metonym that she wished to deterritorialize, that is to estrange from its familiar, known, and local state, and, in Deleuzian terms, to reterritorialize it and make it her own—to restructure and repossess it. She maps her city as a cartography of power, and thereby creates discursive relationships with the existential-ideological vision of Nissim Aloni, whose oeuvre reveals homeland/exile as two major abstract figurations that he constantly confronts.[8]

Aloni's work accents two major strata that might illuminate Shani's ideological-cum-poetic perception. Itzhak Ben Mordechai asserts that Aloni had transformed from perceiving exile as contradiction to homeland, to perceiving homeland itself as exile. Moreover, the following observation on Aloni describes Shani's ongoing dialogue with her birthplace: "[H]omeland and exile that in Aloni's youth had been geographical entities, became throughout the years mental entities. Nevertheless, Aloni's basic feelings towards his homeland had not changed essentially, and his relation to his birthplace—in both phases—remained complex and charged."[9] These tensions between exile and birthplace and between the geographical and mental entities were key axes in Shani's poetry until her death. Like Aloni, Shani's point of departure is that both her geographical birthplace and mental exile are enacted simultaneously through the same geographical space, where she lives and writes.

This perception of homeland as exile sheds important light on Shani's spatial economy in '*Ir zarah*, where the city functions as a major metonymic figuration of a hostile space that rejects its female-subject. Shani's city noticeably corresponds to Aloni's abstract homeland. Shani puts enormous responsibility on her land, her nation, as an entity that constantly casts off and excludes. Her subject is an orphan by birth whose mentality is exilic—without parents, leaders, or founding fathers. Being an orphan, for Shani, strips her poetic persona of all predetermined relations: between her female and universal beings, her national and self-commitment, her femaleness and her male-dominated surroundings. At the same time, it liberates her; her nomadism stands for conscious relinquishment as a standpoint of resistance, more than homelessness or compulsive displacement.[10]

In this context, Shani chooses to open her first book from a liminal position and sets her stance in a form of a "blind raft" as an unstable base and a clear allusion to Aloni's short story, "The Owl," in which the raft is used as a key trope:[11]

אֲלִיבִּי
לְיוֹסְל בֶּרְגְנֶר

נָסֵב אֶל הַשֻּׁלְחָן הַקַּר וְהָרֵיקָן
פָּנֵינוּ חַלּוֹנוֹת זְכוּכִית
יָדֵינוּ מְהַמְּרוֹת
בְּנִחוּשֵׁי עֵינַיִם
תָּמִיד אֶחָד, תָּמִיד שְׁלֹשָׁה,
אֲבָל אַף פַּעַם לֹא בִּשְׁנַיִם.

נָסֵב אֶל הַשֻּׁלְחָן הַמַּר
נַזְמִין בּוּעוֹת אֶל הַדּוּכָן
עֵינֵינוּ מְקַפְּצוֹת כְּאַנְקוֹרִים
מִקֵּן אֶל קֵן
יָדֵינוּ נִשְׁלָפוֹת מִנֶּדְנָן

אֲבָל פִּתְאוֹם נָצוּף כְּרַפְסוֹדָה עֲגֶרֶת
מֵכַּת מְכַרְסְמִים, קְרוּעָה מִיתָדוֹת,
פִּתְאוֹם הַקּוֹל אֲשֶׁר חָיִינוּ אֶת הֵדָיו
עוֹלֶה בְּגַלְגַּלֵּי הַמַּיִם
גּוֹלֵשׁ כַּאֲפֵלָה בַּוִּילוֹנוֹת

הִנָּם בָּאִים הִנָּם בָּאִים
עַכְשָׁו יָדֵינוּ לָרְוָחוֹת
וְלֹא נִשְׁאַל יוֹתֵר מִקֹּטֶן הַגַּרְגְּרִים
נֹאמַר
אֲבָל
הֲרֵי
בְּמַחְתְּרוֹת מִלֵּינוּ הַחוֹפְזוֹת
הָיִינוּ
הֲרֵי
תָּמִיד
חֵרְשִׁים — אִלְּמִים — עִוְרִים.

Alibi
To Yosl Bergner

We'll sit around the cold, empty table
our faces windows of glass
our hands gambling

with guessing eyes
always one, always three,
but never as a couple.

We sit by the bitter table
order bubbles to the podium
our eyes hop like sparrows
from one nest to another
our hands drawn from their scabbard

but suddenly we'll float like a blind raft
struck by rodents, ripped of stakes,
suddenly the voice whose echo we lived
rises in the water rings
glides like darkness in the curtains

here they come here they come
our hands extend now to the winds
and we won't borrow anymore from the smallest grain
we'll say
still
nonetheless
in the underground of our hasty words
we
have
always
heard no evil—spoken no evil—seen no evil.[12]
('*Ir zarah*, 1961)

Dedicated to Yosl Bergner, the poem depicts a familiar scene in a café, where the group of three used to sit. This familiarity becomes intimidating as the poem unfolds and Shani undermines the group's ostensible comfort. The dedication discloses the social context of the poem and clarifies the lyric situation in the first stanza. Yet, the situation evokes a strong sense of instability and lack of intimacy; limbs are used as synecdoche to emphasize the detachment of the group. Their hands are gambling, suggesting hedonism and a sense of immorality; the eyes are guessing as a gesture of unknown future, and their glass faces reflect the changing view that a bird experiences throughout its constant movement. The sociocultural alienation here discloses intimate agony; her complaint that the group had met "never as a couple" could refer to her own frustration over being an outsider even among her friends.[13]

In the second stanza, Shani introduces the sparrow as a social bird that hops swiftly from one nest to another. The nests, like the scabbard, are metonymic of home, whose "dwellers," whether sparrows or hands, wish to leave. The group suddenly changes from a circle of friends to a group of refugees that has survived a storm and is destined to restart their lives in the same familiar/estranged place. This is the cartographic accuracy that Shani creates: her subjects are not migrants or travelers, but insider-exiles, refugees in their own habitat. Refugees problematize the right to belong and the right to enter, and Shani deliberately renounces these "basic," obvious rights. A strong sense of (be)coming fills this arrival and with it, as she clarifies later in the poem, guilt and regret. Aloni's raft in "The Owl" that I already mentioned marks permanent exile; Shani imports that trope, transposing its meaning, so that the raft expresses a sense of liberation and hazard. The floating raft that functions as a romantic trope in Aloni's story stands for Shani's resistance to a sedentary settling and mindset, or a reverse trope of the bourgeois lifestyle that gradually reveals itself as an impossible and hypocritical alternative for Shani and her group. It also creates a textual continuity with Aloni and suggests a spatial metaphor in which streets are imagined as a sea. Applying Aloni's urban imagery to Shani's poem suggests that the poem takes place in the city. Significantly, unlike rhapsody, which connotes harmonious musicality and pathos, Shani creates an anti-epic setting, establishing the "raft" as an antibourgeois trope that accurately portrays her image of a native who feels in exile in her own birthplace.[14]

Even more striking are the poem's final lines:

בְּמַחְתְּרוֹת מִלֵּינוּ הַחוֹפְזוֹת
הָיִינוּ
הֲרֵי
תָּמִיד
חֵרְשִׁים — אִלְּמִים — עִוְרִים.

In the underground of our hasty words
we
have
always
heard no evil—spoken no evil—seen no evil.

Shani alludes to the three proverbial apes from Japanese antiquity, but she also adds a metapoetic reference by mentioning "the underground of our hasty words." That phrase could refer to poetic responsibility or irresponsibility. The raft is used as an alibi, as an evidence of being "elsewhere" when their (birth)place sank.

Homeland, albeit absent, is no less prominent. Shani often replaces her *moledet* with usually unidentified spatial metonyms such as city (in *'Ir zarah*), unidentified land, and sea (in *Yam na'ul*, her second book), figurations "within reach" that present palpable spatial alternatives. To be clear, more often than not Shani's metonyms carry a major civil (and civic) responsibility to protect and shelter, and by not protecting they disappoint their devoted subjects—like a homeland.[15]

But there is more to it. Shani is highly invested in the metapoetic significance of her outsider position and her own alienation. In this context, incomprehensibility or the threat of being rendered incomprehensible (as a poet and translator) metapoetically bridges concrete geographic space and the poetic realm. The following poem illustrates this metapoetic significance:

פרח זר. אינו מבין את שפתי

פֶּרַח זָר. אֵינוֹ מֵבִין אֶת שְׂפָתִי
הַקָּשָׁה כָּאֲבָנִים הָאֵלֶה. אֵינוֹ

קוֹרֵא אֶת אוֹתִיּוֹת הֶחָצָץ. מְחַיֵּךְ
לְעֶזְרָה, טוֹבֵעַ מְשֻׁנֶּה.

לֹא הַשֶּׁמֶשׁ. לֹא הָרוּחַ הַזֹּאת.
הָאָרֶץ הָאַחֶרֶת. בּוֹא, דְּמָמָה,

לְיָדַי בַּמָּקוֹם הַמּוּזָר. הִנֵּה
יְסַפֵּר לִי עַל בַּיִת בְּתוֹךְ הַשֶּׁלֶג.

אֵינֶנִּי מְבִינָה אֶת הָאוֹר הַנִּשְׁבָּר
שָׁם, בַּשֶּׁלֶג. אֲבָל כָּאן, עַכְשָׁו,

הוּא מְעָרֵם יָם, הוּא נִגְרָף,
בַּשֶּׁקֶט הַמֻּטְרָף שֶׁל אַדְמַת-שָׂרָף.

Foreign Flower. Doesn't Understand My Language

Foreign flower. Doesn't understand my language
that is hard like these stones. It doesn't

read the gravel letters. Smiles
for help. Drowns strangely.

Not the sun. Nor this wind.
the other land. Come, silence,

next to me in the strange place. Here
will tell me about a house in the snow.

I don't understand the breaking light
there, in the snow, but here, now,

it piles sea, swept away
in the mad serenity of resin's land.[16]
(*Yam na'ul*, 1963)

In her early poems, Shani uses couplets to convey a trope as a complete idea, in a brief and enveloped syntactical unit. In "Foreign Flower. Doesn't Understand My Language" there is an implicit incompatibility between the inconsistent syntactic divisions and the pace, echoing the interrupted communication between the foreign flower and Shani's lyric "I." Noticeably, the entire poem is built on incompatible spatial figurations and tropes, which creates another realistic (although unidentified) counterspace that mirrors the miscommunication between the "I" and the foreign flower; the metalinguistic layer in the poem is significant since it is juxtaposed with the spatial tropes. Shani unveils the metalinguistic layer in the first line, but even here the line is broken, and the flow is interrupted: "Foreign Flower. Doesn't understand my language." The foreignness of the flower is expressed first and foremost through language. Later, Shani characterizes her language as "hard like these stones." The aestheticization of her own language and the deixis *ha'eleh* (these) clearly places Shani's lyric "I" in the Israeli landscape. The language then acquires a spatial quality that turns it into a space.

The first couplet establishes the important relationship between poetic language, its intelligibility, and geography, which function here as interrelated spaces. In the second, Shani continues to accent biography and geography as two crucial strata in the inner being of both the foreign flower and her lyric "I": the flower, for instance, doesn't read the "gravel letters," a blunt trope that accents the palpability of the letters and at the same time rejects their lyric function. The mental state of the flower is noticeably inconsistent: it "smiles for help" and "drowns strangely." The picture is far from optimistic, but it conveys a certain ability to survive.

The following couplets juxtapose incompatible spatial tropes, along with the unyielding persistency of Shani's lyric "I" to reconcile their differences. Shani's constant use of deixis is her strategy to locate the lyric "I" as native and local, while reaffirming the foreignness of the foreign flower. Since the poem is built on oppositions and intelligibility through the intense use of deictic structures, it is unavoidable to recall Paul de Man's theory of linguistic resistance, where deixis is not only the linguistic mechanism that allows oppositions and distinctions, it refers

> [t]o the fact that language has taken place and that it is something that takes place, that is even something that offers resistance. . . . To language, all of the real is fungible but itself, and the resistance that language opposes to itself—which may take the form of troping—establishes the reality of language to language, which then constructs all other forms of references upon this fundamental model.[17]

According to de Man, Shani may use the incompatible spatial tropes as a form of linguistic resistance from which all other forms of resistance depart. The deixis concretizes her resistance and suggests that this conflict takes place between the lyric and the biographical "I"s, as one resists the other, or rather its own Other. The resistance is intensified with the negations of the sun and "*this* wind" (my emphasis), motifs that mark Shani's immediate Israeli landscape. Following that, when asking the flower to place itself next to her, she calls her location a "strange place." As a countercartography, she situates the origin (homeland) of the foreign flower in a remote and different topography of a house in the snow and frames it with the deixis "here" ("Here/ will tell me about a house in the snow"). At this point the difference between her "here" and the foreign flower's "there" acquires a clear spatial significance, while introducing the concept of "home," and opening up new interpretative possibilities. Shani's lyric "I" admits that she doesn't understand the breaking light "there," in the snow, and reintroduces the conflictual situation with which the poem opens. Significantly, the language begins hard and the light breaks toward the end. If the light marks a spark of hope, then it breaks; yet, the language is resisting and resilient. Grammatically, the final couplet begins in the final sentence of the fifth couplet: "but *here, now,* // *it* (he) piles sea, swept away/ in the mad serenity of resin's land." The accurate meaning of the deixis *it* is blurred, and it could refer to both the breaking light and the foreign flower. Perhaps for Shani the light and the flower are two realizations of the same metaphor that marks the same "Other."

Planted-Twice and Non-Planted: Leah Goldberg and Rina Shani

In "Foreign Flower" it is striking that Shani mentions snow, while her reader knows that this landscape is not in Shani's immediate geographical space. Moreover, the lyrical image is one of storytelling: the foreign flower tells her about its house in the snow while being swept away in the madness of Shani's here and now. The motifs used in "Foreign Flower" evoke Shani's literal and poetic relationship with Leah Goldberg. The poetic role of Goldberg's poetry in Shani's poem is no less interesting than their personal relationship and mutual affinity.[18] A thorough reading of Shani's poems reveals an intertextuality that occasionally collides with her artistic interchanges with Nissim Aloni and Yosl Bergner. Shani found a great interest in Goldberg's rendering of existential-cum-geographical experiences such as foreignness, exile, homeland(s), and intelligibility. Goldberg perceived the land of Israel as "homeland by choice" and as a place of exile.[19]

Goldberg's status as a translator also played a significant role in her relationship with Shani, a prolific translator in her own right. I refer here to the poetic prism they shared regarding the poet as a translator, who, as Adrianna X. Jacobs has suggested, uses "'translation' as both an interlingual movement and a practice that was closely aligned with the desire for the kind of cultural and geographic mobility."[20] I read Jacobs's challenging duality in its wider meaning: the impact of the "translator" on the "poet" and the interlingual mobility that simultaneously allows the positions of insider and outsider, of belonging and nonbelonging. The relation between writing poems and translating them "allows these 'different' landscapes to come—even momentarily—into contact. It is this in-between space of translation that generates the poem, arguably more so than the exilic position—indeed, it becomes a precondition for poetry."[21] Shani believed in this "momentary contact" between two landscapes: between the foreign flower's house in the snow and Shani's mad "resin's land." This momentary contact is perceived through spatial figuration that enables the nomadic movement between them.

Goldberg was famous for her dual affiliation to two homelands, and her refusal to accept the possibility of only one homeland is conveyed in her poem "Pine" as the "heartache of two homelands."[22] According to Natasha Gordinsky, Goldberg's "poems suggest modes of resistance to the bonds of one homeland, by doubling it or by putting other places aside. Goldberg re-writes the oppositions home/exile into a form of belonging in non-belonging, which is a nomadic poetic mode."[23] By using the trope of homeland, Goldberg introduces a complex yet possible sense of simultaneous affiliation with two "homes." Goldberg's well-known negations in "Pine" ("Here I'll not hear the cuckoo's voice/ here the tree will not wear a snowy hat,") are immediately contrasted and balanced ("but in the shadow of these pines/ my entire childhood is revived.") By stating "I was planted twice," she introduces her rooting and uprooting. The Israeli-born Shani, however, clearly could not see even the land of her birth as "home-land." On the contrary, she liberates herself from "the homeland-complex," and creates "alternative routes." The nomadic movement that releases Shani from any type of national commitment also allows her to experience and thus reterritorialize realistic and imaginary spaces and to define her own site in between them.

To gauge affinity between Shani and Goldberg, consider two poems, one at a time, and each poet's approach to the metonym of the city and themes of belonging. In Goldberg's cycle "A Nameless Journey," written in Copenhagen in 1960, the lyric "I" is a foreigner in a foreign city. Interestingly, Goldberg creates and juxtaposes, within the poem's space, multiple spaces that coexist and invert each other. This spatial multiplicity not only encourages a nomadic movement within the metaphoric/realistic space of the poem, but also brings the different spaces in the poem "to a form of co-existence, without necessarily choosing one."[24]

ג

זֶה שָׁבוּעוֹת שֶׁאִישׁ אֵינוֹ פוֹנֶה
אֵלַי בִּשְׁמִי, וְזֶה פָּשׁוּט מְאֹד:
הַתֻּכִּיִּים שֶׁבְּמִטְבַּח בֵּיתִי
עוֹד לֹא לָמְדוּ אוֹתוֹ,
הָאֲנָשִׁים בְּכָל רַחֲבֵי הָעִיר
אֵינָם יוֹדְעִים אוֹתוֹ.
וְהוּא קַיָּם רַק עַל נְיָר, בִּכְתָב,
וְאֵין לוֹ קוֹל, וְאֵין לוֹ צְלִיל וָתָו.

יָמִים אֲנִי הוֹלֶכֶת לְלֹא שֵׁם
בָּרְחוֹב שֶׁאֲנִי יוֹדַעַת אֶת שְׁמוֹ.
שָׁעוֹת אֲנִי יוֹשֶׁבֶת לְלֹא שֵׁם
מוּל עֵץ שֶׁאֲנִי יוֹדַעַת אֶת שְׁמוֹ.
וְלִפְרָקִים אֲנִי חוֹשֶׁבֶת לְלֹא שֵׁם
עַל מִי שֶׁאֵינֶנִּי יוֹדַעַת אֶת שְׁמוֹ.

3

It's been weeks since anyone has addressed me
by name, and it's so simple:
the parrots in my kitchen
haven't yet learned it,
people in all corners of the city
don't know it.
It exists only on paper, in writing,
it has no sound, no note or voice.

For days I walk nameless
in the street whose name I know.
For hours I sit nameless
facing a tree whose name I know.
Sometimes, nameless, I think
of he whose name I do not know.[25]

In the third poem of the cycle, the picture is one of losing identity in a foreign city, or a cruel deterritorialization of what defines us as social beings. This deterritorialization takes place in her own kitchen, a private and highly gendered metonym. She is voiceless, but her identity comes to being through writing. The reterritorialization of this identity starts exactly there, in her writing or in her poems. When Goldberg writes

"It," she regains a meaningful presence in her reader's eyes. In the second stanza, she juxtaposes anonymity and familiarity enacted from her no-name emplacement, which becomes her own intimate site. The nameless identity becomes a liberating possibility that Goldberg repeats in almost every line.

Reading Leah Goldberg's city poems clarifies that Shani molds her own foreignness out of similar poetic perceptions and materials. This is striking since Shani was not an immigrant; she wrote in her birthplace yet felt foreign. Rendering belonging in nonbelonging means to release and redefine a sense of being through concepts of home and its borders. What did Shani preserve of Goldberg's, and what did she discard? How does Shani resolve these two impossibilities of being and belonging released out of nonbelonging? Clearly, Shani realizes that Goldberg's spatial poetic possibilities are not always compatible with her own: Shani's poems are written from a different biographical point of view, and her *moledet* has a single point of reference. Yet, she could identify with Goldberg's point of departure and with the tension between belonging and nonbelonging, fully aware of the biographical differences between them. She develops a figurative space of nonbelonging through the figuration of the alienated city that confronts and destroys its returning female subject. This space allows the nomadic mode of movement in between poetic modes:

העיר הזרה
אֲנִי רָצִיתִי אֶת הָעִיר הַזָּרָה.

כְּשֶׁשָּׁבְתִּי מִיַּמִּים הַרְבֵּה
וְלֹא נָמֵל אֶחָד
רָצִיתִי עִיר זָרָה.
לֹא חֶדֶר
לֹא בַּיִת
לֹא חָצֵר
לֹא סִמְטָה.
אֲנִי רָצִיתִי אֶת כֻּלָּהּ.
אֲבָל כֵּיוָן שֶׁהָיְתָה זָרָה
הִסְתַּפַּקְתִּי בָּרְחוֹב
בְּחֶדֶר
בְּסִמְטָה
וּכְשֶׁהוּגְּפוּ חַלּוֹנוֹתֶיהָ
הָיִיתִי — פִּתְאוֹם
חֶלְדַּת עֲנָנִים

יוֹקֶשֶׁת וְזָרָה
וְאַחַר
שׁוּב נֶחֱצֵיתִי יוֹם יוֹם
וְהֶרֶף-עַיִן — וּשְׁנִיָּה
בַּחֲרַכֵּי הַתְּרִיסִים
שֶׁל הָעִיר הַזָּרָה,כְּשֶׁעָבְרָה הָעִיר הַזָּרָה.
לְמָקוֹם זָר
יָדַעְתִּי שֶׁנָּרוּ חוֹל עַל פָּנַי
שֶׁשָּׂמוּנִי לְחָלָל וְלִמְאֵרָה

וְעִירִי כְּבָרָה.

The Foreign City

I wanted the foreign city.

When I came back from many seas
and not one port
I wanted a foreign city.
Not a room
not a house
not a yard
not an alley.
I wanted all of her [it].
But since she was foreign
I was satisfied with a street
with a room
with an alley
and when her windows were shuttered
I was—suddenly
usty clouds
combative and foreign
and then
I was halved again day by day
and instant—and second
In the shutters' slits
of the foreign city.
When the foreign city moved

> to a foreign place
> I knew that they scattered sand on my face
> that they made me a corpse and a curse
>
> and my city is a sieve.
> ('*Ir zarah*, 1961)²⁶

This is an elegy to an alienating and excluding city. Noticeably, in the first line this city is not any city but a familiar one whose alienation Shani desires: "Ani ratsiti et *ha*'ir *ha*zarah." This familiarity changes as the poem unfolds and *the* city becomes unidentified. Already here, Shani creates two "different cities," one familiar and known and the other unknown. Following the first, separated line, Shani turns to an almost storytelling mode about her return from what seems to have been a long journey. The image of "many seas and not one port" evokes a semi-biblical style that neutralizes the lyric situation from its immediate temporal context, and creates another space in the past, from which the lyric "I" returns. Following the return, the foreign city "loses" its identity and becomes an abstract notion (or space) that Shani's "I" desires. Significantly, the verb *ratsiti* (I wanted) is prominent precisely because it removes any rational explanation for the "I" intentions, and semantically it evokes an erotic meaning to her desire "to have the city." With that phrase, the poem suggests another abstract site of interaction between the subject and the city that is the object of her desire.

The following list of negations ("not a room," "not a house," "not a yard," "not an alley") breaks the metonym of the city into synecdoches (and the imagined space into palpable components), thereby generating counterspaces to the wholeness that she desires: "*kulah*" (all of her.) Each negation presents a motif with a spatial significance. The shift in the poem appears in the tenth line, where she anchors her impossible desire in the foreignness of the city: since the city is foreign, the lyric "I" is satisfied with the counterspaces that she previously negated. In the following lines, the city changes its mode, again in spatial terms: "And when her windows were shuttered/ I was—suddenly/ rusty clouds/ combative and foreign." The lines allude to the fact that, before, the windows were open, but they also reveal that the "I" is now foreign too. The shuttered windows mark the effect of alienation, and mirror the alienation of the subject, who becomes like the city. From this point, when both the subject and the city are foreign, the lyric "I" is brutalized by the city; they are identical, and the space becomes an aggressor. The position of the subject is inverted, and from a desiring subject she becomes a victimized object. The change is evidently linked to the foreignness, which is a quality shared by all the poetic components, but the metonymic function reveals itself as crucial: the city (its people) rejects Shani in repeated acts of violence. Toward the end, the foreignness is multiplied because the city moved to a "foreign place."

There are two possible resolutions to the logical problem of a foreign city that moves to a foreign place. The first reads the verb *moves* in the sense of *becomes*, that is, that the city becomes a place, a foreign site; the "local" foreignness of the city extends, and it becomes a wider foreign space whose foreignness is even more extreme. Significantly, the foreignness carries a spatial significance that projects on the inhabitants of the space: the "I"'s foreignness starts when the city rejects her.

The second possibility involves a heterotopic approach that might illuminate Shani's spatial perception of the city.[27] According to Foucault, heterotopias "always presuppose a system of opening and closing that both isolates them and makes them penetrable. In general, the heterotopic site is not freely accessible like public space."[28] By closing its windows and virtually relocating itself, the city abruptly cancels its accessibility. The "foreign place," in this context, doubles the inaccessibility of the city and thus intensifies the isolation of the lyric "I." Furthermore, according to Foucault, heterotopia "is capable of juxtaposing in a single real place several spaces, several sites that are in themselves incompatible. Thus it is that the theater brings onto the rectangle of the stage . . . a whole series of places that are foreign to one another."[29] Significantly, the foreign city not only "moves" throughout the poem, but also changes its grammatical function, and from a definite noun (*ha'ir*) it transforms into an indefinite noun (*'ir*) before its final version as an "identified" (familiar) city. It is not until the end, that Shani identifies the city as "my city." Out of her agony she reterritorializes her city, but she never dwells or feels at home "there."

Conclusion

Rina Shani's personal and poetic interchanges with Leah Goldberg and Nissim Aloni introduce new forms of poetic transpositions; through her spatial imagery, she presents modes of nonbelonging to allow nomadic, alienated, and dispersed visions that are accountable and committed to the complex, often tragic, reality of her birthplace. She felt affinity for Goldberg but transposed their shared concerns from the possibility of two homelands to the impossibility of one homeland. Shani's nomadic stance moves in-between modes of nonbelonging and intensities of alienation that merge biographical elements with cultural ones. Her spatial economy in her first book allows her to avoid the much-too-obvious political interpretation, which becomes a necessary matter after the war of 1967. At the end of the 1960s, when she is determined to leave Tel Aviv, Shani's nomadic subject is equally accountable for both the victim whose leg was torn from home and her own victimized being that was "halved again day by day" in the shutters' slits of her alienated city.

Notes

I discuss aspects of Shani's work at length in my introductory essay to Rina Shani's *Mivchar shirim* [*Selected Poems*], ed. Riki Traum. See Riki Traum, "'Machshavot shelo nitlakchu': 'al shiratah shel Rina Shani ['Thoughts That Were Not Burned': on Rina Shani's Poetry]," in Rina Shani, *Mivchar shirim* [*Selected Poems*], (Bnei Brak: Hakibbutz Hameuchad, 2019), 7–40. I wish to acknowledge the support and advice of Giddon Ticotsky whose comprehensive knowledge, academic generosity, and love of poetry allowed me to expand my research and consider new perspectives that have sharpened my insights.

1. From "Ani bamizrach velibi bamizrach [I Am in the East and My Heart Is in the East]," in *Shalom le'adoni hamelekh* [*Farewell to a King*], (Tel Aviv: Am Oved 1970), 46. See also Rina Shani, *Mivchar shirim* [*Selected Poems*,] ed. Riki Traum (Bnei Brak: Hakibbutz Hameuchad, 2019), 157. In this essay, all translations are mine unless otherwise stated.

2. *'Ir zarah* [*Foreign City*] (Tel Aviv: Am Oved, 1961); *Yam na'ul* [*Locked Sea*] (Tel Aviv: Hakibbutz Hameuchad, 1963).

3. Shani's poetic and personal relationship with Amir Gilboa had been a constitutive stage in her poetic formation. Her poetic stance as I describe it was highly influenced by his poetics. On Gilboa's poetics in this period, see also Hanan Hever's essay on *Hineh yamim ba'im: Shirim 1942-1946* [*The Days Are Coming: Poems 1942-1946*], Gilboa's archived book. Hever, "'Al hadam ve'al ha'or" ["On the Blood and the Light"], in *Haaretz*, "*Sefarim*," July 19, 2007. Although the book was not yet published then, Shani was likely familiar with the poems because of her close friendship with Gilboa.

4. Natasha Gordinsky and Joyelle McSweeney, "Homeland I Will Name the Language of Poetry in a Foreign Country—Modes of Challenging the Home/Exile Binary in Leah Goldberg's Poetry," in *Leipziger Beiträge zur Jüdischen Geschichte*

und Kultur [Leipzig Studies on Jewish History and Culture], vol. 3, ed. Markus Kirchhoff and Monika Heinker (München: K. G. Saur Verlag, 2005), 252.

5. Charles Altieri, *Self and Sensibility in Contemporary American Poetry* (Cambridge: Cambridge University Press, 1984), 36.

6. See Ann Charters, *The Portable Beat Reader* (New York: Penguin, 1992), xvii. See also Riki Traum, " 'Thoughts That Were Not Burned': on Rina Shani's Poetry," 2019, 20.

7. Nissim Aloni, for instance, had already traveled to Paris at the end of the 1950s, where he became involved with the French theatre and Berthold Brecht, who was also in Paris at the time. See also Sarit Fuchs, *Namer bo'er: moto vechayav shel Nissim Aloni* [Burning Tiger: The Death and Life of Nissim Aloni], (Tel Aviv: Miskal – Yediot Aharonot Books and Hemed Books, 2008).

8. I refer here also to the way Aloni and Shani perceived national seclusion in the sense of "[a] people dwelling apart, who will not reckon themselves among the nations" (Numbers 23:9). See Svetlana Natakovitch, "Akhzar mikol hamelekh/ Nissim Aloni—'al hayetsirah [Cruelest of All—the King: Nissim Aloni-on the Play]," January 7, 2014, in: http://www.tarbutil.cet.ac.il/, Hamerkaz letekhnologiyah chinukhit, 8.1.2018. See also Itzhak Ben Mordechai, "Hamoledet hi hagolah ha'amitit [Homeland is the real exile]," in *'Iyunim bitekumat Yisra'el* 12 (Ben Gurion University: Makhon Ben Gurion, 2002), 567-90.

9. Itzhak Ben Mordechai, ibid., 571. In a later story, "Back to Homeland, in a Train," published in 1983, Aloni shatters the illusion of homeland that as implied by his narrator could serve dreamers. The protagonist, a tormented hunchback, who is on a train back to his homeland from exile, attempts to define the lost space in a palpable figuration that leads him to vision it as the woman who cursed him and caused his exile. At the end of the story, the protagonist states with pathos that he "returns to his real exile since therefore, the homeland is the real exile!" The hunchback, I should note, never reaches his homeland. See Nissim Aloni, "Bechazarah lamoledet, berakevet [Back to the Homeland, in a Train]," in: *Proza*, vol. 5, 1985, 5–6.

10. See Rosi Braidotti, *Nomadic Subjects: Embodiment and Sexual Difference in Contemporary Feminist Theory* (New York: Columbia University Press, 2011), 56. See also Riki Traum, " 'Thoughts That Were Not Burned': on Rina Shani's Poetry," 2019, 11.

11. In: Nissim Aloni, *Hayanshuf: arba'ah sipurim* [*The Owl: Four Stories*] (Tel Aviv: Hakibbutz Hameuchad, 1981), 33–67.

12. Rina Shani, *'Ir zarah*, 10. See also Shani, *Selected Poems*, 2019, 46–47. This poem is also discussed in my introduction, see Riki Traum, ibid., 14.

13. The strong friendship between Bergner and Aloni is discussed in detail by both Ben Mordechai and Bergner. See Ben Mordechai, "Hamoledet hi hagolah ha'amitit," and Yosl Bergner, *What I Meant to Say*, (Or Yehuda: Hed Arzi, 1996), 157–64.

14. It is hard to ignore the assonantal similarity in Hebrew between *rafsodah* (a raft) and *rapsodiyah* (a rhapsody), a similarity that evokes the colorful and improvised nature of the musical rhapsody. I thank Naomi B. Sokoloff for this observation.

15. Shani's artistic interchange with Nissim Aloni also reveals itself through their use of the figuration of the "melekh" (king) as an antihero, or an archetype of an exile. Kings frequently appear in Aloni's work and he defamiliarizes the concept of monarchy for social, political, and class purposes. For readers who are familiar with the artistic and personal relationship between Aloni and Shani, Shani's poem "'*Ir* [City]," in '*Ir zarah*, (94) might recall Aloni's figuration of the king. In her poetry, Shani relies on the semantic range that the figuration of the king enables. The image allows Shani to intensify extremity in linguistic collocations, such as the tension between exile and captive as two opposing mental states associated with power and its abuse. See for instance "Akhzar mikol hamelekh [Cruelest of All—The King]," "Bigdei hamelekh [The Emperor's Clothes]," "Hanesikhah ha'amerika'it [The American Princess]," and "Eddie King"—in which Aloni defamiliarizes the concept of monarchy and often anchors this defamiliarization in social status and class.

16. Rina Shani, *Yam na'ul*, 73. See also Rina Shani, *Selected Poems*, 2019, 126.

17. Paul de Man, *The Resistance to Theory* (Minneapolis and London: University of Minnesota Press, 2002), xvi–xvii.

18. Goldberg was Shani's lecturer and mentor at Hebrew University. Shani refers to Goldberg in her personal notes, but dedications written by Shani to Goldberg reveal the important place that spatial concepts play in their personal interchange. Shani wrote the following words, after the publication of *Yam na'ul* (1963): "Dear Leah—/ on a foreign soil—/ with love/ and appreciation/ from 'all the ends of the earth/ and the distant seas' . . . / Yours, Rina." The different documents and dedications show how important Goldberg's mentoring was in Shani's early poetic career. The dedication is from Goldberg's archive in Makhon Genazim, and I am grateful to Giddon Ticotsky who brought them to my knowledge. See also Riki Traum, "'Machshavot shelo nitlakchu': 'al shiratah shel Rina Shani ['Thoughts That Were Not Burned': on Rina Shani's Poetry]," 2019, 17–18.

19. Natasha Gordinsky's observation on Goldberg's *Mikhtavim minesi'ah medumah* (1937) illuminates the deep poetic understanding between Goldberg and Shani: "Goldberg turns the immigration experience into an artistic device through which she situates herself as a foreigner in the local Israeli literary discourse, while the letters written in Hebrew might be letters on 'intangibility' between the European and Hebrew cultures." Gordinsky concludes that such reading "turned the essential tension between Ruth's [the novel's protagonist, R. T.] will to see the land of Israel as a homeland by choice and her perception of the land as a place of exile, to the organizing poetic-principle of Letters from an Imaginary Journey." Natasha Gordinsky, *Bishloshah nofim: yetsiratah hamukdemet shel Leah Goldberg*

[*In Three Landscapes: Leah Goldberg's Early Writing*] (Jerusalem: Magnes Press, Hebrew University, 2016), 22.

20. Adriana X Jacobs, *Strange Cocktail: Translation and the Making of Modern Hebrew Poetry* (Ann Arbor: University of Michigan Press, 2018), 99.

21. Ibid., 117.

22. See Michael Gluzman, *The Politics of Canonicity: Lines of Resistance in Modernist Hebrew Poetry* (Stanford: Stanford University Press, 2003); Natasha Gordinsky and Joyelle McSweeney, "Homeland I Will Name the Language of Poetry in a Foreign Country—Modes of Challenging the Home/Exile Binary in Leah Goldberg's Poetry," in *Leipziger Beiträge zur Jüdischen Geschichte und Kultur*, 2005; Natasha Gordinsky 2016; Adriana X. Jacobs 2018.

23. Gordinsky 2005, 252–53.

24. Ibid., 250.

25. Leah Goldberg, "Mas'a lelo shem" [A Nameless Journey], in: *Shirim* [Poems]. Vol. 3, ed. Tuvia Ruebner (Tel Aviv: Sifriyat Po'alim, 1986), 33; Leah Goldberg, "A Nameless Journey," in: *Lea Goldberg: Selected Poetry and Drama*, poetry trans. by Rachel Tzvia Back (The Toby Press, New Milford, CT, 2005), 142–143. The poem was first published in *A'l Hamishmar*, on September 21, 1960.

26. Rina Shani, *'Ir zarah*, 49. See also, Shani, *Selected Poems*, 2019, 49.

27. See Gordinsky's discussion of Goldberg's poem in relation to Foucault's heterotopia: Gordinsky, 2005, 247–52.

28. Michel Foucault, "Of Other Spaces: Utopias and Heterotopias," trans. Jay Miskowiec, in: *Diacritics* 16, no. 1 (Spring 1986): 26.

29. Ibid., 25.

Asaf Schurr and the Critique of Postmodernism in Contemporary Hebrew Literature

Yaron Peleg

Although literary histories went out of fashion in Israel and elsewhere with the advent of postmodernism, some time in the beginning of the 1990s, I want to revive that old-fashioned critical tradition, which until thirty or so years ago was passionately engaged in defining and shaping Israeli culture. Much of this critical activity, which has since subsided, was part of a dynamic dialectics that created distinct cultural coordinates.[1]

It would be irrelevant, of course, to revive the practices of literary historians such as Gershon Shaked, for instance. Not only because definitive taxonomies of the kind Shaked composed are likely to be discounted today, but also because they are nigh impossible. The tremendous expansion of Israeli literature since that time has made such attempts impractical. And yet literary histories, like other histories, are not only useful but important for many of the same reasons they were valuable in the past. The expansion and permutation of literature does not change the reflective social and cultural function it has; it only makes the work of the literary historian today harder. A determined historian can deal with these challenges in various ways. One of them is to deliberately narrow the scope of the literature examined and choose a specific time frame and a specific group of authors and treat them as a kind of historical synecdoche, as I tried to do in a previous study about literature between the two intifadas.[2] The approach I take here is an examination of one specific writer, Asaf Schurr, who between 2007 and 2014 published five novels in quick succession,

Amram (Bavel, 2007), *Motti* (Bavel, 2008), *Sigal* (Bavel, 2009), *Thus Said Vincent, the Stupid Cat* (Keter, 2011), *The Building* (Hebrew title: *Why Fish Bird*, Keter, 2014). Both the volume of these works and their integration of content and form make Schurr representative of what looks like an emerging literary trend in Israel that tries to confront the so-called crisis of representation in the postmodern age.[3]

I am referring here to Lyotard's well-known critique of modernism's emphasis on transcendent and universal truths and the prolific literature on postmodernism it has inspired since then.[4] In Israel, postmodernism often took on the guise of post-Zionism, and its critique and countercritique frequently involved politics as well as culture. Because of Israel's history and its particular ideological makeup, these changes were wrapped up in the changing of the ideological guard from Left to Right, in attempts to reverse earlier socialist policies and in the turn toward a more blatant Jewish nationalism since the 1980s.[5]

One of the most pronounced social manifestations of this development has been the rise of identity as the basis for civic or collective action. Instead of the grand national issues, which stood at the center of the labor-Zionist *ancien régime*, the identity of various minority groups within the state became the new inspiration for public mobilization.[6] In Israel, these trends have been expressed by the rise of Mizrachi politics, Mizrachi-religious politics, and Jewish religious politics, as more narrowly focused causes that sought to change established notions of a collective Israeli body politic—from which these sectors were previously excluded. They have also coincided with the hegemonic rise of a populist Right that has manipulated ethnic and religious differences to fortify its electoral dominance.[7]

In the field of literature, these trends have often been expressed by a disengagement from an "official" or "stative" perspective of many of the grand political issues that preoccupied Israeli writers for most of the twentieth century, such as Jewish communal life in Israel, immigration and absorption, the Arab-Israeli conflict, the nature of life under these pressures, etc.[8] Instead, many writers began to explore these issues through more personal aspects of identity as an expression of political engagement. Privileging a sectorial angle from which they examined national-communal affairs, these writers engaged in the concerns of a more specifically identified self as a reaction to the erosion of the Israeli social contract, once referred to as *mamlachtiyut,* or statism.[9]

Like some of his contemporaries, Asaf Schurr seems deeply concerned with these trends, which have changed Israeli society profoundly.

His entire work to date is an attempt to jolt Israeli literature out of its postmodern doldrums, its preoccupation with overly individualized identities and with narratives that play with artistic artifice to the exclusion of collective themes, toward a clearer and more real set of values as a stable basis for reference. It is a point of some irony, then, that most readers of Schurr's novels took them at their postmodern face value.[10] In fact—and this is my claim here—Schurr does something quite different, unique and pathbreaking: he uses postmodernist tools of deconstruction not as an end but as a starting point that at the same time reconnects his work to some of the older but more constructive traditions of Israeli literature. As such, Schurr joins a number of writers who, as I note in the conclusion, also seem concerned with the dissolution of the Zionist metanarrative, and the inability to narrate history that such loss brings with it.[11]

The five novels Schurr published so far engage with this issue primarily through a constant interplay between content and form, and I propose to read the novels as a series. The idea of chapters in a series is suggested not just by the rapid succession of the novels' publication, but also because of other commonalities they share, including the metaphoric quality of the narratives, as well as formal elements such as their evolving self-referential or ars poetic style.

The first three novels, as their titles suggest, focus on individuals, while the last two deal with increasingly wider social units, the family in *Vincent* and the community of an apartment building in *The Building*. But while the characters in the first three novels are given individual names, personal circumstances, distinct personalities, and real physical environments, they remain curiously metaphoric. Time and space in these novels are vague. There are few or no historical or spatial references that can place the stories in a specific historical time, anchor them in a specific location, or tie them to a specific communal context. Lacking fictive specificity, the characters become abstracted, essentialized, and devoid of literary moral value.

Moreover, this metaphoric content is conveyed through a distinct reflexive style, which attracted most of the critical attention when the novels were first published.[12] The first three novels, especially, include an intrusive authorial voice that disrupts the narrative and comments on it with various degrees of involvement. The author makes rare appearances in the fourth novel, *Vincent*. The fifth novel, *The Building*, is the most conventionally styled in the series, lacking the programmatic foreword of the first four books and almost entirely devoid of authorial self-reflection. Comparatively speaking, and commensurate with its role as the last book in the series, it is also more embedded in a contemporary Israeli *Sitz im Leben,* rendering the narrative less obviously metaphoric.[13]

This evolving interplay between form and content is the means by which the series tells a very specific story. While the metaphoric nature of the narratives guided by the voice of a self-conscious author highlights the hollowness of the characters, the gradual change of that style coupled with the change in content eventually revalues the characters, gives them a clearer literary specificity, and brings them closer to life, creating a literary historical subject, so to speak.

The metaphoric nature of the first three novels sets up the moral premise of the series. The first novel, *Amram,* like the two works that follow it, opens with a programmatic foreword:[14]

> Let's settle it right away, already before the first chapter, so that later on you won't carp about knowing or not knowing about it, or if it was gripping or not. We have two people here. In some ways, they do similar things from similar motives, in other ways they do these things from different motives. They do these things with their faces covered, which means there's an identity issue here. One of them does it to fight crime. Seriously, don't laugh. You have to respect that, at least someone is trying to do something very clear, it's not a given, certainly not when everyone else around is preoccupied with proportionality (*midatiyut*). Anyway, eventually one of them will kill the other, and each of them has someone he loves. That's why they do it, from love. (7)

As we eventually find out in the last novel, the series as a whole is concerned with meaningful and enduring connections. *Amram* begins with the statement, "You need someone to love you in order to be who you are," (9) and ends with, "You need to love someone in order to be more than who you are" (226). The book explores the distance between the two through an extreme case of love, which can be described by the paraphrase that the road to heaven is paved with hellish intentions. For the character Amram, it is his overwhelming love for his daughter Tikvah. His work in the archives of the courthouse and his routine exposure to all manner of human depravity, of which he learns from the court cases he files, make him anxious for his daughter's safety. Determined to protect her from every conceivable evil, he becomes a vigilante and prowls the streets at night fighting crime.

For Avichai, it is his love for his wife Ellah. Her wish to conceive, using another man's sperm after Avichai fails to impregnate her, sends him on a murderous search for that man; a search that ends with his own death at the hands of Amram. This is not an accidental death, because the choices both men make at the start of the novel will make them collide by the end of it.[15] Relationships, then, are clearly at the center of *Amram*. Yet these are problematic relationships, to say the least, in which both men lose all sense of proportion. Unable to relate either to the women they love or to their perceived enemies, their relations to and with the world are falsified. While they value the former too highly, they grossly undervalue the latter.

The textual metaphor is created not only by the rudimentary brush strokes that sketch the characters, but also through the occasional interference of the authorial voice, which breaks the proverbial fourth wall to remind readers of the fictive value of the dramatis personae. In one such moment in the middle of the book, the narrative flow stops, the author breaks in and confesses to readers that "this book was already complete when it was suddenly thrown open again, a door was made in it, and in marched the editor dragging me after him to rework it as I please" (159). This direct address to readers goes on for a while and slows the story down until the author asks readers directly to help him "jump-start this novel again by pushing it together down a steep hill" (160).

The final comment of this kind comes toward the very end of the novel, after Amram, who has just murdered Avichai, manages to return home undetected and will presumably go free:

> And maybe that's why everything began, that is, maybe that's the reason for this wrestling match and for the death: because there's a limit to the number of possible stories that the meeting of two people can generate. . . .
>
> At times I wanted this novel to be a tight coil between them, so that the distance between them on the one hand and the wish to get closer on the other will keep it vibrating. And even if I managed to do so, their encounter is still disappointing: they met, the potential was realized, and the novel was closed with a faint thud. (223)

This somewhat rudimentary narrative conceit in *Amram* is developed further in the second novel, *Motti*, which demands a more active involvement from readers in the plot. The novel does so especially by the use of postmodern camp, a deliberately exaggerated postmodernistic style that playfully calls attention to itself. Like *Amram*, this novel opens with a methodological preface as well, which clarifies the text and provides a key for reading it:

> Structurally, this book is strict. Strict and very simple. A symmetrical pyramid with a summit of clouds and a base of Euclidian geometry. Nevertheless, it's a book, not a concert or some sort of performing art. . . . And there's no division between the audience and the stage. You're the performers and the audience all at once, and everything is already out of my control. Therefore, I can only request that you read attentively . . . even with joy. . . . From my perspective, it is all the same now. (3)

Making the discussion about literary conventions clearer still, this ars poetic opening speaks directly about the two key players of any text, without whom the act of reading is not possible, of course: the writer and the reader. The first sentence provides a clear picture of this relationship reflected in the geometric drawing of the pyramid or triangle. While the base of the triangle is visible, real, formed by the demonstrable rules of geometry, the top of the triangle is hidden by clouds. In other words, the relationship between writer and reader create the story, which at this starting point is yet unknown, literally shrouded.

In some ways, Schurr is not innovating here at all. Both this preface and the preface to *Amram* remind us of much older literary conventions, mock-serious confessions like the ones we find in Cervantes's Don Quixote in the early seventeenth century, in Fielding's novels in the eighteenth century, and their mutation into the conventions of the omniscient narrator in the nineteenth century.[16] But the preface to *Motti* adds to these conventions by extending the reader's role and drawing attention to it as fundamental to the series' project. The preface ends with this:

> And because of this the simplicity. . . . There are almost no games here, no deception, there is no deviousness at all in this book. No manipulation. Everything is simple as can be. Everything is on the table. The cards are on the table, the

tablecloth is on the table, everything is on the table, open the refrigerator, there is nothing in it, everything is on the table, everything, look underneath, nothing there either, everything is on the table and in midair the table stands. (4)

The rest of the book, much more explicitly than *Amram*, continues to do just that by providing two narrative strata, an "official" story or plot and a second, metafictional narrative voice that accompanies the first to ensure that readers are constantly made aware of the willing suspension of disbelief inherent to the process of reading. The characters are portrayed as more or less arbitrary whims of the author-narrator and may at any moment be swept away on a new current of his creativity.[17]

The opening of the book eases us into this tension:

Motti loved Menachem like a brother. That is, despite himself. Perhaps they met in the army. This is not uncommon among Israelis. Perhaps they met before that, in school. Possibly even in college. (11)

Again, this kind of literary device is anachronistic. But as we read further into the book, the increasing tension between readers and writer cracks the narrative and breaks it apart. Motti, who is a school teacher, stays at home one day because of a teachers' strike. Presently, he begins a long daydream about his neighbor, Ariella, which unfolds over more than ten pages and stirs in readers a mixture of warmth and pathos: about the two falling in love, having passionate sex, growing old together (51–65).

There is nothing unusual, of course, in a character fantasizing an imaginary life. But what follows is less expected, as the author breaks into the story and comments directly about Motti's fantasies. "Look at this, so many possibilities one can fabricate without committing to any actual story" (64). Less expected still is the next maneuver, in which we learn that Ariella is a schoolgirl and therefore a minor. "And so," the author turns to us again with a sly smile,

has your opinion of [Motti] changed, now that it's been made perfectly clear that she's just a kid? It's important to remember that he hasn't done a thing. Won't, either. Why, she's just a child, why, that's disgusting, the very thought of touching her like that disgusts him, no matter how much he wants to touch her when she grows up, when they're in love. (65)

This is quite literally a demonstration of the teamwork between writer and reader: we have the building blocks, their arbitrary arrangement, the multiple interpretive possibilities they can generate, and most importantly, the moral consequences that result from the combination of both: Motti's relationship to the world is so falsified that Ariella is quite literally commodified for him, a mere object about which he can have romantic and creepy fantasies at the same time.

The series receives its most figurative shape in the third novel, *Sigal*, in which the protagonist is split into two different women, who are then conflated. The result is a symbolic character that illuminates the series' concern not only with the nature of representation but also with kindness, reciprocity, and human connection.[18] In her first appearance as the successful businesswoman, the eponymous Sigal is a derelict mother and a derelict daughter. She treats her small boy as an accessory of her success and speaks to him in cloyingly affectionate language that discloses her impatience with him: "No, my little sweetie . . . we're going home now, you'll play on the swing tomorrow" (31). Asleep, however, he is a perfect ornament to her perfect life: "She leaned against the doorframe and sent a soft look toward her son, who was lying in bed, his golden, angelic hair covering his forehead and thought . . . oh, my beautiful son, you'll have a beautiful life" (34).

As a daughter, Sigal is equally remiss. The nursing home she selects for her father has luxurious amenities meant to paint her as a successful woman and a loving daughter. "Amazing," she thinks to herself complacently as she is visiting her father one day, noting with satisfaction "the pleasant furniture . . . the purr of the air conditioners . . . the clean ceramic tiles . . . the warm, personal and dedicated attention, the cozy atmosphere, and the starched white uniforms" (78–79). But actually staying and talking with her father is another matter, and on her two trips to the nursing home she studiously avoids it by arriving during his nap time. Relieved to see her father asleep, she tells the nurse that she is afraid of "alarming . . . my dear beloved father" (57), and that she is reluctant "to disturb his nap, [which] must be very important to him" (59). On her second visit she is not as lucky and is caught by her father trying to escape his room.

In the second half of the novel, the bitchy Sigal somehow turns into the goodly Na'ama. Sigal is now referred to as a beast (*behema*), and her office romance with the handsome boss, Itamar, makes Na'ama sick. She hates that "slick idiot," that "piece of nothing . . . he and his stupid Sigal.

She is sick of both of them . . . the way they spin their failures into great success, new branding they call it, the idiots" (133–34). In contrast to Sigal, Na'ama is initially portrayed as a kindhearted young woman, who is concerned about the workers who will be laid off because of Sigal's efficiency measures. She is also kind to her mother, to her former boyfriend, and especially to her dog, Nuri, which she loves deeply. So much so, in fact, that when an old resident of her apartment building reports her barking dog to the city, she retaliates by falsely accusing him of harassing her sexually and has him committed to a nursing home. As it turns out, Na'ama is just as nasty as Sigal, if not nastier.

The narrative pyrotechnics Schurr employs in his work highlight some of the problems inherent in postmodern modes of writing, in which "subjectivity [can sometime] become so invaded by the image that modern identity itself is a pretense," as Timothy Bewes writes.[19] The first three novels in the series draw attention to this postmodern crisis of representation in order to highlight Schurr's critique of it and make way for the last two books in the series as a kind of alternative to it.

More precisely, the author of *Amram*, *Motti*, and *Sigal* is decidedly unsatisfied with the postmodern penchant for leaving all possibilities open and considering them all equally plausible. What he says in these novels is that after the story has been deconstructed to the point where everything is "on the table" and the table is "up in the air," the table must eventually fall in some direction or another.[20] Here is where the reader enters: pushed to make aesthetic or moral decisions in order to determine where the "table" falls and filling in the gaps in the story with their own interpretations. Not just in the conventional way, in which all stories are created to some extent in readers' minds, but more proscriptively, like computer games or those open-ended films in which users determine the storyline and choose the ending. Concepts such as morality, truth, belief, are created by the interplay between narrator and reader. Thus, out of the rubble that postmodernism leaves behind, Schurr's novels become constructive by calling readers to participate actively in the building of new narratives and, implicitly, new realities. As it says in the conclusion to *Motti*:

> And do you know what? Perhaps in the end he did meet the grown-up, perfect Ariella, and she was everything he dreamed of, even more, and they had a life together, a good, long life, and they had children or didn't have children, in any event

they raised many dogs and even traveled abroad regularly, maybe adopted a cat or two as well, performed good and important deeds, their days were full of joy, why not. In the end they died, of course. When you go on long enough, all stories end in death. But there could definitely be some sort of happy ending here, I promise. The problem is just knowing where to stop. (184)

Schurr's last two novels demonstrate these possibilities by presenting readers with fuller moralistic tales that are not only written in a more conventional mimetic style, but significantly leave the isolated and nonreferential realm of individuals to dwell on larger and more complete social units, the family in *Vincent* and the community in *The Building*. The preface to the fourth novel, *Thus Said Vincent, the Stupid Cat*, announces it right away:

That's the whole story, which we come back to again and again: man is born. A helpless baby, who then becomes a child. The stories about that child are not many, only the few that we remember, though they're very sweet. And even if some of them are stories about disappointments, we still tell them to say something about innocence, revelations, beginnings.
 . . . The only thing we can tell the child is that "by themselves" doesn't mean "alone" . . . that's why we tell children stories about things that happened a long time ago or never.
 . . . because the single person is never the basis or the foundation, not in the world and not in thought. The first and primary unit is relationship (*zikah*). Everything is a point of contact (*mifgash*) . . .

This last foreword in the series comments on the act and function of writing and on the general nature of fiction much more directly than the previous forewords did. It is also followed by a more formally conventional narrative, about a suburban family, a mother, a father, a sister and a brother, who begin the story alienated from one another and slowly come together as a family. The Feiver family includes a stay-at-home mom, Netta, a psychologist father, Amikam, an anorexic fourteen-year-old daughter, Mattie—who will make a brief appearance in the next novel—and a twentysomething son, Uriah, an ascetic who holes up in the basement of the family's house away from the polluting world, tries to get closer to God, and nurses wounded pets back to health in a sad attempt to connect and feel something in his emptied world. It also includes Vincent, the ghost of a kitten Uriah tried unsuccessfully to save.

Unlike Schurr's earlier novels, the ars poetics of his fourth novel is kept to a minimum with very few authorial incursions. Instead, simpler narrative conventions are used to tell the story. Having previously educated his readers how to read properly, Schurr presents the first text in the series that may be "independently" evaluated without a directing author. To facilitate this kind of reading, Uriah and his prophetic cat provide important clues that turn the text into what Omri Herzog called, "a parody on a prophesy that is devoid of either god or mission."[21]

Vincent, the kitten, dies shortly after Uriah receives him. But soon after his death, Vincent's avatar appears before the astounded Uriah and begins to speak to him in bombastic prophetic register: "I am the storm, said the voice. I am the ever-watchful eye . . . the beat, the sigh, the void between all things . . . the sea without a bottom or a shore. I am hungry and voracious" (100). Despite his initial shock, Uriah's recent search for God has in fact prepared him for this apparition and he soon believes that Vincent was sent to initiate him as a prophet: "I have returned and call upon you, Uriah son of Netta and Amikam, rise, rise and obey" (102). Disconnected literally and metaphorically from the world, unable to distinguish truth from falsehood, Uriah accepts the role. To seal the covenant, the kitten tells him to seize the parrot he has been caring for, to "take his blood and pour it upon the altar and raise it to heaven before God." (103). And Uriah obeys. In a trance, he washes his hands, goes over to the cage, takes his beloved parrot out and wrings its neck. To his surprise, the kitten reacts glibly to Uriah's obedience: "So that's it, eh? said Vincent. I thought it would take a few weeks to convince you. But, stammered Uriah, you told me to. . . . So what, said Vincent, do you get up and slaughter a parrot every time someone speaks to you about God? That's not very nice" (104).

Following Herzog, this droll parody winks at the false messages that in our postpolitical age stand for great truths, but are in fact hollow, utterly disconnected from life's real problems (economic inequality, oppression, power imbalance, etc.). As Timothy Snyder has recently written, postpolitics is a disturbing political extension of postmodernism, whose suspicion of the value of truth encourages various regimes today, in Russia, in the United States, and in Israel too, to promote their own, self-interested lies as personal and national alternative truths.[22] The falseness of Vincent's prophecy resides not only in the nonsense he utters—"I am the thorn that tears your flesh when you take it out, I am a park-bench that no one ever sat on" (106)—but also in the ludicrous fact that it is uttered by a dead cat. Uriah is lured by this nonsense because it panders to his identity as a Jew and to his current search for God or truth.

Moreover, the quasi-biblical register authenticates and personalizes the prophecy as a Jewish/Israeli truth. This false truth is so tempting, in fact, that it overrides Uriah's natural kindness and turns him into a blind and obedient follower. By manipulating him into feeling special and chosen, Vincent easily convinces him to kill something he loves, his pet parrot. Worse still, it makes him treat his menstruating sister as unclean, at which the mother, Netta, puts her foot down. While she was respectful of her son's sociopathic tendencies during his personal search for meaning, she is not willing to tolerate his disrespect for others, not even in the name of a so-called greater Jewish truth. She is livid at his ugly treatment of his sister: "I don't accept it, do you hear me? Netta shouted. . . . Now, get out of here . . . get out . . . or I won't be responsible for my actions" (174).

In the absence of great truths and fixed values, how can we negotiate a world full of signifiers which have lost their signifieds? Schurr's fourth novel suggests that we can begin by focusing on our own surroundings, in this case the family and the relations between its individual members. "This house at night," he writes, "is like a medieval castle with its silent corridors, and all its residents are but princes and princesses who are waiting for their fucking redemption" (64). While the social structure of the family is always at odds with the individual desires of its members, writes Omri Herzog, "a family is a prophecy: a binding contract of future relations, based on a mission of providential fulfilment."[23] Put more expansively, "being human is a set of techniques, something you have to get good at . . . and you cannot do it on your own."[24]

The fifth and last novel, *The Building*, exemplifies the idea of connectivity by expanding the social realm farther afield. This story about homecoming begins with one of several short para-narratives that are inserted intermittently throughout the book as a parallel or adjacent story that accompanies the plot and comments on it. The para-narrative that opens the book connects it to the previous book in the series, *Vincent*, which is an important point in a project about connections or relationships. The novel then continues with a visit by Omer to the apartment block (*shikun*) of his childhood, a late return that takes up the entire book.

Initially, Omer's visit seems depressing. The neighbors are older now, frail and ailing, and Omer himself is rendered miserable and homeless, as he moves between them seeking recognition and comfort. The saddest moment in the book comes when Omer discovers a freakish sci-fi creature, part of his old neighbor Mrs. Saperstein's long-aborted fetus, which for the past twenty years has been kept artificially alive in the building's basement by means of a clever contraption. Feeling sorry for Mrs. Saperstein, who suffered a series of miscarriages, the talented Mr. Greenberg, another old neighbor, built an electric aquarium that kept the brain of her last fetus alive. Trying to protect it from Omer, who stumbles upon it, Mrs. Saperstein falls and breaks the aquarium thereby killing the creature. But in doing so, she also severs the link to a festering past. At that moment, the value of Omer's late return becomes apparent. He is the knight who broke the evil spell that trapped the kingdom in a world of empty signifiers. Since the fetus has been generalized into an abstraction of a child, a "thing" that represents what Bewes calls "a state of degeneration, a prevailing state of nostalgia for what has vanished,"[25] it had to be destroyed and replaced with a real "child," Omer, whose return to the building and his visits to his old neighbors reintroduce a more genuine sense of community to the old *shikun*.

The final question, then, is how the five novels are connected, whether the ambitious literary call, formulated in the first three novels, is continued or answered in the last two, and if so, how? Because the last two novels, contrary to the literary principles articulated in the first three, do not ask readers to participate so much in the stories' construction and present more ready-made and moralistic tales. The answer to this question is in the very process the five novels engage with as a series. After readers are reminded in the first three books of the limitations of postmodern representation, that morality is relative only up to a point and that it is their responsibility to find that point, the last two novels provide readers with a sentimental education, "little portions of love, heartache, laughter, death," which do not only act as vaccines but also as road signs, or as Schurr puts it, "arrows chalked by parents on the pavement in their children's games." These arrows direct us toward specific targets or goals; goals that we actively participate in defining.

The restoration of a clear sense of self and a clear sense of community—a real community, not an imagined one—endows Schurr's characters with a distinct historical subjectivity that has been often missing from recent Israeli literature, but appears to be coming back, not only in Schurr's work but in the work of other contemporary writers, as Oded Nir recently noted.[26] Against what he calls "the crisis of historicity" in contemporary Israeli literature, with its "[fragmented] narratives [that] no longer provide an adequate mediation between personal experience . . . and the possibility of historical agency," Nir points to writers such as Lilach Netanel and Yiftach Ashkenazi, who problematize that possibility. Although, unlike Schurr, neither Netanel nor Ashkenazi offer solutions to the inability to narrate history in the postmodern age, both note the loss that accrues from our failure to imagine a different prospect for ourselves going forward. What distinguishes Schurr, in this respect, is the future vistas that his work suggests. Thus, at the dawn of Zionism's second century, Asaf Schurr and other writers seem to rekindle some of the literature's old commitments to the universal values of modernism and resume, albeit tentatively, the position of literary "prophets," *tsofim lebeyt Yisra'el*.

Notes

1. The contemporary literary critic Arik Glassner considers many of these issues in his PhD dissertation about literary criticism and the media in the postmodern era and tracks the rise and decline of popular literary criticism in Israel and its migration from daily newspapers to the academy from the 1980s onward. Available online at https://arikglasner.files.wordpress.com/2014/06/complete-phd.pdf.

2. Yaron Peleg, *Israeli Culture Between the Two Intifadas: A Brief Romance* (Austin: University of Texas Press, 2008).

3. The formulation with respect to Schurr was first made by Meytal Sharon in her review of his third novel, *Sigal*. See, "Don't Worry about World Affairs, Let's Get Back to What Intellectuals Really Care About," *The Shocking Real Story of* (Hasipur ha'amiti vehameza'aze'a shel) ezine, April 10, 2009. http://www.hahem.co.il/trueandshocking/?p=925.

4. Of particular relevance here is Lyotard's observation about the production of symbols through language in postindustrial societies, where services and creativity—information, knowledge, ideas—become valued forms of capital, as opposed to the actual production of goods, and lead to a new kind of cultural commerce in which the value system tends to be more relative. To deal with this instability, Lyotard formulated his idea of *petits récits*, or small narratives, based on Wittgenstein's language-games theory, which determines the meaning of words in relation to their function within a specific system. See James Williams, *Lyotard: Towards a Postmodern Philosophy* (Cambridge: Polity Press, 1998). On Wittgen-

stein, See P. M. S. Hacker, *Wittgenstein: Rules, Grammar and Necessity* (Chicester: Wiley-Blackwell, 2009), especially chapter 2, "Rules and Grammar," (41–80).

5. The designation Left/Right is useful only up to a point. Labor Zionism developed distinct nationalist characteristics earlier on, as Gershon Shafir, Zeev Sternhell, and others have demonstrated. For representative studies on some of these ideological shifts in Israel see Ella Shohat, *Israeli Cinema: East/West and the Politics of Representation* (Austin: University of Texas Press, 1989), Gadi Taub, *Hamered hashafuf* [*The Dispirited Revolution*] (Tel-Aviv: Hakibbutz Hame'uhad, 1997), Anita Shapira, *Yehudim yeshanim, yehudim chadashim* [*New Jews, Old Jews*] (Tel-Aviv: Am Oved, 1997), Ram Oren, *The Globalization of Israel: McWorld in Tel-Aviv, Jihad in Jerusalem* (London: Routledge, 2008), Tuvia Freeling, *Tshuva le'amit post-tsioni* [*A Reply to a Post-Zionist Colleague*] (Tel-Aviv: Yediot Sfarim, 2003).

6. On the challenges of identity politics, see Kobena Mercer, "Welcome to the Jungle: Identity and Postmodern Politics," in *Identity: Community, Culture, Difference*, ed. Jonathan Rutherford (London: Lawrence and Wishart, 1998), 43–71.

7. It is worth mentioning the economic background to many of these changes, which exacerbated and proliferated them, especially the spread of neoliberalism and "the financialization of everything," as David Harvey puts it; see *A Brief History of Neoliberalism* (Oxford: Oxford University Press, 2007), 33. The bitter irony of the relationship between money and identity was that it fit neatly into the logic of capitalism, which identity politics set out to fight in the first place as one of the most insidious forces of the patriarchy. As it happened, identity politics proved to be the ideology par excellence of the market when new forms of national capitalism emerged as dominant global forces, turning identity into a tool of the populist Right that decried the legacies of the quest for universal values. Harvey gives a succinct explanation of how neoliberal forces coopted the social revolutionary spirit of the 1960s and 1970s in order to free markets rather than people (41–42, for example).

8. For a comprehensive assessment of this, see Peleg, *Intifadas*.

9. For more on this, see a forthcoming volume of articles on cinema and politics in contemporary Israeli culture, edited by Yaron Peleg and Eran Kaplan, "Israeli Cinema and Politics," *Jewish Film & New Media* 6, no. 2 (Spring 2019).

10. On *Amram*, see Omri Herzog, "Hastira hamuvla'at ba'egrof [A Smack Hidden in a Fist]," *Haaretz* online, May 16, 2007; https://www.haaretz.co.il/literature/1.1410149. Maya Feldman, *Milim kedorbanot* [*Poignant*], Ynet Books, Feb. 13, 2007; https://www.ynet.co.il/articles/0,7340,L-3362547,00.html. On *Motti*, see Arik Glassner, "Mada'ei hechalom [Dream Science]," *Ma'ariv Tarbut*, May 16, 2008, 28. On *Sigal*, see Arik Glassner, "Sigal lo matzdik et sakh chalakav [The Whole of Sigal Does Not Justify Its Parts]," *NRG*, Oct. 3, 2009, https://www.makorrishon.co.il/nrg/online/47/ART1/948/316.html. Ran Yagil, "Shuru, habitu ve'al tikre'u

[Behold and Don't Read]," *NRG*, Dec. 09, 2009, https://www.makorrishon.co.il/nrg/online/47/ART1/976/841.html.

11. The analysis is suggested by Oded Nir, "On the Historical Imaginary of Contemporary Israeli Fiction, or, Postmodernism's Aftermath in Novels by Lilach Netanel and Yiftach Ashkenazi," forthcoming in *Prooftexts*.

12. For a comprehensive list of reviews, see Schurr's entry in the online Hebrew literary lexicon at https://library.osu.edu/projects/hebrew-lexicon/01095.php.

13. References to an Israeli life cycle and social phenomena are more numerous in this novel than in the others, including high school rituals, such as the annual hiking trip, as well as army experiences. See pages, 29, 81, 92.

14. All translations are mine, except for *Motti*, Schurr's only novel in English to date, translated by Todd Hasak-Lowy.

15. It turns out that, Eitan, Tikvah's boyfriend, is Ellah's sperm donor. Avichai tries to run him over and when he fails and Eitan is rushed to the hospital, Avichai follows him there in order to complete the job. In the hospital Avichai meets Amram, who came to protect Eitan, and who eventually beats Avichai to death.

16. The preface to Amram acknowledges a similar influence directly: "That's the reason for this preface, and also because it reminds me of Erich Kästner's stories from my childhood: Chapter so and so, which tells of a pack of bills, of a suspicious man and of the real taste of marzipan . . ." (8).

17. The paragraph is taken from a seminar paper on *Motti* by my student, Susannah Pearce, who gave me permission to use it here.

18. "For Schurr, Sigal [and] Na'ama . . . are not people, but purposeful metaphors . . . raised from the dust of nonexistence to help him make several important points. He speaks, for instance, about the crisis or representation in the postmodern world, where readers do not believe writers anymore, because there is no truth or non-truth, and every image is necessarily a reflection, direct or inverted, of another image . . . [merely] pages and paper and written words." Meytal Sharon, "Izvu otchem midiburim al ha'olam, bo'u nachzor lemah shebe'emet me'anyen intelektu'alim [Don't Worry about World Affairs, Let's Get Back to What Intellectuals Really Care About]," *The Shocking Real Story of*, ezine, Oct. 4, 2009. http://www.hahem.co.il/trueandshocking/?p=925. Read in the context of the five novels, the metaphorical nature of the characters is an important part of Schurr's project and not a problem, as Sharon argues.

19. Timothy Bewes, *Reification or the Anxiety of Late Capitalism* (London: Verso, 2002), xi.

20. See Pearce, above.

21. Omri Herzog, "A Prophecy with a Tail [Nevu'a im zanav]," *Haaretz Books* (online), Nov.16, 2011; https://www.haaretz.co.il/literature/prose/1.1567225.

22. Snyder shows how instead of the modern, Western, liberal belief in a constructive movement forward toward a better future, the relative truths promo-

ted by post-politicians arrest their societies by sending them into perpetual loops that are maintained by an us-versus-them tension, meant to keep these societies together. Timothy Snyder, *The Road to Unfreedom, Russia, Europe, America* (Bodley Head, 2018). Harvey says essentially the same, see above, 82–83.

23. Herzog. Or to give it Wittgenstein's analytical formulation, "there is no such thing as meaning independently of determination of how an expression is to be used," Hacker, 43.

24. Terrry Eagleton, *The Illusions of Postmodernism* (Oxford: Blackwell, 1996), 109.

25. Bewes, xiii, xvi.

26. See Nir, *On the Historical Imaginary of Contemporary Israeli Fiction.*

"And the Winner Is . . ."
The Economy of Literary Awards

Nancy E. Berg

No writer who knows the great writers who did not receive the Prize can accept it other than with humility.

—Ernest Hemingway, Nobel Laureate

Literary prizes, already turned into tokens worn out in both material and spirit, will still be given to authors of the works according to age and frailty.

—Dan Miron, Israel Prize Winner,
Pinkas patuach: ʿal hasiporet betaishlach

Literary Prizes

The argument against literary prizes is fierce: Prizes reduce art to a mere beauty contest; they cheapen the art. Furthermore, so the argument goes, the process of selecting a prize winner is at best subjective and at worst corrupt, it is elitist, it is commercial. Awards are also subject to disputes, not only because the judging is so subjective, but because the outcome can be so influential and because awards are so context-dependent. Unstated criteria are often more significant than those that are stated. Finally, prizes are more destructive than constructive: for every winner there are multiple losers.[1]

In direct contrast to the arguments against prizes are those who contend that these prizes in fact celebrate excellence; they show appreciation for the arts; they validate artists and artistic choices; they encourage the artist with money, opportunities, publicity, translation; they serve to establish and spread values, both literary and extraliterary. Whatever our stance on prize culture, the reality is that awards both reflect and influence cultural direction and serve as key interventions in shaping the literary republic.[2]

Indeed, literary prizes not only persist but proliferate.[3] Prizes for Israeli literature, of which there are several dozen given annually, include well-established awards named to honor forebears, awards shepherded by municipalities, national awards overseen by one government ministry or another (culture, education), and of course, the more recent Lotto-funded Sapir Prize. These prizes—as well as other accolades such as fellowships, translations, and honorary degrees—shape the literary landscape, by promoting specific works, guiding reception, and fostering production.

Literary prizes, like anthologies and curricula, help define the canon. The role of literary prizes in canon formation has been well attested, but little studied. This paper is the beginning of such a project. While recognizing the largely reactive nature of literary prizes this paper proposes to read them as an expression of national identity and values,[4] as opportunity for dissent, and as a discussion of changing times and tastes. Recent debates have revealed significant social and cultural fissures; the disputes themselves are telling. In his book *The Economy of Prestige*[5] James English builds on Pierre Bourdieu's theories to examine prize culture. Although he focuses on British and American awards—mostly literary, yet with occasional forays into cinematic, theatrical, and musical arenas—much of what he argues is applicable to the Israeli scene. He points out that prizes disrupt the usual economics of exchange—for example, prizes themselves are not subject to negotiation, neither party can insist on payment, and there is a distinctive "disequilibriousness" in the process when the work of judging is uncompensated—yet they establish a new economics. In this new system the capital is largely symbolic. And the symbolism brings us back from teetering on the edge of the less familiar and less acceptable realms of economics and markets to the more comfortable and laudatory republic of art. So too, the overtly political aspects shed light on both the Israeli literary landscape at seventy, and on literary prizes in general. Israel's relatively small size, deep societal divisions, and dazzling creativity intensify the debates and effects of literary prizes.

Prizes can be likened to beauty contests in that they measure the immeasurable, they force a comparison between unlike items, they are based on aesthetics that are culturally contingent, and they establish or reify national myths and narratives. To illustrate: Miss Israel—the winner of a contest held since 1950—shapes and reflects the Israeli notions of beauty and of Israeli-ness. In 1999, Rana Raslan was the first—and so far only—Arab to win the title; fourteen years later, Yityish Titi Aynaw was the first Ethiopian (and first black) to win. Both cases have served to demonstrate Israeli inclusiveness, even while the token aspect highlights the opposite.

Similarly, the awarding of the Israel Prize for Literature to Emile Habiby in 1992 was taken to signal the inclusion of Arab culture.[6] The jury the year Habiby was honored included Professor Sasson Somekh, one of the foremost authorities of Arabic literature; presumably the possibility of awarding the prize to an Arab writer was inherent in the composition of the committee. The award citation explained the choice:

> Emile Habiby's writing has a modernistic sophisticated style. The writer has succeeded in developing a unique genre by integrating classic Arabic writing style with the best of European satire. . . . Emile Habiby's work, translated from Arabic to Hebrew is accepted as part of modern day Hebrew literature and significantly contributes to Israeli literature of today.[7]

However, controversy erupted in the wake of the prize, mostly on the side of the Arab world, concerned that Habiby's acceptance of the prize implied legitimation of the state of Israel and its government. Habiby's response was to donate the prize money to a Palestinian medical center in the territories. To his critics, as the combination of winning both the Israel Prize and the Palestinian Al-Quds [Jerusalem] Prize suggested, he declared, "A dialogue of prizes is better than a dialogue of stones and bullets."[8] The few Jewish extremists who protested the ceremony were unceremoniously removed from the venue by members of the audience. The unanimous decision met with full acceptance by the prime minister (Yitzhak Shamir) and minister of education (Zevulun Hammer) at the time, both of whom were from the right wing of the political spectrum.[9]

What does it mean to judge a book on its literary merits, to say that one work is better than another? As Barbara Herrnstein Smith would ask, "better for what?"[10] And to what extent do extraliterary factors influence the judging? How does the Zeitgeist—the correlation to the Zionist master narrative, the state of gender politics, the relationship between the collective and the individual—affect the winnowing of the long list to the short list? What role do commercial interests, personal connections, and political interference have in deciding the winner?

Some prizes are more explicitly ideological than others. When serving as minister of culture and sport, Limor Livnat established an award for Zionist creative work (*Pras hayetsirah bitchum hatsionut*). Beginning in 2012, artists in a number of categories—dance, theater, cinema, music, fine arts, and literature—were selected for the honor. From the beginning the Zionist prize was controversial, and a number of well-known and well-respected figures signed a petition in protest: "This prize is one that encourages art to be used for political purposes. We demand its cancellation and request that the designated moneys be directed to the meager fund that supports free artistic creativity in the State of Israel."[11] The ministry replied that artistic merit would be the sole criterion; that the purpose of the prize was "to encourage artistic works . . . expressing the Zionist narrative that unites the Israeli public."[12]

A. B. Yehoshua was awarded the prize the second year—in the category of theater, not literature—for his play *The Two Walked Together*, about the historic meeting of Zeev Jabotinsky and David Ben-Gurion in London in 1932. (The prize for the literature category went to *Mashiv haruach*, a magazine for religious poetry, and to broadcaster Dan Caner for his project reading the entire Hebrew Bible.) While reportedly pleased to win, Yehoshua expressed reservations about the formulation of the prize, suggesting that "there is no such thing as a Zionist creative work [but only] works that deal with the history of Zionism."[13]

The following year, Yehudit Katzir and Shifra Horn shared the honors in the literature category, Haim Gouri surprised the Ministry of Culture when he declined their award for Zionist creative work (*Pras Hayetsirah Hatsionit*).[14] He asserted that his work, a personal reflection on his life and his memories, was not inherently Zionist.[15] "I will not say what my opinion of the prize for Zionist art is," sidestepping the issue, continuing, "I was born a Zionist and will die a Zionist, and all my life I fought for Zionism—but I do not find a connection between this book [*Though I Wished for More of More*] and the prize."[16] He further encouraged the ministry to use the money from his prize to support writers just beginning their careers. The prize has since been discontinued, and nary a trace is left on the website of the Ministry of Culture, Sports, and Tourism.

Some prizes that are less overtly ideological in conception are nonetheless political and contribute to the cultural image. The Israel Prize, by definition, draws a national portrait.[17] Established in the early years of the state by Ben Zion Dinur, then-minister of education (who later went to earn the prize himself), the Israel Prize is given in different fields, the specific categories following four- to seven-year cycles. The lifetime achievement award is annual (since 1972). Overall, the Israel Prize for literature paints a rather conservative picture of the field, populated with mostly male and almost all Ashkenazi writers.[18] With few exceptions, the writers have tended to hold their value.

And yet, controversy was not unknown. Prime Minister Yitzhak Rabin's objections to the choice of Yeshayahu Leibowitz (presumably for the scientist-philosopher's assertion of soldiers' "duty to refuse to serve in the occupied territories") led the scientist to decline the prize;[19] Limor Livnat did her best to block the awarding of the honor to the artist Yigal Tumarkin,[20] and other awards were adjudicated before the Supreme Court. Only in 2015 did politicization reach a new level. That year, Prime Minister Netanyahu, as acting education minister, had oversight of the Israel Prize. Until then, any overt political involvement with the prize was after the fact—after the work of the committees and the announcement of the awardees. Even before the committee did its work, Netanyahu protested that Israel Prize judges were extremists and anti-Zionists, writing:

> Over the years more and more agents extreme in their positions have been appointed to the juries, and among them those who support army-refusers, and too few authentic representatives of the wider sectors of the people.[21]

He posted on Facebook that the prize is controlled by a small, ingrown group of radicals. Against the backdrop of impending elections, the prime minister's office dismissed two judges from the committee that was to award the Israel Prize for literature: professors Ariel Hirschfeld and Avner Holzman. While the former had criticized the prime minister and championed conscientious objectors in print, the latter had never publicly expressed his political opinions. Both were then and are now well-respected academics. Holtzman, the Jacob and Shoshana Schreiber Chair for Contemporary Jewish Culture at Tel-Aviv University, became a full professor of Hebrew literature in 2001. Author of more than a dozen books (and editor of forty), Hirschfeld, also a full professor of Hebrew literature, chaired his department at the Hebrew University in Jerusalem, and published monographs on Agnon, Brenner, Bialik, and Yitzhak Laor.

The third member of the committee, author Gail Hareven, resigned in protest. Yigal Schwartz, Hirschfeld's and Holtzman's counterpart at Ben Gurion University, prolific editor, and memoirist (*Makhelah hungarit*), was the first to withdraw his candidacy, soon to be joined by noted writers such as Sami Michael, Yitzhak Ben-Ner, Haim Be'er, and most prominently David Grossman. Even when the prime minister reversed his objection—in response to the attorney general's advice—the damage was done. Netanyahu's unprecedented interference heightened the politicization of the prize, even while the prime minister was ostensibly trying to counter any such distortion. In the end, the government announced the cancellation of the prize.[22] A few short weeks later, Erez Biton was revealed as the laureate for the Israel Prize in literature, "the first poet of Mizrachi descent" to be so honored.[23] The novelty of his win deflected attention away from the incipient scandal.

One of the most predictive factors of a writer winning a prize is having already won one; prizes beget prizes.[24] It can be argued that the best is naturally accorded recognition multiple times by different bodies. It must be pointed out, however, that prizes legitimate each other as much as they validate their winners. In an exercise of circular axiology, the prestige of a prize is greatly influenced by the reputations and perceived value on those upon whom it is bestowed. The same writers garner prizes again and again. The winningest Israeli writers, Amos Oz, A. B. Yehoshua, and David Grossman, have each won the Bialik, the Brenner, and the Israel Prizes for literature, as well as many of the other most prestigious awards in the country (Agnon, Alterman, Bernstein, Dan David, Emet, Neuman, Sapir) and abroad.

While there are problems in general with literary prizes, almost universal in nature, there are also issues specific to Israel, in large part due to questions of definition and questions of scale. The overlap between "Hebrew" and "Israeli," the relatively large number of prizes in Israel, and the small world in which the residents of its Republic of Letters function all complicate the process of awarding prizes. A central challenge to the culture of literary prizes in Israel is choosing the jury—that is, not just finding people who have no vested interest, personal connections, or stated biases, but also finding enough people, both qualified and willing to be judges, so as to minimize overlap. Many panels include critics, academics, publishing industry personages, and writers. (These are not discrete categories; there is a great deal of intersection: literature professors who work as editors or as critics; writers who publish; critics who become writers, etc.)[25]

A small circle of people who know each other, the *"brangeh"* of the republic of letters, has a limited population.[26] There is the ever-present potential of nepotism, real or metaphorical. Only a small group of people are deemed capable of judging and are willing to do so, even more so in light of an apparent reluctance to find jurors abroad. The pool of options is further limited by the amount of work one is expected to do as a judge or member of a committee. The Sapir, for instance, requires each judge to read scores of books. According to Doline Melnick, the head of the Culture and Arts Department of Mifal Hapayis (the national lottery), each judge is expected to read approximately eighty books.[27]

Just as prizes beget prizes, judging begets judging. The repetition of names potentially leads to a form of stagnation; the individual prize becomes predictable, even stale. The effect of an individual juror shaping the literary landscape becomes magnified.[28] However, according to James English, jurors are motivated by love of the art, a sense of obligation, and/or prestige.[29] Perhaps even more motivating is the opportunity to influence taste, impose one's opinion and shape the canon. The judge represents the influence of the individual in canon formation, and within the institution. The prestige of the judge contributes reciprocally to the prestige of the prize.[30]

Controversies and scandals generally arise from a focus on the credentials of the jurors, their aesthetic taste, or the appearance of a conflict of interest. Conflicts of interest can be social (what English terms intimate capital), professional (e.g., currying favor with one's own editor or publisher), or mutual (reciprocating to a fellow artist when roles are reversed). Each of these—when present—can bias a judge toward choosing a particular winner. An unrestrained grudge or jealousy might have the opposite effect.

Case Study: The Care and Feeding of a Literary Award

> If an artist is good, nobody else can do what he or she does and therefore all comparisons are incoherent. Only the mediocre, pushing forward a commonplace view of life in a commonplace language can really be compared, but . . . "least mediocre of the mediocre" is a discouraging title for a prize.
>
> —Edward St. Aubyn, Wodehouse Prize Winner, *Lost for Words*

Established in 2000 by the National Lottery (Mifal Hapayis), the Sapir Prize was consciously patterned on the Booker[31] and designed to be the most celebrated, if not most elite, prize of its kind.[32] To that end it offers the largest purse of any prize dedicated to Hebrew literature—150,000 NIS (approximately $43,000)—as well as guaranteed distribution and translation. Long- and shortlisted works garner smaller sums (20,000 and 40,000 NIS, respectively).[33] The stated purpose of the prize is "to encourage quality Hebrew literature and the culture of reading in Israel, and thus to contribute to the advancement of Israeli culture."[34] Continuing questions of relevance and worthiness have been punctuated by moments of mistakes and scandal. The balance between what is expected and unexpected, reflecting consensus or stirring controversy, canonical and marginal, the literary and the popular, keeps the prize relevant, keeps people interested and makes the Sapir a wonderful case study.

There is something marvelous about Mifal HaPayis being the sponsor of the Sapir, making literal Julian Barnes's famous statement deriding literary prizes as "posh bingo."[35] So too, the connection with the namesake. Named to honor Pinchas Sapir (1906–1975), the father of the Israeli economy, the commercial value of the prize—beyond its actual purse—begs to be noted. The winning book is widely distributed to municipal libraries, and all of the shortlisted authors are obligated to appear in multiple public forums. To support the culture of reading, municipal libraries are supplied with the books from the short list, and a variety of events showcasing their authors are presented at a number of venues throughout the country. Publicity translates into sales in Israel, and especially through translation.

Haim Sabato's *Te'um kavanot* (*Adjusting Sights*) was the inaugural winner.[36] It was, in many ways, a curious choice. While his first book, a collection of short stories called *Emet me'eretz titzmach* (*Aleppo Tales*), met with success, that is, it was positively reviewed and fairly popular, Sabato has never been part of the mainstream literary establishment. To this day he is not listed on the website of the Institute for the Translation of Israeli Literature (although his four works of fiction have been translated into English), and his full-time job is still running the religious school as *rosh yeshivah* that he helped found. His writing is steeped in autobiography; most articles about him mention that he is descended from a rabbinical family from Aleppo, was born in Cairo, and moved to Israel as a young boy. His language draws from the religious world he describes, interspersing rabbinic Hebrew and references to traditional texts in a manner that has been compared to Agnon. That the winning book was the author's first novel, that the author himself was new to the republic of letters, was Mizrachi, and even more notably, a rabbi-scion of a rabbinic family, and that the style of the work was thick with allusive references and phrases, suggested that the Sapir Prize was deliberately setting itself apart from the crowded field of literary honors.

The following year, the prize was awarded to a much more likely choice, to the much better-known author, David Grossman, who had, as mentioned above, already been the recipient of many awards, both in Israel and abroad. Here again, however, there is an element of surprise. Grossman won for his book *Mishehu larutz 'ito* (*Someone to Run With*) a novel written for the YA (young adult) audience that succeeded in crossing over to the mainstream (adult) audience. Readers of the book were taken on an unexpected tour of Jerusalem's underbelly, by way of the homeless, drug addicts, and runaways.

Gail Hareven's win the third year reportedly surprised "the entire Israeli book industry," besting both Yehoshua's *Hakalah hameshachreret* (*The Liberated Bride*) and Gabriella Avigur-Rotem's *Hamsin utsiporim meshuga'ot* (*Hamsin and Crazy Birds*). Hareven's book had met with "restrained reviews and low sales." There were claims of a feminist conspiracy and reverse discrimination. The two men on the jury—out of five—let their displeasure with the choice be known in yet another small scandal.[37] The winning novel *She'ahavah nafshi* (translated as *Confessions of Noa Weber*) is described as the story of a woman caught between her feminist ideology and her obsessive love. "It's not a casual read; Hareven's insights into desperate yearning are so dead on and painfully astute, the experience can be eviscerating. That the work is also witty and compelling will leave [those] encountering Hareven for the first time, almost certainly pining for more."[38]

And so the Sapir has continued, oscillating between the center and the margins, with an eye to readability. The guidelines of the prize have evolved reflecting changing times, learning from past mistakes, shoring up flaws, and building on success.

The prize money for runners-up has been increased, and a long list has been added. A separate category for first books was created in 2006, as well as Israeli writers translated into Hebrew;[39] the number of books publishers were allowed to submit changed (ten, four in 2010, seven, and then proportional to number of annual titles per house up to fourteen), independently published books became eligible (2015) in recognition of the expanding digital market [40]

The Sapir has weathered miscalculations, disdain, withering criticism, and scandal. James English builds on Bourdieu's observation that "scandal is the instrument *par excellence* of symbolic action" to argue convincingly for the role of *fadicha* in cementing the success of a literary prize.[41] Scandal helps negotiate the route between the loftiness of art and the crassness of the market.[42]

The Sapir Prize's greatest scandal so far led to the unprecedented cancellation of the award in 2009. Yosi Sarid had exercised his prerogative as committee chair to cast the tie-breaking vote in favor of Alon Hilu's *Achuzat Dajani* over Ronit Matalon's *Kol Tsa'adenu*.[43] Hilu's win was unexpected. Ronit Matalon's book arguably has greater aesthetic value. "Forget Sapir. Give Her the Bernstein," proclaimed one article that announced the latter's win of the eponymous prize, implying judgments of both the novels and the prizes.[44] The Bernstein, given annually since 1978 to the best novel by an author under fifty, offers the second-largest purse.

Only a few days after the ceremony in which the winner was announced, *Haaretz* published an article detailing the connections between Sarid and Hilu—not only was Sarid's book published by the same house, but his niece was the editor and chief promoter of *Achuzat Dajani*.[45] The prize was retracted, and in the wake of multiple authors withdrawing their entries (including the entire short list) then canceled for the year. (Matalon's relationship with Ariel Hirschfield, one of the judges, received scant mention: after all, the book didn't win, the relationship was over, and, declared Hirschfeld, many writers have dedicated their books to him.)

The Schadenfreude of those who relished the tarnishing of Sarid's squeaky clean reputation, and the delight of those who had not won, piled on top of the seeming victory of the "Legal Forum for the Land of Israel."[46] The Forum had protested against the left-wing bias of the committee[47] that resulted in the choice of a novel described by its author as dealing with "the narrative of the Other and with the word *nakba*."[48]

Scandals aside, the Sapir has been subject to criticism and controversy almost since its inception. The majority of articles about the award focus on lists, winners, or process; very few actually address the literature. Here is a brief sampling of the criticism.

Menachem Perry, literary scholar, critic, and editor, was one of the first to disparage the prize publicly.[49] In an article in *Haaretz*, he declared the prize to be "no longer relevant" (which does imply, to some extent, that it once was). He argued that books that won—such as Sabato's *Te'um kavanot*—have not stood the test of time ("Five years have passed, has he been shown to be a writer of significance?"), while books such as Yehoshua's *Hakalah hameshachreret* did not win despite their lasting significance. He characterized the 2004 short list as a "list of niches—they chose one veteran, one Mizrachi, one neglected, one political" and sharply criticized the judges for not finding one deserving woman. As editor of the prestigious series Hasifriyah Hechadashah he declared that they would not be submitting to the prize. Doline Melnick countered that the professor had no quarrel with the Sapir the year that Grossman won. Even so, Perry's criticism of the prize has continued unabated; he was especially disparaging of the awarding of the Sapir to Esther Peled for her book *Petach gadol melematah* (*Wide Open Underneath*, Bavel, 2017).

Six months before winning the Levi Eshkol prize in literature (65,000 NIS) writer and critic[50] Amnon Navot wrote an open letter to the managers of the funding of the Sapir. He advocated for the immediate cancellation of the prize, arguing that the gap between its aims and its achievements was causing harm to the public.[51] In his letter he made use of colorful metaphors that included sewage, sailing (rats, whales, and sharks), and dog racing; divided writers into three categories (real, honorary, and conditional); and proposed running the contest along the lines of the Big Brother reality show where the public could SMS their votes. His denigration of the judges' credentials was no less harsh for being implicit, rather, he criticized them as being far from the ideal critic.

He wrote that the literary critic is not a graduate of a course in literary appreciation, a secret advisor to the prize, and/or an arbiter of taste, etc. Instead, according to Navot, the critic deals with the position of literature vis-à-vis reality/existential essence, measuring angles of entry and depths of wounds. "The critic is the one who stands on the blood and explains." Navot denigrated the prize even while making the case for its effectiveness, in his categorizing of current literature into two piles: "those [in the larger pile] written to win the Sapir, and those that—maybe, not for certain—were not."

At the beginning of 2017, poet and publisher Ron Dahan declared the failure of the Sapir to encourage quality literary production and consumption.

He argued that no one remembered who won the Sapir, that the prize was riddled with scandal, the judges' choices were uncourageous, and that the decision was skewed against books that dealt with political and social issues. He felt it a folly that books were considered for reasons other than literary. Furthermore, he argued that since the establishment of the prize there were fewer venues for publishing as smaller presses collapsed, and larger ones merged; original literature was less frequently on the lists of best-sellers. Since, in his view, the Sapir had failed to adapt the Booker to Israel—the prize was not successful in creating lively and interesting literature, he claimed—the funds would be better used to support writers.

The aforementioned Doline Melnick oversees the Sapir and is tasked with defending it against the frequent and expected attacks.[52] He suggests that the smallness of Israel and the likelihood of personal connections is not significant, "because when you take people who will read the books they don't necessarily have to know the author or the publisher or the editor or the *brang'eh*, they need to know how to read a book and to love it." Despite the use of the Booker as a model for the prize, Melnick concludes, "Israel is not England." With that short sentence, he defends the results and reifies the uniqueness of the Israeli literary scene.

Scholars in the field of literary awards see criticism of the prizes as "a fundamental and [even] an obligatory part of the game, a recognizable mode of complicitous participation."[53] The critic engages with the prize and the judging; to critique the outcome validates in some measure the existence and premise of the prize and its process. For all their criticism Perry, Dahan, and Navot are giving the Sapir Prize their serious attention.

Even while Dahan and others argue against the significance of the Sapir Prize (suggesting that the majority of booksellers would be hard-pressed to recognize the prize, much less identify its latest winner), the winning books are routinely decorated with the large sticker trumpeting the award, the translations into Arabic and a second language help spread the title, and the writer is henceforth known as the winner of a prestigious prize. Consider the "scandal" of Galit Distal-Etebaryan who claimed to have won the Sapir twice. The claim reportedly led to opportunities and honors she would not have otherwise received. (In fact, her first book was supported by funding from the National Lottery, as were hundreds of others; another work was long-listed for the prize.)[54] The Sapir continues to garner attention for itself and for its winners.

What does the Sapir prizewinners' list say about Israeli literature? Note that what it says is not always purely literary, and that the criteria are as significant as who wins. For example, after Ruby Namdar's win for *Habayit asher nechrav* (*The Ruined House*), the rules were revised to disqualify writers whose primary residence was abroad, thereby actively resisting the deterritorializing of the literature.[55] The latest winner, Esther Peled, beat out past winners Shimon Adaf and Noa Yedlin, the highly celebrated Sami Berdugo, and the eminently readable Amir Ziv. Relatively unknown, Peled most likely would have been a dark horse candidate at best if not for increased awareness and sensitivity to women in the wake of the #MeToo or Times Up movements. Overall, the Sapir Prize, unlike some others (Bernstein, Bialik) is not meant to be highbrow, and the winners are not all stylists and innovators. As with the Booker, not all judges are literary professionals (writers, scholars, editors, publishers, critics) "because the nation is made of people who are not necessarily literary."[56]

Conclusion

Prizes are multi-edged:
They promote reading but not necessarily the very best reading.
They shape as much as they reflect.

There is no doubt they have impact and help shape the canon. Awards have been proven to increase sales, and especially for works by lesser-known writers.[57] They extend the life of the honored work, or—in some cases—give the book a second chance.[58] There is also the halo effect for other works of the winning writer. In addition to the economic gain they engender,[59] there is also a cultural benefit; prizes add to the prestige of the winner.[60] And clearly, the phrase "award-winning" is meant to confer legitimacy and status, especially for what are considered the more prestigious prizes. In time, the fact of the prize being awarded tends to outlast the criticisms surrounding the process, and writers are introduced according to the latest or largest honor won.[61]

Even as critics point to the discontinuities between major book awards and the canon,[62] they still form keystones to the canon, or at least shortcuts. Curricula both reflect and contribute to the cultural capital of the canon; libraries often rely on lists of awards to help curate their collections. Public libraries thus make these works available to a larger audience, garnering more readership; academic libraries source faculty in preparing syllabi and seeking material for research. Inclusion in courses and scholarship adds to the prestige, visibility, and ultimately sales—cultural, social, and economic capital—of works selected. This is especially true in the case of Israeli prizes.

The sheer volume of works produced necessitates some shortcuts. The supplying of the Sapir short list, for example, to municipal libraries, makes the connection between prizes and library acquisitions even more explicit.

Todd Spires investigates how well his university library (Bradley University) represents major literary awards, concluding, "The end result was a realization that we had done a good job of collecting these titles over the years, but that we could do better."[63] His study makes concrete some of the indirect benefits and influences of literary prizes, the ways that prizes are often used as a shortcut to determining value.

Literary prizes, states Lisa Regan, "tell us about how we value culture more generally on a national and . . . global scale. They signal the direction in which we're traveling culturally, and that is definitely worth our attention."[64] The prize economy has itself become global. There are now multiple prizes patterned on the Booker,[65] award-winners are more likely to be translated and marketed abroad, juries of today actively seek literature from elsewhere. Israeli writers have recently met with great success in the larger world, David Grossman and his translator Jessica Cohen won the Man Booker Prize for the novel *A Horse Walks into a Bar*; Amos Oz won the inaugural Jingdong Literary Prize; his novel *Judas* (shortlisted for the Booker), along with Ayelet Gundar-Goshen's *Waking Lions* were both up for the 2018 International Dublin Literary Award. The success is all the more remarkable with growing international adherence to an un-nuanced politics that censures Israel for its treatment of Palestinians and makes no distinction between the government and the writers, the latter of whom tend to be among the most vocal critics of the former. This is a story that is unfolding and will present complicated dynamics.

The literary prize culture has become much more determinative than ever before, and seemingly fewer voices are included. Whatever we—as scholars, readers, writers—think of literary prizes, they are unlikely to disappear any time soon. However arbitrary the process, the effects last. In the end, literary prizes are not perfect, but at their best, they contribute more than they detract: they keep up interest, support writers and the industry, give rise to discussion, and encourage the reading of literature.

Man Booker winner and critic Julian Barnes declared:

> This is one reason that literary prizes arouse such intense interest and debate: they hold out the promise that it remains possible for reasonable people to arrive at well-argued judgments about literary artifacts.[66]

Notes

1. See for example, Marti LaChance's answer on Quora to the question, "Who are the greatest writers to never have won the Nobel Prize for Literature? What makes/made them great enough to have been worthy of winning the prize, and why do you think they haven't or didn't win the Nobel Prize?" www.quora.com/Who-are-the-greatest-writers-to-never-have-won-the-Nobel-Prize-for-Literature-What-makes-made-them-great-enough-to-have-been-worthy-of-winning-the-prize-and-why-do-you-think-they-havent-or-didnt-win-the-Nobel-Prize.

2. Prizes can be seen as "shorthand for literary merit," Claire Squires, "Literary Prizes and Awards," in *A Companion to Creative Writing*, ed. Graeme Harper (Oxford: Wiley-Blackwell, 2013), 291.

3. "Prizes breed prizes, it seems, and prolifically," Lisa Regan, "Literary prizes are still crucial, despite prevailing skepticism," *The Conversation*, April 15, 2014, http://theconversation.com/literary-prizes-are-still-crucial-despite-prevailing-scepticism-25676; Joel Best, *Everyone's a Winner: Life in Our Congratulatory Culture* (Berkeley: University of California Press, 2011) for his study of prize proliferation as a cultural phenomenon.

4. Studies include: Gillian Roberts, *Prizing Literature: The Celebration and Circulation of National Culture* (2011); Stevie Marsden, "The Saltire Society Literary Awards, 1936–2015: A Cultural History," PhD thesis, University of Stirling, 2016; Paul Washington, "The Postcolonial, the National and Australian Cultural Studies: The Case of the Miles Franklin Award (online), *New Literatures Review* 28–29 (Winter/Summer 1994/1995): 129–39, https://search.informit.com.au/document Summary;dn=960404123;res=IELAPA; cited May 31, 2018.

5. James English, *The Economy of Prestige* (Cambridge: Harvard University Press, 2005).

6. The Israel Prize has been awarded in multiple categories since 1953; the categories themselves appear to rotate in some random order and frequency.

7. http://israelphilately.org.il/en/catalog/articles/546/Emile%20Habiby.

8. Joel Greenberg, "Jerusalem Journal; To a Novelist of Nazareth, Laurels and Loud Boos," *The New York Times*, May 7, 1992, www.nytimes.com/1992/05/07/world/jerusalem-journal-to-a-novelist-of-nazareth-laurels-and-loud-boos.html?sq=Mahmoud+Darwish&scp=32&st=cse; accessed April 28, 2018. See also, Rachel Feldhay Brenner, "The Search for Identity in Israeli Arab Fiction: Atallah Mansour, Emile Habiby, and Anton Shammas," *Israel Studies* 6, no. 3 (2001): 91–112. Project MUSE, muse.jhu.edu/article/14480; Lital Levy, "Exchanging Words: Thematizations of Translation in Arabic Writing from Israel," *Comparative Studies of South Asia, Africa and the Middle East* 23, no. 1 (2003): 106–27. Project MUSE, muse.jhu.edu/article/191276.

9. Ruth Kartun-Blum, "When Shamir Gave the Israel Prize to Habibi," *Haaretz*, Feb. 23, 2015 (Hebrew), www.haaretz.co.il/opinions/.premium-1.2572572.

10. Barbara Herrnstein Smith, *Contingencies of Value: Alternative Perspectives for Critical Theory* (Cambridge: Harvard University Press, 1988).

11. he.wikipedia.org/wiki/פרס_היצירה_בתחום_הציונות.

12. Merav Yudolovitch, "Atsumat omanim neged pras hayetsirah hatsiyonit," *Yediot Aharonot*, Dec. 6, 2011, www.ynet.co.il/articles/0,7340,L-4157692,00.html; accessed April 29, 2018.

13. Shlomo Piotrkovsky, "Eyn davar kazeh yetsirah tsiyonit," *Arutz* 7, April 29, 2013, www.inn.co.il/News/News.aspx/255128.

14. The lesser-known Hannah Livneh became the sole recipient.

15. Hanan Hever concurred, noting that Gouri "no longer represents and establishes in his voice as a poet the imagined Israeli national community with a distinct identity, which for some time is no longer imagined and does not exist." www.haaretz.co.il/literature/study/.premium-1.2729870, Hanan Hever, "Haim Gouri meyuash mitafkid 'Hatsofeh Lebeit Yisra'el,'" *Haaretz*, Sept. 11, 2015.

16. http://blogs.timesofisrael.com/israel-needs-a-tea-party-remembering-haim-gouri-zl/.

17. The prize itself reached the status of popular culture in the film *He'arat shulayim* (Footnote, Cedar, 2011).

18. Of the winners, thirty-three are men (Agnon won twice) and six are women; with only one exception (1972, the poet Yocheved Bat-Miriam), each woman shared the stage with a male counterpart.

19. Uri Avinery, "Israel's Conscientious Objectors," *Counterpunch*, Dec. 29, 2003, www.counterpunch.org/2003/12/29/israel-s-conscientious-objectors/; accessed April 30, 2018.

20. Perhaps his most controversial piece at the time was an exhibit of three pigs wearing phylacteries. See Israel Harel, "The Israel Prize for Divisiveness," *Haaretz*. Feb. 12, 2004, www.haaretz.com/1.4714649; accessed May 31, 2018.

21. www.haaretz.com/.premium-pm-on-israel-prize-too-many-anti-zionist-judges-1.5305033.

22. Aviel Magenzie, "Be'ikvut hit'aravut Netanyahu," March 9, 2015, www.ynet.co.il/articles/0,7340,L-4634923,00.html.

23. "Poet Erez Biton Wins Israel Prize for Literature," March 29, 2015, *Yediot aharonot. Aronot*, www.ynet.co.il/articles/0,7340,L-4642128,00.html; Mitch Ginsburg, "Poet Erez Biton First Sephardi to Win Top Israeli Literary Award, March 30, 2015," *The Times of Israel*, www.timesofisrael.com/erez-biton-wins-israel-prize-amid-surge-of-ethnic-strife/ (Yehuda Burla and A. B. Yehoshua won before him, but for prose, and both were born in Jerusalem).

24. James English, "Winner Take All," in *The Economy of Prestige*, op. cit.

25. See, for example, Yael Fishbein, "Ilu haytah l'akademiyah opozitsiyah," *Davar*, Oct. 14, 1987, 14–15.

26. *Brang'eh* is loosely defined as field, in this case, the related fields of literary production, scholarship, and evaluation.

27. Maya Sela, "Mah mitrachesh me'achorei hakela'im shel prasei hasifrut beYisra'el?" *Haaretz*, Nov. 14, 2014.

28. For example, Nitza Ben Dov served on the jury for the Ramat Gan Prize from its inception in 2010—she is originally from Ramat Gan—until she declared herself finished. Meanwhile she has also adjudicated the following prizes: Sapir, Israel, Bernstein, Leah Goldberg, and Brenner.

29. English, *Economy*, 121.

30. Ibid., 122.

31. The Booker Prize was originally funded by Booker, McConnell Ltd. and was itself inspired by the Prix Goncourt. The latter was established almost a century before the Sapir was born, in 1903, to be awarded to the author of "the best and most imaginative pose work of the year." Initially established to provide funding to support the winner through the writing of a second book, the purse has not kept up with expenses. Instead, due to the sales generated by the prize announcement, the winner "becomes an instant millionaire." https://en.wikipedia.org/wiki/Prix_Goncourt.

32. See Sharon Norris, "The Booker Prize: A Bourdieusian Perspective," *Journal for Cultural Research* 10, no 2 (April 2006): 139–58, for an analysis of corporate sponsorship of prizes based on the theories of Pierre Bourdieu.

33. The Emet Prize, established in 2002, is worth $1 million, but the literature category is not awarded every year. Since its inception the literary laureates include S. Yizhar (2002), David Grossman and Sami Michael (shared, 2007), Sh. Shifra (2010), A. B. Yehoshua and Ronit Matalon (2016).

34. "Takanon 'Pras Sapir Lesifrut shel Mif'al Hapayis' lishnat 2017," https://culture.pais.co.il/Sapir/Documents/2017/tou_sapir_2017_ver2.pdf.

35. Julian Barnes, "Diary," *London Review of Books* 9, no. 20 (Nov. 12, 1987): 21, www.lrb.co.uk/v09/n20/julian-barnes/diary. Said before Barnes won the Booker.

36. It also won the Yitzhak Sadeh Prize, awarded for the best book on a military topic. The prize is often awarded for academic or journalistic works, and only occasionally for novels.

37. Neri Livneh, "Love as science fiction," *Haaretz*, June 19, 2002. https://www.haaretz.co.il/misc/1.803488.

38. Jessa Crispin, "Confessions" of a Woman Obsessed," NPR, April 3, 2009, www.npr.org/templates/story/story.php?storyId=102515201. See also "A very wise book, and it is written in the most beautiful, precise and definitive prose."— Lia Nirgad, *Ha'aretz Literary Supplement*; "Sometimes one has the experience of reading a book and just falling in love with it—because it is so well written, so moving, it gets into your soul. That was my experience when I read *The Confessions of Noa Weber*"—Michael Handelsaltz, "Don't Rely on Luck," *Haaretz*, Aug. 21, 2011. www.haaretz.co.il/misc/1.886288.

39. The latter category was for books written by Israeli citizens in other languages (not Hebrew) over the past five years; Ida Fink was the first and so far only writer to be awarded the prize in this category.

40. "Takanon chadash lePras Sapir: gam lehotsa'ah atsmit," Yotam Schvimmer, May 27, 2015, www.ynet.co.il/articles/0,7340,L-4661743,00.html. Self-published books would be required to prove that they had undergone professional editing and proofing, and were available for purchase at bookstores or through internet sites for book sales. They would also undergo an extra step of vetting by a committee of readers. Up to fourteen self-published books would be sent to the judges.

41. Bourdieu, *Free Exchange*, 84, quoted in English, *Economy*, 192: "Every new prize is already scandalous. The question is simply whether it will attract enough attention for this latent scandalousness to become manifest in the public sphere."

42. James English, "Winning the Culture Game: Prizes, Awards, and the Rules of Art," *New Literary History* 33, no. 1. Reconsiderations of Literary Theory, Literary History (Winter 2002): 109–35.

43. Other finalists: Iris Leal, Nurit Gertz, Amnon Dankner.

44. Maya Sela, "Forget Sapir. Give Her the Bernstein," *Haaretz*, July 16, 2009, www.haaretz.com/israel-news/culture/1.5077952 (English); www.haaretz.co.il/gallery/1.3341080 (Hebrew).

45. Also, Ronit Matalon had dedicated her book to another member of the jury, Ariel Hirschfield, with whom she had had a relationship.

46. The movement was established as a reaction to the 2004 disengagement from Gush Katif.

47. Sarid as MK, Alignment, Ratz, Meretz, and author of book about the *nakba*: *Lefikhakh nitkanasnu: historiah alternativit* (Tel Aviv: Sifrei Hemed, 2008).

48. Lital Grossman and Neta Ahitov, "Sapir Prize: New Revelations and Interim Summary," *HaI'r*, July 9, 2009. Also, Howard Schneider and Samuel Sockol, "Israeli Author's Zionist Novel [sic] Creates Controversy," *Washington Post*, July 15, 2009. Several years later, the Landau Prize in Poetry—also administered by the National Lottery—was withdrawn from Yitzhak Laor. Ostensibly the reversal was due to charges of (unadjudicated) sexual assault, but the prize was also challenged by the Legal Forum for the Land of Israel. In the end the courts awarded the poet 40,000 NIS (approximately $10,000). See Ran Boker, "Yitzhak Laor lo yekabel et Pras Landau," *Yediot Aharonot*, Dec. 22, 2014; Gili Iziovitch, "Mif'al HaPayis yishalem leYitshak Laor," *Haaretz*, June 29, 2016, www.ynet.co.il/articles/0,7340,L-4606044,00.html.

49. "Professor Menachem Perry is the great patriarch of literature in Israel," www.haaretz.com/israel-news/culture/.premium-israeli-literature-s-no-1-prof-menachem-perry-1.5316268.

50. Navot (1952–2017) also won the Prime Minister's Prize for Hebrew Writers (1987, 2002, 2010).

51. Amnon Navot, "Pras Sapir Hu Parodiyah Shel Sifrut," June 19, 2009, www.makorrishon.co.il/nrg/online/47/ART1/905/147.html.

52. The prize is described as "controversial" almost as often as it is labeled as "prestigious" or the "local Booker." See for example, Beth Kissileff, "Orly Castel-Bloom Scoops Always Controversial Sapir Prize," *Forward*, March 4, 2016, https://forward.com/culture/books/335139/orly-castel-bloom-scoops-always-controversial-sapir-prize/.

53. English, *Economy*, 189.

54. Iris Leal, "Zeh shakran vezeh sachro," *Haaretz*, Sept. 24, 2017.

55. See Melissa Weininger's essay in this volume for more discussion of the novel.

56. Maya Sela, "Good Morning (Booker) Israel," *Haaretz*, June 6, 2009. As mentioned above, the prize was founded and funded by the National Lottery. While nearly unavoidable, corporate sponsorship is problematic and paradoxical. Corporations are inherently conservative while the genre of the novel, specifically, and literature in general, is based on innovation, subversion, protest, and the individual voice.

57. Claire Squires, "Book Marketing and the Booker Prize," in *Judging a Book by Its Cover: Fans, Publishers, Designers, and the Marketing of Fiction*, ed. Nickianne Moody (London: Routledge, 2007), 71–83.

58. In Nicholas Barker's life cycle of books he notes that prizes especially affect the stages of reception and survival; Barker, *A Potencie of Life: Books in Society: The Clark Lectures 1986–1987* (London: British Library, 1993), 15.

59. James Surowiecki, "The Power of the Prize," *The New Yorker*, June 18, 2001.

60. Andrew Piper and Eve Portelance, "How Cultural Capital Works: Prize-winning Novels, Bestsellers, and the Time of Reading," *Post 45*, May 12, 2016, http://post45.research.yale.edu/2016/05/how-cultural-capital-works-prizewinning-novels-bestsellers-and-the-time-of-reading/. In a classification of authors by literary prestige significant weight is assigned to major prizes. See Marc Verboord, "Classification of Authors by Literary Prestige," *Poetics* 31 (2003): 259–81. Verboord's study is an attempt to correct the lack of "clear theoretical and empirical grounding" to the notion of canon. Of course, the determination of which prizes are major is not necessarily objective. Also, he does not acknowledge the interdependency of the factors he considers. But it is a sober effort to use big data to quantify what has been both elusive and subjective.

61. Consider Philip Roth's obituaries.

62. See English, *Economy*, 244, https://www.telegraph.co.uk/culture/culturepicturegalleries/10367682/10-great-writers-snubbed-by-the-Nobel-Prize.html; Donald Fleming, "Nobel's Hits and Misses," *Atlantic Monthly*, Oct. 1966, www.theatlantic.com/magazine/archive/1966/10/nobels-hits-and-misses/305482/.

63. Todd Spires, "Major Literary Award Winners in the Medium-Sized Academic Library," *Electronic Journal of Academic and Special Librarianship* 7, no.

2 (Summer 2006), http://southernlibrarianship.icaap.org/content/v07n02/spires_t01.htm; accessed May 8, 2018.

64. Lisa Regan, "Literary Prizes Are Still Crucial, Despite Prevailing Skepticism," *The Conversation*, April 15, 2014, https://theconversation.com/literary-prizes-are-still-crucial-despite-prevailing-scepticism-25676; accessed May 8, 2018.

65. See for example, the International Prize for Arabic Fiction "the Arabic Booker," the Caine Prize or "African Booker," etc.

66. Julian Barnes, "Diary," 21.

Appendix

A Canaanite Story
"The Lord Be Praised"

Eitan Notev

It all came at once. Dawud neither expected it, nor was he concerned about it. He had heard about them and was a little afraid of them; moreover, without ever seeing them, he violently hated them and wanted to kill them. But even in his worst nightmares he did not envision the possibility that they would walk here, into his village, mastering his world, acting as if it was theirs. The sound of cannons from the plains and the low hills, carried upon the wind, sliding over the curved valleys all the way here to the land in the mountains, transformed into unclear and pleasant sounds that did not cause horror in their hearts. Since it all happened so far away and so far down below, and the mountains were so high and serene, the possibility of horror was unimaginable. And when the sounds became frequent, one could mix them with all of the other frequencies that a man tends to accept without a thought, like the rising sun and the blowing wind and the scent of the sheep and goats.

Occasionally at night it was something to think about because then the sounds were accompanied by strange lights. Lights dashing to the sky, with long, spread apart tails, falling down slowly, gloriously, and small, quick lights that crossed the night rapidly and ended with a delayed blast. At dusk, the children would climb onto the sheikh's graveyard to see the faraway sight. Then they would tell one another what they heard from the grown-ups. The Jews will be beaten, they said, and their end will be bitter.

Even before the sounds were heard, there were many strangers passing through the village, raising interest. Most of them were armed men, who came to fight in the plains, to plunder and loot, and to earn a measure of heroic fame. Their mouths were full of hate and rage toward the Zionists, and simultaneously dripping pleasant, flowery sayings about the beloved homeland. The Brits were also a source of curiosity. They accompanied the armed men, guiding them as well as the youngsters with advice and commands.

But refugees came as well. They ran away from the plains, asking for shelter in the safe mountains. They recounted how the yahud deceived them in the dark of night, taking over their villages. The yahud are merciless, so the refugees told; they will not spare women or children. When the day comes, and this day is close, the day when the glorious Arab armies subjugate them, we will retaliate by taking their wealthy colonies in lieu of our poor villages. We will take their women, too, added the men. For now they were paupers, migrating to the big cities beyond the mountains, where there is plenty.

On one occasion, strangers wearing uniforms came. They had an armored car and they all carried the same weapon. These were some of the military men who fought the yahud in the plains. They were received with much respect and everything they wished was done. They made conversation, but did not chatter much about plunder and fame. Rather they were practical, spurring confidence and pride, and everyone knew that they would not disappoint. The children admired them.

The children envied the grown-ups; if only they could, they would take weapons and act like adults. With their good sense of imagination, they described the heroic tales they would take part in. Each morning, when Dawud took the sheep and goats down the slope and into the valley, to pasture, he would picture the goats as the fleeing yahud and he as the one ruling them, herding them. His fists strongly gripped the whip. His black eyes shone in his dark, soft face. But all of these things were just a colorful addition to that which was and remained the unchanging essence of their lives. The boys continued to herd the sheep and goats. The women descended to the valleys to harvest with a sickle and at dusk carried home a jug of water on their heads. When the season came, the men hitched camels to the plows, tilling the earth seeded with stones. At night the hyena laughed and the jackals answered with a howl. Everything as it was a long time ago.

But now things have changed. Now the yahud were here. The village was filled with them and with their deeds. Their patronizing strolling about in the alleys. They walked into yards and houses, acting as if they belonged to them. Their cars were parked in the square and the mukhtar's house was their kitchen. From the balcony of the mosque, one of their scouts would keep watch. And on the summit of the sheikh's graveyard, young prisoners of war dug military positions for them. They terrorized man and animal. The enduring things that should never change faded away, to be replaced by the dread of war. It happened within a night.

Suddenly, without any warning, the sounds were heard. Now the thunders were substantial, accompanied by the cry of torn air and pillars of heavy smoke around wild fire. With them came smaller sounds, thick and plenty, like many rifles shooting in incredible frequency. The sounds fostered an acknowledgment, giving birth to blind fear. The village woke, naturally doing things it had never done before. Possessions were packed swiftly and loaded onto the camels, accompanied by the sounds of women wailing and men cursing. The cattle corrals opened and the flocks fled eastward. The doors were locked and blocked, and everyone, man and animal, began to flow down the narrow alleys into the valleys. Among the runaways, there were also the foreign fighters who passed through the village to fight on the plain. They were the quickest to escape. The explosions continued, some of them falling among the ones seeking refuge for their souls. The voices of the injured, and their pleas not to be left helpless, were heard within the wails and the curses.

Terror rose in their hearts and throats choked when sounds of explosions ended, only to be replaced by bursts of nearby shots, accompanied by sharp shouts in a foreign language. These shouts were quick, eager, piercing through the night like a flock of hungry ravens. As they came closer, they confirmed the terrible rumors of the yahud and their deeds. At once the runaways spread in all directions. A camel went wild, kicking Dawud's thigh, waking him from the terror that paralyzed him. He jumped, hanging in a low branch of a strong Pistacia, settling between its branches. From here he witnessed the occupation of the village.

The flow of runaways disappeared as if it never existed. Now there was more silence than noise. There was only the sound of nailed shoes clapping on the alleys' stones, a few sounds of shooting, doors banging, and some blurred explosions coming from inside homes. The shouts continued but were calmer, not as sharp as before. The sun was about to come out any minute and in dawn's twilight he saw them for the first time—three of them. They had steel helmets and bayonetted rifles. They appeared in the alley, observing the slope. A gaunt cow detached from a clay wall and started moving towards them. Seeing the cow, they began chatting. There was the sound of laughter and suddenly the sound of shot from their direction resulted in the cow ramming its forehead to the ground, falling on its side with quivering feet, and dying. The three turned and walked slowly away.

Red lights from beyond the ridge announced the dawn. Dawud quickly pushed himself deeply into the branches, where he could cling to a solid branch. Doing so he felt the urge to abandon his hiding place and attempt an escape. His yearning eyes looked eastward, the direction in which the other villagers fled, but when he saw a few of the yahud on the ridge, his last hope faded and he felt despair in his heart. He was like an animal, trapped with no chance for escape.

The sunbeams reflected on the steel helmets and bayonets of the yahud on the ridge. The sounds of shooting became more and more sparse. But upon hearing them, flocks of pigeons would fearfully fly away only to land on another roof and sit once again. A car, loaded with singing soldiers, appeared on the road curving up from the plain. In the alley three yahud returned and stood. One leaned sloppily on a nearby wall and the other two turned to the door in the first yard. It was locked. They attempted to pick the lock but for nothing. So with a few crushing kicks, they invaded the house. After a moment they left, rifles on their shoulders, and a crowing hen in each of their hands. The occupation of the village was complete.

He was found after a few hours, when the sun climbed about a third of the way into the sky. Some of them gathered around the dead cow, beginning to skin it. Motionlessly, he examined them, until a tall guy, who behaved and spoke as their commander, gave orders to the others and then sat, resting in the shade of the Pistacia. He removed his steel helmet and leaned his head against the trunk. Then their eyes met and for a moment they looked silently at each other.

Suddenly a wide smile spread on his oval face, which was covered with a thicket of red hair. He put his weapon on a nearby stone. Without getting up, he signaled to him with one finger. His face was very young and his eyes were joyful, but Dawud only looked at him, covered with cold sweat and feeling helpless. The finger below kept on bending and straightening, ordering him down. Terrorized, he started down and as he reached the lowest branch, he fell to the ground. Sitting, with his legs spread in front of him, the red head was taller than Dawud who stood before him. He exclaimed something to his friends, those who were preoccupied with the cow. He pointed to Dawud, then to the tree, and then again to Dawud. They gave him one short, indifferent look. A few of them said some words to the red head and everyone turned, continuing with their business. They were all young adolescents.

"What is your name?" asked the red head in Arabic.

"Dawud Ibn Mahmud," he answered quickly.

"And how are you?" continued the red head, his face becoming serious.

"The Lord be Praised," said Dawud.

"Content?" asked his interrogator.

"The Lord be Praised," answered Dawud.

The red head scratched his forehead; his face seemed to deeply consider things. He eyed Dawud, bewildered. His mouth mumbled a few hesitating syllables and, with a hopeful expression, waited to hear Dawud's answer.

But Dawud was silent.

The red head repeated the same syllables again, stressing each of them. When he saw Dawud's continued silence, he scratched his forehead again, thinking. Suddenly his face lit up. "Many thanks," he said looking at Dawud hopefully.

Dawud did not know how to answer him, so he smiled sadly. The red head accepted the smile, but looked rather bored now. It seemed that he was no longer interested in Dawud. Suddenly, he called one of his people by name and he came quickly towards him. He was a boy with bold face, having a black moustache which curled up. The red head spoke and the mustached one nodded. He spoke to Dawud with an understandable word of urging and instructed him to pass by him. He took his rifle from his shoulder and held it in his right hand.

"Now it will come," thought Dawud.

He began marching, listening to the mustached one walking close behind him. When they passed the alley the barrel touched his shoulder, turning him to the right, towards the mosque. They continued walking, avoiding the corpses of both men and animals, and passed groups of yahud, some carrying chickens in their arms, some standing and talking in the shade of the walls. When they passed, they gave him a look of loathing and posed sarcastic questions. The mustached one answered with laughter and spurred him, directing him with his rifle barrel. They arrived at the mosque's gate, where a soldier stood, holding a bayoneted rifle. The mustached man said a few words and left. The guard pushed

Dawud inside, into the yard, filled with dozens of his fellow villagers and others. The prisoners crouched on the hard ground, with those who were older and respected in the middle, bearded and heavy. They were a group on their own and the others kept their distance. Encircling them were the younger villagers and some of the foreign fighters who tried to assimilate and appear as a part of them. The children were on the margins, near the women. The guard in the gate watched all of them.

Dawud joined the children and soon had a similar expression to theirs: a blend of indifference, scheming expectation, and heavy unease. None of his family members were here, and the rest, including his friends, were now strange to each other, each sunk in his own shattered world. From time to time someone looked into the rifle's barrel, turning away when the guard moved. The bitterness of death hovered above the heads of those crouching in the yard.

Noon came and still they did not kill them. To their astonishment, a large water tank was placed in the yard. They ordered the children to drink first, before the elders, before the adults, and before the women. A short, skinny guy, dark skinned and with big, pretty eyes replaced the guard. This guy knew their language well, although he used a different dialect. Everyone understood him. They listened carefully to a conversation between him and a few of the men crouching near him.

"How did they catch you?" he asked one of the foreign fighters.

"I was sleeping, sir, and voices awakened me. I am a man of peace and not of war. Therefore I took myself away, running from any fight or bloodshed, sir. While running here, I noticed people before me. I bowed and held my arms up, begging them in the name of God not to hurt me."

"Enough!" commanded the dark skinned one.

"Yes, sir," the fighter said submissively.

"You, the elder! Could you count thine years?" the dark skinned one turned to another respected man. It was Abu-Hasan, a senior, wealthy man from the village.

"Should I know, sir? It may be sixty, perhaps ninety, or over one hundred. I am very old indeed."

"You do not appear so old," said the dark skinned one. "An examination of your hair would probably determine that you are seventy-five years old."

"Yes sir," said Abu Hasan.

"And the members of thine family here? Close by you?"

"They are not here, sir. They ran away, but I remained here, as I knew that the yahud are good hearted and merciful. Thou art are good people. You will not do any harm. Righteous, noble thou art . . . !"

"Falsehood," interrupted the dark skinned one. "You did not stay here by your own will. As you were weak and fat and you lagged behind your young family and they left you. That is the way you are, the Arabs!"

"Merciful and gracious thou art . . ." opened the respected man, his voice trembling in fear.

"Unlike you: women rapists and children slayers!" said the dark skinned one with contempt.

At these words, the listeners bowed their heads again and fear snuck once more into their hearts. The foreign fighters looked away so as not to meet the eyes of the guard. Abu Hasan quivered, his mouth whispering, mumbling words of plea. Additional respected men mumbled.

Yet nothing happened. Their guard was silent for a moment, turning his attention to the mountains around the village. Then he pointed at Musa, a young man from the Mukhtar's family.

"Is the pasture good this year?" he asked.

"The Lord be praised," answered Musa.

"Your place is beautiful. It has good air. We will build a settlement here. We will use new methods to fertilize the soil. The stones should be hoed and trees should be planted on the slopes."

"You are correct, sir," replied Musa.

"You Arabs are not capable of doing anything right. You cannot get your act together like us. If only you had built posts around the village to protect the place, rather than protecting just your personal possessions, we would not have conquered it so easily," explained the dark skinned one.

"Understood, sir," said Musa.

"You were fools to fight us. You could have lived with us, peacefully, and we could have taught you how to work the land using machines."

"The Brits are to blame," said Musa, "the sons of dogs . . ."

Hearing him, the Jew's face lightened: "As you say, the wretched Brits bring us only trouble. Our two nations are siblings. It is known: Isaac and Ismael had the same father, and this is their homeland as well as ours . . ."

"Wretched will be the Brits, sons of bitches. Destruction upon their houses, their mothers—" opened Musa enthusiastically. Soon those sitting next to him joined him, then the further ones, all cursing the Brits zealously. They found the secret, the key to the yahud's heart. The mood changed and the fear of the yahud subsided a little. It almost completely faded away when the dark skinned one told them that they would receive food. Then he let anyone who felt it necessary to relieve himself across the fence.

The disaster occurred when the dark skinned one noticed strange words, supposedly in the language of the yahud, weaved in the margins of a khaki shirt that one of the foreign fighters wore. The fighter made an incautious move, changing his sitting position and exposing the marked margins. Seeing it, the dark skinned one jumped as if bitten by a snake. He called two of his friends to stand at the gate and point their guns towards those sitting in the yard. He jumped on the horrified fighter, tearing the shirt off him. With the garment in hand, he rushed out of the yard, seemingly very excited. The two at the gate exchanged words in their language, their faces harsh, intimidating. The prisoners felt the storm coming and shifted uncomfortably. The face of the foreign fighter turned white and his back quivered. Dawud knew him. His name was Jamal and he was one of the leading braggarts; he had good reasons to brag. There were stories about him and his friends, recounting how they ambushed a Jewish car, killing all of its passengers. After plundering the dead and cutting off their ears, they set the car on fire. Then they presented tokens of their victory in the nearby villages and became heroes. Now his neighbors tried to keep their distance from him without calling attention to themselves. An empty circle formed around him and he crouched, banished like a leper, his back quivering, quivering.

The dark skinned one burst into the yard, followed by many Jews, their faces radiating murderous rage, holding guns and ready to shoot. The dark skinned one carried the shirt, pointing at Jamal with excitement. The fighter wept now, bowing down and asking for mercy, blood flowing from holes opened in his chest, neck, and head. The yard was in a panic, like a chicken coop invaded by a hungry fox. Everyone dashed to the fence, trying to climb up. Shots thundered incessantly and people began to fall, heaps of them piling up. But the rest climbed over one another like mad.

Dawud managed to pass the fence and dashed towards the alley leading to the valley. Passing a nearby house, he suddenly found himself face to face with the red headed man who had captured him. The red head stopped, his hand pushing something in his weapon, ready to shoot. Dawud recoiled, moving backwards until his back hit the wall behind him. He had no refuge and the muzzle approaching his forehead blackened his sight. He closed his eyes. But instead of a shot, he heard the laughter of the red head. He opened them again, seeing the wide smile and the joyful eyes of his capturer.

"What is your name?" asked the red head, pointing his weapon down to the ground.

"Dawud Ibn Mahmud," he answered quickly.

"And how are you?" the red head asked.

"The Lord be Praised," answered Dawud.

"Content?" asked the red head, victoriously.

"The Lord be praised."

Translated from Hebrew by Yael Dekel

On Our Bookshelf

Editors' note: Here is a list of authors whose names appear in this volume. This combined list provides a glimpse of the scope of Israeli literature under consideration by our contributors.

Ayat Abou Shmeiss
Shimon Adaf
S. Y. Agnon
Ruth Almog
Nisim Aloni
Natan Alterman
Yehuda Amichai
Aharon Amir
Eli Amir
Aharon Appelfeld
Yiftach Ashkenazi
Maya Arad
Gabriella Avigur-Rotem
Nir Baram
Rivka Basman
Haim Be'er
Almog Behar
Yizhak Ben-Ner
Micha Yosef Berdyczewski
Sami Berdugo
Yosl Bergner
Asfu Beru
Chaim Nachman Bialik

H. Binyomin (B. Hrushovski-Harshav)
Yossl Birshteyn
Erez Biton
Shani Boianjiu
Shahar Bram
Y. H. Brenner
T. Carmi
Siham Daoud
Tzvi Eisenman (Tsevi Ayznman)
Galit Distal-Etebaryan
Alex Epstein
Rukhl Fishman
Alona Frankel
Yankev Friedman
Tomer Gardi
Assaf Gavron
Leah Goldberg
Haim Gouri
Uri Zvi Greenberg
David Grossman
Ayelet Gundar-Goshen
Batya Gur
Adia Gur Horon (Adolphe Gourevitch)

Amir Gutfreund
Emile Habiby
Tehila Hakimi
Avraham Halfi
Shulamit Hareven
Alon Hilu
Yoel Hoffman
Shifra Horn
Amalia Kahana-Carmon
Yoram Kaniuk
Avrom Karpinowitz
Sayed Kashua
Yehudit Katzir
Amos Kenan
Yehoshua Kenaz
Admiel Kosman
Asher Kravitz
Shulamit Lapid
Eleonora Lev
Yanetz Levy
Savyon Liebrecht
Malasha Mali
Mendel Mann
Salman Masalha
Ronit Matalon
Aharon Megged
Sami Michael
Zelda Mishkovsky
Rutu Modan
Yigal Mossinsohn
Ruby Namdar
Lilach Netanel
Eshkol Nevo
Yoram Nimshi (Yaakov Ashman)
Vaan Nguyen
Eitan Notev (Shraga Gafni)
Devorah Omer
Uri Orlev
Yitzhak Orpaz
Amos Oz

Esther Peled
Yonatan Ratosh (Uriel Shelach)
Yotam Reuveni
Avrom Rintsler
Leib Rochman
Carmit Rosen
Dina Rubina
Haim Sabato
Pinchas Sadeh
Asaf Schurr
David Schutz
Nava Semel
Yaakov Shabtai
David Shachar
Natan Shaham
Moshe Shamir
Anton Shammas
Amnon Shamosh
Rina Shani
Mati Shmuelof
Avraham Shlonsky
Yishayahu Shpigel
Ayman Sikseck
Moshe Smilansky
Yehoshua Sobol
Ronni Someck
Avrom Sutzkever
Benjamin Tammuz
Saul Tchernichowsky
Ayelet Tsabari
Dan Tsalka
Yona Wallach
Noa Yedlin
A. B. Yehoshua
Avot Yeshurun
S. Yizhar (Yizhar Smilansky)
Moshe Yungman
Natan Zach
Nurit Zarchi
Amir Ziv

Contributors

Nancy E. Berg, professor of Jewish, Islamic, and Near Eastern Languages and Cultures at Washington University in St. Louis, is the author of *Exile from Exile: Israeli Writers from Iraq* (SUNY Press, 1996), *More and More Equal: The Literary Works of Sami Michael* (Lexington Press, 2005), and numerous essays on Hebrew and Arabic literature appearing in collected volumes and in journals such as *AJS Review, Prooftexts, Hebrew Studies, Edebiyat,* and the *Journal of Arabic Literature.* As Dalck and Rose Feith Family Fellow at the Katz Center for Advanced Judaic Studies she worked on a monograph about Iraqi Jewish memories of Baghdad. Most recently she coedited *What We Talk About When We Talk About Hebrew* (with Naomi B. Sokoloff, University of Washington Press, 2018).

Yael Dekel is a postdoctoral fellow at the Ben-Gurion Research Institute for the Study of Israel and Zionism in Sede Boqer. She has published articles, book reviews, and essays in different journals in English and Hebrew (*Journal of Jewish Identities, Nashim, Mikan,* and more). She is currently working on a book project titled *Canaanite Fiction: History, Theory, Ideology.* Yael is also a translator and editor at the independent publishing house Ra'av. In recent years she was involved in a number of projects, including co-translating Pat Parker's poetry collection *Eifo tihiyu* (*Where Will You Be,* 2014); and editing Makhluf Abitan's collection of essays *Utopia miCasablanca* (*Utopia from Casablanca,* 2016).

Shai Ginsburg, associate professor in the Department of Asian and Middle Eastern Studies at Duke University, publishes on Israel and its culture in its relation to Jewish nationalism and its variants. He is the author of *Rhetoric and Nation: The Formation of Hebrew National Culture, 1880–1990*

(Syracuse University Press, 2014) and co-editor, with Brian Horowitz, of *Bounded Mind and Soul: Russia and Israel, 1880–2010* (Slavica Publishers, 2013). He has translated Paul de Man's collection of essays *The Resistance to Theory* into Hebrew and has written on de Man and deconstruction in the United States.

Yaron Peleg is Kennedy Leigh Reader in Modern Hebrew Studies at the University of Cambridge. His publications include *Directed by God, Jewishness in Contemporary Israeli Film and Television* (University of Texas Press, 2016), *Israeli Culture Between the Two Intifadas* (University of Texas Press, 2008), and *Orientalism and the Hebrew Imagination* (Cornell, 2005). His interests include modern Hebrew literary history, homoeroticism in modern Hebrew literature, the so-called post-Zionist age, as well as gender formation, ethnic identities (Ashkenazi/Mizrachi), and religious identities in Israeli cinema. He is co-editor of the *Journal of Modern Hebrew Studies* and associate editor of *Prooftexts*.

Shachar Pinsker is a professor in the Department of Middle East Studies and the Frankel Center for Judaic Studies at the University of Michigan. He is the author of *A Rich Brew: How Cafés Created Modern Jewish Culture* (NYU Press, 2018) and *Literary Passports: The Making of Modernism: Hebrew Fiction in Europe* (Stanford University Press, 2011). He edited *Women's Hebrew Poetry on American Shores: Poems by Anne Kleiman and Annabelle Farmelant* (Wayne State University Press, 2016), and *In the Place Where Sea and Sky Meet: Israeli Yiddish Stories* (Magness Press, forthcoming), in Hebrew, and he is co-editor of *Hebrew, Gender and Modernity: Critical Responses to Dvora Baron's Fiction* (Maryland, 2007). He is currently at work on a book on *Yiddish in Israeli Literature and Culture*.

Michal Raizen is an associate professor of comparative literature at Ohio Wesleyan University. She works with contemporary Hebrew, Arabic, and Francophone literature and film and has training in ethnomusicology. Raizen's research and teaching center on Arab Jewish studies, Hebrew to Arabic translation, graphic and experimental narratives of the Middle East, intersections of music and literature, and accented cinema. Raizen has an article in *Dibur*, "Jerusalem Writes, Cairo Translates, Berlin Reads: Hebrew to Arabic Literary Translations in the Digital Age." She is currently working on a book project, *Exile Got Your Tongue: The All-Stars of Arabic Song and the Literary-Acoustic*.

Naomi B. Sokoloff is professor of Near Eastern Languages and Civilizations and Comparative Literature at the University of Washington. Her books include *Imagining the Child in Modern Jewish Fiction* (Johns Hopkins University Press, 1992), *Boundaries of Jewish Identity* (coedited with Susan Glenn, University of Washington Press, 2010), and *What We Talk About When We Talk About Hebrew* (coedited with Nancy E. Berg, University of Washington Press, 2018). She is the author of numerous articles and book chapters on Israeli literature, and her current research focuses on animal studies and literary response to the Holocaust.

Riki Traum is a lecturer of English, American, and Jewish Literature at Fairleigh Dickinson University. Her research focuses on poetry of the 1960s in Israel and the United States and on the avant-garde female voices of the era. She is the editor of a volume of the poetry of Rina Shani (1937–1983) and the author of its introductory essay. Dr. Traum is also interested in contemporary protest poetry and in comparative aspects between protest poetry in America and Israel. She writes on immigrants and immigrations in American and Israeli poetry. Dr. Traum teaches creative writing and explores relations between poetry and visual arts, and painting in particular.

Eran Tzelgov is a Hebrew poet, translator, and scholar. He is interested in cultural activism and sees literary works as social agents. His interests include translation and gender studies, postcolonial theory and contemporary Israeli poetry. He has held teaching positions at Northwestern University, Ben-Gurion University, the Open University in Israel and Minshar College of Art. In 2012 he founded the small independent publishing house Ra'av, challenging the often "too homogenized" nature of the Israeli canon. His 2013 collection of poems *Bhirot* was awarded the Israeli Ministry of Culture and Sports award for "New and Upcoming Poets." His translation of Dylan Thomas's *Under Milk Wood* was published by Shocken Books (along with sketches) in summer 2015.

Melissa Weininger is the Anna Smith Fine Lecturer in Jewish Studies and the associate director of the program in Jewish Studies at Rice University. Her research focuses on Modern Hebrew and Yiddish literature, Jewish nationalism, and gender. She is currently at work on a book on diaspora Israeli literature. She teaches courses on Jewish film and literature, women and gender, and modern Israel. Her work has appeared in the journals *Prooftexts*, *Shofar*, and *Studies in the Novel*.

Eric Zakim, associate professor of Hebrew and Comparative Literature at the University of Maryland, currently serves as the director of the program in film studies and is a core faculty member at the Meyerhof Center for Jewish Studies and the Gildenhorn Institute for Israel Studies. He is the author of *To Build and Be Built: Landscape, Literature, and the Construction of Zionist Identity* (University of Pennsylvania Press, 2006) and the co-editor of a special volume of the journal *Prooftexts: David Fogel and the Rise of Hebrew Modernism* (1993). He has published essays on Israeli popular culture, Hebrew poetry, and Marxist and poststructural theory in the study of modernist music.

Wendy I. Zierler serves as the Sigmund Falk Professor of Modern Jewish Literature and Feminist Studies at the New York campus of Hebrew Union College-Jewish Institute of Religion. Her books include *Movies and Midrash: Popular Film and Jewish Religious Conversation* (SUNY, 2017, National Jewish Book Award Finalist); *And Rachel Stole the Idols: The Emergence of Modern Hebrew Women's Writing* (Wayne State University Press, 2004); *Behikansi Atah* (the collected writings of Hava Shapiro, in Hebrew), edited with Carole B. Balin (Resling Press, 2008); and *To Tread on New Ground: Selected Hebrew Writings of Hava Shapiro (1878–1943)*, translated by Wendy Zierler, edited with Carole B. Balin (Wayne State University Press, 2014).

Index

Abou Shmeiss, Ayat, 19
Abramson, Glenda, 80n56
acoustics, 33
Adaf, Shimon, 259
Adaptation, 188
Aderet, Ofer, 200n3
Adorno, 201n7, 203n29
aesthetics, 8, 237, 249, 253, 256; erotic, 185, 186, 198; of language, 2, 216; modernist, 147; Palmach, 32; Rina Shani's, 17, 208, 209, 216
Agnon, S. Y., 6, 179n6, 180n8, 254, 262n18; *Temol shilshom*, 164, 165
Ahad Ha-am, 188
Ahitov, Neta, 264n48
Al-Quds Prize, 249
Alberstein, Chava, 64
Alcalay, Ammiel, 22n22, 57n16
Alef, 16, 103, 106–108, 119n3
alienation, 160n30, 207, 208, 213, 215, 223, 225
Almog, Oz, 77n19
Almog, Ruth, 7; *Nashim*, 9
Aloni, Nissim, 7, 209, 211, 218, 224, 226nn7–9, 226n11, 226n13, 227n15; "The Owl," 211, 214
Alterman, Natan, 3, 29, 38, 68, 277
alternatives, 219; history, 16, 27, 129, 131, 134; homeland, 16, 125, 132, 135, 136; literary, 5, 6, 64, 237; to reality, 150, 153, 169, 214, 240; spatial, 130, 215; to Zionism and Zionist narrative, 7, 20, 38, 108
Althusser, Louis, 30, 41n9, 116, 121n30, 121n32
Altieri, Charles, 210, 226n5
American colonialism, 131
American Imagism, 188
Amery, Jean, 199, 203n30
Amichai, Yehuda, 6, 60, 62–67, 71–75, 98; *Lo me'akhshav, lo mikan*, 72
Amir, Aharon, 106
Amir, Eli, 44–51; *Mafriach hayonim*, 44, 45, 47–48, 51, 55n1, 57n15 (film); *Tarnegol kaparot*, 44, 45, 47–51, 55n1; *Yasmin*, 44, 47, 50–51, 55n1, 56n2
animal, 177; fables, 171, 172; studies, 17, 164, 167, 168, 179n6; themes, 111–12, 164, 165, 178
anthology, 60, 71, 77nn10–11; compilation of, 5, 61, 66; English language, 6
anti-Zionist, 105, 251
anxiety, 89, 184, 191, 193, 195, 196
Appelfeld, Aharon, 6, 11, 85, 175, 181nn22–25
Arab noise, 51, 57n17

INDEX

Arab-Israeli conflict, 67, 144, 158n6, 230
Arabic, 44–50, 53–55; literature, 15, 85, 98, 249; speakers, 16, 19, 51, 112; and translation, 55–56n2, 111, 113, 114–115, 153, 258; and Yiddish, 99
Arad, Maya, 124, 137n5
Aran, Gideon, 161n41
Arendt, Hannah, 202n20
Aristotle's *Poetics*, 180n7
Arpaly, Boaz, 62, 73, 77n14, 79n48; ars poetics, 234, 239
Ars Poetika [movement], 38, 46, 47, 55, 56n6
Ashkenazi, and male, 5, 6, 10, 251; poetic tradition, 36, 38; language [Yiddish], 88
Ashkenazi, Yiftach, 242
Ashman, Yaakov [Yoram Nimshi], 106, 107, 108, 120n20
authenticity, 4, 14, 53, 195, 210; claims to, 130; questions of, 110, 240
authorship, 185, 187
autobiography, narrator, 83, 84; semi-, 44, 52; writing, 17, 163–164, 177, 264, 179n3
Averbach, David, 62, 77n15
Avigur-Rotem, Gabriella, 12; *Chamsin utsiporim meshuga'ot*, 255
Avinery, Uri, 262n19
awards. *See* Literary Prizes
Axelrod, Liraz, 181n20
Axler, Craig H., 77n13

Badiou, Alain, 203n29
Balibar, Etienne, 121n33
Bar-Am, Gali Drucker, 99n7, 101n34
Bar-El, Adina, 160n38
Bar-Yosef, Eitan, 158n8
Barabash, Uri, 101n36

Baram, Nir, 11
Barker, Nicholas, 265n58
Barnea, Or, 181n21
Barnes, Julian, 254, 260, 263n35, 266n66
Barthes, Roland, 191, 192, 193, 202n17
Barzilai, Gad, 158n6
Barzilai, Maya, 99n6
Bashkin, Orit, 57n12
Basman, Rivka, 91, 92
Bass, Warren, 201n14
Bat-Miriam, Yocheved, 262n18
Bataille, George, 34, 42n21
Be'er, Haim, 85, 252
Beat poets, 210
Behar, Almog, 44–47; *Tchachla veHezkel*, 52–55, 55n1, 56n2, 58n21
Beit Tefilah (Tel Aviv), 59, 64; belonging, 126, 130, 133, 136; Shani and, 17, 208–209, 219, 221, 224, 225
Belsey, Catherine, 116, 121n31
Ben Dov, Nitza, 79n46, 263n28
Ben Mordechai, Itzhak, 211, 226nn8–9, 226n13
Ben-Gurion, David, 147, 148, 250
Ben-Ner, Yitzhak, 6, 252
Benjamin, Walter, 199
Berdugo, Sami, 11, 259
Berdyczewski, Micah Yosef, 138n7
Bereshit, Haim, 101n33
Berg, Nancy E., 22n14, 46, 56n8
Berger, Alan L., 179n4
Bergner, Yosl, 91, 209, 212, 213, 218, 226n13
Bernstein Prize, 252, 256, 259
Beru, Asfu, 11
Besser, Yaakov, 22n12
Best, Joel, 261n3
Bewes, Timothy, 237, 241, 244n19, 245n25
Bhabha, Homi, 124

Biale, David, 171, 181n18
Bialik Prize, 252, 259
Bialik, Haim Nahman, 64, 90
Bible, Hebrew of, 66, 67, 104, 111, 112, 210; reference to, 57n15, 98, 105, 106; register of, 114, 127, 223, 240; story, 30, 79n40, 127–128, 132
Bildungsroman, 48
Binyomin, H. [Binyamin Hrushovski-Harshav], 15, 91, 92, 93–95, 98
biography, 108, 209, 217, 221, 225
Birah, Iftah, 179n6
Birshteyn, Yossl [Yosi Birstein], 15, 83–84, 91, 92, 95–97, 99n1, 101n30
birthplace, 207–208, 209, 211, 214, 221, 225
Biton, Erez, 52, 252
Black Panthers, 210
Bogue, Roland, 117, 121n36
Boianjiu, Shani, 3, 124, 137n4
Boker, Ran, 264n48
Booker Prize, 254, 258, 259, 260, 263n31
bookshelf, 9–10, 12, 277ff
borders, conceptual, 44, 67, 137, 167, 221; cultural, 12, 125; geographic, 44, 50, 134; linguistic, 44, 84, 85; metaphoric, 39, 65, 134, 167; political, 44, 50, 125, 150
boundaries, blurred, 164, 167, 187; geographic, 133, 144; of Hebrew, 19, 44, 55; of literature, 3, 14, 16, 124; symbolic, 133; transgression of, 56n7, 187
Bourdieu, Pierre, 248, 256, 264n41
Boydem, 130
Boym, Svetlana, 121n27
Braidotti, Rosi, 226n10
Bram, Shahar, 3
Brand, Roy, 199, 202n24, 203n28
Brecht, Berthold, 226n7
Bregman, Ahron, 158n6

Brenner, Y. H., 8, 252
Brenner Prize for Literature, 263n28
Brenner, Rachel Feldhay, 121n38, 261n8
British colonial authorities, 17, 144, 145
Buchman Prize, 180nn14–15
Budick, Emily Miller, 181n17
Burla, Yehuda, 262n23

Caine Prize (African Booker), 266n65
Calderon, Nissim, 29, 34, 41n5, 41n15
Cammy, Justin, 100nn13, 17
Canaan, 114, 147
Canaanites, art, 105, 106; criticism of, 105, 119n2; fiction, 19, 106, 107, 108, 109, 117; and Hebrew, 104, 107, 114; ideology, 16, 104, 105, 106, 107; membership, 109, 115, 116; movement, 16, 104, 107, 109, 115, 116; and Palestinians, 106, 107, 108; writers, 108, 116
Caner, Dan, 25
canon, 2–14, 16–20, 103–111, 157n1, 200, 248–253; challenges to, 108, 118, 128, cultural capital of, 259; and identity politics, 10; factors in, 5–12, 248, 254; and interiority, 190; Israeli writers in, 17, 18, 60, 110; limitations of, 4, 259; -making, 5–12, 248, 253, 259; margins of, 103, 117, 254; opening, 11, 128, 259; outside of, 14, 16, 17, 184, 210; prayer, 18; questioning, 2–4, 10, 12, 20, 248; and *stalagim*, 190, 198, 200; texts, 2, 5–12, 108, 164; unmaking of, 5, 9, 259; as verb, 3, 11, 12
Carmi, T., 93
Cartography, 155, 211, 214, 217
Castel-Bloom, Orly, 265n52; *Dolly City*, 12

censorship, 62, 77n12, 185
Charters, Ann, 226n6
Chaver, Yael, 94, 100n14
childhood, 16–17, 19, 143; children's literature, 14, 16, 154, 157, 160–161n39, 163; and the canon, 14; experiences, 17, 175, 177; fantasy in, 17, 145, 151; features of, 70, 165, 169, 174, 178; home, 52, 240; magazine, *Mishmar liyeladim*, 144; memoir, 14, 174, 202n15; memories, 66, 94, 108, 171; poetry, 146–147, 159n17; as topic, 160n30, 170, 219
citizenship, 45, 48, 103
Cixous, Hélène, 37, 42n29
Coetzee, J. M., 181n17
Cohen, Jessica, 260
Cohen, Uri, 179n6
collective, 11, 117, 230–231; expression of, 11, 38, 44, 132, 188, 190; and individual, 8, 19, 185–187, 197–201, 250; Jewish, 64, 89; memory 109; myth of, 210; national, 157, 159
Crispin, Jessa, 263n38
curriculum, 3, 4, 198, 248, 259

Dagnino, Arianna, 125, 138n9
Dahan, Ron, 257–258
Dankner, Amnon, 264n43
Danziger, Yitzhak, 106, 119n7
Daoud, Siham, 19
Darr, Yael, 145, 158n10, 159n15, 159n17, 161n45
De Beauvoir, Simone, 42n34
De Man, Paul, 217, 227n17
death, 150, 241; of character, 151, 175, 195, 233, 238–239, 244n15; in liturgy, 73–75; metaphorical, 12, 88, 136; of poet 34, 211; and war, 107, 109, 149–150; and Yiddish, 83, 89

defamiliarization, 115, 175, 211, 227
Dekel, Yael, 16, 19
Deleuze & Guattari, 104, 117, 121nn34–37, 211
desire, 63, 134, 196, 198, 209–210, 233; anxiety of, 199; conflicting, 132; expression of, 49; for silence, 33; individual, 151, 187, 199, 233, 240; and its objects, 191, 193, 223; poet's, 36, 54; repression of, 17, 186; sexual, 184, 194, 195, 197; and shame, 183; transgressive, 71, 185, 223
destabilization, 136–137
deterritorialization, 45, 117, 118, 121n37, 211, 220; of literature, 259
Di goldene keyt, 91
Diamond, James S., 120n9
diaspora, 49, 93, 107, 122–126, 132–133, 138n7; and homeland, 128–129, 136–137; language of, 88, 89, 130, 135; literature, 6, 11, 116, 123; rejection of, 106, 124
digital market, 255
Dinur, Ben Zion, 251
Dinur, Yehiel [Ka-Tzetnik], 198, 199, 202n21
disengagement Plan, 155
disruption, 186
Distal-Estebyan, Galit, 258
dogs, in Agnon, 164–165; in Kravitz, 179n5; in literature, 180n8; in Mann, 95; in Schurr, 237–238; in *stalagim*, 198
Dunayer, Joan, 180n13
Dworkin, Andrea, 186, 200n5

echo, 9, 28, 37, 114, 131, 174; intertextuality, 46, 61, 127; in poetry, 213, 216
economy, 143; of desire, 196; of exchange, 248; Israeli, 45, 152, 188,

239, 243n7, 254; and literature, 65n7; of prizes, 259–260; spatial, 211; and violence, 152, 153
Eichmann trial, 184, 185, 193, 195, 198–199
Eichner, Itamar, 160n36
Einstein, Arik, 60
Eisenman, Tzvi [Tzevi Ayznman], 15, 91, 92, 97–98, 101n31
Eitan, Rafael, 152
Elegy, 73, 223
Eliot, T. S., 21n6, 28, 40n1
Elkad-Lehman, 160n32
Emet Prize, 263n33
England, 210, 258
English, 16, 85; anthology in, 6; audience, 13, 15, 106; Israeli literature in, 3, 11, 16, 124; translation from, 125, 210; translation into, 12, 153, 178n1, 254; transliterated, 136; with translation, 72
English, James, 248, 253, 256, 261n5, 262n24, 263n29, 264nn41–42, 265n53, 265n62
Ephratt, Michal, 119n8
Epstein, Alex, 11
escapism, 16
Eshed, Eli, 158n4, 194, 196, 198, 200n1, 201n11, 202n22, 202n24
Eshed, Haggai, 160n33
E-srael, 124, 129–137, 138n14; *Tschok shel akhbarosh*, 164, 165, 178
estrangement, 32, 115, 118 121n27, 211, 214; from Arabic, 44, 45
ethnicity, 2, 4, 8, 38, 84–85, 187, 230
Even-Zohar, Itamar, 6, 21n6, 22n12
exile, 8, 53, 55, 83; and home(land), 17, 125, 128, 211; as homeland, 211; negation of, 88; permanent, 214; reverse, 46, 48, 52; self-, 134
exoticism, 155, 184

Ezrahi, Sidra DeKoven, 77n17
Ezrahi, Yaron, 200n7

fantasy, 131, 136, 151, 199, 235; in children's literature, 16, 17, 143–161; as political, 157
Faulkner, William, 188
Feldman, Maya, 243n10
Feldman, Yael, 179n3, 22n22
feminist criticism, 37, 185, 186, 160n30
fiction, nature of, 238
Fink, Ida, 263n39
First Intifada, 152
Fischof, Ohad, 201n9
Fish, Stanley, 21n6
Fishbein, Yael, 262n25
Fishman, Rukhl, 91, 92
Fleming, Donald, 265n62
foreignness, 32, 198, 207–224; flower, 216–220; genre, 197; history, 105, 144; identity, 131, 209, 217, 221–224; make, 114, 115, 184, 187–188; person, 111, 115, 219
forgetting, 60, 132, 176
Foucault, Michel, 121n33, 224, 228nn27–29
Francis, Christine Doyle, 157n2
Frankel, Alona, 17, 19; *Ishah*, 163, 176–177, 178n1; *Na'arah*, 163, 176, 177, 178n1; *Once Upon a Potty*, 174; *Yaldah*, 163, 166–176, 177, 178, 178nn1–2
free indirect discourse, 190
Freeling, Tuvia, 243n5
Friedman, Yankev, 91, 92
Fuchs, Sarit, 226n7

Gafni, Shraga, 103, 106, 108, 109. *See also* Eitan Notev
Galron-Goldschlager, Yosef, 23n28
Gamad, 200n4

Gaon, Gili, 56n11
Gardi, Tomer, 124, 137n4
Gavron, Assaf, 11
Genesis, 67, 71, 73, 87–88, 127–128
gender, feminine, 39, 40, 67; masculine, 30–31, 36–40, 41n19, 42n34, 193
geography, 104, 211, 215; boundaries of, 2, 16, 215, 217–218; fanciful, 155; and language, 19, 134, 217; of literature, 20, 103; and silence, 32; transcending, 125, 208, 209
German Expressionism, 188
Germany, 21, 123, 181n16, 193
Gertz, Nurit, 106, 264n43
Al-Ghazali, Nazem, 45, 52, 53
Gilboa, Amir, 225n3
Ginsberg, Allen, 210
Ginsburg, Mitch, 262n23
Ginsburg, Shai, 16, 17, 19, 21n4, 84, 99n5, 159n23, 201n7
Glassner, Arik, 242n, 243n10
Gluzman, Michael, 228n22
Golan, Arnon, 101n29, 101n33
Goldberg, Leah, 18, 29, 93, 154, 208, 224; as mentor, 227n18; *Mikhtavim menisa'ah medumah*, 227n19; "Nameless Journey," 219–221; *Nisim venifla'ot*, 160n38; "Pine," 219; and Rina Shani, 208, 209, 218–221, 224–225; as translator, 218
Gomel, Elana, 157n1
Gordinsky, Natasha, 219, 225n4, 227n19, 228nn22–24, 228n27
Gorodish, Shmuel Gonen, 150
Gouri, Haim, 6, 27, 31–33, 250; *Shoshanat ruchot*, 32
Gover, Yerach, 22n22
Graff, Rani, 157n1
Green, Dror, 34, 41n18
Greenberg, Joel, 261n8
Greenberg, Uri Zvi, 90

Grossman, David, 10, 85, 252, 255, 257, 263n33; '*Ayen 'erekh ahavah*, 9, 164, 165, 178, 179n6 (*see also under* love); *Sus nikhnas lebar* [*A Horse Walks into a Bar*], 260
Grossman, Lital, 264n48
Grumberg, Karen, 56n4
Guillory, John, 21n6
Gundar-Goshen, Ayelet, 260
Gur, Batya, 9
Gurevich, Zali, 161n41
Gurevitch, Danielle, 157n1
Gutfreund, Amos, 9

Ha'olam hazeh, 187, 188
Habiby, Emile, 249
hafla, 15, 43, 44, 45, 48, 49
Hakimi, Tehila, 14, 27, 38–40
Halevi-Wise, Yael, 23n29
Halevi, Yehuda, 208
Halfi, Avraham, 60, 63, 68–71
Halperin, Liora, 99n5
Hammer, Zevulun, 249
Handelsaltz, Michael, 263n38
Har'el, Shlomo, 159n17
haredi, 59
Harel, Israel, 262n20
Harel, Na'ama, 180n6
Hareven, Gail, 252; *She'ahavah nafshi*, 255
Harris, Rachel, 21n4, 21n7
Harshav, Benjamin, 101n36. *See also* H. Binyomin, Hrushovsky
Harvey, David, 243n7
Hassan, Roy, 46
Hausner, Gideon, 202n20
Hayiti kalbato shel kolonel Schultz, 185, 187, 200n3
Hazzaz, Haim, 23n28
Hebraism, 4, 104, 124
Helman, Anat, 101n23, 201n8
Hemingway, Ernest, 247

Herman, David, 180n11
Herzog, Omri, 239, 240, 243n10, 244n21, 243n23
Hess, Tamar, 178n3
heterotopia, 224, 228nn27–28
Hever, Hanan, 106, 108, 111, 201n7, 262n15; on Gilboa, 225n3; on Gouri, 262n15; "Ivrit," 121n38; on labor poetry, 158n13; "Minority Discourse," 130n23; "Teritoriyaliyut," 120nn14–15, 120n19
Higgins, Ian, 161n40
Hillel, Ayin, 154, 160n38
Hilu, Alon, 11; *Achuzat Dajani*, 256
Hirsch, Eli, 36, 42n22
Hirschfeld, Ariel, 251–252, 256
historiography, 4, 10, 13, 14, 17, 27, 92
Ho!, 99
Hoffman, Yoel, 85
Hollander, Uri, 160n39
Holocaust, after, 178; animal studies, 17, 164, 176, 177; and Canaanites, 106; child's experience in, 175; compared to *nakba*, 95; second generation, 9; stalagim, 185–200; survivors, 19, 98, 101nn34–35, 106, 134, 164–165; Yiddish after, 84, 85, 87–90, 98
Holtzman, Avner, 121n39, 251
homeland, 44, 45, 48; alternative, 50, 123–137; and exile, 8, 17, 125, 128, 211, 219; linguistic, 127; multiple, 18, 219, 225; resistance to, 209–225
homeless, 241
Honeyman, Susan, 157n2
Horn, Shifra, 250
Horon, Adia Gur [Adolphe Gourevitch], 104
Hovav, Lea, 159n17
humor, 89, 135, 145, 155, 177–178

hunger, 31, 33, 170
Hunt, Peter, 157n2
Hurwitz, Yair, 209

identity, fluidity of, 194, 195, 199; Israeli, 38, 59, 88, 136, 199, 210; Jewish, 20, 62, 116, 125, 130, 133, 240; lack of, 199, 200, 201n7, 203n29, 220, 223; national, 18–20, 104, 131, 248; new Hebrew, 105, 115; other, 14, 29, 209; politics of, 4, 10, 230, 243nn6–7
imaginary, 136, 175, 178, 196
imagination, 108, 109, 148; failure of, 242; poetic, 214
imagined community, 18, 61, 241
imagined journey, 149
imaginary spaces, 143, 145, 151, 155–157, 175, 219, 223
immigrants, 44, 95, 163, 176; experience of 47, 49, 116, 227; as political issue, 38, 230; writers, 93, 210, 221, 227
individual, 7, 11, 127, 150, 157, 177, 178; and collective, 113, 186, 190, 197, 200, 250; vs. collective, 11, 19, 30, 185, 187; desire of, 17, 151, 186; experience of, 127, 199; and family, 238, 240; and statehood generation, 31, 37, 185, 198, 201nn7–8; as subject, 116, 117, 190, 231
Institute for Translation of Israeli Literature, 6, 23n28, 254
International Dublin Literary Award, 260
International Prize for Arabic Fiction (Arabic Booker), 266n65
interpellation, 30–31, 116–117
intersubjectivity, 199
intertextuality, 19, 60, 121n38, 218
irony, 29, 36, 84, 114, 131, 169–171, 193, 231, 243

Israel Prize, 249, 251
'Iton 77, 22n11
Iziovitch, Gili, 264n48

Jabotinsky, Zeev, 250
Jacob's dream, 127–128
Jacobs, Adrianna X., 218, 228nn20–22
Jacobson, David, 76n3
Jay, Martin, 202n18, 203n29
Jingdong Literary Prize, 260
Jury, of literary prizes, 255, 259

Ka-Tzetnik, *Beit Habubot*, 198
Kahana-Carmon, Amalia, 7; *Sadot magnetiyim*, 7
Kalbato shel Schultz, 183, 188, 200n3
Kaniuk, Yoram, 6, 12, 178n3; *Adam ben kelev*, 164, 165, 178
Kaplan, Eran, 243n9
Kareem, Sarah Tindal, 161nn40, 43
Karpinowitz, Avrom, 91
Kartun-Blum, Ruth, 29, 41n6, 261n9
kashrut, 170
Kashua, Sayed, 19
Katzir, Yehudit, 23n28, 250
Kauffman, Lane, 203n29
Keissar, Adi, 38, 46
Kenan, Amos, 7, 107, 120n17
Kenaz, Yehoshua, 9
Keren-Yaar, Dana, 151, 159nn17, 159n22, 159n27
Keydar, Eli, 187
kibbutz, 49, 49, 51, 59, 63, 149–150
Kibbutz Ma'ayan, 150; Kibbutz Yagur, 90
Kissileff, Beth, 265n52
Knowles, Ronald, 161n40
Kosman, Admiel, 21n3
Kravitz, Asher, 179nn5–6
Kristal, Merav, 198, 203n27
Kronfeld, Chana, 22n22, 73, 76n8, 77n12, 101n25, 101n27; *Full Severity of Compassion*, 62

Kulbak, Moyshe, 90
Kurzweil, Baruch, 119n2
Kuwaity brothers, 45

Labor Zionism, 6, 63, 146, 158n13, 240, 243n5
Lacan, Jacques, 196, 203n25
Lachower, Fishel, 12
Landau Prize in Poetry, 264n48
landscape, 15; American, 126, 129, 130, 133–135, 137; European, 93, 108, 138; and language, 15, 116; in literary, 18, 248, 253; literature, 15, 123, 125, 136, 216, 219
Laor, Dan, 119n6, 119n8, 178n2
Laor, Yitzhak, 264n48
Lapid, Shulamit, 9, 23n28
Leach, Neil, 139n16
Leal, Iris, 264n43, 265n54
Leavis, F. R., *The Great Tradition*, 3
Legal Forum for the Land of Israel, 256
Leibowitz, Yeshayahu, 251
Lev, Eleonora, 11
Levi Eshkol Prize, 257
Levi, Etti, 54, 58n22
Levi, Primo, 199, 203n30
Levi, Yanetz, 16; *Harpatka'ot Dod Ariyeh*, 153–156
Levy, Lital, 46–47, 56n9, 99n6, 261n8
Library, 54, 84, 254, 259, 260; catalogue, 161, 187, 188, 201
Libsker, Ari, *Stalagim*, 194, 198
Liebrecht, Savyon, *Tapuchim min hamidbar*, 9
Likrat, 95
linguistic registers, 19, 46, 54, 58n21, 111, 114, 239, 240
literary prizes, 4, 5, 18, 247–260; arguments against, 247–259; arguments for, 248, 259, 260; juries, 252–253. *See also* prizes by names
Livnat, Limor, 250, 251

Livneh, Hannah, 262n14
love, 44, 48, 255; of animals, 152–153, 167, 177, 237, 240; divine, 75; of family, 48, 232, 233, 235, 236, 241; of literature, 253, 258, 263n38; as motive, 67, 232, 233, 235, 241
Lubin, Orly, 37, 42n28
Luz, Zvi, 70, 71, 78n33, 79n39
Lyotard, Jean-François, 230, 242n4

Ma'abarah, 44, 46, 47, 49, 50, 51, 55. See also transit camp
Magenzie, Aviel, 262n22
Mali, Malasha, 91
mamlachtiyut [statism], 230
Man Booker Prize, 260
Mann, Mendel, 15, 91, 95, 101n28
Mapam, 144
marginality, 3, 45, 254; genres, 11, 14, 17, 157n1; political, 103, 105, 106, 117
Marsden, Stevie, 261n4
Masalha, Salman, 19
masculinity, 30, 36–40, 41n19, 42n34, 193
Mashiv haruach, 250
Matalon, Ronit, 201n9, 263n33; Kol tsa'adenu, 256
McSweeney, Joyelle, 225n4, 228n22
Megged, Aharon, 7, 85, 120n21
Melnick, Doline, 253, 257, 258
memoir, 14, 17, 163–178, 181n25, 202n15, 252
memory, 44, 48; childhood, 66, 108, 168, 172–173, 176, 250; collective, 109; cultural, 45, 52, 55; historical, 52, 95, 97; Jewish, 60, 90; traumatic, 87, 164 165
Mendelson-Maoz, Adia, 99n5
Mercer, Kobena, 243n6
metafictional narrative, 235
metalinguistic, 216
metapoetic, 30, 215

Michael, Sami, 252, 263n33; Hasut, 6, 7
millennial literature, 18
Milman, Yosef, 62, 77n16
mimicry, 53, 174, 179n4
minor literature, 11, 20, 104, 117, 121nn34–37
minority discourse, 111, 115, 230
Mintz, Alan, 181n22
Miron, Dan, 11, 27, 41n8, 100n13, 100n16, 100n18, 119n8, 247
mizrachi, 6, 56n5, 230; literature, 43–55; music, 43, 47, 52; voice, 15, 43, 45, 55; writers, 9, 38, 47, 252, 255, 257
Modan, Rutu, 11
Modern Hebrew Literature (journal), 5, 6, 99n4, 161n44
modernism, 88, 90, 147, 159n17, 188, 230, 241, 249
morality, 67, 71, 196–197, 231–241; lack, 195, 213; and nationalism, 132; uncertainty in, 111
Morris, Benny, 158n6
Moshkin, Alex, 99n6
Mossinsohn, Yigal, 16, 158n5; Derekh gever, 190; Hasamba, 143–145
mute, 19, 54, 69–70, 83, 111–112
muzikah mizrachit [Mizrachi music], 43, 53
myth, 2, 37; American, 130, 135; Jewish, 74, 87, 119n7, 125, 130; national, 105, 108, 144, 210, 249

Nakba, 31, 95, 256, 264n47
Namdar, Ruby, 16, 124, 138n10; Habayit asher nechrav, 124, 125–129, 130, 132–133, 136–137, 258–259
Nashawi, Yaacov, 54, 58n22
Natakovich, Svetlana, 226n8
nationalism, American, 132
nativism, 104, 105, 106

nature, 39–40, 70
Naveh, Hannah, 22n13
Navot, Amnon, 257, 258, 264nn50–51
neoliberalism, 243n7
Netanel, Lilach, 242
Netanyahu, Benjamin, 251
Nevo, Eshkol, 11; *Homesick*, 12
Nevo, Gideon, 180n6
new Jew, 124, 144
New Wave, 3
Newberg, Adina, 60, 76n5
Nguyen, Vaan, 11
Nimshi, Yoram, 120n16
Nir, Oded, 201n7, 242, 244n11, 245n26
Nirgad, Lia, 263n38
Noah, Mordecai Manuel, 129, 132, 133, 134
Nobel Prize, 247, 261n1
nonbelonging, 209, 219, 221, 224
noncanonical, 17, 184
nonhuman, 168–169, 172, 176, 178
Nooshin, Laudan, 51, 57n19
Norich, Anita, 99n2
normalization, 56, 166
Norris, Sharon, 263n32
North America, 4, 18, 35
nostalgia, 63, 89, 110, 199, 241
Notev, Eitan [Shraga Gafni], 6, 103, 106, 110, 115, 116, 120n24
Novershtern, Avraham, 99n4

Occupation, 50, 110, 111, 113
Ohana, David, 119n7
Olmert, Ehud, 155–156, 157
Omer, Devorah, 16, 153, 154, 159n20; *Kol mah shehayah (ulai)*, 149–151
Onheyb, 88
Oren, Ram, 243n5
Orlev, Uri, 6
Orpaz, Yitzhak, 6

Oz, Amos, 6, 178n3, 188, 190, 252, 260

Palestinians, 144, 149, 152, 166, 260; and Canaanites, 106–118; in comparison with Native Americans, 131; writers, 249; in Yiddish literature, 95–97
Palmach Generation, 32, 38, 185, 186, 190, 201n7
Paris, 210, 226n7
parody, 35, 107, 108, 146, 155, 239
Patterson, Charles, 180n16
Pearce, Susannah, 244n17, 244n20
Pedaya, Haviva, 36, 38–39, 42n25, 42n52
Peled, Esther, 259; *Petach gadol melematah*, 257
Peleg Yaron, 6, 18, 19, 21n9, 23n30, 242n2, 243nn8–9
Perry, Menachem, 9, 10, 256–257, 258, 264
Petersen, Laura, 179n6, 180n9
pilgrimage, 136
Pilowsky, Aryeh, 100n14
Pinchevski, Amit, 199, 202n24, 203n28
Pines, Noam, 180n6
Pinsker, Shachar, 15, 19, 21n9, 100n8, 100n21, 101n22, 101n25, 101n36, 137n1
pioneers, 63, 135, 202n15
Piotrkovsky, Shlomo, 262n13
Piper, Andrew, 265n60
piyyut, 15, 63, 72, 74, 77
Pnueli, Sh. Y., 89, 100 n15
poetics, 54; Amichai's, 62, 73; by generation, 29, 32, 22, 209; Gilboa's, 225n3; *hafla*, 44, 45, 55; of minutiae, 168, 175; modernist, 147; Shani's, 208; Shlonsky's, 146, 147, 159n17; Zach's, 38, 41, 188; Zarchi's, 160n30

Pollin-Galay, Hannah, 100n13
popular literature, 198, 254
pornography, 184, 197, 200; feminist criticism of, 185–186; of the Holocaust, 187, 193–194
Portelance, Eve, 265n60
postcolonialist, 45, 49
posthumanist, 165, 278; postmodernist, 7, 18, 229–231, 234, 237, 239, 241–242
post-globalist, 18
post-nationalist, 18, 159, 243
post-Zionist, 7, 186, 230
prayer, 15, 18, 59, 63, 78n21
prestige, 253
Prime Minister's Prize for Hebrew Writers, 264n50
Psalm 92, 68–71
Psalm 95, 64–65, 66
Psalm 137, 48, 52, 55, 132–133
pseudonyms, 187, 190

Qibya massacre (1953), 95

Rabbinic Hebrew, 254
Rabin, Yitzhak, 251
Raizen, Michal, 15, 19, 56n10
Ramazani, Jahan, 60–61, 76n35
Raspe, Rudolf Erich, *Surprising Adventures of Baron Munchausen*, 154
Ratosh, Yonatan [Uriel Shelach, Uriel Halperin], 104, 106, 107, 115–116, 119n3, 119n5, 120n26, 121n28
Rechnitzer, Haim O., 78n33
reflexivity, 231
refugees, 57n15, 90, 95, 97–98, 144, 214
Regan, Lisa, 260, 261n3, 266n64
Regev, Menahem, 157n3, 159n17
Regev, Motti, 21n1, 123, 137n3

resistance, 178, 209, 210, 211, 217, 219
reterritorialization, 104, 118, 209, 211, 220, 224
Reuveni, Yotam, 7
Rintsler, Avrom, 91, 92
Roberts, Claire, 261n4
Rochman, Leib, 90
rock and roll, 210
Rojanski, Rachel, 99n7, 100n20, 101n32
Rokem, Na'ama, 99n6
Ronell, Anna, 99n6
Rosen, Carmit, 27, 35–38
Rosenblatt, Louise, 60, 61, 63, 76n7, 78n24
Roskies, David, 99n4, 100n21
Roth, Philip, 183
Rovner, Adam, 131, 135, 138n8, 139n17
Rozin, Orit, 201n8
Rubina, Dina, 3

Sabato, Haim, *Te'um kavanot*, 254–255, 256
Sacerdoti, Yaakova, 161n40
Sadeh, Pinchas, 6; *Hachayim kemashal*, 10
Sagi, Avi, 76n3, 78n23
St. Aubyn, Edward, 253
Salima Pasha, 45, 48, 51, 52, 53, 57n14
Sapir Prize, 18, 178n2, 181n21, 248, 253, 254–260; origins, 254
Sapir, Pinchas, 254
Sarid, Yossi, 256
Sarland, Charles, 157–158n3
Sax, Boria, 180n16
scandal, military, 18; of literary prizes, 252–256, 258, 264n41
Schleiermacher, Friedrich, 114, 121n26
Schneider, Howard, 264n48

Scholem, Gershom, 80n54
Schulz, Bruno, 164
Schurr, Asaf, 12, 18, 229–242; *Amram*, 230, 232–234, 237; *Motti*, 230, 234–236, 237–238; *Sigal*, 230, 236–237; *Thus Said Vincent, the Stupid Cat*, 230; *The Building*, 230, 238
Schutz, David, 7
Schvimmer, Yotam, 264n40
Schwartz, Yigal, 21n9, 23n28, 180n6, 252
Second Intifada, 155
secular, 59, 60, 105
Seelig, Rachel, 99n6
Sela, Maya, 160n36, 263n27, 264n44, 265n56
self-sacrifice, 11
Semel, Nava, 9, 16, 124
Seroussi, Edwin, 21n1
Shabtai, Yaakov, *Zikhron dvarim*, 6, 7, 10, 85
Shachar, David, 6
Shachter, Allison, 137n1
Shafir, Gershon, 243n5
Shaham, Natan, 7
Shaked, Gershon, 22n17, 22n27, 41n13, 201n7, 229; *Hasiporet ha'ivrit*, 5; *Leshon hamar'ot*, 7–9, 10
Shalev, Meir, 202n15
Shalev, Zeruya, 23n28
shame, and desire, 183
Shamir, Moshe, 7, 41n12, 98; *Hu halakh basadot*, 10
Shamir, Yitzhak, 249
Shamir, Ziva, 119n8
Shammas, Anton, 9, 19, 118
Shamosh, Amnon, 9
Shandler, Jeffrey, 85, 100n9
Shani, Rina, 17–18; "Alibi," 212–215; "City," 227n15; "Foreign City," 221–223; "Foreign Flower," 215–218; "I am in the East," 207–208, 225n1; *'Ir zarah*, 207, 210; *Shalom le'adoni hamelekh*, 207; as translator, 210; *Yam na'ul*, 207
Shapira, Anita, 243n5
shared bookshelf, 5
Sharon, Ariel, 155
Sharon, Meytal, 242n3, 244n18
Shavit, Yaacov, 106, 119n9, 120n10, 121n29
Shavit, Zohar, 44, 158n7, 161nn39
Shmuelof, Mati, 21n3, 124, 137n5
Shenhav, Yehuda, 57n15
Shifra, Sh., 263n33
Shikhmanter, Rima, 158n9, 159n24, 159n27, 161n44
Shklovsky, Victor, 115, 121n27
Shlonsky Avraham, 16, 29, 68, 119n2, 154, 159n17; *Ani veTali*, 145–148, 158n11
Shohat, Ella, 56n3, 243n5
Shokeid, Moshe, 77n19
Shpigel, Yishayahu, 91
Sikseck, Ayman, 19
silence, 13, 19, 27–40, 165, 181n25; of Mizrachi voice, 40, 52–53; of women's voice, 39–40; of Yiddish language, 92
silent language, 83–84
sing-alongs, 77n19
Singer, I. B., 177, 181n17, 182n27
Smilansky, Moshe, 111
Smith, Barbara Herrnstein, 21n6, 249–250, 262n10
Snyder, Timothy, 244–245n22
Sobol, Yehoshua, 9
Sockol, Samuel, 264n48
Sokoloff, Naomi, 19, 79n49, 161n45, 179n6, 180n10
Someck, Ronni, 9
Somekh, Sasson, 249
space, ambivalence of, 161n41
speciesism, 168

Spiegelman, Art, *Maus*, 165
Spires, Todd, 260, 265n63
Squires, Claire, 261n2, 265n57
stalagim, 17, 183–200; *Stalag 10*, 188; *Stalag banot hasatan*, 191
Statehood Generation, 16, 31, 41n7, 95; critique of, 35, 36; poetry of, 28, 30, 40n2, 40n4; relation to Palmach Generation, 185–186, 188, 190, 201n7
statehood, 3, 17, 21n1, 124
Stavi, Zisi, 23n28
Steir-Livny, Liat, 106, 120n10
Stern Gang [Lehi], 109
Stern, David, 61, 77n10, 77n11
Sternhell, Zeev, 243n5
Stott, Jon, 157n2
subjectivity, 17, 117; dialectical, 187, 191, 200; historical, 237, 241; Israeli, 187, 201n9; Jewish, 199
Surowiecki, James, 265n59
Sutzkever, Avrom, 15, 86–90, 92, 98, 100nn11–12
Swift, Jonathan, *Gulliver's Travels*, 154, 157

Tabory, Joseph, 77n10
talush, 138n7
Tammuz, Benjamin, 7, 106
Taub, Gadi, 243n5
tefilat haderekh, 48
Tel Aviv, 7, 43, 133, 135–136, 144, 208; Beit Tefilah of, 59, 64, 78; Yiddish, in, 90
television, 3, 5, 7–8, 10
territory, 2, 109, 147, 152, 210; alternative, 135–136; enemy, 148; gain, 105, 107, 144, 145; and history, 148, 156; and language, 117; occupied, 107, 152, 249, 251; relinquish, 156
Teveth, Shabtai, 201nn7, 14

Tmol Shilshom café, 52
Toby Press, 12, 23n28
transit camp, 43, 44, 46, 47, 57n16, 95, 101n34. See also *Ma'abarah*
tansgression, 49, 67, 71, 184–188, 195
translation, 10, 109, 218, 219; anxiety of, 89; English, 12, 72, 139; fictive, 17, 19, 111–113, 187; foreignizing, 111–115; lack, 49, 51, 54, 55; as prize, 254, 258; theories of, 16, 114; and Yiddish, 85, 88–90
translingual, 124
transnational, 13, 20; Hebrew literature, 85, 123, 124, 125, 137n1; home, 126, 136; Israeli literature, 3; Yiddish literature, 98
Traugott, John, 157, 161n46
Traum, Riki, 17, 19, 225n, 226n6, 226n10, 226n12, 227n18
trauma, of 1948, 96, 97, 197; of 1973, 7, 8; childhood, 34, 165, 170, 172, 177; of Holocaust, 164, 199; memory of, 44, 48, 87; response to, 17, 19, 37, 173, 175; of uprooting, 15
travel, 53, 129, 210, 260; as alternative home, 130; as escapism, 16; literature, 155; prayer for, 48
Tsabari, Ayelet, 124, 137n4
Tsalka, Dan, 6, 178n3
Tumarkin, Yigal, 251
Tzamir, Hamutal, 28, 31, 40n2
Tzelgov, Eran, 14, 19
Tzoref, Yehezkel, 159n17

Umm Kulthum, 43, 48, 51, 52
untranslatability, 5, 55, 114–115, 158, 202n15

validation, 248, 252, 258
values, 7, 9, 26, 60, 115; challenged, 20, 107, 150, 168, 231–233, 237;

values *(continued)*
  and national identity, 3, 6, 18; and prizes, 248, 251, 252, 254, 256, 260; universal, 157, 242
Vater, Roman, 106, 120n11
vegetarianism, 177; Hitler's, 181n16
Verboord, Marc, 265n60
Vogel, David, 11

Wallach, Yona, 9, 27, 33–35, 209
War, of Attrition [1969–70], 149; of Independence [1948], 90, 95, 97, 107–109, 116, 144; Sinai [1956], 147; Six Day [1967], 47, 500, 150, 207, 210
Washington, Paul, 261n4
Weininger, Melissa, 16, 18, 19, 99n6, 138n6, 265n55
West, Cornel, 21n6
White, Hayden, 191, 194
Whitman, Walt, 126–127, 138n11
Wieseltier, Meir, 209
Williams, James, 242n4
Williams, Linda, 186, 200n6
Wisse, Ruth, 90, 100n19
Wittgenstein, Ludwig, 242–243n4

Yablonka, Hanna, 101n34
Yagil, Ran, 243–244n10
Yeats, William Butler, "The Second Coming," 129
Yediot aharonot, 9, 10
Yedlin, Noa, 259
Yehoash [Solomon Bloomgarden], 87, 88, 89
Yehoshua, A. B., 6, 10, 111, 188, 190, 250, 252, 262n23; *Hakalah hameshachreret*, 255, 257; *Hame'ahev* [The Lover], 6, 7

Yeshurun, Avot, 85
Yiddish, 15–16, 83–99, 125, 130, 210
Yildiz, Yasmin, 85, 100n10
yishuv, 6, 118
Yitzhak Rabin, 59
Yitzhak Sadeh Prize, 263n36
Yizhar, S., 7, 23n28, 98, 263n33; "Hashavuy" (The prisoner), 111, 114, 190; "Khirbet Khizeh," 110–111; *Yemei Tsiklag*, 8
Young Hebrews, 103, 104
Young Poets (of the 60s), 3, 209
Yudolovitch, Merav, 262n12
Yung Yisroel, 91–92, 95, 100–101n21
Yungman, Moshe, 91

Zach, Natan, 3, 14, 27, 32–37, 40, 98, 188; "One Moment," 28–23; poetics, 38, 41n7
Zakim, Eric, 19, 123, 137n2
Zarchi, Nurit, 16, 149–151, 160nn28–31
Zemer, Hannah, 22n15
Zierler, Wendy, 15, 18, 79n40
Ziolkowski, Theodore, 180n8
Zionism, 4, 8, 242; and Arab nationalism, 49; and Canaanism, 103–109, 117, 118; origins of, 132, 135, 250
Zionist discourse, 4, 108, 109, 110
Zionist fiction 103
Zionist literary prize 250
Zionist metanarrative (also master narrative), 2, 6, 7, 10, 12, 16, 18, 250; alternative to 7, 20, 49; diminished significance of 10, 12, 45, 231; eclipsed, 20, 45; with land and language, 123
Ziv, Amnon, 259